Fodor's 99

London

The complete guide, thoroughly up-to-date

Packed with details that will make your trip

The must-see sights, off and on the beaten path

What to see, what to skip

Vacation itineraries, walking tours, day trips

Smart lodging and dining options

Essential local do's and taboos

Transportation tips

Key contacts, savvy travel advice

When to go, what to pack

Clear, accurate, easy-to-use maps

Fodor's Travel Publications, Inc.
New York • Toronto • London • Sydney • Auckland
www.fodors.com

Fodor's London

EDITOR: Robert I. C. Fisher

Author: Kate Sekules
Editorial Contributors: Robert Andrews, David Brown, Jacqueline Brown, Helayne Schiff, M. T. Schwartzman, Brandy Whittingham
Editorial Production: Stacey Kulig
Maps: David Lindroth Inc., *cartographer*; Robert Blake, *map editor*
Design: Fabrizio La Rocca, *creative director*; Guido Caroti, *associate art director*; Jolie Novak, *photo editor*
Production/Manufacturing: Rebecca Zeiler
Cover Photograph: Richard T. Norwitz

Copyright

ISBN 0–679–00127–1

Special Sales

Fodor's Travel Publications are available at special discounts for bulk purchases for sales promotions or premiums. Special editions, including personalized covers, excerpts of existing guides, and corporate imprints, can be created in large quantities for special needs. For more information, contact your local bookseller or write to Special Markets, Fodor's Travel Publications, 201 East 50th Street, New York, NY 10022. Inquiries from Canada should be directed to your local Canadian bookseller or sent to Random House of Canada, Ltd., Marketing Department, 2775 Matheson Boulevard East, Mississauga, Ontario L4W 4P7. Inquiries from the United Kingdom should be sent to Fodor's Travel Publications, 20 Vauxhall Bridge Road, London SW1V 2SA, England.

PRINTED IN THE UNITED STATES OF AMERICA

10 9 8 7 6 5 4 3 2 1

CONTENTS

Maps

ON THE ROAD WITH FODOR'S

WHEN I PLAN A VACATION, the first thing I do is cast around among my friends and colleagues to find someone who's just been where I'm going. That's because there's no substitute for a recommendation from a good friend who knows your tastes, your budget, and your circumstances, someone who's just been there. Unfortunately, such friends are few and far between. So it's nice to know that there's *Fodor's London '99.*

In the first place, this book won't stay home when you hit the road. It will accompany you every step of the way, steering you away from wrong turns and wrong choices and never expecting a thing in return. It includes a wonderful, full-color map from Rand Mc-Nally, the world's largest commercial mapmaker. Most important of all, it's written and assiduously updated by the kind of people you *would* hit up for travel tips if you knew them. They're as choosy as your pickiest friend, except they've probably seen a lot more of Britain's booming capital. In these pages, they don't send you chasing down every town and sight in London but have instead selected the best ones, the ones that are worthy of your time and money. To make it easy for you to put it all together in the time you have, they've created itineraries and neighborhood walks that you can mix and match in a snap. Just tear out the map at the perforation, and join us on the road in London. Will this be the vacation of your dreams? We hope so.

About Our Writers

Our success in helping to make your trip the best of all possible vacations is a credit to the hard work of our extraordinary writers and editors.

Since **Kate Sekules** lives with a foot on either side of the Atlantic, her mission is getting the best of both worlds—and Fodor's is much the winner. Thanks to her knack for coming up with the most—both *bon* and *juste*—her wit is much in demand: *Vogue, W, Travel Holiday, Harper's Bazaar, Travel & Leisure,* and *The New Yorker*

are just some of the publications she writes for. Happily, she found enough time to do the lion's share of writing for this guidebook. Her idea of a smashing Saturday in old Londontown? The latest avant-garde art show at the Serpentine Gallery, dinner at Wódka, then a Baroque-period concert at Kenwood House.

A New York native, **Brandy Whittingham** is working on a doctoral dissertation on London's Victorian architecture. For this edition, she has written the introductions to chapters 2 through 8, plus the Close-Up, Great Itineraries, and What's Where sections. Her oft-told tale to first-time travelers: "W. S. Gilbert—of the celebrated Gilbert and Sullivan team—once wrote of a novice British bobbie who lost his way in London's Soho and ended up wandering the streets for twenty years. Caution: the believe-it-or-not twists, turns, and windings of London's layout can outwit even an expert's sense of direction!"

Being a settler in London, says writer and editor **Jacqueline Brown,** is mainly different from being a true native in that one really tries to get the most out of what the city has to offer. After 20 years of living in the capital, her favorite targets are those culinary and cultural arenas which lie far beyond bully beef and Buckingham Palace. When she is not working as a freelance editor or helping to update the Gold Guide section of this book, Jacqueline can be found strolling the parklands of a National Trust stately home with her young family.

Editor **Robert I. C. Fisher,** weaned on a steady diet of Masterpiece Theater productions, remains convinced that every word uttered with an English accent is a pearl. After working on three other Fodor's guidebooks to Great Britain and London, he knows that if Dickens had used a PC for his wordy tomes, he would have had a mean case of carpal tunnel syndrome. A raging Anglophile, Robert believes Queen Vicky was the true author of *Alice's Adventures in Wonderland.* Along the way, he's written on a variety of Europe-based subjects for such magazines as *Town & Country* and *Art in America.*

Connections

We're pleased that the American Society of Travel Agents continues to endorse Fodor's as its guidebook of choice. ASTA is the world's largest and most influential travel trade association, operating in more than 170 countries, with 27,000 members pledged to adhere to a strict code of ethics reflecting the Society's motto, "Integrity in Travel." ASTA shares Fodor's devotion to providing smart, honest travel information and advice to travelers, and we've long recommended that our readers—even those who have guidebooks and traveling friends—consult ASTA member agents for the experience and professionalism they bring to your vacation planning.

On Fodor's Web site (www.fodors.com), check out the new Resource Center, an online companion to the Gold Guide section of this book, complete with useful hot links to related sites. In our forums, you can also get lively advice from other travelers and more great tips from Fodor's experts worldwide.

How to Use This Book

Organization

Up front is the **Gold Guide,** an easy-to-use section arranged alphabetically by topic. Under each listing you'll find tips and information that will help you accomplish what you need to in London. You'll also find addresses and telephone numbers of organizations and companies that offer destination-related services and detailed information and publications.

The first chapter in the guide, **Destination: London** helps get you in the mood for your trip. In this section, you'll find several features: New and Noteworthy cues you in on trends and happenings, What's Where gets you oriented, Pleasures and Pastimes describes the activities and sights that really make London unique, Great Itineraries maps out exciting tours of the city, Fodor's Choice showcases our top picks, and Festivals and Seasonal Events alerts you to special events you'll want to seek out.

The **Exploring chapter** is divided into neighborhood sections; each recommends a walking tour and then lists neighborhood sights alphabetically, including sights that are off the beaten path. The remaining chapters are arranged in alphabetical order by subject (dining, lodging, nightlife and the arts, outdoor activities and sports, shopping, and side trips).

Icons and Symbols

★   Our special recommendations
✕   Restaurant
🏠   Lodging establishment
🐤   Good for kids (rubber duck)
☞   Sends you to another section of the guide for more information
✉   Address
☎   Telephone number
🕐   Opening and closing times
💷   Admission prices (those we give apply to adults; substantially reduced fees are almost always available for children, students, and senior citizens)

Tying each chapter together are Fodor's easy-to-use maps: Each sight or attraction is marked by a circle with a number—simply connect the dots in numerical sequence and you have the ideal city walk. In addition, numbers in white and black circles—③ and ❸, for example—that appear on the maps, in the margins, and within the tours correspond to one another, for easy reference.

Restaurant Reservations and Dress Codes

Reservations are always a good idea; we mention them only when they're essential or are not accepted. Book as far ahead as you can, and reconfirm as soon as you arrive. Unless otherwise noted, the restaurants listed are open daily for lunch and dinner. We mention dress only when men are required to wear a jacket or a jacket and tie.

Credit Cards

The following abbreviations are used: **AE,** American Express; **DC,** Diners Club; **MC,** MasterCard; and **V,** Visa.

Don't Forget to Write

You can use this book in the confidence that all prices and opening times are based on information supplied to us at press time; Fodor's cannot accept responsibility for any errors. Time inevitably brings changes, so always confirm information when it matters—especially if you're making a detour to visit a specific place.

Were the restaurants we recommended as described? Did our hotel picks exceed your expectations? Did you find a museum we recommended a waste of time? Keeping a travel guide fresh and up-to-date is a big job, and we welcome your feedback, positive *and* negative. If you have complaints, we'll look into them and revise our entries when the facts warrant it. If you've discovered a special place that we haven't included, we'll pass the information along to our correspondents and have them check it out. So send us your thoughts via e-mail at editors@fodors.com (specifying the name of the book on the subject line) or on paper in care of the London editor at Fodor's, 201 East 50th Street, New York, NY 10022. In the meantime, have a wonderful trip!

Karen Cure
Editorial Director

Central London

King's Cross Station

St. Pancras Station

Pentonville Rd.

City Rd.

King's Cross Rd.

St. John's St.

Rosebery Ave.

Goswell Rd.

East Road

Old St.

Hoxton St.

City Rd.

Gt. Eastern St.

Shoreditch High St.

Kingsland Rd.

Commercial St.

Coram's Fields

Judd St.

Woburn Pl.

Gray's Inn Rd.

Guilford St.

Southampton Row

Farringdon Rd.

Theobald's Rd.

Clerkenwell Rd.

Barbican Centre

Moorgate

Liverpool St. Station

Bishopsgate

Houndsditch

British Museum

New Oxford St.

High Holborn

Kingsway

Drury Ln.

Holborn Viaduct

London Wall

Bank of England

Leadenhall St.

Fenchurch St.

Charing Cross Rd.

Old Bailey

Newgate St.

Cheapside

Cornhill

Shaftesbury Ave.

Covent Garden

Aldwych

Law Courts

Fleet St.

St. Paul's

Queen Victoria St.

Cannon St.

Tower of London

Tower Hill

Strand

Victoria Embankment

Blackfriars Br.

Blackfriars Station

Upper Thames St.

Southwark Br.

Cannon St. Station

Lower Thames St.

London Br.

Tower Br.

National Gallery

Charing Cross Stn.

Trafalgar Square

Waterloo Br.

South Bank Arts Complex

Stamford St.

Southwark St.

River Thames

St. Thomas St.

Tooley St.

London Bridge Station

Whitehall

York Rd.

Waterloo Rd.

The Cut

Blackfriars Rd.

Union St.

Borough High St.

Bridge Rd.

Waterloo Station

Westminster Br.

Houses of Parliament

Westminster Abbey

Millbank

Lambeth Palace Rd.

Westminster Br. Rd.

Lambeth Rd.

Borough Rd.

London Rd.

Tower

New Kent Rd.

Horseferry Rd.

Lambeth Br.

Kennington Rd.

Imperial War Museum

Old Kent Rd.

Tate Gallery

Albert Embankment

Walworth Rd.

Rd.

Vauxhall Br.

Kennington Ln.

Kennington Park Rd.

N

Vauxhall Station

Kennington Oval

Ln.

0   1 mile

0   1 km

SMART TRAVEL TIPS A TO Z

Basic Information on Traveling in London, Savvy Tips to Make Your Trip a Breeze, and Companies and Organizations to Contact

Half the fun of traveling is looking forward to your trip—making plans, learning about your destination. The following travel tips will give you helpful pointers on many of the questions that arise at this stage. Your journey may begin at a Great Britain tourist office: the addresses and telephone numbers for main branches are listed below under **Visitor Information.** Happy landings!

AIR TRAVEL

BOOKING YOUR FLIGHT

Price is just one factor to consider when booking a flight: frequency of service and even a carrier's safety record are often just as important. Major airlines offer the greatest number of departures. Smaller airlines—including regional and no-frills airlines—usually have a limited number of flights daily. On the other hand, so-called low-cost airlines usually are cheaper, and their fares impose fewer restrictions, such as advance-purchase requirements. Safety-wise, low-cost carriers as a group have a good history—about equal to that of major carriers.

When you book, **look for nonstop flights** and **remember that "direct" flights stop at least once.** Try to **avoid connecting flights,** which require a change of plane. Two airlines may jointly operate a connecting flight, so ask if your airline operates every segment—you may find that it flies you only part of the way. International flights on a country's flag carrier are almost always nonstop; U.S. airlines often fly direct.

Ask your airline if it offers electronic ticketing, which eliminates all paperwork. There's no ticket to pick up or misplace. You go directly to the gate and give the agent your confirmation number—a real blessing if you've lost your ticket or made last-minute changes in travel plans. There's no worry about waiting on line at the airport.

CARRIERS

When flying internationally, you must usually choose between a domestic carrier, the national flag carrier of the country you are visiting, and a foreign carrier from a third country. National flag carriers have the greatest number of nonstops. Domestic carriers may have better connections to your hometown and serve a greater number of gateway cities. Third-party carriers may have a price advantage.

British Airways (☏ 800/AIRWAYS) is the national flag carrier and offers mostly nonstop flights from 18 U.S. cities to Heathrow and Gatwick airports, along with flights to Manchester, Birmingham, and Glasgow. As the leading British carrier, it offers myriad add-on options, helping to bring down ticket costs. In addition, it has a vast program of discount airfare/hotel packages.

➤ MAJOR AIRLINES: **American Airlines** (☏ 800/433–7300; 0181/572–5555 in London) to Heathrow, Gatwick. **British Airways** (☏ 800/247–9297; 0345/222–1111 in London) to Heathrow, Gatwick. **Continental** (☏ 800/231–0856; 0800/776464 in London) to Gatwick. **Delta** (☏ 800/241–4141; 0800/414767 in London) to Heathrow, Gatwick. **Northwest Airlines** (☏ 800/447–4747; 0990/561000 in London) to Gatwick. **United** (☏ 800/241–6522; 0845/844–4777 in London) to Heathrow. **TWA** (☏ 800/892–4141; 0181/814–0707 in London or 01293/535535) to Gatwick. **Virgin Atlantic** (☏ 800/862–8621; 01293/747747 in London) to Heathrow, Gatwick.

CHARTERS

Charters usually have the lowest fares but are the least dependable. Departures are infrequent and seldom on time, flights can be delayed for up to 48 hours or can be canceled for any reason up to 10 days before you're scheduled to leave. Itineraries and prices can change once you've booked your flight.

In the U.S., the Department of Transportation's Aviation Consumer Protection Division has jurisdiction over charters and provides a certain degree of protection. The DOT requires that money paid to charter operators be held in escrow, so if you can't pay with a credit card, **always make your check payable to a charter carrier's escrow account.** The name of the bank should be in the charter contract. If you have any problems with a charter operator, contact the DOT (☞ Airline Complaints, *below*). If you buy a charter package that includes both air and land arrangements, remember that the escrow requirement applies only to the air component.

CHECK IN & BOARDING

Airlines routinely overbook planes, assuming that not everyone with a ticket will show up, but sometimes everyone does. When that happens, airlines ask for volunteers to give up their seats. In return these volunteers usually get a certificate for a free flight and are rebooked on the next flight out. If there are not enough volunteers, the airline must choose who will be denied boarding. The first to get bumped are passengers who checked in late and those flying on discounted tickets, so **get to the gate and check in as early as possible,** especially during peak periods.

Although the trend on international flights is to drop reconfirmation requirements, many airlines still ask you to reconfirm each leg of your international itinerary. Failure to do so may result in your reservation being canceled.

Always **bring a government-issued photo ID to the airport.** You may be asked to show it before you are allowed to check in.

CONSOLIDATORS

Consolidators buy tickets for scheduled international flights at reduced rates from the airlines, then sell them at prices that beat the best fare available directly from the airlines, usually without restrictions. Sometimes you can even get your money back if you need to return the ticket. Carefully read the fine print detailing penalties for changes and cancellations, and **confirm your consolidator reservation with the airline.**

➤ CONSOLIDATORS: **Cheap Tickets** (☎ 800/377–1000). **Up & Away Travel** (☎ 212/889–2345). **Discount Travel Network** (☎ 800/576–1600). **Unitravel** (☎ 800/325–2222). **World Travel Network** (☎ 800/409–6753).

COURIERS

When you fly as a courier, you trade your checked-luggage space for a ticket deeply subsidized by a courier service. It's all perfectly legitimate, but there are restrictions: you can usually book your flight only a week or two in advance, your length of stay may be set for a certain number of days, and you probably won't be able to book a companion on the same flight.

CUTTING COSTS

The least-expensive airfares to London are priced for round-trip travel and usually must be purchased in advance. It's smart to **call a number of airlines, and when you are quoted a good price, book it on the spot**—the same fare may not be available the next day. Airlines generally allow you to change your return date for a fee. If you don't use your ticket, you can apply the cost toward the purchase of a new ticket, again for a small charge. However, most low-fare tickets are nonrefundable. To get the lowest airfare, **check different routings.** Compare prices of flights to and from different airports if your destination or home city has more than one gateway. Also price off-peak flights, which may be significantly less expensive.

Travel agents, especially those who specialize in finding the lowest fares (☞ Discounts & Deals, *below*), can be helpful for booking a plane ticket. When you're quoted a price, **ask your agent if the price is likely to get any lower.** Good agents know the seasonal fluctuations of airfares and can usually anticipate a sale or fare war.

However, waiting can be risky: the fare could go *up* as seats become scarce, and you may wait so long that your preferred flight sells out. A wait-and-see strategy works best if your plans are flexible. If you must arrive and depart on certain dates, don't delay.

ENJOYING THE FLIGHT

For more legroom, **request an emergency-aisle seat.** Don't sit in the row in front of the emergency aisle or in front of a bulkhead, where seats may not recline.

If you don't like airline food, **ask for special meals when booking.** These can be vegetarian, low-cholesterol, or kosher, for example.

When flying internationally, try to maintain a normal routine, to help fight jet lag. At night, **get some sleep.** By day, **eat light meals, drink water (not alcohol), and move around the cabin** to stretch your legs.

Many carriers have prohibited smoking on all of their international flights; others allow smoking only on certain routes or certain departures, so **contact your carrier regarding its smoking policy.**

FLYING TIMES

Flying time to London is about 6½ hours from New York, 7½ hours from Chicago, and 10 hours from Los Angeles.

HOW TO COMPLAIN

If your baggage goes astray or your flight goes awry, complain right away. Most carriers require that you **file a claim immediately.**

➤ AIRLINE COMPLAINTS: U.S. Department of Transportation Aviation Consumer Protection Division (✉ C-75, Room 4107, Washington, DC 20590, ☎ 202/366–2220). Federal Aviation Administration Consumer Hotline (☎ 800/322–7873).

AIRPORTS & CITY TRANSFERS

AIRPORTS

International flights to London arrive at either **Heathrow Airport,** 15 mi west of London, or at **Gatwick Airport,** 27 mi south of the capital. Most flights from the United States go to Heathrow, which is divided into four terminals, with Terminals 3 and 4 handling transatlantic flights (British Airways uses Terminal 4). Gatwick is London's second gateway. It has grown from a European airport into an airport that serves 21 scheduled U.S. destinations. A third, new, state-of-the-art airport, **Stansted,** is to the east of the city. It handles mainly European and domestic traffic, although there is a scheduled service from New York. There are fast connections from all the London airports into the capital.

➤ AIRPORT INFORMATION: Heathrow Airport (☎ 0181/759–4321). Gatwick Airport (☎ 01293/535353). Stansted Airport (☎ 01279/680500).

CITY TRANSFERS

Heathrow: The least expensive route into London is via the **Piccadilly line** of the **Underground** (London's subway system). Trains on the "Tube" run every four to eight minutes from all four terminals; the painless 40-minute trip costs £3.30 one-way and connects with London's extensive tube system. The quickest way into London is the new **Heathrow Express** (☎ 0845/600–1515), which ferries travelers in just 15 minutes to and from Paddington Station (in the city center and hub for many of London's Underground city lines). One-way tickets cost £10 for standard class and £20 for first class. Service is daily, from 5:10 AM to 10:40 PM, with departures every 15 minutes.

London Transport (☎ 0171/222–1234) runs two bus services from the airport; each costs £6 one-way and £10 round-trip and travel time each direction is about one hour. The **Airbus A1** leaves for Victoria Station, with stops along Cromwell Road, at Earls Court, and at Hyde Park Corner, every 30 minutes 5:40 AM–8:30 PM. The **Airbus A2** leaves for King's Cross and Euston, with stops at Marble Arch, and Russell Square every 30 minutes 6 AM–9:30 PM.

Gatwick: Fast, nonstop **Gatwick Express** trains leave for Victoria Station every 15 minutes 5:20 AM–12:50 AM; then hourly 1.35 AM–4.35 AM. The 30-minute trip costs £9.50 one-way. A frequent local train also runs all night. Hourly bus services (6:30 AM to 10 PM) are provided by **Flightline 777** to Victoria Coach Station. This takes about 90 minutes and costs £7.50 one-way.

Stansted: London's newest airport, opened in 1991, serves mainly European destinations. The **Stansted Skytrain** to Liverpool Street Station runs every half hour and costs £10 one-way although, at press time, fares were set to increase.

Cars and taxis drive into London on M4; the trip can take more than an hour, depending on traffic, from Heathrow. The taxi fare is about £40, plus tip. From Gatwick, the taxi fare is at least £80, plus tip; traffic can be very heavy.

BUS TRAVEL

BUS LINES

In central London, buses are traditionally bright red double- and single-deckers, though there are now many privately owned buses of different colors. Not all buses run the full length of their route at all times; check with the driver or conductor. On some buses you pay the conductor after finding a seat, on others you pay the driver upon boarding. Bus stops are clearly indicated; the main stops have a red LT symbol on a plain white background. When the word "Request" is written across the sign, you must flag the bus down. Buses are a good way of seeing the town, but **don't take one if you are in a hurry.**

Single fares start at 60p for short hops (90p in the central zone). London is divided into six concentric zones for both bus and tube fares: the more zones you cross, the higher the fare. Regular single-journey or round-trip **One Day Travelcards** (£3.50–£4.30) allow unrestricted travel on bus and tube after 9:30 AM and all day on weekends and national holidays. **LT Cards** (£4.50–£7.30) do not have any restricted times of travel except on N–prefixed Night Buses.

Traveling without a valid ticket makes you liable for an on-the-spot fine (£10 at press time), so always pay your fare before you travel. For more information, there are **LT Travel Information Centres** at the following tube stations: Euston, Hammersmith, King's Cross, Oxford Circus, Piccadilly Circus, St. James's Park, Victoria, and Heathrow (in Terminals 1 and 2); open 6 AM–12 AM, or call 0171/222–1234.

DISCOUNT PASSES

Visitor Travelcards (£3.90) are the same as the One Day Travelcards, but with the bonus of a booklet of money-off vouchers to major attractions (available only in the United States, for three, four, and seven days; contact **BritRail Travel International**, ✉ 1500 Broadway, New York, NY 10036, ☎ 212/382–3737).

NATIONAL EXPRESS

If you plan on traveling out of London to various destinations—including the side trips covered in Chapter 8—note that **National Express** (☎ 0990/808080) is the largest British coach operator.

NIGHT BUSES

Night Buses can prove helpful when traveling in London from 11 PM to 5 AM—these buses add the prefix "N" to their route numbers and don't run as frequently and don't operate on quite as many routes as day buses. You'll probably have to transfer at one of the Night Bus nexuses: Victoria, Westminster, and either Piccadilly Circus or Trafalgar Square. Weekly and monthly Travelcards are good for Night Buses, but One Day and Weekend Travelcards are not; Night Bus single fares are also a bit higher than daytime ones. Note: avoid sitting alone on the top deck of a Night Bus unless you want to experience the happily rare misfortune of being mugged in London.

CAMERAS & COMPUTERS

EQUIPMENT PRECAUTIONS

Always **keep your film, tape, or computer disks out of the sun.** Carry an extra supply of batteries, and **be prepared to turn on your camera, camcorder, or laptop** to prove to security personnel that the device is real. Always **ask for hand inspection of film,** which becomes clouded after successive exposure to airport X-ray machines, and **keep videotapes and computer disks away from metal detectors.**

➤ PHOTO HELP: **Kodak Information Center** (☎ 800/242–2424). *Kodak Guide to Shooting Great Travel Pictures,* available in bookstores or from Fodor's Travel Publications (☎ 800/533–6478; $16.50 plus $4 shipping).

CAR RENTALS

When considering a rental car, it's worth noting that unless you are going to be traveling extensively outside London, a car in the city is often more of a liability than an asset. Remember that Britain drives on the left, and the rest of Europe on the right. Therefore, you may want to leave your rented car in Britain and pick up a left-side drive if you cross the Channel (☞ Driving, *below*).

Rates in London begin at $54 a day and $176 a week for an economy car, usually with manual transmission. Air-conditioning and unlimited mileage generally come with the larger sized automatic car. This does not include 17.5% tax on car rentals.

➤ MAJOR AGENCIES: **Alamo** (☎ 800/522–9696, 0800/272–2000 in the U.K.). **Avis** (☎ 800/331–1084, 800/879–2847 in Canada, 008/225533 in Australia). **Budget** (☎ 800/472–3325, 0800/181181 in the U.K.). **Dollar** (☎ 800/800–6000; 0990/565656 in the U.K., where it is known as Eurodollar). **Hertz** (☎ 800/654–3001, 800/263–0600 in Canada, 0345/555888 in the U.K., 03/9222–2523 in Australia, 03/358–6777 in New Zealand). **National InterRent** (☎ 800/227–3876; 0345/222525 in the U.K., where it is known as Europcar InterRent).

CUTTING COSTS

For the best deal, **book through a travel agent who is willing to shop around.**

Also **ask your travel agent about a company's customer-service record.** How has the company responded to late plane arrivals and vehicle mishaps? Are there often lines at the rental counter? During holiday periods, does a confirmed reservation guarantee you a car?

Be sure to **look into wholesalers,** companies that do not own fleets but rent in bulk from those that do and

often offer better rates than traditional car-rental operations. Prices are best during off-peak periods. Rentals through wholesalers must be paid for before you leave the United States.

➤ RENTAL WHOLESALERS: **Auto Europe** (☎ 207/842–2000 or 800/223–5555, FAX 800/235–6321). **Europe by Car** (☎ 212/581–3040 or 800/223–1516, FAX 212/246–1458). **DER Travel Services** (✉ 9501 W. Devon Ave., Rosemont, IL 60018, ☎ 800/782–2424, FAX 800/282–7474 for information or 800/860–9944 for brochures). **Kemwel Holiday Autos** (☎ 914/835–5555 or 800/678–0678, FAX 914/835–5126).

INSURANCE

You are generally responsible for any damage to or loss of a rented car. Before you rent, **see what coverage you already have** under the terms of your personal auto-insurance policy and credit cards.

Collision policies that car-rental companies sell for European rentals typically do not cover stolen vehicles. Before you buy additional coverage for theft, check with your credit-card company and personal auto insurance—you may already be covered.

REQUIREMENTS

In London your own driver's license is acceptable. An International Driver's Permit is a good idea; it's available from the American or Canadian automobile association, and, in the United Kingdom, from the Automobile Association or Royal Automobile Club. International permits are universally recognized, and having one may save you a problem with the local authorities.

SURCHARGES

Before you pick up a car in one city and leave it in another, **ask about drop-off charges or one-way service fees,** which can be substantial. Note, too, that some rental agencies charge extra if you return the car before the time specified in your contract. To avoid a hefty refueling fee, **fill the tank just before you turn in the car,** but be aware that gas stations near the rental outlet may overcharge.

THE CHANNEL TUNNEL

Short of flying, the "Chunnel" is the fastest way to cross the English Channel: 35 minutes from Folkestone to Calais, 60 minutes from motorway to motorway, or 3 hours from London's Waterloo Station to Paris's Gare du Nord.

➤ CAR TRANSPORT: Le Shuttle (☎ 0990/353535 in the U.K.).

➤ PASSENGER SERVICE: In the U.K., Eurostar (☎ 0345/881881), InterCity Europe (✉:Victoria Station, London, ☎ 0171/834–2345, 0171/828–0892 for credit-card bookings). In the U.S., BritRail Travel (☎ 800/677–8585), Rail Europe (☎ 800/942–4866).

CHILDREN & TRAVEL

CHILDREN IN LONDON

Be sure to plan ahead and **involve your youngsters** as you outline your trip. When packing, include things to keep them busy en route. On sightseeing days try to schedule activities of special interest to your children. If you are renting a car don't forget to **arrange for a car seat** when you reserve.

➤ LOCAL INFORMATION: Kidsline (☎ 0171/222–8070; ⏲ open 4–6 PM during school time; 9 AM–4 PM during holidays). Visitorcall, London Tourist Board's info line, offers two options: What's on for Children (☎ 0839/123404) and Places for Children to Go (☎ 0839/123424), both 49p per minute.

The *Children's Guide to London,* by Christopher Pick (Cadogan Books, ✉ 16 Lower Marsh, London SE1 7RJ; £3.50); *Book of London,* by Usborne Publishers, a hands-on children specialist (8 Saffron Hill, London EC1 8RT, call ☎ 0171/430–2800 for a catalog; £6.99, with a pocket-size Hot-Shot version at £1.99); and *Kids' London,* by Elizabeth Holt and Molly Perham (St. Martin's Press, ✉ 175 5th Ave., New York, NY 10010; $5.95), cover the subject. Up-to-date information is available in *Kids Out!* magazine, available monthly at better newsstands (£1.75). *Time Out* weekly listings magazine has a section of child-friendly activities and trips (£1.80). The information sheet, *Chil-dren's London* (available free from the London Tourist Board, Tourist Information Centre, Victoria Station Forecourt, London SW1V 1JT and other London TICs) gives a complete story.

➤ BABY-SITTING: The Nanny Service (✉ 6 Nottingham St., London W1M 3RB, ☎ 0171/935–3515). **Nanny Connection** (✉ Stern House, 85 Gloucester Rd., London SW7 4SS, ☎ 0171/835–2277). **Universal Aunts** (✉ Box 304, London SW4 0NN, ☎ 0171/738–8937).

FLYING

If your children are two or older, **ask about children's airfares.** As a general rule, infants under two not occupying a seat fly at greatly reduced fares or even for free.

In general the adult baggage allowance applies to children paying half or more of the adult fare. When booking, **ask about carry-on allowances for those traveling with infants.** In general, for babies charged 10% of the adult fare you are allowed one carry-on bag and a collapsible stroller, which may have to be checked; you may be limited to less if the flight is full.

Experts agree that it's a good idea to use safety seats aloft for children weighing less than 40 pounds. Airlines, however, can set their own policies: U.S. carriers allow FAA-approved models but usually require that you buy a ticket, even if your child would otherwise ride free, since the seats must be strapped into regular seats. Airline rules vary, so it's important to **check your airline's policy about using safety seats during takeoff and landing.** Safety seats cannot obstruct the movement of other passengers in the row, so get an appropriate seat assignment as early as possible.

When making your reservation, **request children's meals or a free-standing bassinet** if you need them; the latter are available only to those seated at the bulkhead, where there's enough legroom. Remember, however, that bulkhead seats may not have their own overhead bins, and there's no storage space in front of you—a major inconvenience.

GROUP TRAVEL

When planning to take your kids on a tour, look for companies that specialize in family travel.

➤ FAMILY-FRIENDLY TOUR OPERATORS: **Grandtravel** (✉ 6900 Wisconsin Ave., Suite 706, Chevy Chase, MD 20815, ☎ 301/986–0790 or 800/247–7651) for people traveling with grandchildren ages 7–17. **Families Welcome!** (✉ 92 N. Main St., Ashland, OR 97520, ☎ 541/482–6121 or 800/326–0724, ℻ 541/482–0660). **Rascals in Paradise** (✉ 650 5th St., Suite 505, San Francisco, CA 94107, ☎ 415/978–9800 or 800/872–7225, ℻ 415/442–0289).

HOTELS

Most hotels in London allow children under a certain age to stay in their parents' room at no extra charge, but others charge them as extra adults; be sure to **ask about the cutoff age for children's discounts.**

➤ BEST CHOICES: Hotels that are noticeably family- and child-friendly include **Forte Hotels** (☎ 0171/301–2000), **Hart House Hotel** (✉ 51 Gloucester Place, Marylebone, London W1H 3PE, ☎ 0171/935–2288), **Basil Street Hotel** (✉ Basil St., Knightsbridge, London SW3 1AH, ☎ 0171/581–3311),, **Edward Lear** (✉ 30 Seymour St., London W1H 5WD, ☎ 0171/402–5401), and the **Langland Hotel** (✉ 29–31 Gower St., Bloomsbury, London WC1E 6HG, ☎ 0171/636–5801). The **AA Guide to Hotels and Restaurants,** (£8.99 from AA shops and good bookstores) has regularly inspected and graded selections which signpost child-friendly places. Also, on the Net, www.theaa. co.uk/hotels. Check out those that pass the beady Which? eye in **The Which? Hotel Guide** (£14.99; www.which.net); or for a hotel/kindergarten exclusively for children, **Pippa Pop-ins,** (✉ 430 Fulham Rd., London SW6 1DU, ☎ 0171/385–2457/8).

CONSUMER PROTECTION

Whenever possible, **pay with a major credit card** so you can cancel payment or get reimbursed if there's a problem, provided that you can provide documentation. This is the best way to pay, whether you're buying travel arrangements before your trip or shopping at your destination.

If you're doing business with a particular company for the first time, **contact your local Better Business Bureau and the attorney general's offices** in your state and the company's home state, as well. Have any complaints been filed?

Finally, if you're buying a package or tour, always **consider travel insurance** that includes default coverage (☞ Insurance, *below*).

➤ LOCAL BBBs: **Council of Better Business Bureaus** (✉ 4200 Wilson Blvd., Suite 800, Arlington, VA 22203, ☎ 703/276–0100, ℻ 703/525–8277).

CUSTOMS & DUTIES

When shopping, **keep receipts** for all of your purchases. Upon reentering the country, **be ready to show customs officials what you've bought.** If you feel a duty is incorrect, appeal the assessment. If you object to the way your clearance was handled, get the inspector's badge number. In either case, first ask to see a supervisor, then write to the appropriate authorities, beginning with the port director at your point of entry.

IN THE U.K.

There are two levels of duty-free allowance for travelers entering Great Britain: one for goods bought outside the EU, the other for goods bought in the EU (Belgium, Greece, the Netherlands, Denmark, Italy, Portugal, France, the Irish Republic, Spain, Germany, or Luxembourg).

In the first category, you may import duty-free: 200 cigarettes or 100 cigarillos or 50 cigars or 250 grams of tobacco; 2 liters of table wine and, in addition, (a) 1 liter of alcohol over 22% by volume (most spirits), (b) 2 liters of alcohol under 22% by volume (fortified or sparkling wine or liqueurs), or (c) 2 more liters of table wine; 50 milliliters of perfume; ¼ liter of toilet water; and other goods up to a value of £145, but not more than 50 liters of beer or 25 cigarette lighters.

In the second category, the EU has set guidelines for the import of certain goods. Following side trips entirely within the EU, you no longer need to go through customs on your return to the United Kingdom; however, if you exceed the guideline amounts, you may be required to prove that the goods are for your personal use only ("personal use" includes gifts). The guideline levels are: 800 cigarettes, 400 cigarillos, 200 cigars, and 1 kilogram of smoking tobacco, plus 10 liters of spirits, 20 liters of fortified wine, 90 liters of wine, and 110 liters of beer, plus goods to the value of £75. By June 1999 this duty-free allowance could be scrapped, so the U.K. falls in line with the rest of the EU single market.

No animals or pets of any kind can be brought into the United Kingdom without a lengthy quarantine. The penalties are severe and are strictly enforced. Similarly, fresh meats, plants and vegetables, controlled drugs, and firearms and ammunition may not be brought into Great Britain.

You will face no customs formalities if you enter Scotland or Wales from any other part of the United Kingdom, though anyone coming from Northern Ireland should expect a security check.

IN AUSTRALIA

Australia residents who are 18 or older may bring back $A400 worth of souvenirs and gifts (including jewelry), 250 cigarettes or 250 grams of tobacco, and 1,125 ml of alcohol (including wine, beer, and spirits). Residents under 18 may bring back $A200 worth of goods.

➤ INFORMATION: **Australian Customs Service** (Regional Director, ✉ Box 8, Sydney, NSW 2001, ☎ 02/9213–2000, FAX 02/9213–4000).

IN CANADA

Canadian residents who have been out of Canada for at least 7 days may bring in C$500 worth of goods duty-free. If you've been away less than 7 days but more than 48 hours, the duty-free allowance drops to C$200; if your trip lasts 24–48 hours, the allowance is C$50. You may not pool allowances with family members. Goods claimed under the C$500 exemption may follow you by mail; those claimed under the lesser exemptions must accompany you. Alcohol and tobacco products may be included in the 7-day and 48-hour exemptions but not in the 24-hour exemption. If you meet the age requirements of the province or territory through which you reenter Canada, you may bring in, duty-free, 1.14 liters (40 imperial ounces) of wine or liquor or 24 12-ounce cans or bottles of beer or ale. If you are 16 or older you may bring in, duty-free, 200 cigarettes and 50 cigars.

You may send an unlimited number of gifts worth up to C$60 each duty-free to Canada. Label the package UNSOLICITED GIFT—VALUE UNDER $60. Alcohol and tobacco are excluded.

➤ INFORMATION: **Revenue Canada** (✉ 2265 St. Laurent Blvd. S, Ottawa, Ontario K1G 4K3, ☎ 613/993–0534, 800/461–9999 in Canada).

IN NEW ZEALAND

Although greeted with a "Haere Mai" ("Welcome to New Zealand"), homeward-bound residents with goods to declare must present themselves for inspection. If you're 17 or older, you may bring back $700 worth of souvenirs and gifts. Your duty-free allowance also includes 4.5 liters of wine or beer; one 1,125-ml bottle of spirits; and either 200 cigarettes, 250 grams of tobacco, 50 cigars, or a combo of all three up to 250 grams.

➤ INFORMATION: **New Zealand Customs** (✉ Custom House, ✉ 50 Anzac Ave., Box 29, Auckland, New Zealand, ☎ 09/359–6655, ☎ 09/309–2978).

IN THE U.S.

U.S. residents may bring home $400 worth of foreign goods duty-free if they've been out of the country for at least 48 hours (and if they haven't used the $400 allowance or any part of it in the past 30 days).

U.S. residents 21 and older may bring back 1 liter of alcohol duty-free. In addition, regardless of your age, you are allowed 200 cigarettes and 100 non-Cuban cigars. Antiques, which the U.S. Customs Service defines as objects more than 100 years old, enter duty-free, as do original works of art done entirely by hand.

You may also send packages home duty-free: up to $200 worth of goods for personal use, with a limit of one parcel per addressee per day (and no alcohol or tobacco products or perfume worth more than $5); label the package PERSONAL USE, and attach a list of its contents and their retail value. Do not label the package UNSOLICITED GIFT, or your duty-free exemption will drop to $100. Mailed items do not affect your duty-free allowance on your return.

➤ INFORMATION: **U.S. Customs Service** (Inquiries, ⊠ Box 7407, Washington, DC 20044, ☎ 202/927–6724; complaints, Office of Regulations and Rulings, ⊠ 1301 Constitution Ave. NW, Washington, DC 20229; registration of equipment, Resource Management, ⊠ 1301 Constitution Ave. NW, Washington DC 20229, ☎ 202/927–0540).

DISABILITIES & ACCESSIBILITY

ACCESS IN LONDON

Compared to New York City, London has a way to go in helping people with disabilities, but is moving toward making the city more accessible. Most underground (subway) stations have vast escalators and steps, but contact the London Transport system (☎ 0171/918–3312) for their booklet, "Access to the Underground," which gives facts about elevators and ramps at individual tube stations. The grand, regal London Black Cabs are perfectly accommodating in their spacious interiors for people using wheelchairs, and many London hotels have wheelchair ramps. Read the British Tourist Authority's booklets "London Made Easy" and "Access in London" for the final word on accessibility. Note that the BTA will provide lists of London hotels for people with disabilities; these hotels often post the sign "H" at their door to welcome such travelers.

➤ LOCAL RESOURCES: The biggest organization in Britain is **RADAR**, or the Royal Association for Disability

and Rehabilitation, command central for travel information and advice on accommodations through the British Isles and Europe (⊠ 12 City Forum, 250 City Rd., London, EC1, ☎ 0171/250–3222). Contact **London Transport's Unit for Disabled Passengers** (⊠ 172 Buckingham Palace Rd., London SW1W 9TN, ☎ 0171/918–3312) for details on **Stationlink**, a wheelchair-accessible "midibus" service, as well as information on other access information. Another important organization is **Holiday Care Service** (⊠ Imperial Building, Victoria Road, Horley, Surrey RH6 7PZ, ☎ 01293/774535). **Artsline** (☎ 0171/388–2227) provides information on the accessibility of arts events.

MAKING RESERVATIONS

When discussing accessibility with an operator or reservations agent, **ask hard questions.** Are there any stairs, inside *or* out? Are there grab bars next to the toilet *and* in the shower/tub? How wide is the doorway to the room? To the bathroom? For the most extensive facilities meeting the latest legal specifications, **opt for newer accommodations,** which are more likely to have been designed with access in mind. Older buildings or ships may have more limited facilities. Be sure to **discuss your needs before booking.**

➤ COMPLAINTS: **Disability Rights Section** (⊠ U.S. Department of Justice, Civil Rights Division, ⊠ Box 66738, Washington, DC 20035–6738, ☎ 202/514–0301 or 800/514–0301, TTY 202/514–0383 or 800/514–0383, ℻ 202/307–1198) for general complaints. **Aviation Consumer Protection Division** (☞ Air Travel, *above*) for airline-related problems. **Civil Rights Office** (⊠ U.S. Department of Transportation, Departmental Office of Civil Rights, S-30, ⊠ 400 7th St. SW, Room 10215, Washington, DC, 20590, ☎ 202/366–4648, ℻ 202/366–9371) for problems with surface transportation.

TRAVEL AGENCIES & TOUR OPERATORS

As a whole, the travel industry has become more aware of the needs of travelers with disabilities. In the U.S., the Americans with Disabilities Act requires that travel firms serve the needs of all travelers. Some agencies and operators specialize in making travel arrangements for individuals and groups with disabilities.

➤ TRAVELERS WITH MOBILITY PROBLEMS: **Access Adventures** (✉ 206 Chestnut Ridge Rd., Rochester, NY 14624, ☎ 716/889–9096), run by a former physical-rehabilitation counselor. **Accessible Journeys** (✉ 35 W. Sellers Ave., Ridley Park, PA 19078, ☎ 610/521–0339 or 800/846–4537, FAX 610/521–6959), for escorted tours exclusively for travelers with mobility impairments. **CareVacations** (✉ 5019 49th Ave., Suite 102, Leduc, Alberta T9E 6T5, ☎ 403/986–6404, 800/648–1116 in Canada) has group tours and is especially helpful with cruise vacations. **Flying Wheels Travel** (✉ 143 W. Bridge St., Box 382, Owatonna, MN 55060, ☎ 507/451–5005 or 800/535–6790, FAX 507/451–1685), a travel agency specializing in customized tours and itineraries worldwide. **Hinsdale Travel Service** (✉ 201 E. Ogden Ave., Suite 100, Hinsdale, IL 60521, ☎ 630/325–1335), a travel agency that benefits from the advice of wheelchair traveler Janice Perkins.

➤ TRAVELERS WITH DEVELOPMENTAL DISABILITIES: **Sprout** (✉ 893 Amsterdam Ave., New York, NY 10025, ☎ 212/222–9575 or 888/222–9575, FAX 212/222–9768).

DISCOUNTS & DEALS

Be a smart shopper and **compare all your options** before making any choice. A plane ticket bought with a promotional coupon may not be cheaper than the least expensive fare from a discount ticket agency. For high-price travel purchases, such as packages or tours, keep in mind that what you get is as important as what you save. Just because something is cheap doesn't mean it's a bargain.

CLUBS & COUPONS

Many companies sell discounts in the form of travel clubs and coupon books, but these cost money. You must use participating advertisers to get a deal, and only after you recoup the initial membership cost or book price do you begin to save. If you plan to use the club or coupons frequently, you may save considerably. Before signing up, find out what discounts you get for free.

➤ DISCOUNT CLUBS: **Entertainment Travel Editions** (✉ 2125 Butterfield Rd., Troy, MI 48084, ☎ 800/445–4137; $20–$51, depending on destination). **Great American Traveler** (✉ Box 27965, Salt Lake City, UT 84127, ☎ 801/974–3033 or 800/548–2812; $49.95 per year). **Moment's Notice Discount Travel Club** (✉ 7301 New Utrecht Ave., Brooklyn, NY 11204, ☎ 718/234–6295; $25 per year, single or family). **Privilege Card International** (✉ 237 E. Front St., Youngstown, OH 44503, ☎ 330/746–5211 or 800/236–9732; $74.95 per year). **Sears' Mature Outlook** (✉ Box 9390, Des Moines, IA 50306, ☎ 800/336–6330; $19.95 per year). **Travelers Advantage** (✉ CUC Travel Service, ✉ 3033 S. Parker Rd., Suite 1000, Aurora, CO 80014, ☎ 800/548–1116 or 800/648–4037; $59.95 per year, single or family). **Worldwide Discount Travel Club** (✉ 1674 Meridian Ave., Miami Beach, FL 33139, ☎ 305/534–2082; $50 per year family, $40 single).

CREDIT-CARD BENEFITS

When you use your credit card to make travel purchases you may get free travel-accident insurance, collision-damage insurance, and medical or legal assistance, depending on the card and the bank that issued it. American Express, MasterCard, and Visa provide one or more of these services, so **get a copy of your credit card's travel-benefits policy.** If you are a member of an auto club, always **ask hotel and car-rental reservations agents about auto-club discounts.** Some clubs offer additional discounts on tours, cruises, and admission to attractions.

DISCOUNT RESERVATIONS

To save money, **look into discount-reservations services** with toll-free numbers, which use their buying power to get a better price on hotels, airline tickets, even car rentals. When booking a room, always **call the hotel's local toll-free number** (if one is available) rather than the central reservations number—you'll often get a better price. Always ask about special packages or corporate rates.

When shopping for the best deal on hotels and car rentals, **look for guaranteed exchange rates,** which protect you against a falling dollar. Your rate is locked in, even if the price goes up in the local currency.

➤ AIRLINE TICKETS: ☎ **800/FLY–4–LESS.**

➤ HOTEL ROOMS: **Hotels Plus** (☎ **800/235–0909**). **Hotel Reservations Network** (☎ **800/964–6835**). **Steigenberger Reservation Service** (☎ **800/223–5652**). **Travel Interlink** (☎ **800/888–5898**).

PACKAGE DEALS

Packages and guided tours can save you money, but don't confuse the two. When you buy a package, your travel remains independent, just as though you had planned and booked the trip yourself. Fly/drive packages, which combine airfare and car rental, are often a good deal. In cities, ask the local visitor's bureau about hotel packages. These often include tickets to major museum exhibits and other special events.

DRIVING

The best advice on driving in London is: don't. Because the capital grew up as a series of villages, there never was a central plan for London's streets, and the result is a winding mass of chaos, aggravated by a passion for one-way streets.

If you must risk life and limb, however, note that the speed limit is 30 mph in the royal parks, as well as in all streets—unless you see the large 40 mph signs (and small repeater signs attached to lampposts) found only in the suburbs. Other basic rules: pedestrians have right-of-way on "zebra" crossings (black-and-white stripes that stretch across the street between two Belisha beacons—orange-flashing globe lights on posts). The curb on each side of the zebra crossing has zigzag markings. It is illegal to park within the zigzag area or to pass another vehicle at a zebra crossing. At other crossings pedestrians must yield to traffic, but they do have right-of-way over traffic turning left at con-

trolled crossings—if they have the nerve.

Traffic lights sometimes have arrows directing left or right turns; get into the turn lane if you mean to go straight ahead—don't try to catch a glimpse of the road markings in time. The use of horns is prohibited between 11:30 PM and 7 AM.

You can park at night in 30-mph zones, provided you are within 25 yards of a lighted street lamp, but not within 15 yards of a road junction (within central London this includes parking on single yellow lines—but never on a double—after 6 PM or 8 PM. Watch for the No Waiting signposts on the sidewalk that tell you when restrictions are relaxed). To park on a bus route, you must show side (parking) lights, but you'll probably get a ticket anyway unless it's after 7 PM, or whenever the signpost indicates it's permitted. On "Red Routes"—busy stretches with red lines painted in the street—you may not even stop to let a passenger out. During the day—and probably at all times—it is safest to believe that you can park nowhere except at a meter, in a garage, or where you are sure there are no lines or signs; otherwise, you run the risk of a towing cost of about £100, or a wheel clamp, which costs about the same, since you pay to have the clamp removed, plus the one or two tickets you'll have earned first. It is also illegal to park on the sidewalk, across entrances, or on white zigzag lines approaching a pedestrian crossing. If you must drive, an indispensable, insider's reference book is the **London Parking Guide** (£4.99, Two Heads Publishing), usually found in better bookstores.

ELECTRICITY

To use your U.S.-purchased electric-powered equipment, **bring a converter and adapter.** The electrical current in London is 230 volts (about twice the voltage used for American equipment), 50 cycles alternating current (AC); wall outlets use three-pin plugs, shaver sockets take two round, over-size prongs.

If your appliances are dual-voltage, you'll need only an adapter. Don't use 110-volt outlets, marked FOR SHAVERS

ONLY, for high-wattage appliances such as blow-dryers. Most laptops operate equally well on 110 and 220 volts and so require only an adapter. For converters and adapters, go to your local electrical supply store.

EMBASSIES

➤ AUSTRALIA: **Australia House** (✉ Strand, WC2, ☎ 0171/379–4334).

➤ CANADA: **MacDonald House** (✉ 38 Grosvenor Sq., W1, ☎ 0171/258–6600).

➤ NEW ZEALAND: **New Zealand House** (✉ 80 Haymarket, SW1, ☎ 0171/930–8422).

➤ UNITED STATES: **U.S. Embassy** (✉ 24 Grosvenor Sq., W1, ☎ 0171/499–9000); for passports, go to the **U.S. Passport Unit** (✉ 55 Upper Brook St., W1, ☎ 0171/499–9000).

EMERGENCIES

➤ DOCTORS & DENTISTS: **Doctor's Call** (☎ 0181/900–1000); **Medical Express**, a private, for-profit outfit (✉ 117A Harley St., W1, ☎ 0171/499–1991); **Eastman Dental Hospital** (☎ 0171/915–1000).

➤ EMERGENCIES: Dial **999** for police, fire, or ambulance.

➤ HOSPITALS: For emergency hospital care, with first treatment free under the National Health Service regulations: **Royal Free Hospital** (✉ Pond St., NW3, ☎ 0171/794–0500) and **University College Hospital** (✉ Grafton Way, WC1, ☎ 0171/387–9300). Most other London hospitals also have emergency rooms.

➤ 24-HOUR PHARMACIES: In Britain, drugstores are called chemists. The leading chain is Boots, but the best bet for hours until midnight is **Bliss the Chemist** (✉ 5 Marble Arch, W1, ☎ 0171/723–6116).

GAY & LESBIAN TRAVEL

➤ GAY- AND LESBIAN-FRIENDLY TOUR OPERATORS: **Hanns Ebensten Travel** (✉ 513 Fleming St., Key West, FL 33040, ☎ 305/294–8174, FAX 305/292–9665), one of the oldest operators in the gay market.

➤ GAY- AND LESBIAN-FRIENDLY TRAVEL AGENCIES: **Corniche Travel** (✉ 8721 Sunset Blvd., Suite 200, West Holly-wood, CA 90069, ☎ 310/854–6000 or 800/429–8747, FAX 310/659–7441). **Islanders Kennedy Travel** (✉ 183 W. 10th St., New York, NY 10014, ☎ 212/242–3222 or 800/988–1181, FAX 212/929–8530). **Now Voyager** (✉ 4406 18th St., San Francisco, CA 94114, ☎ 415/626–1169 or 800/255–6951, FAX 415/626–8626). **Yellowbrick Road** (✉ 1500 W. Balmoral Ave., Chicago, IL 60640, ☎ 773/561–1800 or 800/642–2488, FAX 773/561–4497). **Skylink Travel and Tour** (✉ 3577 Moorland Ave., Santa Rosa, CA 95407, ☎ 707/585–8355 or 800/225–5759, FAX 707/584–5637), serving lesbian travelers.

HEALTH

MEDICAL PLANS

No one plans to get sick while traveling, but it happens, so **consider signing up with a medical-assistance company.** Members get doctor referrals, emergency evacuation or repatriation, 24-hour telephone hot lines for medical consultation, cash for emergencies, and other personal and legal assistance. Coverage varies by plan, so **review the benefits of each.**

➤ MEDICAL-ASSISTANCE COMPANIES: **International SOS Assistance** (✉ 8 Neshaminy Interplex, Suite 207, Trevose, PA 19053, ☎ 215/245–4707 or 800/523–6586, FAX 215/244–9617; ✉ 12 Chemin Riant-bosson, 1217 Meyrin 1, Geneva, Switzerland, ☎ 4122/785–6464, FAX 4122/785–6424; ✉ 10 Anson Rd., 14-07/08 International Plaza, Singapore, 079903, ☎ 65/226–3936, FAX 65/226–3937).

HOLIDAYS

New Year's Day, Good Friday, Easter Monday, May Day (first Monday in May), spring and summer bank holidays (last Monday in May and August, respectively), Christmas, and Boxing Day (day after Christmas).

INSURANCE

Travel insurance is the best way to **protect yourself against financial loss.** The most useful plan is a comprehensive policy that includes coverage for trip cancellation and interruption, default, trip delay, and medical expenses (with a waiver for preexisting conditions).

Without insurance, you will lose all or most of your money if you cancel your trip, regardless of the reason. Default insurance covers you if your tour operator, airline, or cruise line goes out of business. Trip-delay covers unforeseen expenses incurred due to bad weather or mechanical delays. **Compare the fine print regarding trip-delay coverage when comparing policies.**

For overseas travel, one of the most important components of travel insurance is its medical coverage. Supplemental health insurance will pick up the cost of your medical bills should you get sick or injured while traveling. U.S. residents should note that Medicare generally does not cover health-care costs outside the United States, nor do many privately issued policies. Residents of the United Kingdom can buy an annual travel-insurance policy valid for most vacations taken during the year in which the coverage is purchased. If you are pregnant or have a pre-existing condition, make sure you're covered. Australian travelers should buy travel insurance, including extra medical coverage, whenever they go abroad, according to the Insurance Council of Australia.

Always **buy travel insurance directly from the insurance company**; if you buy it from a cruise line, airline, or tour operator that goes out of business you probably will not be covered for the agency or operator's default, a major risk. Before you make any purchase, **review your existing health and home-owner's policies** to find out whether they cover expenses incurred while traveling.

➤ TRAVEL INSURERS: In the U.S., **Access America** (✉ 6600 W. Broad St., Richmond, VA 23230, ☎ 804/285–3300 or 800/284–8300). **Travel Guard International** (✉ 1145 Clark St., Stevens Point, WI 54481, ☎ 715/345–0505 or 800/826–1300). In Canada, **Mutual of Omaha** (✉ Travel Division, ✉ 500 University Ave., Toronto, Ontario M5G 1V8, ☎ 416/598–4083, 800/268–8825 in Canada).

➤ INSURANCE INFORMATION: In the U.K., **Association of British Insurers** (✉ 51 Gresham St., London EC2V 7HQ, ☎ 0171/600–3333). In Australia, the **Insurance Council of Australia** (☎ 613/9614–1077, FAX 613/9614–7924).

LODGING

APARTMENT & HOUSE RENTALS

If you want a home base that's roomy enough for a family and comes with cooking facilities, **consider a furnished rental.** These can save you money, especially if you're traveling with a large group of people. Home-exchange directories list rentals (often second homes owned by prospective house swappers), and some services search for a house or apartment for you (even a castle if that's your fancy) and handle the paperwork. Some send an illustrated catalog; others send photographs only of specific properties, sometimes at a charge. Up-front registration fees may apply. For agencies that specialize in London B&B listings, *see* Chapter 4.

➤ RENTAL AGENTS: **At Home Abroad** (✉ 405 E. 56th St., Suite 6H, New York, NY 10022, ☎ 212/421–9165, FAX 212/752–1591). **Drawbridge to Europe** (✉ 5456 Adams Rd., Talent, OR 97540, ☎ 541/512–8927 or 888/268–1148, FAX 541/512–0978). **Europa-Let/Tropical Inn-Let** (✉ 92 N. Main St., Ashland, OR 97520, ☎ 541/482–5806 or 800/462–4486, FAX 541/482–0660). **Hometours International** (✉ Box 11503, Knoxville, TN 37939, ☎ 423/690–8484 or 800/367–4668). **Interhome** (✉ 124 Little Falls Rd., Fairfield, NJ 07004, ☎ 973/882–6864 or 800/882–6864, FAX 973/808–1742). **Property Rentals International** (✉ 1008 Mansfield Crossing Rd., Richmond, VA 23236, ☎ 804/378–6054 or 800/220–3332, FAX 804/379–2073). **Rental Directories International** (✉ 2044 Rittenhouse Sq., Philadelphia, PA 19103, ☎ 215/985–4001, FAX 215/985–0323). **Rent-a-Home International** (✉ 7200 34th Ave. NW, Seattle, WA 98117, ☎ 206/789–9377 or 800/488–7368, FAX 206/789–9379). **Vacation Home Rentals Worldwide** (✉ 235 Kensington Ave., Norwood, NJ 07648, ☎ 201/767–9393 or 800/633–3284, FAX 201/767–5510). **Villas and Apartments Abroad** (✉ 420 Madison Ave.,

Suite 1003, New York, NY 10017, ☎ 212/759–1025 or 800/433–3020, FAX 212/755–8316). **Villas International** (✉ 950 Northgate Dr., Suite 206, San Rafael, CA 94903, ☎ 415/499–9490 or 800/221–2260, FAX 415/499–9491). **Hideaways International** (✉ 767 Islington St., Portsmouth, NH 03801, ☎ 603/430–4433 or 800/843–4433, FAX 603/430–4444; membership $99; travelers arrange rentals among themselves).

HOME EXCHANGES

If you would like to exchange your home for someone else's, **join a home-exchange organization,** which will send you its updated listings of available exchanges for a year and will include your own listing in at least one of them. It's up to you to make specific arrangements.

➤ EXCHANGE CLUBS: **HomeLink International** (✉ Box 650, Key West, FL 33041, ☎ 305/294–7766 or 800/638–3841, FAX 305/294–1148; $83 per year).

HOSTELS

No matter what your age, you can **save on lodging costs by staying at hostels.** In some 5,000 locations in more than 70 countries around the world, Hostelling International (HI), the umbrella group for a number of national youth hostel associations, offers single-sex, dorm-style beds and, at many hostels, "couples" rooms and family accommodations. Membership in any HI national hostel association, open to travelers of all ages, allows you to stay in HI-affiliated hostels at member rates (one-year membership is about $25 for adults; hostels run about $10–$25 per night). Members also have priority if the hostel is full; they're eligible for discounts around the world, even on rail and bus travel in some countries.

➤ HOSTEL ORGANIZATIONS: **Hostelling International—American Youth Hostels** (✉ 733 15th St. NW, Suite 840, Washington, DC 20005, ☎ 202/783–6161, FAX 202/783–6171). **Hostelling International—Canada** (✉ 400-205 Catherine St., Ottawa, Ontario K2P 1C3, ☎ 613/237–7884, FAX 613/237–7868). **Youth Hostel Association of England and Wales** (✉

Trevelyan House, ✉ 8 St. Stephen's Hill, St. Albans, Hertfordshire AL1 2DY, ☎ 01727/855215 or 01727/845047, FAX 01727/844126); membership in the U.S. $25, in Canada C$26.75, in the U.K. £9.30).

MAIL

Greater London is divided into 32 boroughs—33, counting the City of London, which has all the powers of a London borough. More useful for finding your way around, however, are the subdivisions of London into various postal districts. Throughout the guide we've listed the full postal code for places you're likely to be contacting by mail, although you'll find the first half of the code more important. The first one or two letters give the location: N = north, NW = northwest, etc. Don't expect the numbering to be logical, however. You won't, for example, find W2 next to W3.

Stamps may be bought from main or subpost offices (the latter are located in stores), from stamp machines outside post offices, and from many newsagents stores and newsstands. Mailboxes are known as post or letter boxes and are painted bright red; large tubular ones are set on the edge of sidewalks, while smaller boxes are set into post-office walls.

POSTAL RATES

Postal rates are: airmail letters up to 10 grams to North America, 43p; postcards 37p, aerogrammes 36p. Letters within Britain are 26p for first class, 20p for second class. Always check rates in advance, however, as they are subject to change.

RECEIVING MAIL

If you're uncertain where you'll be staying, you can have mail sent to you c/o Poste Restante, The **London Main Post Office** at Trafalgar Square (✉ 24–28 William IV St., London WC2N 4DL), open Mon.–Sat. 8:30–9. They will hold international mail for one month (☎ 0171/930–9580). This service can be arranged at any main or sub–post office. (☎ 0345/740–740). You can also collect letters at **American Express** (✉ 6 Haymarket, SW1Y 4BS, ☎ 0171/930–4411, or any other branch). The service is free to cardholders and traveler's-check holders; all others pay a small fee.

MONEY

The units of currency in Great Britain are pound sterling (£) and pence (p): £50, £20, £10, and £5 bills; £2, £1 (100p), 50p, 20p, 10p, 5p, 2p, and 1p coins. At press time, the exchange rate was about U.S. $1.65 and Canadian $2.35 to the pound (also known as quid).

COSTS

A movie in the West End costs £5–£9.50 (less on Monday and at matinees); a theater seat, from £6.50 to about £33, more for hit shows; admission to a museum or gallery, around £3 (though some are free and others request a "voluntary contribution"); coffee, £1–£2; a pint of light (lager) beer in a pub, £2 and more; whiskey, gin, vodka, and so forth, by the glass in a pub, £2.50 and up (the measure is smaller than in the United States); house wine by the glass in a pub or wine bar, around £2, in a restaurant, £3.50 or more; a Coke, around 80p; a ham sandwich from a sandwich bar in the West End, £2; a 1-mi taxi ride, £4; an average Underground or bus ride, £1.60, a longer one, £2.50.

London now ranks as one of the world's most expensive hotel capitals. Finding budget accommodations—especially during July and August—can be difficult; you should try to book well ahead if you are visiting during these months. Many London hotels offer special off-season (October–March) rates, however. Dining out at top restaurants can be prohibitively expensive, but there are new chains of French-Italian-style café-brasseries, along with a large number of pubs and ethnic restaurants that offer excellent food at reasonable prices. Fast-food facilities of every nationality are widespread. Post and pre–theater menus, offering two courses for a set price, are worth taking advantage of.

CREDIT & DEBIT CARDS

Should you use a credit card or a debit card when traveling? Both have benefits. A credit card allows you to delay payment and gives you certain rights as a consumer (☞ Consumer Protection, *above*). A debit card, also known as a check card, deducts funds directly from your checking account and helps you stay within your budget. When you want to rent a car, though, you may still need a credit card. Although you can always *pay* for your car with a debit card, some agencies will not allow you to *reserve* a car with a debit card.

Otherwise, the two types of plastic are virtually the same. Both will get you cash advances at ATMs worldwide if your card is properly programmed with your personal identification number. (For use in London, your PIN must be four digits long or less.) Both offer excellent, wholesale exchange rates. And both protect you against unauthorized use if the card is lost or stolen. Your liability is limited to $50, as long as you report the card missing.

➤ ATM LOCATIONS: **Cirrus** (☎ 800/424–7787). **Plus** (☎ 800/843–7587) for locations in the U.S. and Canada, or visit your local bank.

EXCHANGING MONEY

For the most favorable rates, **change money through banks.** Although fees charged for ATM transactions may be higher abroad than at home, Cirrus and Plus exchange rates are excellent, because they are based on wholesale rates offered only by major banks. You won't do as well at exchange booths in airports or rail and bus stations, in hotels, in restaurants, or in stores, although their hours may be more convenient. To avoid lines at airport exchange booths, **get a bit of local currency before you leave home.**

➤ EXCHANGE SERVICES: **Chase *Currency To Go*** (☎ 800/935–9935; 935–9935 in NY, NJ, and CT). **International Currency Express** (☎ 888/842–0880 on the East Coast, 888/278–6628 on the West Coast). **Thomas Cook Currency Services** (☎ 800/287–7362 for telephone orders and retail locations).

TRAVELER'S CHECKS

Do you need traveler's checks? It depends on where you're headed. If you're going to rural areas and small towns, go with cash; traveler's checks are best used in cities. Lost or stolen checks can usually be replaced within 24 hours. To ensure a speedy refund, buy your own traveler's checks—don't let someone else pay for them: irregularities like this can cause delays. The person who bought the checks should make the call to request a refund.

PACKING

London can be cool, damp, and overcast, even in summer. You'll need a heavy coat for winter and a lightweight coat or warm jacket for summer. Always **bring an umbrella and, if possible, a raincoat.** Pack as you would for an American city: jackets and ties for expensive restaurants and nightspots, casual clothes elsewhere. Jeans are popular in London and are perfectly acceptable for sightseeing and informal dining. Blazers and sport jackets are popular here with men. For women, ordinary street dress is acceptable everywhere. If you plan to stay in budget hotels, take your own soap.

In your carry-on luggage **bring an extra pair of eyeglasses or contact lenses** and **enough of any medication you take** to last the entire trip. You may also want your doctor to write a spare prescription using the drug's generic name, since brand names may vary from country to country. **Never put prescription drugs or valuables in luggage to be checked.** To avoid customs delays, carry medications in their original packaging. And don't forget to copy down and carry addresses of offices that handle refunds of lost traveler's checks.

LUGGAGE

How many carry-on bags you can bring with you is up to the airline. Most allow two, but the limit is often reduced to one on certain flights. Gate agents will take excess baggage—including bags they deem oversize—from you as you board and add it to checked luggage. To avoid this situation, make sure that everything you carry aboard will fit under your seat. Also, get to the gate early, and request a seat at the back of the plane; you'll probably board first, while the overhead bins are still empty. Since big, bulky baggage attracts the attention of gate agents and flight attendants on a busy flight, make sure your carry-on is really a carry-on. Finally, a carry-on that's long and narrow is more likely to remain unnoticed than one that's wide and squarish.

On international flights baggage allowances may be determined not by piece but by weight—generally 88 pounds (40 kilograms) in first class, 66 pounds (30 kilograms) in business class, and 44 pounds (20 kilograms) in economy.

Airline liability for baggage is limited to $1,250 per person on flights within the United States. On international flights it amounts to $9.07 per pound or $20 per kilogram for checked baggage (roughly $640 per 70-pound bag) and $400 per passenger for unchecked baggage. You can buy additional coverage at check-in for about $10 per $1,000 of coverage, but it excludes a rather extensive list of items, shown on your airline ticket.

Before departure, **itemize your bags' contents** and their worth, and label the bags with your name, address, and phone number. (If you use your home address, cover it so that potential thieves can't see it readily.) Inside each bag, **pack a copy of your itinerary.** At check-in, **make sure that each bag is correctly tagged** with the destination airport's three-letter code. If your bags arrive damaged or fail to arrive at all, file a written report with the airline before leaving the airport.

PASSPORTS & VISAS

U.S. and Canadian citizens need only a valid passport to enter Great Britain for stays of up to 90 days. For international travel, **carry a passport even if you don't need one** (it's always the best form of ID), and make **two photocopies of the data page** (one for someone at home and another for you, carried separately from your passport). If you lose your passport, promptly call the nearest embassy or consulate and the local police.

PASSPORT OFFICES

The best time to apply for a passport or to renew is during the fall and winter. Before any trip, be sure to check your passport's expiration date and, if necessary, renew it as soon as possible. (Some countries won't allow you to enter on a passport that's due to expire in six months or less.)

➤ AUSTRALIAN CITIZENS: **Australian Passport Office** (☎ 13/1232).

➤ CANADIAN CITIZENS: **Passport Office** (☎ 819/994–3500 or 800/567–6868).

➤ NEW ZEALAND CITIZENS: **New Zealand Passport Office** (☎ 04/494–0700 for information on how to apply, 0800/727–776 for information on applications already submitted).

➤ U.S. CITIZENS: **National Passport Information Center** (☎ 900/225–5674; calls are charged at 35¢ per minute for automated service, $1.05 per minute for operator service).

SENIOR-CITIZEN TRAVEL

To qualify for age-related discounts, **mention your senior-citizen status up front** when booking hotel reservations (not when checking out) and before you're seated in restaurants (not when paying the bill). Note that discounts may be limited to certain menus, days, or hours. When renting a car, **ask about promotional car-rental discounts,** which can be cheaper than senior-citizen rates.

➤ EDUCATIONAL PROGRAMS: **Elderhostel** (✉ 75 Federal St., 3rd floor, Boston, MA 02110, ☎ 617/426–8056). **Interhostel** (✉ University of New Hampshire, ✉ 6 Garrison Ave., Durham, NH 03824, ☎ 603/862–1147 or 800/733–9753, FAX 603/862–1113).

SIGHTSEEING TOURS

BY BUS

Guided sightseeing tours offer passengers a good introduction to the city from double-decker buses, which are open-topped in summer. Tours run daily and depart from Haymarket, Baker Street, Grosvenor Gardens, Marble Arch, and Victoria. You may board or alight at any of about 21 stops to view the sights, and then get back on the next bus. Tickets (£12) may be bought from the driver. These tours include stops at places such as St. Paul's Cathedral and Westminster

Abbey. Prices and pickup points vary according to the sights visited, but many pickup points are at major hotels.

➤ TOUR OPERATORS: **Evan Evans** (☎ 0181/332–2222), **Frames Rickards** (☎ 0171/837–3111), **The Original London Sightseeing Tour** (☎ 0181/877–1722), and **The Big Bus Company** (☎ 0181/944–7810). **Black Taxi Tour of London** (☎ 0171/289–4371).

BY CANAL

In summer, narrow boats and barges cruise London's two canals, the Grand Union and Regent's Canal; most vessels (they seat about 60) operate on the latter, which runs between Little Venice in the west (nearest tube: Warwick Avenue on the Bakerloo Line) and Camden Lock (about 200 yards north of Camden Town tube station). Fares are about £5 for 1½-hour cruises.

➤ CRUISE OPERATORS: **Canal Cruises** (☎ 0171/485–4433). **Jason's Trip** (☎ 0171/286–3428). **London Waterbus Company** (☎ 0171/482–2660).

BY FOOT

One of the best ways to get to know London is on foot, and there are many guided and themed walking tours from which to choose.

➤ TOUR OPERATORS: **City Walks** (☎ 0171/700–6931). **Original London Walks** (☎ 0171/624–3978). **Streets of London** (☎ 0181/346–9255).

BY RIVER

All year round, but more frequently in April to October, boats cruise the Thames, offering a different view of the London skyline. Most leave from Westminster Pier, Charing Cross Pier, and Tower Pier. Downstream routes go to the Tower of London, Greenwich, and the Thames Barrier; upstream destinations include Kew, Richmond, and Hampton Court. Most of the launches seat between 100 and 250 passengers, have a public-address system, and provide a running commentary on passing points of interest. Depending upon the destination, river trips may last from one to four hours.

➤ RIVER CRUISE OPERATORS: **Catamaran Cruisers** (from Charing Cross to Greenwich (☎ 0171/839–3572). **Thames Cruises** (☎ 0171/930–3373 for the Thames Barrier and Greenwich). **Westminster Passenger Boat Services** (☎ 0171/930–4097).

A **Sail and Rail** ticket combines the modern wonders of Canary Wharf by Docklands Light Railway with a trip on the river. Tickets are available year-round from Westminster Pier or DLR stations, Canary Wharf, Island Gardens and Tower Gateway (☎ 0171/363–9700); ticket holders also get discounted tickets to the London Aquarium at Westminster, the Tower Bridge Experience, and the National Maritime Museum, Greenwich.

EXCURSIONS

London Regional Transport, Green Line, Evan Evans, and **Frames Rickards** all offer day excursions by bus to places within easy reach of London, such as Hampton Court, Oxford, Stratford, and Bath.

TRAVEL AGENCIES

To save money, **look into deals available through student-oriented travel agencies.** To qualify you'll need a bona fide student ID card. Members of international student groups are also eligible.

➤ STUDENT IDs & SERVICES: **Council on International Educational Exchange** (✉ CIEE, ✉ 205 E. 42nd St., 14th floor, New York, NY 10017, ☎ 212/822–2600 or 888/268–6245, 🖷 212/822–2699), for mail orders only, in the United States. **Travel Cuts** (✉ 187 College St., Toronto, Ontario M5T 1P7, ☎ 416/979–2406 or 800/667–2887) in Canada.

➤ STUDENT TOURS: **Contiki Holidays** (✉ 300 Plaza Alicante, Suite 900, Garden Grove, CA 92840, ☎ 714/740–0808 or 800/266–8454, 🖷 714/740–2034). **AESU Travel** (✉ 2 Hamill Rd., Suite 248, Baltimore, MD 21210-1807, ☎ 410/323–4416 or 800/638–7640, 🖷 410/323–4498).

TAXES

AIRPORT

An airport departure tax of £20 (£10 for within UK and EU countries) per person is payable, and may be subject to more government tax increases, although it is included in the price of your ticket.

VALUE-ADDED TAX (VAT)

The British sales tax (VAT, Value Added Tax) is 17½%. The tax is almost always included in quoted prices in shops, hotels, and restaurants.

You can **get a VAT refund** by either the Retail Export or the more cumbersome Direct Export method. Most large stores provide these services, but only if you request them, and will handle the paperwork. For the Retail Export method, you must ask the store for Form VAT 407 (you must have identification—passports are best), to be given to customs at your last port of departure. (Lines at major airports can be long, so allow plenty of time.) The refund will be forwarded to you in about eight weeks, minus a small service charge, either in the form of a credit to your charge card or as a British check, which American banks usually charge you to convert. With the Direct Export method, the goods go directly to your home; you must have a Form VAT 407 certified by customs, police, or a notary public when you get home and then sent back to the store, which will refund your money. For inquiries, call the local Customs & Excise office listed in the telephone directory.

TAXIS

Those big black taxicabs are as much a part of the London streetscape as the red double-decker buses, yet many have been replaced by the new boxy, sharp-edged model, while the beauty of others is marred by the advertising they carry on their sides. Hotels and main tourist areas have cab stands (just take the first in line), but you can also **flag one down from the roadside.** If the yellow FOR HIRE sign on the top is lit, the taxi is available. Cab drivers often cruise at night with their signs unlit so that they can choose their passengers and avoid those they think might cause trouble. If you see an unlit, passengerless cab, hail it: you might be lucky.

FARES

Fares start at £1.40 and increase by units of 20p per 281 yards or 55.5 seconds until the fare exceeds £8.60. After that, it's 20p for each 188 yards or 37 seconds. A 60p surcharge is added on weekday nights 8–midnight and until 8 PM on Saturday. Over Christmas and New Year's Eve, it rises to £2—and there's 40p extra for each additional passenger. Note that fares are usually raised in April of each year. Tips are extra, usually 10% to 15% per ride.

TELEPHONES

COUNTRY CODES

The country code for Great Britain is 44. London has two area codes, 0171 for inner London and 0181 for outer London. You don't have to dial either if you are calling inside the same zone. Drop the 0 from the prefix and dial only 171 or 181 (or any other British area code) when calling from overseas. To give one example: let's say you're calling Buckingham Palace—0171/839–1377—from the U.S. to inquire about tours and hours. First, dial 011 (the international access code), then 44 (Great Britain's country code), then 171 (London's center city code), then the remainder of the telephone number.

DIRECTORY & OPERATOR INFORMATION

For information anywhere in Britain, dial 192. For the operator, dial 100. For assistance with international calls, dial 155.

INTERNATIONAL CALLS

AT&T, MCI, and Sprint international access codes make calling the United States relatively convenient, but you may find the local access number blocked in many hotel rooms. First ask the hotel operator to connect you. If the hotel operator balks, ask for an international operator, or dial the international operator yourself. One way to improve your odds of getting connected to your long-distance carrier is to travel with more than one company's calling card (a hotel may block Sprint, for example, but not MCI). If all else fails, call from a pay phone in the hotel lobby.

➤ ACCESS CODES: **AT&T Direct** (☎ In the U.K., there are AT&T access numbers to dial the U.S. using three different phone types—Mercury: 0500/890011; British Telecom: 0800/890011; and AT&T: 0800/0130011; ☎ 800/435–0812 for other areas). **MCI WorldPhone** (☎ In the U.K., dial 0800/890222 to dial the U.S via MCI.; ☎ 800/444–4141 for other areas). **Sprint International Access** (☎ In the U.K., there are Sprint access numbers to dial the U.S. using two different phone types—Mercury: 0500/890877; and British Telecom: 0800/890877); ☎ 800/877–4646 for other areas).

LONG-DISTANCE CALLS

For long-distance calls within Britain, dial the area code (which begins with 01), followed by the number. The area code prefix is only used when you are dialing from outside the city. In provincial areas, the dialing codes for nearby towns are often posted in the booth.

PUBLIC PHONES

There are three types of phones: those that accept (a) only coins, (b) only British Telecom (BT) phone cards, or (c) BT phone cards and credit cards.

The coin-operated phones are of the push-button variety; the workings of coin-operated telephones vary, but there are usually instructions in each unit. Most take 10p, 20p, 50p, and £1 coins. Insert the coins *before* dialing (minimum charge is 10p). If you hear a repeated single tone after dialing, the line is busy; a continual tone means the number is unobtainable (or that you have dialed the wrong—or no—prefix). The indicator panel shows you how much money is left; add more whenever you like. If there is no answer, replace the receiver and your money will be returned.

All calls are charged according to the time of day. Standard rate is weekdays 8 AM–6 PM; cheap rate is weekdays 6 PM–8 AM and all day on weekends when it's even cheaper. A local call before 6 PM costs 15p for three minutes; this doubles to 30p for the same from a pay phone. A daytime call to the United States will cost 24p a minute, on a regular phone (weekends are cheaper); 80p on a pay phone.

Card phones operate with special cards that you can buy from post offices or newsstands. They are ideal for longer calls, are composed of units of 10p, and come in values of £2, £5, £10, and more. To use a card phone, lift the receiver, insert your card, and dial the number. An indicator panel shows the number of units used. At the end of your call, the card will be returned. Where credit cards are taken, slide the card through, as indicated.

TIPPING

Many restaurants and large hotels (particularly those belonging to chains) will automatically add a 10%–15% service charge to your bill, so **always check in advance before you hand out any extra money.** You are, of course, welcome to tip on top of that for exceptional service. If you are dissatisfied with the service, however, refuse to pay the service charge, stating your reasons for doing so; you will be within your rights legally.

Do not tip movie or theater ushers, elevator operators, or bar staff in pubs—although you may buy them a drink if you're feeling generous. Washroom attendants may display a saucer, in which it's reasonable to leave 20p or so.

Here's a guide for other tipping situations: **Restaurants:** 10%–15% of the check for full meals if service is not already included (when you're paying by credit card, check to see if a service tip has not already been included in the bill before you fill in the correct amount in the total box of your credit slip voucher); a small token if you're just having coffee or tea. **Taxis:** 10%–15%, or perhaps a little more for a short ride. **Porters:** 50p–£1 per bag. **Doormen:** £1 for hailing taxis or for carrying bags to check-in desk. **Bellhops:** £1 for carrying bags to rooms, £1 for room service. **Hairdressers:** 10%–15% of the bill, plus £1–£2 for the hair-washer.

TOUR OPERATORS

Buying a prepackaged tour or independent vacation can make your trip to London less expensive and more hassle-free.

Operators that handle several hundred thousand travelers per year can use their purchasing power to give you a good price. Their high volume may also indicate financial stability. But some small companies provide more personalized service; because they tend to specialize, they may also be more knowledgeable about a given area.

The more your package or tour includes, the better you can predict the ultimate cost of your vacation. Make sure you know exactly what is covered, and **beware of hidden costs.** Are taxes, tips, and service charges included? Transfers and baggage handling? Entertainment and excursions? These can add up.

Prices for packages and tours are usually quoted per person, based on two sharing a room. If traveling solo, you may be required to pay the full double-occupancy rate. Some operators eliminate this surcharge if you agree to be matched with a roommate of the same sex, even if one is not found by departure time.

BOOKING WITH AN AGENT

Travel agents are excellent resources. In fact, large operators accept bookings made only through travel agents. But it's a good idea to **collect brochures from several agencies,** because some agents' suggestions may be influenced by relationships with tour and package firms that reward them for volume sales. If you have a special interest, **find an agent with expertise in that area;** ASTA (☞ Travel Agencies, *below*) has a database of specialists worldwide.

Make sure your travel agent knows the accommodations and other services. Ask about the hotel's location, room size, beds, and whether it has a pool, room service, or programs for children, if you care about these. Has your agent been there in person or sent others you can contact?

Do some homework on your own, too: local tourism boards can provide information about lesser-known and small-niche operators, some of which may sell only direct.

THE GOLD GUIDE / SMART TRAVEL TIPS

BUYER BEWARE

Each year consumers are stranded or lose their money when tour operators—even very large ones with excellent reputations—go out of business. So **check out the operator.** Find out how long the company has been in business, and ask several travel agents about its reputation. If the package or tour you are considering is priced lower than in your wildest dreams, **be skeptical.** Try to **book with a company that has a consumer-protection program.** If the operator has such a program, you'll find information about it in the company's brochure. If the operator you are considering does not offer some consumer protection, ask for references from satisfied customers.

In the U.S., members of the National Tour Association and United States Tour Operators Association are required to set aside funds to cover your payments and travel arrangements in case the company defaults. It's also a good idea to choose a company that participates in the American Society of Travel Agent's Tour Operator Program (TOP). This gives you a forum if there are any disputes between you and your tour operator; ASTA will act as mediator.

➤ TOUR-OPERATOR RECOMMENDATIONS: **American Society of Travel Agents** (☞ Travel Agencies, *below*). **National Tour Association** (⊠ NTA, ⊠ 546 E. Main St., Lexington, KY 40508, ☎ 606/226–4444 or 800/755–8687). **United States Tour Operators Association** (⊠ USTOA, ⊠ 342 Madison Ave., Suite 1522, New York, NY 10173, ☎ 212/599–6599 or 800/468–7862, FAX 212/599–6744).

GROUP TOURS

Among companies that sell tours to London, the following are nationally known, have a proven reputation, and offer plenty of options. The classifications used below represent different price categories, and you'll probably encounter these terms when talking to a travel agent or tour operator. The key difference is usually in accommodations, which run from budget to better, and better-yet to best.

➤ SUPER-DELUXE: **Abercrombie & Kent** (⊠ 1520 Kensington Rd., Oak Brook, IL 60521-2141, ☎ 630/954–2944 or 800/323–7308, FAX 630/954–3324). **Travcoa** (⊠ Box 2630, 2350 S.E. Bristol St., Newport Beach, CA 92660, ☎ 714/476–2800 or 800/992–2003, FAX 714/476–2538).

➤ DELUXE: **Globus** (⊠ 5301 S. Federal Circle, Littleton, CO 80123-2980, ☎ 303/797–2800 or 800/221–0090, FAX 303/347–2080). **Maupintour** (⊠ 1515 St. Andrews Dr., Lawrence, KS 66047, ☎ 913/843–1211 or 800/255–4266, FAX 913/843–8351). **Tauck Tours** (⊠ Box 5027, 276 Post Rd. W, Westport, CT 06881-5027, ☎ 203/226–6911 or 800/468–2825, FAX 203/221–6828).

➤ FIRST-CLASS: **Brendan Tours** (⊠ 15137 Califa St., Van Nuys, CA 91411, ☎ 818/785–9696 or 800/421–8446, FAX 818/902–9876). **British Airways Holidays** (☎ 800/247–9297). **Caravan Tours** (⊠ 401 N. Michigan Ave., Chicago, IL 60611, ☎ 312/321–9800 or 800/227–2826, FAX 312/321–9845). **CIE Tours** (⊠ 108 Ridgedale Ave., Morristown, NJ 07960, ☎ 201/292–3438 or 800/243–8687). **Collette Tours** (⊠ 162 Middle St., Pawtucket, RI 02860, ☎ 401/728–3805 or 800/832–4656, FAX 401/728–1380). **DER Travel Services** (⊠ 9501 W. Devon Ave., Rosemont, IL 60018, ☎ 800/782–2424, FAX 800/282–7474 for information or 800/860–9944 for brochures). **Gadabout Tours** (⊠ 700 E. Tahquitz Canyon Way, Palm Springs, CA 92262-6767, ☎ 619/325–5556). **Insight International Tours** (⊠ 745 Atlantic Ave., #720, Boston, MA 02111, ☎ 617/482–2000 or 800/582–8380, FAX 617/482–2884 or 800/622–5015). **Trafalgar Tours** (⊠ 11 E. 26th St., New York, NY 10010, ☎ 212/689–8977 or 800/854–0103, FAX 800/457–6644).

➤ BUDGET: **Cosmos** (☞ Globus, *above*). **Trafalgar** (☞ *above*).

PACKAGES

Like group tours, independent vacation packages are available from major tour operators and airlines.

Those listed below offer vacation packages in a broad price range.

➤ AIR/HOTEL: **American Airlines Vacations** (☎ 800/321–2121). **British Airways Holidays** (☞ *above*). **Celtic International Tours** (✉ 1860 Western Ave., Albany, NY 12203, ☎ 518/463–5511 or 800/833–4373, FAX 518/463–8461). **Continental Vacations** (☎ 800/634–5555). **Delta Vacations** (☎ 800/872–7786). **DER Travel Services** (✉ 9501 W. Devon Ave., Rosemont, IL 60018, ☎ 800/782–2424. **TWA Getaway Vacations** (☎ 800/438–2929). **United Vacations** (☎ 800/328–6877). **US Airways Vacations** (☎ 800/455–0123).

THEME TRIPS

➤ ANTIQUES: **Travel Keys Tours** (✉ Box 162266, Sacramento, CA 95816, ☎ 916/452–5200).

➤ COOKING SCHOOLS: **Le Cordon Bleu** (✉ 404 Airport Executive Pk., Nanuet, NY 10954, ☎ 800/457–2433).

➤ CUSTOMIZED PACKAGES: **Alekx Travel** (✉ 519A S. Andrews Ave., Fort Lauderdale, FL 33301, ☎ 954/462–6767, FAX 954/462–8691). **Great British Vacations** (✉ 4800 S.W. Griffith Dr., #125, Beaverton, OR 97005, ☎ 503/643–8080 or 800/452–8434). **Travel Contacts** (✉ Box 173, Camberley, Surrey GU15 1YE, ☎ 0127667–7217, FAX 012766–3477), which represents 150 tour operators, can satisfy just about any special interest in Great Britain.

➤ HOMES AND GARDENS: **Coopersmith's England** (✉ Box 900, Inverness, CA 94937, ☎ 415/669–1914, FAX 415/669–1942). **Expo Garden Tours** (✉ 70 Great Oak, Redding, CT 06896, ☎ 203/938–0410 or 800/448–2685, FAX 203/938–0427).

➤ LEARNING: **IST Cultural Tours** (✉ 225 W. 34th St., New York, NY 10122-0913, ☎ 212/563–1202 or 800/833–2111, FAX 212/594–6953).

➤ PERFORMING ARTS: **Dailey-Thorp Travel** (✉ 330 W. 58th St., #610, New York, NY 10019-1817, ☎ 212/307–1555 or 800/998–4677, FAX 212/974–1420). **Keith Prowse Tours** (✉ 234 W. 44th St., #1000, New York, NY 10036, ☎ 212/398–1430 or 800/669–7469, FAX 212/302–4251).

➤ TENNIS: **Championship Tennis Tours** (✉ 8040 E. Morgan Trail #12, Scottsdale, AZ 85258, ☎ 602/443–9499 or 800/468–3664, FAX 602/443–8982). **Sportstours** (✉ 2301 Collins Ave., #A1540, Miami Beach, FL 33139, ☎ 800/879–8647, FAX 305/535–0008). **Steve Furgal's International Tennis Tours** (✉ 11828 Rancho Bernardo Rd., #123-305, San Diego, CA 92128, ☎ 619/675–3555 or 800/258–3664).

TRAVEL AGENCIES

A good travel agent puts your needs first. Look for an agency that has been in business at least five years, emphasizes customer service, and has someone on staff who specializes in your destination. In addition, **make sure the agency belongs to a professional trade organization,** such as ASTA in the United States. If your travel agency is also acting as your tour operator, *see* Buyer Beware in Tour Operators, *above*).

➤ LOCAL AGENT REFERRALS: **American Society of Travel Agents** (ASTA, ☎ 800/965–2782 24-hr hot line, FAX 703/684–8319). **Association of Canadian Travel Agents** (✉ Suite 201, 1729 Bank St., Ottawa, Ontario K1V 7Z5, ☎ 613/521–0474, FAX 613/521–0805). **Association of British Travel Agents** (✉ 55–57 Newman St., London W1P 4AH, ☎ 0171/637–2444, FAX 0171/637–0713). **Australian Federation of Travel Agents** (☎ 02/9264–3299). **Travel Agents' Association of New Zealand** (☎ 04/499–0104).

TRAVEL GEAR

Travel catalogs specialize in useful items, such as compact alarm clocks and travel irons, that can **save space when packing.** They also offer dual-voltage appliances, currency converters, and foreign-language phrase books.

➤ CATALOGS: **Magellan's** (☎ 800/962–4943, FAX 805/568–5406). **Orvis Travel** (☎ 800/541–3541, FAX 540/343–7053). **TravelSmith** (☎ 800/950–1600, FAX 800/950–1656).

THE GOLD GUIDE / SMART TRAVEL TIPS

UNDERGROUND AND TRAIN TRAVEL

Known colloquially as the "Tube," London's extensive Underground system is by far the most widely used form of city transportation. Its easily marked routes, crystal-clear signage, and extensive connections make it a delight to travel. Trains run both beneath and aboveground out into the suburbs, and all stations are clearly marked with the London Underground circular symbol. (In Britain, the word "subway" means "pedestrian underpass.") Trains are all one class; smoking is *not* allowed on board or in the stations.

There are 10 basic lines—all named. The Central, District, Northern, Metropolitan, and Piccadilly lines all have branches, usually taking you to the outlying sections of the city, so **be sure to note which branch is needed for your particular destination.** Electronic platform signs tell you the final stop and route of the next train, and some signs conveniently indicate how many minutes you'll have to wait for the train to arrive. Begun in the Victorian era, the Underground is still being expanded and improved. The East London line, which runs from Shoreditch and Whitechapel south to New Cross re-opened after major reconstruction in March 1998. September 1998 is the latest date for the opening of the Jubilee line extension: this state-of-the-art subway will sweep from Green Park to Southwark, with connections to Canary Wharf and the Docklands and the much hyped Millennium Experience megadome, and on to the east at Stratford. One of the newest lines is the Docklands Light Railway, which runs from Stratford in east London and from Bank and Tower Gateway to Island Gardens. Scheduled for completion in January 2000, the new DLR extension will pass the *Cutty Sark* in Greenwich and then continue on to the razzmatazz of the Millennium Experience (North Greenwich station), terminating at Lewisham.

FARES

For both buses and tube fares, London is divided into six concentric zones; the fare goes up the farther out you travel. Ask at Underground ticket counters for the London Transport booklets that give details of all the various ticket options for the tube. Traveling without a valid ticket makes you liable for an on-the-spot fine (£10 at press time).

For one trip between any two stations, you can buy an ordinary single (one-way ticket) for travel anytime on the day of issue; if you're coming back on the same route the same day, an ordinary return (round-trip ticket) costs twice the single fare. Singles vary in price from £1.30 to £3.30—expensive if you're making several journeys in a day. There are several passes good for both the tube and the bus; ☞ Passes, *below.*

HOURS

Trains begin running just after 5 AM Monday–Saturday; the last services leave central London between midnight and 12:30 AM. On Sunday, trains start two hours later and finish about an hour earlier. Frequency of trains depends on the route and the time of day, but normally you should not have to wait more than 10 minutes in central areas.

INFORMATION

A pocket map of the tube network is available free from most Underground ticket counters. A large map is on the wall of each platform.

There are LT (London Transport) Travel Information Centres at the following tube stations: Euston, Hammersmith, King's Cross, Oxford Circus, Piccadilly Circus, St. James's Park, and Victoria, open 7:15 AM–10 PM; and at Heathrow (in Terminals 1,2 and 4), open 6 AM–3 PM). For information on all London tube and bus times, fares, and so on, dial 0171/222–1234 (24 hours). For travelers with disabilities, get the free leaflet, "Access to the Underground" (☎ 0171/918–3312).

PASSES

Several **Travelcards** for tube and bus travel are available at tube and rail stations, as well as some newsstands. These allow unrestricted travel on the tube, most buses, and national railways in the Greater London zones and are valid weekdays after 9:30 AM, weekends, and all public holidays. They cannot be used on airbuses, night buses, or for certain special services. A **One Day Travelcard** (£3.50–£4.30); **Weekend Travelcards**, for the two days of the weekend and on any two consecutive days during public holidays (£5.20–£6.40). **Family Travelcards**: one day ticket for one or two adults with one to four children (£2.80–£3.40 with one child, additional children cost 60p each). The **Carnet** is a book of 10 single tickets valid for central Zone 1 (£10) to use any time over a year. Up-to-date prices can be found on the LT Web site www.londontransport.co.uk. The **Visitor's Travelcard** may be bought in the United States and Canada for three, four, and seven days' travel; it is the same as the LT Card and has a booklet of discount vouchers to London attractions. In the United States, the Visitor's Travelcard costs $25, $32, and $49, respectively; in Canada, C$29, C$36, and C$55, respectively. Apply to travel agents or, in the United States, to **BritRail Travel International** (✉ 1500 Broadway, New York, NY 10036, ☎ 212/382–3737).

BRITRAIL

The main telephone number for **Britrail** train information, prices, and schedules in Britain is ☎ 0345/484950. Outside the U.K., dial ☎ 0161/236–3522. The main administrative office number is ☎ 0171/928–5151.

VISITOR INFORMATION

TOURIST INFORMATION

➤ IN THE U.S.: **British Tourist Authority (BTA)** (✉ 551 5th Ave., 7th Floor, New York, NY 10176, ☎ 212/986–2200 or 800/462–2748; ✉ 625 N. Michigan Ave., Suite 1510, Chicago, IL 60611 (personal callers only); ✉ 620 Cranberry Place, Roswell, GA 30076 (no personal callers), ☎ 404/594–8818; ✉ Columbus Center, 1 Alhambra Plaza, Suite 1465, Coral Gables, FL 33134 (personal callers only).

➤ IN CANADA: (✉ 111 Avenue Rd., 4th floor, Toronto, Ontario M5R 3J8, ☎ 416/925–6326).

➤ IN THE U.K.: (✉ Thames Tower, Black's Rd., London W6 9EL, ☎ 0181/846–9000).

➤ IN LONDON: Go in person to the **London Tourist Information Centre** at Victoria Station Forecourt for general information (in summer, Mon.–Sat. 8–7 and Sun. 8–5; winter, Mon.–Sat. 8–6 and Sun. 8:30–4) or to the **British Travel Centre** (✉ 12 Regent St., SW1Y 4PQ) for travel, hotel, and entertainment information (weekdays 9–6:30, weekends 10–4; May–Sept., Sat. 9–5).

➤ BY PHONE: The London Tourist Board's **Visitorcall** (☎ 0839/123456) phone guide to London gives information about events, theater, museums, transport, shopping, and restaurants. A three-month events calendar (☎ 0839/401279) and an annual version (☎ 0839/401278) are available by fax (set fax machine to polling mode, or press start/receive after the tone). Visitorcall charges are 39p–49p per minute, depending on the time of the call. Note that this service is only accessible in the U.K.

U.S. GOVERNMENT

Government agencies can be an excellent source of inexpensive travel information. When planning your trip, **find out what government materials are available.**

➤ PAMPHLETS: **Consumer Information Center** (✉ Consumer Information Catalogue, Pueblo, CO 81009, ☎ 719/948–3334 or 888/878–3256) for a free catalog that includes travel titles.

WEB SITES

Do check out the World Wide Web when you're planning. You'll find everything from up-to-date weather forecasts to virtual tours of famous cities. Fodor's Web site, www.fodors.com, is a great place to start your online travels. For more information specifically on London, visit:

The British Tourist Authority Web site is at **www.visitbritain.com.** Their new "gateway" Web site, **www.usagateway.vistibritain.com.,** focuses on information most helpful to Britain-bound U.S. travelers.

For London events and news months in advance, visit the following culture and entertainment Web sites **www.timeout.co.uk, www.officiallondontheatre.co.uk,** and **www.ukcalling.co.uk.royal-albert.**

For the latest information about shops, restaurants, art events peruse Britain's glossy monthly magazines—*Tatler, Harpers & Queen, British Vogue, World of Interiors, British House & Garden, The Face.* Many better newsstands also feature the Sunday editions of the leading British newspapers, such as the *London Times,* the *Evening Standard,* the *Independent,* and the *Manchester Guardian;* the "Arts" sections of these papers often have advance news of future events. In addition, these London newspapers have Web sites of their own, full of tips and reviews of the hottest eateries, chicest restaurants, newest hotels. For the hotel scene in London, visit **www.demon.co.uk/hotel-uk.**

WHEN TO GO

The heaviest tourist season in Britain runs mid-April–mid-October, with another peak around Christmas—though the tide never really ebbs. The spring is the time to see the countryside and the royal London parks and gardens at their freshest; early summer to catch the roses and full garden splendor; the fall for near-ideal exploring conditions. The British take their vacations mainly in July and August, and the resorts are crowded. London in summer, however, though full of visitors, is also full of interesting things to see and do. But be warned: air-conditioning is rarely found in places other than department stores, modern restaurants, hotels, and cinemas in London, and in a hot summer you'll swelter. The winter can be rather dismal and is frequently wet and usually cold, but all the theaters, concerts, and exhibitions go full speed.

CLIMATE

London's weather has always been contrary, and in recent years it has proved red hot and cool by turns. It is virtually impossible to forecast what the pattern might be, but you can be fairly certain that it will not be what you expect! The main feature of the British weather is that it is generally mild—with some savage exceptions, especially in summer. It is also fairly damp—though even that has been changing in recent years, with the odd bout of drought. The following list includes the average daily maximum and minimum temperatures for London.

➤ FORECASTS: **Weather Channel Connection** (☎ 900/932–8437), 95¢ per minute from a Touch-Tone phone.

Climate in London

Jan.	43F	6C	May	62F	17C	Sept.	65F	19C
	36	2		47	8		52	11
Feb.	44F	7C	June	69F	20C	Oct.	58F	14C
	36	2		53	12		46	8
Mar.	50F	10C	July	71F	22C	Nov.	50F	10C
	38	3		56	14		42	5
Apr.	56F	13C	Aug.	71F	21C	Dec.	45F	7C
	42	6		56	13		38	4

1 Destination: London

THE CITY OF VILLAGES

L ONDON IS AN ENORMOUS city—600 square mi—on a tiny island, hosting about 7 million Londoners, ⅛ of the entire population of England, Scotland, and Wales; but it has never felt big to me. It is fashioned on a different scale from other capital cities, as if, given the English penchant for modesty and understatement, it felt embarrassed by its size. Each of the 32 boroughs that comprise the whole has its own attitude, and most are subdivided into yet smaller enclaves exhibiting yet more particular behaviors, so that there is really no such person as a generic Londoner. Stay here long enough, and Professor Higgins's feat of deducing Eliza Dolittle's very street of birth from the shape of her vowels will seem like nothing special. It's a cliché, but London really is a city of villages.

I have lived in several of these, and I am fluent in the language of a few others, but my village, Holland Park, is the one I know best, and it illustrates as well as any how London is changing. Holland Park is small—just a few streets surrounding the former grounds of Holland House, a Jacobean mansion whose remains (it was bombed during World War II) now house a restaurant, a gallery, an open-air theater, and a youth hostel. North of the park, Holland Park Avenue metamorphoses into the windy local high street, Notting Hill Gate, then into bleak Bayswater Road, abutted on its right by Kensington Gardens and Hyde Park, before breaking, where the main London gallows once stood, into irritating, commercial Oxford Street. But here, for a few West Eleven moments (postal-district terminology you'd do well to master to help with navigation), it is a broad, plane tree–lined boulevard strung with vast white-stucco late-Victorian houses and looking an awful lot like Paris.

In our sophisticated age, the European ambience of Holland Park Avenue has been seized upon by niche marketers, and we now have two French patisseries, three international newsstands, a BMW showroom, and a candlelighted Provençal restaurant within a couple of blocks. The

history racket is doing similar things all over town, history being what London has to sell now that it no longer cuts much ice in the world economy. It would be sentimental to prefer the avenue's old hardware store and late-night family grocer (open till 9!) to the fancy Continental shops that have replaced them—London's got to move with the times, after all.

Both good and bad come with the new territory. The Pakistani family who used to take turns minding the grocery store bought the block a decade later. Those Patels are now a well-known London dynasty, with most of the capital's newsstands in their empire—a satisfying reversal of roles from the British Raj days. Meanwhile, homeless Londoners (the number is about 100,000, and rising) work the overpriced yuppie supermarket threshold selling their magazine, *The Big Issue,* for a profit of 25p per guilty conscience. As one of the many villages built during Victoria's reign, Holland Park is a neighborhood unaccustomed to urban blight. But much of London has weathered several centuries of coping with the indigent population.

That's one of the best things about the city: everything has been seen before, and history is forever poking its nose in. Whatever you're doing, you're doing it on top of a past layered like striated rock. You can see the cross sections clearly sometimes, as in the City, where lumps of Roman wall nest in the postmodern blocks of the street helpfully named London Wall. Walk toward the Thames to Cheapside, which you can tell was the medieval marketplace if you know the meaning of "ceap" ("to barter"), and there's the little Norman church of St. Mary-le-Bow, rebuilt by Wren and then again after the Blitz, but still ringing the Bow Bells. Then look to your right, and you'll be gobsmacked by the dome of St. Paul's. Of course, all you really wanted was to find a place for lunch—nearly impossible on a weekend in this office wasteland.

Instead of going weak-kneed at the sights, Londoners are apt to complain about such privations while pretending simultaneously that no other city in the United

Kingdom exists. Edinburghers and Liverpudlians can complain till Big Ben tolls 13, but Londoners continue to pull rank with a complacency that amuses and infuriates visitors in about equal measure. London definitely *used* to be important. The vein of water running through its center has always linked the city with the sea, and it once gave British mariners a head start in the race to mine the world's riches and bring them home. The river proved convenient for building not only palaces (at Westminster, Whitehall, Hampton Court, Richmond, Greenwich) but an empire, too.

The empire dissolved, but the first Thames bridge is still there, in almost the same spot that the emperor Claudius picked in AD 43, and although the current drab concrete incarnation dates only from 1972, it's still called London Bridge. The Tudor one was much better—something I learned before I was 10 from visits to the Museum of London, which used to be in nearby Kensington Palace. I liked the old bridge because of the row of decapitated heads stuck on poles above the gatehouse, which you could see on the model. It added a frisson to history, which more recent exhibitions, like the amazingly popular London Dungeon, have rather cynically packaged.

The old London Bridge lasted 600 years. Lined with shops and houses, it presided over a string of fairs *on* the Thames, when winters were colder and the water froze thick. Nowadays we rarely see a snowfall, though we'll talk endlessly about its possibility. We are genuinely obsessed by the weather because we have so much of it, though most of it is damp. Snow varies the scenery, stops any tube train with an overground route, makes kids of everyone with a makeshift toboggan and access to a park (99% of the population), and fosters a community spirit normally proscribed by the city's geography and its citizens' cool. Winters were colder as recently as the '60s, when waiting for the crust to thicken enough to skate on the Round Pond in Kensington Gardens—now good only for model-boat sailors and duck feeders— was only a matter of time.

The corollary to our temperate winter, though, is a fresh confidence in summer sufficient to support herds of sidewalk tables. Holland Park Avenue no longer has the monopoly on Parisian ambience. All over town, an epidemic of Continental-style café chains serving croissants and *salade frisée* has devoured the traditional tobacco-stained pubs serving warm bitter and bags of pork scratchings. Most of the remaining pubs have turned into faux-Edwardian parlors with coffee machines and etchings or, more recently, wood-floored bars serving flavored vodkas and Tuscan food. The change has been going on for about a decade, and it suits London, as does its momentous discovery that restaurants are allowed to serve good food in smart surroundings and not charge the earth.

London is increasingly a European city, as if England were no longer stranded alone in the sea. In fact, ever since airplanes superseded ships, this island race has been undergoing an identity crisis, which reached its apogee in the '70s when Prime Minister Edward Heath sailed us irrevocably into the Common Market. Occasionally Britain still holds out against some European Community legislation or other, attempting to reassert differences that are following executions at the Tower and British Colonial supremacy into history. But however much the social climate changes, London is built on a firm foundation. Until the ravens desert the Tower of London— which is when, they say, the kingdom will fall—we have Westminster Abbey and St. Paul's and the Houses of Parliament, the Georgian squares and grand Victorian houses, the green miles of parks, the river, the museums and galleries and theaters, and 32 boroughs of villages to keep us going.

—Kate Sekules

NEW AND NOTEWORTHY

London has undergone a huge resurgence and is now acclaimed as the center of Europe. It all started with Tony Blair, the dynamic Labour prime minister, and with the National Lottery, which continues to fund exciting projects. England is also in the grip of millennium fever, which will only intensify as the numbers creep toward the big 2000.

Among the several buildings due to open on or around the big day is the **Millennium Dome,** at Greenwich. This multimillion-pound 320-meter structure designed by architect-provocateur Richard Rogers is terribly controversial. A cornucopia of architectural installations is being set up around the dome, including one by the avant-garde three-woman outfit, Muff. What there is to see now—the Dome's shell—is not worth the long trip downstream, unless you're planning to revisit the wonders of the Royal Observatory, the Prime Meridien, or the Maritime Museum (☞ Greenwich *in* Chapter 2). If you do head out that way, you could drop in on the Millennium Experience Visitor Centre (Pepys House, Royal Naval College), with its graphic displays, models, videos, and interactive monitors designed for the locals, with employment information and the like on offer. May 2000 will see the 10-day **Millennium Maritime Festival** in the vicinity, with 2,000 vessels moored in and around Docklands.

Docklands—the neighborhood in the southeast that contains Canary Wharf and the U.K.'s tallest building—has been picking up steam as a tourist destination in its own right, welcoming a third more visitors last year than the year before. The Canary Wharf Tourist Information Centre (☎ 0171/512–9800) remains in place, as does the helpful TourEast London (☎ 0171/512–8512), which exists largely to promote the attractions of the charming East End. In January 2000, the Museum in Docklands will open to suck up all this disparate information and dispense it to you. Until then, why not view the Dome as part of the Tower of London's new package deal with Catamaran Cruisers; it includes a Yeoman Warder tour of the Crown Jewels in the morning, and a cruise to Greenwich in the afternoon, for a reasonable £12.50 (☎ 0345/023842 for 24-hr reservations).

Other major building projects include the new Tate Gallery being installed in the former Bankside Power Station, and the refit of the South Bank Centre. There is also still plenty going on around the OXO Tower. These works were in various stages of construction at press time. For a cyber-glimpse of the whole shebang, visit **London Interactive** (20 Bury St., SW1).

The new **BBC Experience** is a guided tour of the Broadcasting House of the British Broadcasting Corporation including the Marconi Collection of early audiovisual equipment, and interactive bits where you can play at directing *EastEnders*, the popular cockney TV soap, or cast yourself in a role on *Desert Island Discs*. Modern art buffs will want to take in Islington's first major museum, the **Estorick Collection of Italian Art,** (Northhampton Lodge, 39a Cannonbury Sq., N1, ☎ 0171/704–9522) features those naughty Futurists in a renovated Georgian building. Check out the new **British Library,** which already offers selected services to readers, although everything won't be completely operational until mid-1999. Other recent news on the museum horizon? At the V &A, its famed **Raphael Gallery** has been restored, and they've recently opened new **British Art and Design Galleries** and an expanded **Boilerhouse,** for contemporary design purposes. The National Portrait Gallery has a new toy, the Piers Gough–designed **Victorian and Early 20th Century Galleries.** Last and largest, the Natural History Museum has come through with the biggest project since it opened in 1881, the **Earth Galleries,** which examine earthly phenomena, like volcanoes, tornadoes, deserts, and then take you out into space and onto other planets.

The performing arts Muses seem to be, for all intents and purposes, practically homeless in London these days. The world-renowned **Royal Opera House** is still shuttered, owing to an ongoing renovation. Its resident troupes are taking up temporary shelter, gypsylike, at other theaters in the interim. For the 1998–99 season, the **Royal Opera** will present full opera productions at the Barbican Theatre, the Shaftesbury Theater, and Royal Albert Hall, and concert versions at Royal Festival Hall, Barbican Hall, and Royal Albert Hall. The **Royal Ballet** has been performing in the Labatt's Apollo Theatre in Hammersmith and Royal Festival Hall; for the 1998–99 season, most productions should be concentrated in the newly refurbished Sadler's Wells Theatre. The English National Opera—or **ENO**, as it is called—has abandoned the Coliseum, its home since 1968. Possible sites for a new house, funded by the Lottery, include several places along the South Bank, King's Cross, or the sadly disused yet magisterial Battersea Power Station. Further clouds: the **Royal Shakespeare Theatre** will no longer offer a summer season and the Old Vic theater may close, with a resultant eviction of some of London's livelier theater troupes.

Try a **Supersky Trip** (Spring Gardens, Vauxhall Bridge SE11, ☎ 0345/023842) in a tethered balloon that goes aloft a few hundred feet for 15 minutes. For childish thrills, there's **Nanco Station**—a 35,000-square-ft noise-filled and neon-lit cavern of 200-odd video games, jet-ski and cyber-cycle simulators, bumper cars, and something else called "Techno Bowl," based above the Aquarium in the old County Hall. In total contrast, by now **WineWorld** should be open in Southwark—an adults-only museum for oenophiles, featuring the Wine Odyssey, an audiovisual tour of the history and culture of the noble grape.

Back in the former County Hall, above the Aquarium and Nanco Station, are two new hotels, the **County Hall Marriott** and the **Travel Inn Capital.** Other hotels were the luxurious One Aldwych, the more modest Stakis Islington, and a slew of budget-level hotels outside the city center: a 224-room Holiday Inn Express in the City and a 50-room one in Victoria; the Park Plaza Hotel and a Travel Inn Capital in Euston; plus the swankier Chelsea Village (which is actually in Fulham); and a flagship 314-room Posthouse Forte hotel next to Canary Wharf that is expected to open in spring 1999.

How many new, trendy, talked-out, flavor-of-the-month gastrodomes can the city support? Read up on them in the food supplements of the newspapers, especially the Saturday and Sunday editions, or log onto the London Tourist Board's restaurant Web site at **www.londondining.co.uk/london/dining/.** The new places are so numerous we can barely keep up with them, but we've reviewed some of the best and most talked about: **Aubergine, Bluebird, Maison Novelli, Quo Vadis,** and **Zafferano.** Two of the trendiest 1998 openings were Notting Hill Gate's **Pharmacy** and the Great Portland Street **MASH,** the former a reasonable simulacrum of an actual pharmacy, the latter, the latest see-and-be-seen place. **Circus** in Soho is minimalist and style conscious. **Pasha** features oh-so-fashionable North African cuisine. Some new luxe pubs have heated up the scene, such as **The Enterprise** and **The Cow.** There's a new **Livebait** (great fish!) in Covent Garden, and Jan Woroniecki of Wódka fame has opened another spot, as yet unnamed, in Blackfriars (which is slugging it out with Spitalfields as London's newest, coolest nabe). Enjoy the city of cities, and congratulations on arriving before the millennium.

WHAT'S WHERE

London is actually a city whose celebrated sites and distinct neighborhoods each has its own character, lore, and rhythm. There is the heraldic splendor of Westminster, the chic of artistic Chelsea, the architectural elegance of Belgravia and Mayfair, the cosmopolitan charm of Soho, and the East End, home base of the cockney—to name just a few. The number of choices is awesome, and it takes some thinking through. Happily, the city's expansive tube and bus systems bring far-flung sights within easy reach of one another. Keep in mind, however, that London's contrasts can best be savored by strolling from one district to another.

First pick a starting point such as Piccadilly Circus, which the British think of as "the hub of the universe." Keeping your wits about you—the Circus is a swirl of traffic rather fetchingly surrounded by grand Edwardian-era buildings—face in the direction of the area of central London you want to explore, and start moving. To the north runs Regent Street, curving up one side of ritzy, mostly residential Mayfair. To the south is Lower Regent Street, leading toward Whitehall, the parks, and the palaces. To the east are Shaftesbury Avenue and Leicester Square, for theaters and Soho; to the west is Piccadilly itself, heading out to Hyde Park and Knightsbridge. This is also a great place to board a double-decker sightseeing bus—just remember to have some sort of protective wrap handy: atop these buses it's always windy.

Westminster and Royal London

No matter how you first approach London—historically, geographically, emotionally—all things start at Westminster, one of the truly ancient centers of the city. There is as much history in these few acres as there is in many complete cities.

To view the 1,000 rooms of the Houses of Parliament would require at least a week—but an hour is all that's needed to enjoy the best show staged for free in the world's most renowned ego chamber, the House of Commons. Then there is Westminster Abbey, crammed with memorials and monuments to the great, the famous, and the totally forgotten surrounded by spectacular Gothic splendor. Whitehall is both an avenue and the heartbeat of the British government; here is the prime minister's official residence, No. 10 Downing Street, and the Horse Guards, where two mounted sentries of the Queen's Life Guard provide London's most frequently taken-up photo op. Whitehall leads to Trafalgar Square and the incomparable National Gallery. From the grand Admiralty Arch, the Mall leads straight to Buckingham Palace, as unprepossessing on the outside as it is sumptuous inside (as the summer tours now let you see). With beautifully kept St. James's Park at its center, the Westminster area exudes a feeling of timeless dignity and offers frequent glimpses of pinnacles and towers over treetops and, of course, the deep tones of Big Ben counting off the quarter hours.

Belgravia

Just a short carriage ride from Buckingham Palace is the most splendidly aristocratic enclave to be found in London: Belgravia. Built in the mid-1800s, untouched by neon, it basks today in an authentic vintage patina. Here are block after block of grand, porticoed mansions, many currently serving as embassies, all painted Wedgwood-china white (to signify they remain the property of the Dukes of Westminster). Pedigree-proud locations include Belgrave Square, Grosvenor Crescent, and Belgrave Place, but also check out the chic alleyways, called "mews" from the time when they housed Milord's horse and carriage (nowadays dukes live in these former stables while the oil-rich occupy the houses).

Bloomsbury

The self-centered freethinking set that made the name of Bloomsbury world famous has left hardly a trace, but this remains the heart of learned, literary London. The University of London is here; so are the Law Courts, and Mankind's Attic—the British Museum, home of the Elgin Marbles, the Rosetta Stone, and the Magna Carta. Until the British Library moves to its new venue at St. Pancras, a greater number of books can probably be found in Bloomsbury than in all the rest of London. Virginia Woolf and T. S. Eliot would be pleased to note that some of London's most beautiful domestic architecture, elegant houses that would have been familiar to Dr. Johnson, still line the area's prim squares. At No. 48 Doughty Street, Charles Dickens's house, is the tall upright clerk's desk where he worked on *Oliver Twist*.

Bloomsbury is really part of Holborn, the core of Legal London. On the quiet courts, leafy gardens, and magnificent halls that compose the Inns of Court is the finest group of historic buildings in the city in an almost unspoiled setting—the closest thing to the spirit of Oxford that London has to offer. In Holborn, you'll also find several of London's fascinating "time-machines": Sir John Soane's Museum, a mansion that whisks you back to the mid-1800s, and the delightful Victorian-era Pollock's Toy Museum.

Chelsea

Chelsea has always beckoned to freethinkers and fashion-fringers—from Sir Thomas More to Isadora Duncan. Major sights include Christopher Wren's magisterial Royal Hospital—now the site of the Chelsea Flower Show—and Cheyne Walk, where Henry James and Dante Gabriel Rossetti once lived. Now an extremely expensive place to live, the area on Saturdays continues to draw an army of trendaholics to King's Road, whose boutiques gave birth to the paisleyed '60s and the pink-headed-punk '70s.

The City

Known as "the Square Mile," the City is to London what Wall Street is to Manhattan. And as the site of the Celtic settlement the Romans called Londinium, this is the oldest part of London. Unfortunately, thanks to blocks of high-rise apartments and steel skyscrapers, it now looks like the newest part. Yet within and around the capital-C City are some of London's most memorable attractions—St. Paul's Cathedral, the storybook Tower Bridge, the Royal Shakespeare Company (at the Barbican Centre), St. Giles-without-Cripplegate, and St. Mary-le-Bow. At the east border of the City is the legendary Tower of London, where the young Princes of the

Bloody Tower, and Sir Thomas More and Anne Boleyn, all met untimely ends.

Covent Garden

In not much more than a decade, Covent Garden—which lies just to the east of Soho—has gone from a down-at-the-heels district to one of the busiest, most raffishly enjoyable parts of the city. Continental-style open-air cafés create a very un-English atmosphere. Warehouses, once cavernous and grim, now accommodate fashion boutiques and a huge variety of shops favored by the "trendoisie." A network of narrow streets, arcades, and pedestrian malls, the area is dominated by the Piazza—scene of a food market in the 1830s, then a flower market in the 1870s. Today, the indoor/outdoor complex overflows with clothing shops and crafts stalls. The London Transport Museum and the famed Royal Opera House (undergoing extensive renovations at press time) are conveniently nearby. Eliza "My Fair Lady" Dolittle wasn't the only one singing in the neighborhood.

The East End

In the East End, you'll find sights and sounds that are as much a part of the real London as a November fog. Although its 19th-century slums—immortalized by Charles Dickens and the evocative etchings of Gustave Doré—are a relic of the past, the area still possesses a haunting beauty and a warm spirit of humor and friendliness. Here you'll find, on Sundays, the 20th-century version of a medieval fair, called Petticoat Lane, and other fascinating sights including the Geffrye Museum—an overlooked venue of wonderful historic interiors—Hawksmoor's Christ Church, and the Blind Beggar, the Victorian den of iniquity where Salvation Army founder William Booth was moved to preach his first sermon. Off the main thoroughfare, tap into the true pulse of East End life by exploring the lanes and alleys that still make up one of the world's most fascinating melting pots.

Greenwich

A quick 8-mi jaunt down the Thames will bring you past the National Maritime Museum and the *Cutty Sark* to Greenwich's Old Royal Observatory, where if time stood still, all the world's timepieces would be off. When you tire of straddling the hemispheres at the Greenwich Meridian, take a stroll through the acres of parkland that cover the area or, on weekends, the crafts and antiques markets. Sir Christopher Wren's Royal Naval College and Inigo Jones's Queen House, both scale architectural heights. The pretty streets of Greenwich Village house numerous bookstores and antiques shops. The journey to Greenwich is most appealing if you approach by river.

Hampstead

One of the great glories of England is the English village, and on the northern outskirts of London you'll find one of the most fetching: Hampstead. Today, its flower-spangled Georgian houses, its picturesque tidiness, and its expensive French delicatessens attract personages from the arts and wealthy entrepreneurs. For sheer pleasure, exploring Hampstead is hard to top, as an amble along Church Walk—possibly the finest (and certainly the prettiest) row of 18th-century houses in London—will prove. London's most beautiful painting by Vermeer is on view at Kenwood House (its park hosts grand concerts and fireworks in the summer), and the latest cutting-edge art is at the Saatchi Collection. Here, too, are the Freud Museum and the Keats House. You can go bird-watching in the 800-plus emerald acres of Hampstead Heath. In the nearby neighborhood of St. John's Wood, you can visit Abbey Road to snap the famed crossing outside the studios where John, Paul, George, and Ringo recorded nearly all of their music.

Hyde Park, Kensington Gardens

When in need of elbow room, Londoners head for their green "lungs"—Hyde Park and Kensington Gardens. They form an open swath across central London; together with St. James's Park, Green Park, and Buckingham Palace Gardens, they make up almost 600 beauty-filled acres that offer a taste of serene remoteness from the great city. The handsome trees and quiet walks in these spots will refresh you as thoroughly as, centuries ago, these grounds refreshed Henry VIII after a hard day's shenanigans. In the Regency era, splendid horseflesh and equipages were the grand attraction; today, the soapbox orators (most oratorical on Sunday mornings) at Hyde Park Corner remain grand entertainment. Sooner or later, however, everyone heads to the Long Water in Kensington Gardens for one of London's most beloved sights: the Peter Pan statue (E. M. Barrie had the sprite living on a nearby island). Then circumnavigate the Round Pond, or swim in the Serpentine, or try to catch a glimpse of the Household Cavalry on Rotten Row.

Knightsbridge and Kensington

Within the district's cavalcade of streets lined with decorous houses are tucked-away corners—small squares that would not be out of place in a sleepy cathedral town; delightful pubs nestled away in back lanes; and antiques shops, their windows aglow with the luminous colors of oil paintings. Not surprisingly, the capital's snazziest department stores are also here, Harrods and Harvey Nichols (the latter being chic London's center of gravity). The area's main attraction is the great museum complex of South Kensington. Raphael and Constable canvases, Ossie Clark couture, and William Morris chairs all beckon at the Victoria and Albert Museum, a grand pile whose forte is the decorative arts and whose predominant audience is an especially decorative crowd. Next to the V&A come three museums devoted to science, including the Natural History Museum (kids will head for its Creepie Crawlies exhibit first). Most delightful are two historic homes: Leighton House, Lord Leighton's stunning Persian extravaganza, and the Linley Sambourne House, whose elegant Edwardian interiors were featured in *A Room with a View*. Regroup at Kensington Palace—its state rooms and royal dress collection (where Princess Diana's mementoes are displayed) are open to view—than repair to its elegant Orangery for a pot of Earl Grey.

Notting Hill and Holland Park

These are two of London's most fashionable, coveted residential areas. Notting Hill, around Portobello Road, is a trendsetting square mile of multiethnicity, galleries, small exciting shops, and see-and-be-seen-in restaurants. The style-watching media dubbed the natives—by and large, musicians, novelists, and fashion plates—Notting Hillbillies. If Notting Hill is for the young, neighboring Holland Park is entirely the opposite—its leafy streets are full of expensive white-stucco Victorians that lead to bucolic Holland Park itself.

Regent's Park

Helping to frame the northern border of the city, Regent's Park is home to the much-loved zoo, the much-loved rose-bedecked Queen Mary's Gardens, and the much-loved Regent's Park Open-Air Theatre. A walk around the perimeter of the park is a must for devotees of Classical architecture; the payoff is a view of John Nash's Terraces, a grandiose series of white-stucco terraced houses, built around 1810. The "People of Quality" for whom these stately buildings were intended demanded London homes as nearly as possible resembling their grand country estates, and Nash magnificently obliged. In summer, be sure to take in Queen Mary's Gardens. Next, head over to the theater for a picture-perfect performance of *A Midsummer Night's Dream*. Year-round, the park is a favorite spot for mothers with strollers, joggers, and hand-holding senior citizens enjoying the fresh air. Watch out for those airborne objects—softballs, footballs, and cricket balls.

St. James's and Mayfair

St. James's and Mayfair form the core of the West End, the city's smartest and most desirable central area—St. James's to the south of Piccadilly and north of the Mall, Mayfair to the north of Piccadilly and south of Oxford Street. Neither is stuffed with must-sees, though there is no shortage of history and gorgeous architecture, but they *are* custom-built for window-shopping, expansive strolling, and getting a peek into the lifestyles of London's rich and famous—18th- *and* 20th-century versions. Although many will say Mayfair is only a state of mind, the heart of Mayfair has shifted from the 19th-century's Park Lane to Carlos Place and Mount Row. The shops of New and Old Bond streets lure the wealthy; even if you bid on a letter at Sotheby's signed by one of the Brontë sisters, or stop in at Graff's for a weighty diamond, the window-shopping is next best to the real thing and is free. Mayfair is primarily residential, so its homes are off-limits except for two satisfyingly grand houses: Apsley House, the Duke of Wellington's home, built by Robert Adam in 1771, and once known as No. 1, London, and, on gorgeous Manchester Square, the Wallace Collection, situated in a palatial town house filled with Old Masters and fine French furniture. The district of St. James's—named after the centuries-old palace that lies at its center—remains the ultimate enclave of the old-fashioned gentleman's London. Here you'll find Pall Mall, with its many noted clubs, including the Reform Club—where Jules Verne's Phileas Fogg wagered he could go around the world in 80 days—and Jermyn Street, where you can follow in the Duke of Windsor's sartorial footsteps by purchasing a half-dozen shirts made at Turnbull & Asser.

Soho and Theatreland

Once the setting for London's red-light district, Soho these days is more stylish than seedy, and it is now home to film and record bigwigs (Sir Paul McCartney's offices are here). The area is not especially rich architecturally, but it has an intriguing atmosphere. Built up around quaint Soho Square, the density of Continental residents means some of London's best restaurants—whether pricey Italian, budget Chinese, or the latest opening—are in the vicinity. Nearby is Carnaby Street, still hoping to stage a revival of swinging '60s psychedelic fashion. Shaftesbury Avenue cuts through the southern part of Soho; this is Theatreland—home to almost 50 West End theaters, and a stand-in for Mecca for those who love Shakespeare, Maggie Smith, and *Oliver!* To the south of Theatreland lies Leicester Square, London's answer to Times Square, and Charing Cross Road, the bibliophile's dream.

The South Bank

You won't say "How very British" in this section of town across the Thames from London Bridge, which was totally rebuilt after the bombs of World War II flattened the remains of medieval Southwark. However, if William Shakespeare returned today, he would be delighted to find a complete reconstruction of his Globe Theatre, which was inaugurated in 1996, not far from where the original closed in 1642. In fact, this side of the Thames—walk along the riverside embankment for great views of the city—has become a perch for diehard culture vultures: the Design Museum is here, and the gigantic Bankside Power Station building (hard by the Globe) is being readied to become the new Tate Gallery. Also here is the South Bank Arts Complex—the country's chief arts center, with its important Museum of the Moving Image, Royal National Theatre, and Royal Festival Hall, and London's newest culinary hot spot, the OXO Tower Restaurant and Brasserie. And who could resist the London Dungeon—a waxwork extravaganza full of scenes featuring plenty of blood-'n'-guts and medieval dismemberments—where "a perfectly horrible experience" is guaranteed.

The Thames Upstream

London has been Britain's power center for centuries, so it is only natural that many visitable places associated with royalty and the ruling establishment—among them, Chiswick, Kew Gardens, Osterley Park, Richmond, and Putney—should be found close to the capital. The link between London and these idyllic retreats is Father Thames—who offers a river cruise as a particularly nice way to escape the city on a sweltering summer day. These palaces and country houses are enveloped with serenity and rolling greenery, which explains the astronomical prices that some of the local real estate commands. Stroll around and get lost in a daydream while breathing the rural air or find your way out of the famous maze at Hampton Court Palace, England's version of Versailles.

PLEASURES AND PASTIMES

Food, Glorious Food: The Delights of Dining

London now ranks among the world's top dining scenes. A new generation of chefs has precipitated a fresh approach to food preparation, which you could call "London style," though most refer to it as "Modern British."

Today, almost everything on the culinary front has changed. The old standards have been given a nouvelle spin—although roast suckling pig topped with strawberry-papaya and served on a bed of chili noodles may not be everyone's cup of tea. The nouvelle push has taken the starch—literally—out of many of the city's menus, and this new energy is even finding a vogue for old standbys like angels-on-horseback (crisp bacon wrapped around oysters).

Savvy Londoners looking for a dinner bargain go for the nearest tandoori house—

this Indian food goes beyond the cliché into national-dish territory. Londoners have now enlarged their purview to encompass most of the world; in the space of two weeks, diners can cover as much tongue-tingling ground as in a two-week package tour of exotic, far-flung places.

In fact, so many people are eating ethnic that the indigenous caff (the British diner)—which offers such grab-and-gulp goodies as fish-and-chips, chip butties (Wonder Bread with margarine and fries), or chips and ketchup—has become less ubiquitous in central London than good sandwich bars. Today, such native delicacies as the cockles, winkles, and smoked eels found in the cockney stalls of the East End appear as just one more exotic cuisine in the pantheon.

Cheers!: The Pub Experience

Londoners could no more live without their "local" than they could forgo dinner. The pub—or public house, to give it its full title—is ingrained in the British psyche as social center, bolt-hole, second home. Pub culture—revolving around pints, pool, darts, and sports—is still male dominated; however, as a result of the gentrification trend started in the late '80s by the major breweries (which own most pubs), transforming many ancient smoke- and spittle-stained dives into fantasy Edwardian drawing rooms, women have been entering their welcoming doors in increasing numbers. This decade, the trend has been toward the bar, superficially identified by its cocktail list, creative paintwork, bare floorboards, and chrome fittings. The social function is the same: these are English pubs, but not as we formerly knew them.

When doing a London pub crawl, you must remember one thing: arcane licensing laws forbid the serving of alcohol after 11 PM (10:30 on Sunday; there are different rules for restaurants)—a circumstance you see in action at 10 minutes to 11, when the "last orders" bell signals a stampede to the bar. After many decades, however, some relaxation of these unpopular laws is in evidence with weekend "extensions" being granted, especially in Soho, plus a slew of clubs/bars/pubs that get around them by charging a moderate cover after 11 PM.

The Performing Arts: From the Boards to the Bard

There is a strength and fluidity about the performing arts in London that makes them very difficult to pin down. An actor playing Lear with the Royal Shakespeare Company one day could quite possibly appear in a television farce the next; an opera that has played to the small exclusive audience at Glyndebourne in the English countryside might reappear the next week at the Royal Albert Hall, delighting millions through radio. In music and drama, opera and ballet, there are endless opportunities for visitors to enjoy themselves to the hilt.

THEATER➤ Shakespeare, of course, supplies the backbone to the theatrical life of the city. There can hardly have been a day since the one on which the Bard breathed his last when one of his plays, in some shape or form, was not being performed. On the London stage, they have survived being turned into musicals (from Purcell to rock), they have made the reputations of generations of famous actors (and broken not a few), and they have seen women playing Hamlet and men playing Rosalind. If the Bard of Bards remains the headliner at Stratford-upon-Barbican, the London theater scene is amazingly varied. From a West End *Oliver!* revival to an East End feminist staging of *Ben-Hur,* London remains a theatergoer's town.

If you're a theater junkie and want to put together a West End package, the *Complete Guide to London's West End Theatres* has seating plans and booking information for all of the houses. It costs £9.95 from the **Society of London Theatres** (✉ Bedford Chambers, The Piazza, Covent Garden, London WC2 E8HQ, ☎ 0171/836–0971).

MUSIC➤ London is home to four world-class orchestras. The London Symphony Orchestra is in residence at the Barbican Centre, while the London Philharmonic lives at the Royal Festival Hall—one of the finest concert halls in Europe. Between the Barbican and South Bank, there are concert performances almost every night of the year. The Barbican also presents chamber music concerts in partnership with such celebrated orchestras as the City of London Sinfonia. The Royal Albert Hall during the Promenade Concert season (July–September) is a don't-miss pleasure. Also look for the lunchtime concerts held throughout the city in either smaller concert halls, arts-center foyers, or churches; they usually cost less than £5 or arc free. St. John's, Smith Square, and St. Martin-in-the-Fields are the major venues for these, and they also present evening concerts.

BALLET AND OPERA➤ For decades, London's leading troupes, the Royal Opera and the Royal Ballet, have shared grandiose quarters at the Royal Opera House in Covent Garden. Now the grand Opera House has been closed for a major two-year renovation, and the resident companies are scurrying for other venues. Plans are in the offing for a completely new venue for the ballet.

Best Foot Forward: Walking Through London

London is a great walking city because so many of its real treasures are untouted details: tiny alleyways barely visible on the map; garden squares; churchyards; shop windows; sudden vistas of skyline or park. However, it is big, VERY BIG. And often rather damp. With the obvious precautions of comfortable, weatherproof shoes and an umbrella, this activity might well become your favorite pastime.

GREAT ITINERARIES

In a city with as many richly stocked museums and marvels as London, visitors risk seeing half of everything and all of nothing. One could easily spend two solid weeks exploring the many layers of the city, but if time is limited you'll need to plan carefully. *See* Chapter 2 for complete information about individual sights and detailed neighborhood walking tours.

If You Have 1 Day

Touring the largest city in England in the space of a single day sounds like an impossible goal, but it can actually—almost—be done in the span of one sunrise to sunset. Begin at postcard London, the **Houses of Parliament,** best viewed from Westminster Bridge. If you're lucky, you'll hear **Big Ben** chiming. Move on to centuries-old **Westminster Abbey**—where coronations are staged—then tube it from the Westminster stop to Charing Cross (if you want to catch a glimpse of Her Majesty's two mounted sentries at Horse Guards Parade, bus it up Whitehall) to arrive at **Trafalgar Square** for Nelson's Column and hundreds of pigeons. Take in the treasures of the **National Gallery,** which ranks with the collections of the Louvre and the Uffizi, or take a fast tour of the adjacent **National Portrait Gallery.** Break for lunch in the **Brasserie** of the National Gallery, then take a short taxi trip over to a sight dear to your heart: the Wallace Collection or Tate Gallery; Apsley House, the home of the Duke of Wellington, or Sir John Soane's Museum, or the London Dungeon or Madame Tussaud's. For a mid-afternoon session, choose between two royal monuments. Heading west from Trafalgar Square, taxi through the impressive Admiralty Arch down the **Mall** to what there is believed to be the world's most photographed building, **Buckingham Palace.** During summer weeks, when the state rooms are open to the public, you can ogle their full pomp. **Theatreland** awaits palace trekkers with a hit West End musical—a refreshing finale to the day. Second choice: eastward (take the tube to the Tower Hill stop) lies the **Tower of London,** home to the Beefeaters, the Crown Jewels, and the six resident ravens that nest on high. At dusk, after leaving the Tower, head across the way to the East End for a guaranteed spine-chiller, a Jack the Ripper guided walking tour.

If You Have 3 Days

A breakneck first day in London has been outlined above. On your second day tour the **British Museum,** home of such wonders as the Rosetta Stone, the Elgin Marbles, and the Lindow Man. In Bloomsbury other treats beckon: **Pollock's Toy Museum,** the **Charles Dickens House,** and, on Gordon Square, former address of Virginia Woolf and Lytton Strachey, the **Percival David Foundation of Chinese Art.** For an early lunch, take the tube from Russell Square to Leicester Square in Soho for dim sum in Chinatown. Next, for a dose of magisterial grandeur, hop back on the tube to arrive at **St. Paul's Cathedral.** Walk off lunch by strolling south through Blackfriars—a quaint district full of crooked streets, historic courtyards, and minuscule cul-desacs—to the River Thames. After downing a refreshing pint at the **Black Friar** (possibly London's most spectacular 19th-century pub), cross Blackfriars Bridge to Southwark's riverside embankment for a splendid view of St. Paul's dome. Keep an eye out for **Cardinal's Cap Alley**—the house Sir Christopher Wren, architect of St. Paul's, built so he could easily check on the cathedral's construction. A stone's throw away is the rebuilt **Shakespeare's Globe Theatre**; if you're not catching an open-air performance (held only in warm-weather months), tour the adjoining museum. Head eastward along the river, cross Southwark Bridge, then take the tube from the Mansion House stop to **Covent Garden.** Dine at one of the area's chic restaurants, then watch the colorfully costumed street performers called buskers, take in some jazz at Ronnie Scott's in Soho, or run down to an evening recital at one of London's historic churches.

Start your third day with Buckingham Palace's **Changing of the Guard,** held April–July at 11:30 daily, and August–March at the same hour on alternate days. View a selection of Her Majesty's treasures in the **Queen's Gallery** and the nearby **Royal Mews.** Wander up Park Lane into **Mayfair,** one of London's ritziest neighborhoods, and stroll past Grosvenor Square and Oxford Street to Manchester Square and the **Wallace Collection,** whose gilded interiors are stuffed with 18th-century art. For a pub break, visit the **Devonshire Arms,** a Henry Higgins's–parlour look-alike on Duke Street, a few blocks south of the Wallace. Return south, then east to scout three great shopping destinations: **Bond Street** for world-class glitz, **Regent Street** for savvy sophistication, and **Carnaby Street** for some rocker-style street gear. For an evening highlight, book a performance of the **Royal Shakespeare Company** at the Barbican Centre.

If You Have 7 Days

Each section of London provides distinct clues to the city's past. In your first three days, you've made a start on piecing together the story of this great, crowded, endlessly fascinating city. Now you're ready to build on that foundation. Kick off Day 4 at the South Kensington museums: the **Victoria and Albert,** the **Natural History Museum,** and the **Science Museum.** All three cultural palaces could easily consume an entire day, so you'll need to pick one to do it justice. Then head over to Knightsbridge to either of the mercantile-and-fashion giants **Harrods** or **Harvey Nichols.** Move on to **Kensington Gardens,** where almost everyone throws a kiss to the famous statue of **Peter Pan,** and to **Kensington Palace,** once the address of Princess Diana, where the state rooms are open to view year-round. For a perfect late afternoon pot of tea, check out the palace's elegant Orangery. For modern-art buffs, the **Serpentine Gallery** should be the next stop. Along the way, let yourself venture into the many winding lanes and narrow courts in the area, and smell the roses.

Day 5 dawns at **the City**—London's ancient core. Built up around St. Paul's, the area has numerous attractions, including **Dr. Johnson's House,** the **Old Bailey,** the **Museum of London,** and several Christopher Wren churches. The nearby East End beckons with its **Petticoat Lane** sprawling market (open weekends); the **Geffrye Museum,** a must for decorative-arts lovers; and the **Spitalfields** restoration. After lunch at the Whitechapel Gallery Café, head west on the tube to Holborn (Chancery Lane, Temple stops) to visit the **Inns of Court** and the **Temple,** the historic foundations of Legal London. Farther along lies that storybook icon, **Tower Bridge,** which you must cross to reach the South Bank, where the **London Dungeon** awaits—this medieval waxworks show is devoted to the more gory aspects of British history—and there were plenty of them!

On Day 6, leave the city behind for pleasures along the Thames: choose either to visit **Greenwich,** or the storied palace and gardens of **Hampton Court.** Or else opt to head for the outskirts of northern London and the relentlessly picturesque village of **Hampstead,** where you'll find **Kenwood**—a noble Robert Adam house—as well as the **homes of Keats and Freud,** and the bustling **Camden Lock** market. (Nearby, in swank St. John's Wood, is **Abbey Road,** beloved address to Beatlemaniacs.) Just south of Hampstead is **Regent's Park,** surrounded by Nash's Terraces—a must for Regency-era buffs and admirers of splendid urban creations.

Begin your last day by taking the tube to the Knightsbridge stop and heading south for an early morning stroll through **Belgravia**; few tourists venture here, but it's

London at its most *Upstairs, Downstairs*. Head over to the endless cavalcade of glitzy emporiums of **Sloane Street** and **Sloane Square** for some world-class shopping. **Chelsea**, along King's Road, is where much of London comes to shop and stroll. After viewing Wren's historic **Royal Hospital**, relax over lunch at a King's Road pub, move on to **Cheyne Walk**, where leading 19th-century artists lived, then bus over to Millbank to take in the **Tate Gallery**'s incomparable collection of British paintings. As dusk settles, head over to the **South Bank Arts Complex**, where you might finish up your visit with a play in the Olivier Theatre or a concert in the Queen Elizabeth Hall.

FODOR'S CHOICE

No two people will agree on what makes a perfect vacation, but it's fun and helpful to know what others think. Here's a compendium drawn from the must-see lists of hundreds of tourists. We hope you'll have a chance to experience some of these great memories-in-the-making yourself while visiting London. For detailed information about entries, refer to the appropriate chapters within this guidebook.

Long Live the Queen!
★ **Changing of the Guard.** Adding a dash of color to the gloomiest of London days, this ceremony is mounted (daily, depending on the season) at both Whitehall and Buckingham Palace.

★ **The Mall.** Look down this grand thoroughfare to Buckingham Palace from underneath Admiralty Arch and you'll see what the Queen sees during all those royal ceremonies.

★ **Trooping the Colour.** Marking the Queen's birthday in June (the real one is in April), this is the capital's most spectacular military occasion, with bands playing, flags fluttering, and massed ranks of soldiers in scarlet coats and immense "busbies."

Quintessential London
★ **The Houses of Parliament at sunset.** Cross the Thames to Jubilee Gardens to see this view of London at its storybook best.

★ **Sunday Afternoon at Speakers' Corner, Hyde Park.** A space especially reserved for anyone with anything to say that they *must* say publicly makes for great entertainment. Speakers seem to be most oratorical on Sunday afternoons.

★ **St. Paul's Cathedral Thames-side.** The most thrilling vantage point to take in St. Paul's is at Cardinal Cap's Alley, across the Thames on the southern embankment, right by Shakespeare's Globe.

★ **An Afternoon Performance at Shakespeare's Globe.** This new, spectacular, open-to-the-skies reconstruction of Shakespeare's beloved "wooden O" magically transports you back to Elizabethan London. In 16th-century fashion, audience participation is welcome: jump in and hiss Iago—you'll have plenty of company.

★ **Tower Bridge at Night.** A dramatically floodlighted Tower Bridge confronts you as you come out of the Design Museum on a winter's night.

Fascinating Walks
★ **Beatles' Magical Mystery Tour.** This wonderful stroll down Memory Lane offered by Original London Walks includes the London Palladium, No. 3 Savile Row— the Fab Four's London headquarters—and Abbey Road.

★ **A Belgravia Promenade.** Far from the madding crowd, Belgravia represents all that is gracious in London living. A vision out of a Regency-period engraving, Belgrave Place is one of the most moneyed addresses in town and adorned with elegant mansions and picturesque mews.

★ **In and Around Hampstead Heath.** Just like John Le Carré, you can climb the rolling hills of Hampstead Heath, from Hampstead Village to Kenwood, perhaps in time for a summer concert.

★ **Jack the Ripper Walk.** Several organizations offer tours of "Jack's London"— the East End and its grisly settings for the Whitechapel murders. Unforgettable!

London Splendor
★ **Apsley House.** Known as No. 1 London, this was the august residence of the Duke of Wellington, fabled conqueror of Napoléon. The house's centerpiece, the Waterloo Gallery, is one of the grandest rooms in Europe.

★ **Denis Sever's House.** One of the most amazing experiences in London is going on a candlelight tour of this time-burnished jewel of a house.

★ **Linley Sambourne House.** A little masterpiece of Victoriana, this former residence of *Punch* cartoonist Linley Sambourne is unusually charming.

★ **Sir John Soane's Museum.** Eccentric architect of the Bank of England, Sir John left his house to the nation on condition nothing be changed; the result is a phantasmagoria of colors, unusual perspectives, and artifacts from many centuries.

★ **Spencer House.** The London house to end all London houses, this glamorous 18th-century Palladian pile was built by Princess Diana's ancestors. Now restored to all its glory by Lord Rothschild, it proves the 18th-century Spencers were no slouches in the flash department.

★ **Wallace Collection.** The serene 18th-century mansion, Hertford House, that shelters this sumptuous collection, is as much a part of the appeal as its rich array of porcelain, paintings, furniture, and sculptures.

Magnificent Museums

★ **British Museum.** You could move into this grand pile and never tire of all that it has to offer, from the Rosetta Stone to the Mildenhall Treasure. Best of all are the beautiful Elgin Marbles from ancient Greece.

★ **Tate Gallery.** The greatest glories of English painting are here, from Elizabethan portraits to the most avant avant-garde works.

★ **National Gallery.** Da Vincis, Rubenses, and Rembrandts fill the rooms here—an incomparably rich treasure trove of Old Masters.

Top Hotels

★ **Claridge's.** The same fine qualities that attracted the King of Morocco, among many others, to this world-renowned Mayfair hotel are sure to make you feel right at home, too. ££££

★ **Covent Garden Hotel.** Discerning travelers now call this the most stylish hotel in London. ££££

★ **The Dorchester.** It's a true accomplishment that so much gold leaf and marble, linens and brocades have managed the effect of sophisticated intimacy in this hotel that has all of Hyde Park as its front garden. ££££

★ **The Savoy.** Secure a river suite at this historic, late-Victorian hotel overlooking the Thames, and you'll get one of the best stays—and views—in London. ££££

★ **The Beaufort.** It's fair to use this set of Victorian houses, run by a wonderfully friendly all-female staff, as a home away from home, especially if you live practically next door at Harrods. £££

★ **The Franklin.** Everything is romantic here, from the quiet garden to tea in the lounge to the sweet smell of the Floris toiletries that you'll find in your room. £££

★ **The Pelham.** Designed to capture the essence of English country housedom, Tim and Kit Kemp's boutique hotel offers the comforting feel of a tranquil country retreat with all the advantages of being in the center of South Kensington. £££

★ **Basil Street.** So many people return to this Knightsbridge hotel that there is a standard discount for repeat guests—what more need be said. ££

★ **The Commodore.** Secreted in a quiet square behind Bayswater Road, this family-run hotel has some great value duplex-style rooms. ££

★ **The Vicarage.** Friendly and homey, this Kensington B&B has kept high standards for years. £

Great Restaurants and Pubs

★ **La Tante Claire.** Pierre Kaufman may be London's best chef. The decor is light and sophisticated, the service impeccable, the French wine list impressive, but the food is the point. Walk your meal off afterward along the nearby Thames embankment. ££££

★ **Oak Room.** Marco Pierre White enjoys Jagger-like fame as he ventures where few chefs have gone before. His kitchen is dizzingly creative: Be prepared for grand style—foie gras, caviar, and truffles—done with a truly adventurous hand. The room—a Belle-Epoque extravaganza—is one of London's most beautiful. ££££

★ **Le Caprice.** This glamorous place has stood the test of time—the food is great, the ambience even better. The other reason everyone comes here is that everyone else does, which leads to the best people-watching in town. £££

★ **Quaglino's.** This isn't the biggest, but it is still the best of Sir Terence Conran's London hot spots. Now past its fifth birthday, "Quags" is *the* out-of-towners' post-theater or celebration destination, while Londoners like its late hours. £££

★ **Rules.** Come, escape from the 20th century. London's answer to Maxim's in Paris, this enjoys an incomparably beautiful setting, one that has welcomed everyone from Dickens to the Duke of Windsor. The food is good but the decor is truly delicious. £££

★ **Zafferano.** London's best Italian restaurant has attracted Princess Margaret, Eric Clapton, Joan Collins, and any number of snazzy neighborhood Belgravians. The decor is ho-hum, but try pumpkin ravioli with a splash of amaretto. £££

★ **Maison Novelli.** Jean Christophe Novelli is one of the new cult heroes of mod Brit cusine, and foodies flock to up-and-coming Islington to check out his Rabelasian dishes. ££–£££

★ **The American Bar.** This dazzling bar at the Stafford Hotel, covered with college ties, toys, and antique U.S. memorabilia, is one of London's most delightful interiors. ££

★ **The Cow.** Notting Hillbillies and other stylish folk adore this luxe "gastro-pub." A serious chef whips up Tuscan/British specialties but some diners prefer the half-dozen Irish rock oysters with a pint of Guinness. ££

★ **Wódka.** Laid back and stylish, this serves London's only modern Polish food. Order from the separate menu a carafe of the purest vodka in London (and watch the check inflate). ££

★ **The Black Friar.** The ornate building with a statue of a friar on the front near Blackfriars tube station is one of London's most splendiferous pubs—all colored marble, inlaid mother-of-pearl, and stained glass. The pub grub is minimal, but the pints and the fetching locals are great. £

★ **Geales.** Fish-and-chips as you always imagined it awaits you here. The decor is stark, but the fish will have been swimming just hours beforehand. £

★ **George Inn.** London at its time-machine best, this inn sits in a courtyard where Shakespeare's plays were performed. The building dates from the 17th century, and it is London's last remaining galleried inn. £

FESTIVALS AND SEASONAL EVENTS

Top seasonal events in and around London include the Chelsea Flower Show in May, Derby Day at Epsom Racecourse, Wimbledon Lawn Tennis Championships and Henley Regatta in June, and a new innovation, the London Arts Season, which combines many events in theater, art, and music with good deals on hotels and meals out.

There is a complete list of ticket agencies in *Britain Events,* available in person only from the **British Travel Centre.** ⊠ *12 Regent St. Tube: Piccadilly Circus.* When in London, check the weekly magazine *Time Out,* available at newsstands, for an ongoing calendar of special events. Or, for 49p per minute, call London Tourist Board's 24-hour **VisitorCall** (☎ 0839/123400 in U.K. only) service, which offers the latest on events throughout the city.

WINTER

➤ Mid-Dec.: **Olympia International Show Jumping Championships,** international equestrian competition in Olympia's Grand Hall. For information, ☎ 0171/370–8209.

➤ Jan. 1: **The London Parade** is a good ole U.S.-style extravaganza complete with cheerleaders, floats, and marching bands, led by the Lord Mayor of Westminster.

It starts on the south side of Westminster Bridge at 12:30, finishing in Berkeley Square around 3 PM. No tickets required.

➤ Jan. 31: **Charles I Commemoration** is held on the anniversary of the monarch's execution and brings out Londoners dressed in 17th-century garb for a march tracing his last walk from St. James's Palace to the Banqueting House in Whitehall.

➤ Feb.–Mar.: **London Arts Season** showcases the city's extensive arts scene, with bargain-price tickets and special events. ⊠ *British Travel Centre, 12 Regent St., SW1Y 4PQ,* ☎ 0171/839–6181 (Arts Season only).

SPRING

➤ Mar. 18–28 and Sept. 16–26: **Chelsea Antiques Fair,** a twice-yearly fair with wide range of pre-1830 pieces for sale. ⊠ *Old Town Hall, King's Rd., Chelsea SW3 4PW,* ☎ 01444/482514.

➤ Mid-Mar.: **Open House** is a rare one-day chance to view historic London interiors of buildings usually closed to the public. ☎ 0181/341–1371.

➤ Mar.: **Camden Jazz Festival** is 10 days of concerts sponsored by the Borough of Camden. For information, ☎ 0171/860–5866.

➤ Early Apr.: **Chaucer Festival** allows Londoners to don medieval garb and parade from Southwark Cathedral to the Tower of London, where jugglers and strolling minstrels party the day away. ☎ 01227/470379.

➤ Mid-Apr.: **London Marathon,** a New York–style marathon through London's streets. Runners from 68 countries start in Greenwich and Blackheath at 9–9:30 AM, then run via Docklands and Canary Wharf, the Tower of London and Parliament Square to finish in the Mall.

➤ Mid-Apr.: **Head of the River Boat Race** offers the spectacle of 420 eight-man crews from Oxford and Cambridge universities dipping their 6,720 oars in the Thames as they race from Mortlake to Putney. The best view is from Surrey Bank above Chiswick Bridge (tube to Chiswick); check out *Time Out* for the starting time, which depends on the tide.

➤ Mar. 27–23: **British Antique Dealers' Association Fair,** the newest of the major fairs, is large and prestigious, with many affordable pieces. ⊠ *Duke of York's Headquarters, King's Rd., Chelsea SW3,* ☎ 0171/589–6108.

➤ Apr. 21: **Queen's Birthday** earns a showy 41-gun salute at Hyde Park. In June (*see* below), Elizabeth II's ceremonial B-day is celebrated by Trooping the Colour.

➤ MID-MAY: **Punch and Judy Festival** is held on the second Sunday in May and offers a May Fayre Procession in the morning, services at St. Paul's Church, then puppet shows until dusk. A lovely event for children of all ages! ✉ *Covent Garden Piazza,* ☎ *0171/375–0441.*

➤ MID-MAY: **Royal Windsor Horse Show,** a major show-jumping event attended by some members of the Royal Family. ✉ *Show Box Office, 4 Grove Parade, Buxton, Derbyshire SK17 6AJ,* ☎ *01298/72272.*

➤ MAY 25–28: **Chelsea Flower Show,** Britain's most prestigious flower show is always graced by the Royals and covers 22 acres. ✉ *Royal Hospital Rd., Chelsea SW3,* ☎ *0171/630–7422.*

SUMMER

➤ LATE MAY–LATE AUG.: **Glyndebourne Festival Opera** is a unique opportunity to see international stars in a bucolic setting and in a brand-new theater. Tickets go fast and early. ✉ *Glyndebourne Festival Opera, Lewes, Sussex BN8 5UU,* ☎ *01273/812321.*

➤ LATE MAY–LATE AUG.: **Shakespeare Under the Stars** gives you the chance to see the Bard of Bard's plays performed at Regent's Park Open Air Theatre. Performances are usually Monday–Saturday at 8 PM, with matinees on Wednesday, Thursday,

and Saturday. ✉ *Inner Circle, NW1,* ☎ *0171/486–2431.*

➤ EARLY JUNE: **Beating Retreat by the Guards Massed Bands,** when more than 500 musicians parade at Horse Guards, Whitehall. ✉ *Tickets from Household Division Fund, Block 8, Wellington Barracks, Birdcage Walk, SW1E 6HQ,* ☎ *0171/414–3253.*

➤ EARLY JUNE: **Derby Day** is the best-known event on the horse-racing calendar. ✉ *Information from United Racecourses Ltd., Racecourse Paddock, Epsom, Surrey KT18 5NJ,* ☎ *013727/26311.*

➤ MID-JUNE: **Trooping the Colour,** Queen Elizabeth's colorful official birthday parade, is held at Horse Guards, Whitehall, usually on the second or third Saturday of June. Write for tickets *only* between January 1 and February 28, enclosing a self-addressed stamped envelope. ✉ *Ticket Office, Headquarters, Household Division, Horse Guards, London SW1A 2AX,* ☎ *0171/414–2497.*

➤ MID-JUNE: **Royal Meeting at Ascot** brings the horsey set and their enormous hats out in force during the third week in June (Tuesday–Friday; Thursday is the high-fashion Ladies Day). General admission is available but reserve months in advance; for tickets (you must be sponsored) to the Royal Enclosure, write to Her Majesty's Representative, Ascot Office, St. James's Palace, London SW1 (☎ *0171/930–9882).* ✉

Ascot Racecourse, Ascot, Berkshire SL5 7JN, ☎ *01344/622211.*

➤ MID JUNE–EARLY SEPT.: **Kenwood Lakeside Concerts** offers fireworks and classical concerts under the stars in the park of London's regal stately house. ✉ *Kenwood House, Hampstead La.,* ☎ *0181/348–1286.*

➤ JUNE 10–19: **The Grosvenor House Antiques Fair** is one of the most prestigious antiques fairs in Britain. ✉ *Grosvenor House Hotel, Park La., London W1A 3AA,* ☎ *0171/499–6363.*

➤ JUNE 21–JULY 4: **Wimbledon Lawn Tennis Championships,** held at the All England Lawn Tennis and Croquet Club in Wimbledon. Write early to enter the lottery for tickets for Centre and Number One courts; tickets for outside courts are available daily at the gate. ✉ *Church Rd., Wimbledon, London SW19 5AE,* ☎ *0181/946–2244.*

➤ LATE JUNE–LATE JULY: **City of London Festival** fills the City with theater, poetry, classical music, and dance performed by international artists. ☎ *0171/377–0540.*

➤ EARLY JULY: **Hampton Court Palace Flower Show** is a five-day event that nearly rivals the Chelsea Flower Show for glamour. ✉ *East Molesey,* ☎ *0171/834–4333.*

➤ JUNE 30–JULY 4: **Henley Royal Regatta,** an international rowing event and top social occasion, at Henley-upon-Thames, Oxfordshire. For information, ☎ *01491/572153.*

➤ MID-JULY–MID-SEPT.: **Henry Wood Promenade Concerts,** a marvelous series of concerts at the Royal Albert Hall. ⊠ *Box Office, Royal Albert Hall, Kensington Gore SW7 2AP,* ☎ *0171/589–8212.*

➤ JULY 20–AUG. 1: **The Royal Tournament** features military displays and pageantry by the Royal Navy, the Royal Marines, the Army, and the Royal Air Force. ⊠ *Earl's Court Exhibition Centre, Warwick Rd., London SW5 9TA,* ☎ *0171/370–8226.*

AUTUMN

➤ EARLY OCT.: **Pearly Harvest Festival Service** draws a crowd of coster-mongers to the Church of St. Martin-in-the-Fields on the first Sunday in October. The Pearly Kings and Queens strut their famous costumes. ⊠ *Trafalgar Square,* ☎ *0171/930–0089.*

➤ EARLY NOV.: **London to Brighton Veteran Car Run,** a run from Hyde Park in London to Brighton in East Sussex. No tickets required. For information, ☎ 01753/681736.

➤ EARLY NOV.: **Lord Mayor's Procession and Show.** At the lord mayor's inauguration, a procession takes place from the Guildhall in the City to the Royal Courts of Justice. No tickets required. For information, ☎ 0171/606–3030.

➤ NOV. 5: **Guy Fawkes Day** celebrates a foiled 1605 attempt to blow up Parliament. Fireworks are held throughout London, but the place to be is the bonfire festivity on Primrose Hill near Camden Town.

2 Exploring London

If London contained only its landmarks—Buckingham Palace, Big Ben, the Tower of London—it would still rank as one of the world's top destinations. But England's capital is much more. It is a bevy of British bobbies, an ocean of black umbrellas, and an unconquered continuance of more than 2,000 years of history. A city that loves to be explored, London beckons with great museums, royal pageantry, and off-the-beaten-path delights: Call on the Duke of Wellington's house, track Jack the Ripper's shadow in Whitechapel, then get Beatle-ized at Abbey Road. East End, West End, you'll find London is a Dickens of a place.

Updated by
Kate Sekules

LONDON IS AN ANCIENT CITY whose history greets you at every turn. To gain a sense of its continuity, stand on Waterloo Bridge at the hour of sunset. To the east, the great globe of St. Paul's Cathedral glows golden in the fading sunlight as it has since the 17th century, still majestic amid the towers of glass and steel that hem it in. To the west stand the mock-medieval ramparts of Westminster, home to the "Mother of Parliaments," which has met here or hereabouts since the 1250s. Past them both snakes the swift, dark Thames, as it flowed past the first Roman settlement nearly 2,000 years ago.

For much of its history, innumerable epigrams and observations have been coined about London by both her enthusiasts and detractors. The great 18th-century author and wit Samuel Johnson, said that a man who is tired of London is tired of life. Oliver Wendell Holmes said, "No person can be said to know London. The most that anyone can claim is that he knows something of it." In all likelihood a more appropriate tribute paid to London would note that the capital of Great Britain is—simply stated—one of the most interesting places on earth. There is no other place like it in its agglomeration of architectural sins and sudden intervention of almost rural sights, in its medley of styles, in its mixture of the green loveliness of parks and the modern gleam of neon. Thankfully, the old London of Queen Anne and Georgian architecture can still be discovered under the hasty routine of later additions.

Discovering it takes a bit of work, however. Modern-day London still largely reflects its medieval layout, a willfully difficult tangle of streets. This swirl of spaghetti will be totally confusing to anyone brought up on the rigidity of a grid system. Even Londoners, most of whom own a copy of the indispensable A–Z street finder (they come under different names), get lost in their own city. But London's bewildering street pattern will be a plus for the visitor who wants to experience its indefinable historic atmosphere. London is a walker's city and will repay every moment you spend exploring on foot. The visitor to London who wants to penetrate beyond the crust of popular knowledge is well advised not only to visit St. Paul's Cathedral and the Tower, but also to set aside some of his or her limited time for random wandering. Walk in the city's back streets and mews, around Park Lane and Kensington. Pass up Buckingham Palace for Kew, the smallest royal palace, beautifully situated in the botanical gardens. Take in the National Gallery, but don't forget London's "time machine" museums, such as the 19th-century homes of Linley Sambourne and Sir John Soane. For out-and-out glamour, pay a call on the palatial Wallace Collection and Apsley House, the historic abode of the Duke of Wellington. Abandon the city's identikit chain stores to discover unique shopping emporiums, such as the gentlemen's outfitters of St. James's. In such ways can you best visualize the shape or, rather, the various shapes, of Old London, a curious city that engulfed its own past for the sake of modernity but still lives and breathes the air of history.

Today, that sense of modernity is stronger than ever. Everyone is talking about swinging-again London. *Vanity Fair* recently proclaimed it "the coolest, hottest city in the world," and *Newsweek* announced that the capital was the *only* place to be. Tony Blair's Labour Party has ushered in a blast of youthful optimism and verve. A booming economy has helped the city's art, style, fashion, and dining scenes to make headlines around the world. London's chefs have become superstars; its fashion designers have conquered Paris (John Galliano, Alexander McQueen, and Stella McCartney recently grabbed the reins at Dior, Givenchy, and Chloë); avante-garde artists have stormed the august Royal Academy of Arts (once noted for its stuffy predilection for still lifes and puritanical abhorrence of the nude), which recently displayed Damien Hirst's formaldehyde-preserved tiger shark and Marcus Hindley's gigantic portrait of a notorious child killer; the city's raging after-hours scene is packed with music mavens ready to catch the Next Big Thing after Oasis and the Spice Girls; and enfants terribles are turning upside down the National Theatre with radical stagings. Even Shakespeare is ready for the millennium: the Bard's own Globe—the fabled "Wooden O"—has been reconstructed on the banks of the Thames just 200 yards from where it stood in the 16th century. Its 1996 preview season opened with *Two Gentlemen of Verona* and had cast members sporting Ray-Ban sunglasses and sneakers.

On the other hand, while the outward shapes may be altered and the inner spirit may be warmer—the 1997 funeral of Diana, Princess of Wales, was far removed from the conventional picture of a somewhat staid city of people who don't display their emotions—the bedrock of London's character and tradition remains the same. Deep down, Britons have a sense of the continuity of history. Even in the modern metropolis, some things rarely change. The British bobby is alive and well. The tall, red, double-decker buses still lumber from stop to stop, though their aesthetic match at street level, the glossy red telephone booths, is slowly disappearing. And, of course, teatime is still a hallowed part of the day, with, if you search hard enough, toasted crumpets still honeycombed with sweet butter. Then, of course, there is that greatest living link with the past—the Royal Family. Don't let the tag of "typical tourist" stop you from enjoying the pageantry of the Windsors, one of the greatest free shows in the world. Line up for the Changing of the Guard and poke into the Royal Mews for a look at the Coronation Coach. Pomp reaches its zenith in mid-June when the Queen celebrates her official birthday with a parade called Trooping the Colour. Royalty watching is by no means restricted to fascinated foreigners. You only have to open London's tabloid newspapers to read reports of the latest rumors. Then again, more and more people are feeling that what goes on inside Buckingham Palace is no one's affair but the Queen's.

In the end, the London you'll discover will surely include some of our enthusiastic recommendations, but be prepared to be taken by surprise as well. The best that a great city has to offer often comes in unexpected ways. Armed with energy and curiosity, and the practical information and helpful hints in the following pages, one thing remains certain: To quote Dr. Johnson again, you can find "in London all that life can afford."

WESTMINSTER AND ROYAL LONDON

This tour might be called "London for Beginners." If you went no farther than these few acres, you would see many of the most famous sights, from the Houses of Parliament, Big Ben, Westminster Abbey, and Buckingham Palace to two of the world's greatest art collections, housed in the National and Tate galleries. You can truly call this area Royal London, as it is neatly bounded by the triangle of streets that make up the route that the Queen usually takes when journeying from Buckingham Palace to the Abbey or to the Houses of Parliament on state occasions. The three points on this royal triangle are Trafalgar Square, Westminster, and Buckingham Palace. If you have time to visit only one part of London, undoubtedly this should be it. There is as

22

Central London Exploring *(Boxes Refer to Detail Maps)*

King's Cross
Station

Pentonville Rd.

City Rd.

The East End

King's Cross Rd.

Gray's Inn Rd.

St. John's St.

East Road

Old St.

City Rd.

Hoxton St.

Kingsland Rd.

Shoreditch High St.

Eastern St.

Commercial St.

cras
on

ury
don

Coram's
Fields

Guilford St.

Southampton Row

Theobald's Rd.

Rosebery Ave.

Farringdon Rd.

Goswell Rd.

Clerkenwell Rd.

Liverpool
St.
Station

London Wall

Moorgate

Bishopsgate

Houndsditch

Holborn

High

Drury Ln.

Holborn

Holborn Viaduct

Newgate St.

Old
Bailey

The City

Cheapside

Cornhill

Gracechurch St.

Leadenhall St.

Fenchurch St.

**Soho and
Covent Garden**

Fleet St.

Queen Victoria St.

Cannon St.

Tower Hill

Strand

Victoria Embankment

Upper Thames St.

Cannon St.
Station

Lower Thames St.

Waterloo Br.

Blackfriars Br.

Southwark Br.

London Br.

River Thames

Tower Br.

**South
Bank
Arts
Complex**

Southwark St.

Union St.

St. Thomas St.

Tooley St.

London
Bridge
Station

York Rd.

The Cut

The South Bank

Borough High St.

Bridge Rd.

Tower Bridge Rd.

Waterloo
Station

Waterloo Rd.

Blackfriars Rd.

Borough Rd.

London Rd.

Westminster Br. Rd.

Lambeth Rd.

Kennington Rd.

Millbank

Rd.

Lambeth Br.

**Imperial
War
Museum**

New Kent Rd.

Old Kent Rd.

er and
ondon

Walworth Rd.

Kennington Ln.

Kennington Park Rd.

N

**Vauxhall
Station**

Kennington
Oval

0   1 mile

0   1 km

much history in these few acres as in many entire cities, as the statues of kings, queens, soldiers, and statesmen that stand guard at every corner attest—this is concentrated sightseeing, so pace yourself. The main drawback to sightseeing here is that half the world is doing it at the same time. So, even if you're tired after a long day on your feet, try to come back in the evening, after the crowds have dispersed, to drink in the serenity and grandeur at your leisure. You'll get to see it in a new light, literally, as much of Royal London is spectacularly floodlighted at night.

Westminster is by far the younger of the capital's two centers, postdating the City by some 1,000 years. Edward the Confessor put it on the map when he packed up his court from its cramped City quarters and moved it west a couple of miles, founding the abbey church of Westminster—the minster west of the City—in 1050. Subsequent kings continued to hold court here until Henry VIII decamped to Whitehall Palace in 1512, leaving Westminster to the politicians. And here they are still; not in the palace, which burned almost to the ground in 1834, but in the Victorian mock-Gothic Houses of Parliament, whose 320-ft-high Clock Tower is as much a symbol of London as the Eiffel Tower is of Paris.

Numbers in the text correspond to numbers in the margin and on the Westminster and Royal London map.

A Good Walk

Trafalgar Square ① is the obvious place to start for several reasons. It is the geographical core of London and home to many political demonstrations, a raucous New Year's Eve party, and the highest concentration of bus stops and pigeons in the capital. After taking in the instantly identifiable **Nelson's Column** ② in the center (read about the area on a plaque marking its 150th anniversary), head for the **National Gallery** ③, on the north side—this is Britain's greatest trove of masterpieces. Detour around the corner to see the **National Portrait Gallery** ④—a parade of the famous that can be very rewarding to anyone interested in what makes the British tick. East of the National Gallery, still on Trafalgar Square, see the much-loved church of **St. Martin-in-the-Fields** ⑤, then, stepping through grand **Admiralty Arch** ⑥ down on the southwest corner, enter the royal pink road, **the Mall**, with St. James's Park on your left. On your right is the **Institute of Contemporary Arts** ⑦, known as the ICA and housed in the great Regency architect John Nash's **Carlton House Terrace** ⑧. At the foot of the Mall is one of London's most famous sights, **Buckingham Palace** ⑨, home, of course, to the monarch of the land and punctuated by the ornate, white marble **Queen Victoria Memorial** ⑩. Turning left and left again, almost doubling back, follow the southern perimeter of St. James's Park around Birdcage Walk, passing the **Queen's Gallery** ⑪—with changing exhibitions from Her Majesty's vast art collection—and the HQ of the Queen's Guard, the **Wellington Barracks** ⑫ on your right, and, in turn, the hulking **Home Office** and **Queen Anne's Gate** ⑬. Cross Horse Guard's Road at the eastern edge of the park, walk down Great George Street, with **St. Margaret's Church** ⑭ on your right, and across **Parliament Square** to come to another of the great sights of London, the **Houses of Parliament** ⑮—a mock-medieval extravaganza, down to the last detail (neo-Gothic umbrella stands), designed by two celebrated Victorian-era architects—built along the Thames and including the famous Clock Tower, known the world over as Big Ben. Try to stick around for the sonorous chiming of the bell: For millions of citizens of the British empire, the sound of Big Ben's chimes is a link with the heart and soul of the commonwealth. A clockwise turn around the square brings you to yet

Westminster and Royal London

another major landmark, breathtaking **Westminster Abbey** ⑯. Complete the circuit and head north up Whitehall, passing the **Cabinet War Rooms** ⑰, where you'll see a simple monolith in the middle of the street—the **Cenotaph,** designed by Edwin Lutyens in 1920 in commemoration of the 1918 armistice. The gated alley on your left is **Downing Street** ⑱, where England's modest "White House" stands at No. 10. Soon after that, you pass **Horse Guards Parade** ⑲, the setting for the Queen's birthday celebration, Trooping the Colour, with the perfect classical Inigo Jones **Banqueting House** ⑳, scene of Charles I's execution, opposite. It's well worth it to backtrack a little ways down Whitehall, down Abington Street, to Millbank and the **Tate Gallery** ㉑—the most famous museum of British art—which is going to split in two for the millennium (when the new Bankside Power Station branch opens across the Thames in Southwark).

TIMING

You could achieve this walk of roughly 3 mi in just over an hour, but you could just as easily spend a week's vacation on this route alone. Allow as much time as you can for the two great museums—the National Gallery requires at *least* two hours; the National Portrait Gallery can be whizzed round in less than one. Westminster Abbey can take half a day—especially in summer, when lines are long, both to get in and to get around. In summer, you can get inside Buckingham Palace, too, a half day's operation increased to a whole day if you see the Royal Mews and the Queen's Gallery or the Guards' Museum. If the Changing of the Guard is a priority, make sure you time this walk correctly.

HOW TO GET THERE

This is an easy neighborhood to access, especially if you start at Trafalgar Square, where many buses stop. The central neighborhood tube stop, Charing Cross (on the Jubilee, Northern, and Bakerloo lines), exits at the beginning of Northumberland Avenue, on the southeast corner. Practically all buses stop around here, including Nos. 3, 6, 9, 12, 13, 15, 23, 24, 29, 53, 88, 94, and 139. Alternative tube stations are St. James's Park (on the District and Circle lines)—which is the best for Buckingham Palace—or the next stop, Westminster, which deposits you right by the bridge, in the shadow of Big Ben.

Sights to See

❻ **Admiralty Arch.** Gateway to the Mall—no, not an indoor shopping center but one of the very grand avenues of London—this is one of London's stateliest urban set pieces. Situated on the southwest corner of Trafalgar Square, the arch, which was named after the adjacent Royal Navy headquarters, was designed in 1910 by Sir Aston Webb as part of a ceremonial route to Buckingham Palace. As you pass under the enormous triple archway—though not through the central arch, opened only for state occasions—the atmosphere changes along with the color of the road, for you are exiting frenetic Trafalgar Square and entering the Mall (rhymes with shall)—the elegant avenue that leads directly to the palace.

⓴ **Banqueting House.** This is all that remains today of the Tudor Palace of Whitehall, which was (according to one foreign visitor) "ill-built, and nothing but a heap of houses." James I commissioned Inigo Jones (1573–1652), one of England's great architects, to do a grand remodeling. Influenced by Andrea Palladio's work during a sojourn in Tuscany, Jones brought Palladian sophistication and purity back to London with him. The resulting graceful and disciplined classical style of Banqueting House must have stunned its early occupants. James I's son, Charles I, enhanced the interior by employing the Flemish painter Peter Paul Rubens to glorify his father all over the ceiling. As it turned out, these allegorical paintings, depicting a wise monarch being received into heaven, were the last thing Charles saw before he was beheaded by Cromwell's Parliamentarians in 1649. But his son, Charles II, was able to celebrate the restoration of the monarchy in this same setting 20 years later. ⊠ *Whitehall, SW1,* ☎ *0171/930–4179.* 🎫 *£3.25.* ☻ *Mon.–Sat. 10–5; closed on short notice for banquets, so call first. Tube: Westminster.*

❾ Buckingham Palace. Supreme among the symbols of London, indeed of Britain generally and of the Royal Family, Buckingham Palace tops many must-see lists—although the building itself is no masterpiece and has housed the monarch only since Victoria (1819–1901) moved here from Kensington Palace at her accession in 1837. Its great gray bulk sums up the imperious splendor of so much of the city: stately, magnificent, and ponderous. When Victoria moved in, the place was a mess. George IV, at *his* accession in 1820, had fancied the idea of moving to Buckingham House, his parents' former home, and had employed John Nash, as usual, to remodel it. The government authorized only "repair and improvement"; Nash, that tireless spendthrift, overspent his budget by about half a million pounds. George died, Nash was dismissed, and Edward Blore finished the building, adding the now familiar east front (facing the Mall). Victoria arrived to faulty drains and sticky doors and windows, but they did not mar her affection for the place, nor that of her son, Edward VII. The Portland stone facade dates only from 1913 (it, too, was part of the Aston Webb scheme), and the interior was renovated and redecorated only after it sustained World War II bomb damage. Indeed, compared to other great London residences, this is very much a Johnny-come-lately affair.

The palace contains some 600 rooms, including the State Ballroom and, of course, the Throne Room. You'll find pomp and circumstance here but little else. These state rooms are where much of the business of royalty is played out—investitures, state banquets, receptions, lunch parties for the famous, and so on. The royal apartments are in the north wing; when the Queen is in, the royal standard is raised. Until fairly recently all the quarters were off-limits to the public, but a 1992 fire at Windsor Castle created an urgent need for cash. And so the state rooms are now on show from August to early October, a period when the royal family is away. (Visitors can now even prebook their tour reservations with a credit card by phone.) Without an invitation to one of the Queen's garden parties, however, you won't see much of the magnificent 45-acre grounds. The state rooms are graced with some of Her Majesty's most famous Old Master paintings, but other artworks are sometimes on view in special temporary exhibitions held at the **Queen's Gallery** (☞ *below*), near the south side of the palace. The **Changing of the Guard**, which, with all the ceremony monarchists and children adore, remains one of London's best free shows, culminates in front of the palace. Marching to live music, the Queen's Guard proceeds up the Mall from St. James's Palace to Buckingham Palace. Shortly afterward, the new guard approaches from Wellington Barracks via Birdcage Walk. Once the old and new guards are in the forecourt, the gold guard symbolically hands over the keys to the palace. The ceremony takes places daily at 11:30 AM April–July and on alternating days August–March, but the guards sometimes cancel due to bad weather; check the signs in the forecourt or call 089/150–5452. Arrive by 10:30 AM for a decent view. Early birds should grab a section of the gate facing the palace, since most of the hoopla takes place inside the fence. There are those who may scoff at this clockwork ceremony, but for the Briton who treasures the continuity of history, pageantry means permanence. ⊠ *Buckingham Palace Rd., SW1,* ☎ *0171/839–1377,*

0171/321–2233 credit-card reservation line (AE, MC, V). ☎ £9. ☉ Early Aug.–early Oct. (confirm dates, which are subject to Queen's mandate), daily 9:30–4. Tube: St. James's Park, Victoria.

⑰ **Cabinet War Rooms.** It was from this small maze of 17 bomb-proof underground rooms—in back of the hulking Foreign Office—that Britain's World War II fortunes were directed. During air raids, the Cabinet met here—the Cabinet Room is still arranged as if a meeting were about to convene; in the Map Room, the Allied campaign is charted; the Prime Minister's Room holds the desk from which Winston Churchill (1874–1965) made his morale-boosting broadcasts; and the Telephone Room has his hot line to FDR. The great man only slept here on a number of occasions; he preferred the comfort of Downing Street, even at the height of the German blitz.☒ *Clive Steps, King Charles St., SW1,* ☎ *0171/930–6961.* ☎ *£4.40.* ☉ *April–Aug., daily 9:30–5:15; Sept.–Mar., daily 10–5:15. Tube: Westminster.*

❽ **Carlton House Terrace.** This is a glorious example of Regency architect John Nash's genius. Between 1812 and 1830, under the patronage of George IV (Prince Regent until George III's death in 1820), Nash was responsible for a series of West End developments, of which these white-stucco facades and massive Corinthian columns may be the most imposing. It was a smart address, needless to say, and one that Prime Ministers Gladstone (1856) and Palmerston (1857–75) enjoyed. Today Carlton House Terrace is home to the Royal College of Pathologists, the Royal Society, the Turf Club, and, at No. 12, the **Institute of Contemporary Arts** (☞ *below*), better known as the ICA. ☒ *The Mall, W1. Tube: Charing Cross.*

⑱ **Downing Street.** Looking like an unassuming alley but barred by iron gates at both its Whitehall and Horse Guards Road approaches, this is where **No. 10 Downing Street,** London's modest version of the White House, stands. Only three houses remain of the terrace built circa 1680 by Sir George Downing, who spent enough of his youth in America to graduate from Harvard—the second man ever to do so. **No. 11** is the residence of the chancellor of the exchequer (secretary of the treasury); **No. 12** is the party whips' office. No. 10 has officially housed the Prime Minister since 1732. (The gates were former Prime Minister Margaret Thatcher's brainstorm.) Just south of Downing Street, in the middle of Whitehall, you'll see the **Cenotaph,** a stark white monolith designed in 1920 by Edward Lutyens to commemorate the 1918 armistice. On Remembrance Day (the Sunday nearest November 11) it is strewn with red poppies to honor the dead of both world wars, with the first wreath laid by the Queen. (Wherever you are on that day, you'll be inveigled to buy a plastic poppy to support veterans' charities.)

⑲ **Horse Guards Parade.** Once the tiltyard of Whitehall Palace, where jousting tournaments were held, the Horse Guards Parade is now notable mainly for the annual Trooping the Colour ceremony, in which the Queen takes the Royal Salute, her official birthday gift, on the second Saturday in June. (Like Paddington Bear, the Queen has two birthdays; her real one is on April 21.) There is pageantry galore, with marching bands, the occasional guardsman fainting clean away in his weighty busby, and throngs of onlookers. Covering the vast expanse of the square that faces Horse Guards Road, opposite St. James's Park at one end and Whitehall at the other, the ceremony is televised and also broadcast on Radio 4. Visitors may also attend the queenless rehearsals on the preceding two Saturdays. At the Whitehall facade of Horse Guards, two mounted sentries known as the Queen's Life Guard provide what may be London's most frequently exercised photo opportunity. They change, quietly, at 11 AM Monday–Saturday, 10 on Sunday.

★ ⑮ **Houses of Parliament.** Postcard London come to life, the Houses of Parliament are, arguably, the city's most famous and photogenic sight, with the Clock Tower—which everyone erroneously calls Big Ben—keeping watch on the corner and Westminster Abbey ahead of you across Parliament Square. The most romantic view of the complex is from the opposite (south) side of the river, a vista especially dramatic at night when the storybook spires, pinnacles, and towers of the great building are floodlighted green and gold—a fairy-tale vision only missing the presence of Peter Pan and Wendy on their way to Never-Never Land.

The Palace of Westminster, as the complex is still properly called, was established by Edward the Confessor during the 11th century, when he moved his court here from the City. It has served as the seat of English administrative power, on and off, ever since. In 1512, Henry VIII (1491–1547) abandoned it for Whitehall, and it ceased to be an official royal residence after 1547. At the Reformation, the Royal Chapel was secularized and became the first meeting place of the Commons. The Lords settled in the White Chamber. These, along with everything but the **Jewel Tower** and **Westminster Hall**, were destroyed in 1834 when "the sticks"—the arcane abacus beneath the Lords' Chamber on which the court had kept its accounts until 1826—was incinerated, and the fire got out of hand.

After the 1834 fire, architects were invited to submit plans for new Houses of Parliament in the grandiose "Gothic or Elizabethan style." Charles Barry's were selected from among 97 entries, partly because Barry had invited the architect and designer Augustus Pugin to add the requisite neo-Gothic curlicues to his own Renaissance-influenced style. As you can see, it was a happy collaboration, with Barry's classical proportions offset by Pugin's ornamental flourishes—although the latter were toned down by Gilbert Scott when he rebuilt the bomb-damaged House of Commons after World War II. The two towers were Pugin's work. The **Clock Tower,** now virtually the symbol of London, was completed in 1858 after long delays due to bickering over the clock's design. (Barry designed the faces himself in the end.) It contains the 13-ton bell known as Big Ben, which chimes the hour (and the quarters). Some say Ben was "Big Ben" Caunt, heavyweight champ; others, Sir Benjamin Hall, the far-from-slim Westminster building works commissioner. At the southwest end of the main Parliament building is the 336-ft-high **Victoria Tower,** newly agleam from its recent restoration and cleaning. The rest of the complex was scrubbed down some years ago; the revelation of the honey stone under the dowdy, smog-blackened facades, which seemed almost symbolic at the time, cheered London up no end.

There are two Houses, the Lords and the Commons. The former consists of more than 1,000 peers (nowadays there are more "life peers," with recently bestowed titles, than aristocrats); the latter is made up of 650 elected Members of Parliament (MPs). The party with the most MPs forms the government, its leader becoming Prime Minister; other parties form the Opposition. Since 1642, when Charles I tried to have five MPs arrested, no monarch has been allowed into the House of Commons. The state opening of Parliament in November consequently takes place in the House of Lords. Visitors aren't allowed many places in the Houses of Parliament, though the Visitors' Galleries of the House of Commons do afford a view of the best free show in London, staged in the world's most renowned ego chamber. The opposing banks of green leather benches seat only 346 MPs—not that this is much of a problem, since absentees far outnumber the diligent. When MPs vote, they exit by the "Aye" or the "No" corridor, thus being counted by the party "whips" (yes, it is a fox-hunting term); when they speak, it is not directly to each other but through the Speaker, who also decides who will get the floor each day. Elaborate procedures notwithstanding, debate is often drowned out by the amazingly raucous and immature jeers and insults familiar to TV viewers since 1989, when cameras were first allowed into the House of Commons.

Other public areas of the 1,100-room labyrinth are rather magnificently got up in high neo-Gothic style and punctuated with stirring frescoes commissioned by Prince Albert. You pass these en route to the Visitors' Galleries—if, that is, you are patient enough to wait in line for hours (the Lords line is shorter) or have applied in advance for the special "line of route" tour—open only to overseas visitors—by writing to the Public Information Office (House of Commons, Westminster, SW1A 2PW) at least a month in advance of your visit. The tour takes you through the Queen's Robing Room, Royal Gallery, House of Lords, Central Hall (where MPs meet their constituents—the lucky ones get to accompany their MP to a prestigious tea on the terrace), House of Commons, and out into the spectacular Westminster Hall. Watch for the "VR" (Victoria Regina) monograms in the carpets and carving belying the "medieval" detailing as 19th-century work. Permits for tours of up to 16 people are available Friday afternoons while the House is sitting. The time to catch the action is "Question Time"—when the Prime Minister defends himself against the slings and arrows of his "right honorable friends" on Wednesday between 3 and 3:30 PM. Foreigners are required to secure tickets from their respective embassies. The next best time to visit is either chamber's regular "Question Time," held Monday–Thursday 2:30–3:30. The easiest time to get into the Commons is during an evening session—Parliament is still sitting if the top of the Clock Tower is illuminated. For a special exhibition devoted to "History of Parliament: Past and Present," head to the Jewel Tower, across the street from Victoria Tower, on Abingdon Street (also called Old Palace Yard), just south of Parliament Square; there is a small admission charge. ⊠ *St. Stephen's Entrance, St. Margaret St., SW1,* ☎ *0171/219–3000, 0171/219–4272 (Commons information), 0171/ 219–3107 (Lords information).* ▨ *Free.* ☉ *Commons Mon.–Thurs. 2:30–10, Fri. 9:30–3 (although not every Fri.); Lords Mon.–Thurs. 2:30–10. Closed Easter wk, July–Oct., and 3 wks at Christmas. Tube: Westminster.*

❼ Institute of Contemporary Arts (ICA). Behind its incongruous white-stucco facade, at No. 12 Carlton House Terrace, the ICA has provided a stage for the avant-garde in performance, theater, dance, visual art, and music since it was established in 1947. There are two cinemas, an underused library of video artists' works, a bookshop, a café and a bar, and a team of adventurous curators. ⊠ *The Mall, W1,* ☎ *0171/930– 3647.* ▨ *1-day membership £1.50, additional charge for entry to specific events.* ☉ *Daily noon–9:30, later for some events. Tube: Charing Cross.*

NEED A BREAK?	The **ICAfé** is windowless but brightly spotlighted, with a self-service counter offering good hot dishes, salads, quiches, and desserts. The bar upstairs, which serves baguette sandwiches, has a picture window overlooking the Mall. Both are packed before popular performances and are subject to the £1.50 one-day membership fee.

The Mall. This street was laid out around 1660 for the game of *pell mell* that also gave Pall Mall its name, and it quickly became the place to be seen. Samuel Pepys, Jonathan Swift, and Alexander Pope all wrote about it, and it continued as the beau monde's social playground into the early 19th century, long after the game it was built for had gone out of vogue. Something of the former style survives on those summer days when the Queen is throwing a Buckingham Palace garden party: hundreds of her subjects throng the Mall, from the grand and titled to the humble and hardworking, all of whom have donned hat and frock to take afternoon tea with the monarch—or somewhere near her—on the lawns of Buck House. The old Mall still runs alongside the graceful, pink, 115-ft-wide avenue that replaced it in 1904 for just such occasions.

★ ❸ **National Gallery.** Jan Van Eyck's *Arnolfini Marriage,* Leonardo da Vinci's *Madonna of the Rocks,* Velázquez's *"Rokeby Venus,"* Constable's *Hay Wain* . . . you get the picture. There are about 2,200 other paintings in this museum—many of them instantly recognizable and among the most treasured works of art anywhere. The museum's low, gray, colonnaded neoclassic facade fills the north side of Trafalgar Square. The institution was founded in 1824, when George IV and a connoisseur named Sir George Beaumont persuaded a reluctant government to spend £57,000 to acquire part of the recently deceased philanthropist John Julius Angerstein's collection. These 38 paintings, including works by Raphael, Rembrandt, Titian, and Rubens, were augmented by 16 of Sir George's own and exhibited in Angerstein's Pall Mall residence until 1838, when William Wilkin's building was completed. By the end of the century, enthusiastic directors and generous patrons had turned the National Gallery into one of the world's foremost collections, with works from painters of the Italian Renaissance and earlier, from the Flemish and Dutch masters, the Spanish school, and of course the English tradition, including Hogarth, Gainsborough, Stubbs, and Constable.

In 1991, following years of wrangling and the rehanging of the entire collection, the Sainsbury Wing was opened. It had been financed by the eponymous British grocery dynasty to house the early Renaissance collection, and designed—eventually—by the American architect Robert Venturi after previous plans were abandoned. (Prince Charles didn't liked these modernist designs. "A monstrous carbuncle on the face of a much-loved friend" was his infamous comment.)

The collection is really too overwhelming to absorb in a single viewing. It is wise to acquaint yourself with the layout—easy to negotiate compared with other European galleries—and plot a route in advance. The **Micro Gallery,** a computer information center in the Sainsbury Wing, might be the place to start. You can access in-depth information on any work here, choose your favorites, and print out a free personal tour map that marks the paintings you most want to see. Careful, though—you could spend hours in here scrolling through this colorful if pixelized history of art.

The following is a list of 10 of the most familiar works, to jog your memory, whet your appetite, and offer a starting point for your own exploration. The first five are in the Sainsbury Wing. In chronological order: (1) **Van Eyck** (circa 1395–1441), *The Arnolfini Marriage.* A solemn couple holds hands, the fish-eye mirror behind them mysteriously illuminating what can't be seen from the front view. (2) **Uccello** (1397–1475), *The Battle of San Romano.* In a work commissioned by the Medici family, the Florentine commander on a rearing white warhorse leads armored knights into battle with the Sienese. (3) **Bellini** (circa 1430–1516), *The Doge Leonardo Loredan.* The artist captured the Venetian doge's beatific expression (and snail-shell "buttons") at the beginning of his 20 years in office. (4) **Botticelli** (1445–1510), *Venus and Mars.* Mars sleeps, exhausted by the love goddess, oblivious to the lance wielded by mischievous putti and the buzzing of wasps. (5) **Leonardo da Vinci** (1452–1519), *The Virgin and Child*. This haunting black chalk cartoon is partly famous for having been attacked at gunpoint, and it now gets extra protection behind glass and screens. (6) **Caravaggio** (1573–1610), *The Supper at Emmaus*. A cinematically lighted, freshly resurrected Christ blesses bread in an astonishingly domestic vision from the master of chiaroscuro. (7) **Velázquez** (1599–1660), *The Toilet of Venus*. "The Rokeby Venus," named for its previous home in Yorkshire, has the most famously beautiful back in any gallery. She's the only surviving female nude by Velázquez. (8) **Constable** (1776–1837), *The Hay Wain*. Rendered overfamiliar by too many greeting cards, this is the definitive image of golden-age rural England. (9) **Turner** (1775–1851), *The Fighting Téméraire*. Most of the collection's other Turners were moved to the Tate Gallery (☞ *below*); the final voyage of the great French battleship into a livid, hazy sunset stayed here. (10) **Seurat** (1859–1891), *Bathers at Asnières*. This static summer day's idyll is one of the pointillist extraordinaire's best-known works.

Glaring omissions from the above include some of the most popular pictures in the gallery, by Piero della Francesca, Titian, Holbein, Bosch, Brueghel, Rembrandt, Vermeer, Canaletto, Claude, Tiepolo, Gainsborough, Ingres, Monet, Renoir, and van Gogh. You can't miss the two most spectacular works on view—due to their mammoth size—Sebastiano del Piombo's *Sermon on the Mount* and Stubbs's stunning *Whistlejacket*. These great paintings aren't the only thing glowing in the rooms of the National Gallery—thanks to government patronage and new lottery monies, salons here now gleam with stunning brocades and opulent silks. Rubens's *Samson and Delilah* has never looked better. ⊠ *Trafalgar Sq., WC2,* ☎ *0171/747–2484, or 0171/747–2885 (recorded general information).* 🎫 *Free; charge for special exhibitions.* ☉ *Mon.–Sat. 10–6, Sun. 2–6; June–Aug., Wed. until 8; 1-hr guided tour starts at Sainsbury Wing weekdays at 11:30 and 2:30, Sat. 2 and 3:30. Tube: Charing Cross.*

NEED A
BREAK?

The **Brasserie** in the Sainsbury Wing of the National Gallery offers a fashionable lunch—mussels, gravlax, charcuterie, salads, a hot special—plus baguette sandwiches, pastries, tea, coffee, and wine, in a sophisticated, spacious room on the second floor.

★ ❹ **National Portrait Gallery.** An idiosyncratic collection that presents a potted history history of Britain through its people, past and present, this museum is an essential visit for all history and literature buffs. As an art collection it is eccentric, as the subject, not the artist, is the point, and there are notable works (a Holbein portrait of Henry VIII, Stubbs and Hockney self-portraits) mixed up with photographs, busts, caricatures, and amateur paintings. (The miniature of Jane Austen by her sister Cassandra, for instance, is the only likeness that exists of the great novelist.) Many of the faces are obscure and will be just as unknown to English visitors because the portraits outlasted their sitters' fame—not so surprising when the portraitists are such greats as Reynolds, Gainsborough, Lawrence, and Romney. But the annotation is comprehensive, the layout is easy to negotiate—chronological, with the oldest at the top—and there is a new, separate research center for those who get hooked on particular personages. Don't miss the new Victorian and early 20th-century portrait galleries nor the photography gallery. ⊠ *St. Martin's Pl., WC2,* ☎ *0171/306–0055.* 🎫 *Free.* ☉ *Mon.–Sat. 10–5:45, Sun. 12–5:45. Tube: Charing Cross, Leicester Sq.*

❷ **Nelson's Column.** Trafalgar Square takes its name from the Battle of Trafalgar, Admiral Lord Horatio Nelson's great naval victory over the

French in 1805. Appropriately, the dominant landmark here is this famous column, a 145-ft-high granite perch from which E. H. Baily's 1843 statue of Nelson (1758–1805), one of England's favorite heroes, keeps watch; three bas-reliefs depicting his victories at Cape St. Vincent, the Battle of the Nile, and Copenhagen (and a fourth, his death at Trafalgar itself in 1805) sit around the base. All four bas-reliefs were cast from cannons he captured. The four majestic lions, designed by the Victorian painter Sir Edwin Landseer, were added in 1867. The calling cards of generations of picturesque pigeons have been a corrosive problem for the statue; this may have been finally solved by the statue's new gel coating.

⓭ **Queen Anne's Gate.** Standing south of Birdcage Walk, by St. James's Park, are these two pretty 18th-century closes, once separate but now linked by a statue of the last Stuart monarch. (Another statue of Anne, beside St. Paul's, inspired the doggerel "Brandy Nan, Brandy Nan, you're left in the lurch, your face to the gin shop, your back to the church,"— proving that her attempts to disguise her habitual tipple in a teapot fooled nobody.)

❿ **Queen Victoria Memorial.** You can't overlook this monument if you're near Buckingham Palace, which it faces from the traffic island at the west end of the Mall. The monument was conceived by Sir Aston Webb as the nucleus of his ceremonial route down the Mall to the Palace, and it was executed by the sculptor Thomas Brock, who was knighted on the spot when the memorial was revealed to the world in 1911. Many wonder why he was given that honor, since the thing is Victoriana incarnate: The frumpy queen glares down the Mall, with golden-winged Victory overhead and her siblings Truth, Justice, and Charity, plus Manufacture, Progress-and-Peace, War-and-Shipbuilding, and so on—in Osbert Sitwell's words, "tons of allegorical females . . . with whole litters of their cretinous children"—surrounding her. ⊠ *The Mall and Spur Rd. Tube: St. James's Park, Victoria.*

⓫ **Queen's Gallery.** This is the former chapel at the south side of Buckingham Palace, which has been open to visitors since 1962. The gallery is only open for special, temporary exhibitions (focusing on small parts of the collection, such as Her Majesty's Michelangelo drawings); call for information on current exhibitions and opening dates. Sign-of-the-times note: Now that she is a taxpayer, HRH's artwork, along with all her other possessions (for example, Buckingham Palace), are officially part of a business known as Royal Collection Enterprises. ⊠ *Buckingham Palace Rd., SW1,* ☎ *0171/799–2331.* ☑ *£3.50, combined ticket for Queen's Gallery and Royal Mews £6.20.* ☉ *Tues.– Sat. 9:30–4:30, Sun. 2–4:30. Closed Dec. 24–Mar. 4. Tube: St. James's Park, Victoria.*

☙ **Royal Mews.** Unmissable children's entertainment, this museum is the home of Her Majesty's Coronation Coach. Standing nearly next door to the Queen's Gallery, the Royal Mews were designed by famed Regency-era architect John Nash. Mews were originally falcons' quarters (the name comes from their "mewing," or feather shedding), but horses gradually eclipsed birds of prey. Now some of the magnificent royal beasts live here alongside the fabulous bejeweled, glass and golden coaches they draw on state occasions. ⊠ *Buckingham Palace Rd., SW1,* ☎ *0171/ 839–1377.* ☑ *£3.70, combined ticket for Queen's Gallery and Royal Mews £6.20.* ☉ *Oct.–Mar., Wed. noon–4; Apr.–Oct., Tues.–Thurs. noon–4. Closed Mar. 25–29, Oct. 1–5, Dec. 23–Jan. 5. Tube: St. James's Park, Victoria.*

St. James's Park. London's smallest, most ornamental park, and the oldest of its royal ones, St. James's Park makes a spectacular frame for the towers of Westminster and Victoria—especially at night, when the illuminated fountains play and the skyline beyond the trees looks like a floating fairyland. Henry VIII drained a marsh that festered here next to the lepers' hospital that St. James's Palace replaced and bred his deer on the newly dry land. Later kings tinkered with it further, with James I installing an aviary and zoo (complete with crocodiles); Charles I laying out formal gardens, which he then had to traverse to his execution at the Banqueting House (☞ *above*) in 1649; and Charles II employing André Lenôtre, Louis XIV's Versailles landscaper, to remodel it completely with avenues, fruit orchards, and a canal. Its present shape more or less reflects what John Nash designed under George IV, turning the canal into a graceful lake (which was cemented in at a depth of 4 ft in 1855, so don't even think of swimming) and generally naturalizing the gardens.

More than 30 species of birds—including flamingos, pelicans, geese, ducks, and swans (which belong to the Queen)—now congregate on Duck Island at the east end of the lake, attracting ornithologists at dawn. Later on summer days the deck chairs (which you must pay to use) are crammed with office workers lunching while being serenaded by music from the bandstands. But the best time to stroll the leafy walkways is after dark, with Westminster Abbey and the Houses of Parliament rising above the floodlighted lake, and peace reigning.

⑭ **St. Margaret's Church.** Dwarfed by its northern neighbor, Westminster Abbey, this church was founded during the 12th century and rebuilt between 1486 and 1523. St. Margaret's is the parish church of the Houses of Parliament and much sought after for weddings; Samuel Pepys married here in 1655, Winston Churchill in 1908. The east Crucifixion window celebrates another union, the marriage of Prince Arthur and Catherine of Aragon. Unfortunately, it arrived so late that Arthur was dead, and Catherine had married his brother, Henry VIII. Sir Walter Raleigh is among the notables buried here, only without his head, which had been removed at Old Palace Yard, Westminster, and kept by his wife, who was said to be fond of asking visitors, "Have you met Sir Walter?" as she produced it from a velvet bag.

❺ **St. Martin-in-the-Fields.** One of Britain's best-loved churches, this was completed in 1726; James Gibbs's classical temple-with-spire design became a familiar pattern for churches in early Colonial America. Though it seems dwarfed by the surrounding structures of Trafalgar Square, the spire is actually slightly taller than Nelson's Column, which it overlooks. It is a welcome sight for the homeless, who have sought soup and shelter here since 1914. The church is also a haven for music lovers; the internationally known Academy of St. Martin-in-the-Fields was founded here, and a popular program of lunchtime (free) and evening concerts continues today. The church's musty interior has a wonderful atmosphere for music making—but the wooden benches can make it hard to give your undivided attention to the music. St. Martin's is often called the royal parish church, partly because Charles II was christened here—not because his mistress, Nell Gwyn, lies under the stones, alongside William Hogarth, Thomas Chippendale (the cabinetmaker), and Jack Sheppard, the notorious highwayman. Also in the crypt is the **London Brass-Rubbing Centre,** where you can make your own souvenir knight from replica tomb brasses, with metallic waxes, paper, and instructions provided for about £1; and the **St. Martin's Gallery** showing contemporary work. There is also a crafts market in the courtyard behind the church. ⊠ *St. Martin-in-the-Fields, Trafalgar Sq., WC2,* ☎ *0171/930–0089, 0171/839–8362 credit-card bookings for evening concerts.* ☉ *Church daily 8–8; crypt Mon.–Sat. 10–8, Sun. noon–6. Tube: Charing Cross, Leicester Sq.*

NEED A
BREAK?

St. Martin's **Café-in-the-Crypt** serves full meals, sandwiches, snacks, and even wine by the glass, Monday–Saturday 10–8 and Sunday noon–6.

Smith Square. An elegant enclave of perfectly preserved early 18th-century town houses still looks like the London of Dr. Johnson. The address is much sought after by MPs, especially of the Tory persuasion; No. 32 is the Conservative Party Headquarters. The Baroque church of **St. John's, Smith Square,** completed around 1720, dominates charmingly. It is well known to Londoners as a chamber-music venue; its popular lunchtime concerts are often broadcast on the radio.

In the Crypt of St. John's is the **Footstool**—about the only place to find refreshments around here. It has an interesting and reasonably priced lunchtime menu and also serves evening meals on concert nights.

★ ㉑ **Tate Gallery.** By the river, on traffic-laden Millbank, the Tate Gallery of Modern British Art, to give it its full title, opened in 1897, funded by the sugar magnate Sir Henry Tate. "Modern" is slightly misleading, as one of the three collections here consists of British art from 1545 to the present, including works by William Hogarth, Thomas Gainsborough, Sir Joshua Reynolds, and George Stubbs from the 18th century and by John Constable, William Blake (a mind-blowing collection of his visionary works), and the Pre-Raphaelite painters from the 19th century. Also from the 19th century is the second of the Tate's collections, the Turner Bequest, consisting of J. M. W. Turner's personal collection; he left it to the nation on the condition that the works be displayed together. The James Stirling–designed **Clore Gallery** (to the right of the main gallery) has fulfilled his wish since 1987, and it should not be missed.

The Tate's modern collection is international and so vast that it is never all on display at once. The annual rehanging goes some way toward solving the problem of the gallery's embarrassment of riches, but it also means that a favorite work may not be on view, although the most famous and popular works are on permanent display. Happily, come the year 2000, the Tate's space issue will be resolved with the opening of a new gallery, opposite St. Paul's, in the former Bankside Power Station, currently undergoing a £100 million transformation to the plans of Swiss architects Herzog & de Meuron. Even now, though, you can see work by an abundance of late 19th- and 20th-century artists and a good deal more. Your tour will deal you multiple shocks of recognition (Rodin's *The Kiss,* Lichtenstein's *Whaam!*). To enhance the picture, you can rent a "Tateinform," a handheld audio guide, with commentaries by curators, experts, and some of the artists themselves, to enhance the picture. Here's a short list of names: Matisse, Picasso, Braque, Léger, Kandinsky, Mondrian, Dalí, Bacon, de Kooning, Pollock, Rothko, Moore, Hepworth, Warhol, Freud, Hockney. About a 20-minute walk south of the Houses of Parliament, the Tate is also accessible if you tube it to the Pimlico stop, then take a five-minute walk through Chelsea to the museum. ⊠ *Millbank, SW1,* ☎ *0171/821–1313 or 0171/821–7128.* ◲ *Free; special exhibitions £3–£7.* ☉ *Mon.–Sat. 10–5:50, Sun. 2–5:50. Tube: Pimlico.*

❶ **Trafalgar Square.** This is the center of London, by dint of a plaque on the corner of the Strand and Charing Cross Road from which distances on U.K. signposts are measured. It is the home of the **National Gallery** (☞ *above*) and of one of London's most distinctive landmarks, **Nelson's Column** (☞ *above*). Permanently alive with people, Londoners and tourists alike, and roaring traffic, it remains London's "living room"—great events, such as New Year's, royal weddings, elections, sporting triumphs—will always see the crowds gathering in the city's most famous square.

Today it's a commanding open space, built on the grand scale demanded by its central position in the capital of an empire that once reached to the farthest corners of the globe. Long ago, however, the site housed the Royal Mews, where Edward I (1239–1307) kept his royal hawks and lodged his falconers. (Not the numberless Edward the Confessor of Westminster Abbey fame, who died in 1066; this one, known as "Longshanks," died of dysentery in 1307.) Later, all the kings' horses were stabled here, in increasingly smart quarters, until 1830, when John Nash had the buildings torn down as part of his Charing Cross Improvement Scheme. Nash cleverly exploited the square's natural incline—it slopes down from north to south—making it a succession of high points from which to look down the imposing carriageways that run dramatically away from it toward the Thames, the Houses of Parliament, and Buckingham Palace. Upon Nash's death, the design baton was passed to Sir Charles Barry and then to Sir Edwin Lutyens.

There's a pathetic history attached to the **equestrian statue of Charles I**, which stands near Whitehall on the southern slope of the square (on a pedestal *possibly* designed by Sir Christopher Wren and *possibly* carved by Grinling Gibbons). After Charles's High Treasurer ordered it (from Hubert le Sueur), the Puritan Oliver Cromwell tumbled Charles from the throne and commissioned a scrap dealer with the appropriate name of Rivett to melt the king down. Rivett made a fortune peddling knickknacks wrought, he claimed, from its metal, only to produce the statue miraculously unscathed after the restoration of the monarchy—and to make more cash reselling it to the authorities. In 1767 Charles II had it placed where it stands today, near the spot where his father was executed in 1649.

Today, street performers enhance the square's intermittent atmosphere of celebration, which is strongest in December, first when the lights on the gigantic Christmas tree (an annual gift from Norway to thank the British for harboring their Royal Family during World War II) are turned on, and then, less festively, when thousands see in the New Year.

⑫ Wellington Barracks. These are the headquarters of the Guards Division, the Queen's five regiments of elite foot guards (Grenadier, Coldstream, Scots, Irish, and Welsh) who protect the sovereign and patrol her palace dressed in tunics of gold-purled scarlet and tall fur "busby" helmets of Canadian brown bearskin. (London fact: The two items together cost more than £4,000.) If you want to learn more about the guards, you can visit the **Guards Museum**; the entrance is next to the Guards Chapel. ⊠ *Wellington Barracks, Birdcage Walk,* ☎ *0171/ 930–4466, Ext. 3430.* ☞ *£2.* ☉ *Daily 10–4. Tube: St. James's Park.*

★ ⑯ Westminster Abbey. Announced by the teeming human contents of tour buses, off the south side of Parliament Square, this is where nearly all of England's monarchs were crowned amid great heraldic splendor; most are buried here, too. The main nave is packed with atmosphere, crowds, and memories, as it has witnessed many splendid coronation ceremonies, royal weddings, and, more recently, the funeral of Diana, Princess of Wales. As the most ancient of London's great churches, the place is crammed with spectacular medieval architecture. Other than the mysterious gloom of the vast interior, the first thing to strike most people is the fantastic proliferation of statues, tombs, and commemorative tablets: In parts, the building seems more like a stonemason's yard than a place of worship. But it is in its latter capacity that this landmark truly comes into its own. Although attending a service is not something to undertake purely for sightseeing reasons, it provides a glimpse of the Abbey in its full majesty, accompanied by music from the Westminster choristers and the organ that Henry Purcell once

Westminster Abbey

played. During a service, you won't be bothered by the frequent and jarring loudspeaker announcements made during peak hours, requesting "a minute of silence" from the teeming masses. Note that some parts are closed on Sunday except to worshipers.

The origins of Westminster Abbey are uncertain. The first church on the site may have been built as early as the 7th century by the Saxon King Sebert (who may be buried here, alongside his queen and sister); a Benedictine abbey was established during the 10th century. There were certainly preexisting foundations when Edward the Confessor was crowned in 1040, moved his palace to Westminster, and began building a church. Only traces have been found of that incarnation, which was consecrated eight days before Edward's death in 1065. (It appears in the Bayeaux Tapestry.) Edward's canonization in 1139 gave a succession of kings added incentive to shower the Abbey with attention and improvements. Henry III, full of ideas from his travels in France, pulled it down and started again with Amiens and Rheims in mind. In fact, it was the master mason Henry de Reyns ("of Rheims") who, between 1245 and 1254, put up the transepts, north front, and rose windows, as well as part of the cloisters and Chapter House; and it was his master plan that, funded by Richard II, was resumed 100 years later. Henry V (reigned 1413–1422) and Henry VII (1485–1509) were the chief succeeding benefactors. The Abbey was eventually completed in 1532. After that, Sir Christopher Wren had a hand in shaping the place; his West Towers were completed in 1745, 22 years after his death. The most riotous elements of the interior were, similarly, much later affairs.

The Nave is your first sight on entering; you need to look up to gain a perspective on the truly awe-inspiring scale of the church because the eye-level view is obscured by the 19th- (and part 13th-) century choir screen, past which point admission is charged. Before paying, look at the poignant **Tomb of the Unknown Warrior,** an anonymous World War I martyr who lies buried here in memory of the soldiers fallen in both world wars. Nearby is one of the very few tributes to a foreigner, a plaque to Franklin D. Roosevelt.

There is only one way around the Abbey, and as there will almost certainly be a crocodile of shuffling visitors at your heels, you'll need to be alert to catch the highlights. Pass through the Choir, with its mid-19th-century choir stalls, into the North Transept. Look up to your right to see the painted-glass Rose Window, the largest of its kind; on the left is the first of the extravagant 18th-century monuments in the North Transept chapels. For a fee, you can then proceed into one of the architectural glories of Britain, the **Henry VII Chapel,** passing the huge white marble tomb of Elizabeth I, buried with her half sister, "Bloody" Mary I; then the tomb of Henry VII with his queen, Elizabeth of York, by the Renaissance master Torrigiano (otherwise known for having been banished from Florence after breaking Michelangelo's nose). All around are magnificent sculptures of saints, philosophers, and kings, with wild mermaids and monsters carved on the choir stall misericords (undersides), and with exquisite fan vaulting above—one of the miracles of Western architecture. (Keep an eye open for St. Wilgefort, who was so concerned to protect her chastity that she prayed to God for help and woke up one morning with a full growth of beard.)

Next you enter the **Chapel of Edward the Confessor,** where beside the royal saint's shrine stands the **Coronation Chair,** which has been briefly graced by nearly every regal posterior. Edward I ordered it around 1300; it used to shelter the Stone of Scone (pronounced Skoon), upon which Scottish kings had been crowned since time began, but this precious relic was returned in 1996 to Scotland's Edinburgh Castle for good.

The tombs and monuments of which Westminster Abbey is packed (some would say stuffed) began to appear at an accelerated rate starting in the 18th century. One earlier occupant, though, was Geoffrey Chaucer, who in 1400 became the first poet to be buried in **Poets' Corner.** Most of the other honored writers have only their memorials here, not their bones: William Shakespeare and William Blake (who both had a long wait before the dean deemed them holy enough to be here at all), John Milton, Jane Austen, Samuel Taylor Coleridge, William Wordsworth, Charles Dickens. All of Ben Jonson is here, though—buried upright in accord with his modest demand for a 2 × 2-ft grave site. ("O rare Ben Jonson," reads his epitaph, in a modest pun on the Latin *orare,* "to pray for.") Sir Isaac Newton, James Watt, and Michael Faraday are among the scientists with memorials. There is only one painter: Godfrey Kneller, whose dying words were, "By God, I will not be buried in Westminster."

After the elbow battle you are guaranteed in Poets' Corner, you exit the Abbey by a door from the South Transept. Outside the west front is an archway leading into the quiet green **Dean's Yard** and the entrance to the **Cloisters,** where monks once strolled in contemplation. You may do the same and catch a fine view of the massive flying buttresses above in the process. You may also, for a modest fee, take an impression from one of the tomb brasses in the **Brass-Rubbing Centre** (☎ 0171/222–2085). Also here is the entrance to Westminster School, formerly a monastic college, now one of Britain's finest public (which means the exact opposite) schools; Christopher Wren and Ben Jonson number among the old boys. The **Chapter House,** a stunning octagonal room supported by a central column and adorned with 14th-century frescoes, is where the King's Council and, after that, an early version of the Commons met between 1257 and 1547. In the **Undercroft,** which survives from Edward the Confessor's original church, note the deliciously macabre effigies made from the death masks and actual clothing of Elizabeth I, Charles II, and Admiral Lord Nelson (complete with eye patch), among others. Finally, the **Pyx Chamber** next door contains the Abbey's treasure, just as it used to when it became the royal strong room during the 13th century. Note that photography is only permitted on Wednesday 6–7:45 PM. ⊠ *Broad Sanctuary, SW1,*☎ *0171/222–5152.* ☞ *£5.* ☉ *Mon., Tues., Thurs., and Fri. 9–4; Wed. 9–7:45; Sat. 9–2 and 3:45– 5; Sun. all day for services only. Undercroft, Pyx Chamber, Chapter House, and Treasury April–Oct., daily 10:30–5:30; Nov.–Mar., daily 10:30–4:30. Closed weekdays to visitors during services. Tube: Westminster.*

Westminster Cathedral. This massive cathedral is hard to miss—once you are almost upon it, that is. It's set back from the left side of the street in a 21-year-old paved square that has fallen on hard times. The cathedral is the seat of the Cardinal of Westminster, head of the Roman Catholic Church in Britain; consequently it is London's principal Roman Catholic church. The asymmetrical redbrick Byzantine hulk, dating only from 1903, is banded with stripes of Portland stone and abutted by a 273-ft-high campanile at the northwest corner, which you can scale by elevator. Faced with the daunting proximity of the heavenly Westminster Abbey, the architect, John Francis Bentley, flew in the face of fashion by rejecting neo-Gothic in favor of the Byzantine idiom, which still provides maximum contrast today—not only with the great church, but with just about all of London. The interior is partly unfinished but worth seeing for its atmosphere of broody mystery, its mosaics, and its noted Eric Gill reliefs depicting the Stations of the Cross. ⊠ *Ashley Pl.,* ☎ *0171/834–7452.* ☞ *Tower £2.* ☉ *Cathedral daily; tower Apr.–Sept., daily.*

ST. JAMES'S AND MAYFAIR

St. James's and Mayfair form the very core of London's West End, the city's smartest central area. No textbook sights here; rather, these neighborhoods epitomize so much of the flavor that is peculiarly London's—the sense of being in a great, rich, (once) powerful city is almost palpable as you wander along its posh and polished streets. Here is the highest concentration of grand hotels, department stores, exclusive shops, glamorous restaurants, commercial art galleries, auction houses, swanky offices—all accoutrements that give this area an unmistakable air of wealth and leisure, even on busy days.

A late-17th-century ghost in the streets of contemporary St. James's would not need to bother walking through walls because practically none have moved since he knew them. Its boundaries, clockwise from the north, are Piccadilly, Haymarket, the Mall, and Green Park: a neat rectangle, with a protruding spur satisfyingly located at Cockspur Street. The rectangle used to describe "gentlemen's London," where Sir was outfitted head and foot (but not in between, since the tailors were, and still are, north of Piccadilly in Savile Row) before repairing to his club. In fact, this has been a fashionable part of town from the first, largely by dint of the eponymous palace, St. James's, which was a royal residence—if not *the* palace—from the time of Henry VIII until the beginning of the Victorian era. In 1996, St. James's once again became a truly royal residence, as Prince Charles took up quarters here, shortly after leaving the Kensington Palace digs he once shared with his then wife.

Mayfair, like St. James's, is precisely delineated—a trapezoid contained by Oxford Street and Piccadilly on the north and south, Regent Street and Park Lane on the east and west. Within its boundaries are streets both broad and narrow, but mostly unusually straight and gridlike for London, making it fairly easy to negotiate.

Numbers in the text correspond to numbers in the margin and on the St. James's and Mayfair map.

A Good Walk

Look at any street map and you'll quickly see what a random pattern the streets of St. James's and Mayfair form. The easiest approach would be the serendipitous one—follow your instincts and see where they take you. Here, however, is a tour that incorporates all the highlights. Starting in Trafalgar Square, you'll find Cockspur Street off the southwest corner; follow it to the foot of **Haymarket.** On your right is London's oldest shopping arcade, the splendid Regency Royal Opera Arcade, which John Nash finished in 1818. Now you come to **Pall Mall** ①, a showcase of 18th- and 19th-century patrician architecture and home to such famous gentlemen's retreats as the Reform Club, halfway along on the right, from which Phileas Fogg set out to go around the world. At the end of Pall Mall, you collide with the small Tudor brick **St. James's Palace** ②. Continue along Cleveland Row by the side of the palace to spy on York House, home of the Duke and Duchess of Kent, then turn left into Stable Yard Road to Lancaster House, built for the Duke of York in the 1820s but more notable as the venue for the 1978 conference that led to the end of white rule in Rhodesia/Zimbabwe; and Clarence House, designed by John Nash and built in 1825 for the Duke of Clarence (who became William IV) and which is now home to the Queen Mother. Now, head north up along St. James's Street to St. James's Place, where, if you turn left, you can spot, at No. 27, one of London's most spectacular 18th-century mansions, **Spencer House** ③, home of Diana's ancestors; the interior can be viewed on tours given on Sunday only through the year (except August and January).

Cross back over St. James's Street to King Street—No. 8 is Christie's, the fine art auctioneers who got £25 million for van Gogh's *Sunflowers*; Duke Street on the left harbors further exclusive little art salons—but straight ahead is **St. James's Square** ④, one of London's oldest and home of the London Library. Leave the square by Duke of York Street to the north, and turn left on **Jermyn Street** ⑤, the world center of gentlemen's-paraphernalia shops. Set back from the street is the lovely **St. James's Church** ⑥. A right on Duke Street brings you to Piccadilly. Turn right again, and you'll pass the exclusive department store that supplies the Queen's groceries, Fortnum and Mason, on the right, and the **Royal Academy of Arts** ⑦, opposite, with famous **Piccadilly Circus** ⑧ ahead. Turn around—Wellington Arch and **Apsley House (Wellington Mu-**

St. James's and Mayfair

Apsley House, **9**
BBC Experience, **17**
Bond Street, **10**
Burlington Arcade, **11**
Jermyn Street, **5**
Marble Arch, **15**
Museum of
Mankind, **12**
Pall Mall, **1**
Piccadilly Circus, **8**

Royal Academy of
Arts, **7**
St. James's Church, **6**
St. James's Palace, **2**
St. James's Square, **4**
Selfridges, **13**
Speakers' Corner, **14**
Spencer House, **3**
Wallace Collection, **16**

seum) ⑨, the gloriously opulent mansion the Duke of Wellington once called home, are ahead in the distance. Cross the street and head north up the shopping mecca of **Bond Street** ⑩, with **Burlington Arcade** ⑪ to the right. You could detour by turning right before you reach Oxford Street into Burlington Gardens, where you'll find the **Museum of Mankind** ⑫, or go into Brook Street (the composer Handel lived at No. 25), which leads to Hanover Square. Turning right down St. George Street brings you to the porticoes of St. George's Church, where Percy Bysshe Shelley and George Eliot, among others, had their weddings. A right turn after the church down Mill Street brings you into Savile Row, the fashionable center for custom-made suits and coats since the mid-19th century. No. 3 is mecca for Beatlemaniacs: the former head-quarters of Apple Records and the site of John, Paul, George, and Ringo's legendary rooftop concert (the building now houses a financial institution and is not open to the public). From Savile Row, head westward on Grosvenor Street to Duke Street: slightly to the south, you'll find one of Mayfair's beauty spots—Carlos Place (site of the Connaught) and neighboring Mount Row, both adorned with some veddy, veddy elegant residences. Here, too, is Mount Street, a pedigree-proud shopping avenue; take South Audley Street one block south to discover St. George's Gardens, a fine place for a picnic. Head over to Hyde Park to take in **Speakers' Corner** ⑭ and **Marble Arch** ⑮. Shop-till-you-droppers can then explore Oxford Street (**Selfridges** ⑬ and **Marks & Spencer** are here), while art lovers will want to continue north to Manchester Square for the magnificent **Wallace Collection** ⑯. TV aficionados should, instead, make a beeline for the new **BBC Experience** ⑰.

TIMING

Although this walk doesn't cover an enormous distance, you'll probably do a lot of doubling back and detouring down beckoning alleys—and into interesting shops. If you want to do more than window-shop, we suggest most emphatically a weekday jaunt, starting in the morning, so you get time for visits to the Royal Academy and the Wallace Collection or perhaps the Museum of Mankind and some of the commercial art galleries in and around Cork Street. The walk alone should take less than two hours. Add at least an hour for Apsley House, another two for the Wallace Collection, and one to two for the Museum of Mankind. Any of those could easily consume an afternoon, if you have one to spare. Shopping could take all week.

HOW TO GET THERE

You could start walking around this area from Trafalgar Square (☞ Westminster and Royal London, *above*), or get the Piccadilly or Bakerloo lines to the Piccadilly Circus tube stop, the Piccadilly to the Hyde Park Corner stop, or the Central Line to any of the stops along Oxford Street—Marble Arch, Bond Street (also Jubilee Line), Oxford Circus (also Victoria and Bakerloo lines), or Tottenham Court Road (also Northern Line). The Green Park stop on the Piccadilly, Victoria, or Jubilee lines is also central to many of this neighborhood's sights. The best buses are the Nos. 8, 9, 14, 19, 22, and 38 along Piccadilly, especially the 8, which loops around via New Bond Street to Oxford Street, and skims the eastern border of Green Park down Grosvenor Place.

Sights to See

★ ⑨ **Apsley House (Wellington Museum).** Once known, quite simply, as No. 1, London, this was long celebrated as the best address in town. Built by Robert Adam in the 1770s and later refaced and extended, this was where the Duke of Wellington lived from the 1820s until his death in 1852. As the Wellington Museum, it has been kept as the Iron Duke liked it, his uniforms and weapons, his porcelain and plate, and his extensive art collection, partially looted during military campaigns, displayed heroically. In 1996, the house underwent a superlative restoration—even the railings outside are painted pale green as the duke once had them. Unmissable, in every sense, is the gigantic Canova statue of a nude (but fig-leafed) Napoléon Bonaparte, Wellington's archenemy, which presides over the grand staircase. Here, too, is the Waterloo Gallery, a state dining room that is a veritable orgy of opulence—it was the first importation to London of the French Louis style, setting the fashion for most succeeding Park Lane mansions. Apsley House got iron shutters in 1830 after rioters, protesting the Duke's opposition (he was briefly Prime Minister) to the Reform Bill, broke the windows. Yes, the British loved him for defeating Napoléon, but mocked him with the name "Iron Duke"—referring not to his military prowess, but to those shutters. Across the way is the 1828 Decimus Burton Wellington Arch. ⊠ *149 Piccadilly, W1,* ☏ *0171/499–5676.* ⊡ *£4.* ☉ *Tues.– Sun. 11–4:30.*

⑰ **BBC Experience.** For those who have been weaned on a steady diet of Masterpiece Theatre presentations, the BBC is the greatest television producer in the world. These fans, and those of the BBC's countless other programs, will be happy to know that the BBC has just opened the doors of its own in-house museum to celebrate the BBC's 75th anniversary. There's an audiovisual show that traces the BBC's history, an interactive section—want to try your hand at commentating on a sports game, presenting a weather forecast, or making your own director's cut of a segment of *East Enders?*—and, of course, a massive gift shop. This museum will probably be deluged by crowds for the first few years—conveniently, admission is on a prebooked and timed system. ⊠ *Broadcasting House, Portland Pl., W1,* ☏ *0870/603–0304; outside U.K., 01222/55771.* ⊡ *Free.* ☉ *Daily 9:30–5:30. Tube: Oxford Circus.*

Berkeley Square. As anyone who's heard the old song knows, the word rhymes with "starkly." Not many of its original mid-18th-century houses are left, but look at Nos. 42–46 (especially No. 44, which the architectural historian Sir Nikolaus Pevsner thought London's finest terraced house) and Nos. 49–52 to get some idea of why it was once London's top address—not that it's in the least humble now. Snob nightclub Annabels is one current resident.

⑩ **Bond Street.** This world-class shopping haunt is divided into northern "New" (1710) and southern "Old" (1690) halves. New Bond Street boasts **Sotheby's,** the world-famous auction house, at No. 35, but there are other opportunities to flirt with financial ruin on Old Bond Street: the mirror-lined Chanel store, the vainglorious marble acres of Gianni Versace and the boutique of his more sophisticated compatriot Gucci, plus Tiffany's British outpost and art dealers Colnaghi, Léger, Thos. Agnew, and Marlborough Fine Arts. **Cork Street,** which parallels the top half of Old Bond Street, is where London's top dealers in contemporary art have their galleries—you're welcome to browse, but dress appropriately.

⑪ **Burlington Arcade.** Perhaps the finest of Mayfair's enchanting covered shopping alleys is the second oldest in London, built in 1819. It's still patrolled by top-hatted beadles, who prevent you from singing, running, or carrying open umbrellas or large parcels (to say nothing of lifting English fancy goods from the mahogany-fronted shops).

Faraday's Laboratory. In the basement of the Royal Institution is a reconstruction of the laboratory where the physicist Michael Faraday discovered electromagnetic induction in 1831—with echoes of Franken-stein. ⊠ *21 Albermarle St., W1,* ☎ *0171/409–2992.* ⊠ *£1.* ☉ *Week-days 1–4.*

Grosvenor Square. This square (pronounced Grove-na) was laid out in 1725–31 and is as desirable an address today as it was then. Americans certainly thought so—from John Adams, the second president, who as ambassador lived at No. 38, to Dwight D. Eisenhower, whose wartime headquarters was at No. 20. Now the ugly '50s block of the U.S. Embassy occupies the entire west side, and a British memorial to Franklin D. Roosevelt stands in the center. The little brick chapel used by Eisenhower's men during World War II, the 1730 Grosvenor Chapel, stands a couple of blocks south of the square on South Audley Street, with the entrance to pretty **St. George's Gardens** to its left. Across the gardens is the headquarters of the English Jesuits, and society-wedding favorite, the mid-19th-century Church of the Immaculate Conception, known as Farm Street because that is the name of the street on which it stands.

Heinz Gallery. The gallery of the Royal Institute of British Architects has a changing program of exhibitions, and interesting, often cutting-edge, evening lectures. ⊠ *21 Portman Sq., W1,* ☎ *0171/580–5533.* ⊠ *Free.* ☉ *Weekdays during exhibitions 11–5, Sat. 10–1. Closed Aug. Tube: Bond St.*

⑤ Jermyn Street. This is where the gentleman purchases his traditional fashion accessories. He buys his shaving sundries and hip flask from Geo. F. Trumper, briar pipe from Astley's, scent from Floris (for women, too—both the Prince of Wales and his mother are customers of Floris), whose interiors are exceedingly historic and beautiful, or Czech & Speake, shirts from Turnbull & Asser, and deerstalker and panama from Bates the Hatter. Don't forget the regal cheeses from Paxton & Whit-field (founded in 1740 and a legend among dairies). Shop your way east along Jermyn Street, and you're practically in Piccadilly Circus.

⑮ Marble Arch. The name denotes both the traffic whirlpool where Bayswater Road segues into Oxford Street and John Nash's 1827 arch, which moved here from Buckingham Palace in 1851. Search the sidewalk on the traffic island opposite the cinema to find the stone plaque that marks (roughly) the place where the Tyburn Tree stood for four centuries, until 1783. This was London's central gallows, a huge wooden structure with hanging accommodations for 21. Hanging days were holidays, the spectacle supposedly functioning as a crime deter-rent for the hoi polloi. It didn't work, alas. Oranges, gingerbread, and gin were sold, alongside "personal favors," to vast, rowdy crowds, and the condemned, dressed in finery for his special moment, was treated more as hero than as villain. Cross over (or under—there are signs to help in the labyrinth) to the northeastern corner of Hyde Park to ☞ Speakers' Corner, *above.* Believe it or not, there are two tiny apart-ments in Marble Arch, rented out by the National Trust.

⑫ Museum of Mankind. More than overspill from the British Museum, with the best bits of the ethnographic collection, this museum is housed in a masterpiece of Victorian architecture and contains amazing arti-facts from non-Western civilizations. Long-running, imaginatively cu-rated exhibitions are held on the first floor. When the long-awaited new British Library is up and running, the Department of Ethnography will be kicked back to the British Museum, so take advantage now. ⊠ *6 Burlington Gardens, WC1,* ☎ *0171/437–2224.* ⊠ *Free.* ☉ *Mon.–Sat. 10–5, Sun. 2:30–6. Tube: Tottenham Court Rd.*

NEED A
BREAK?

The suitably themed **Café de Colombia** is usually as peaceful as the Museum of Mankind it inhabits—unless you collide with a school visit. Salads and pastries, Colombian coffee, and wine and beer are on the lunch menu.

❶ Pall Mall. Like its near-namesake, *the* Mall, Pall Mall rhymes with "shall" and derives its name from the cross between croquet and golf that the Italians, who invented it, called *pallo a maglio,* and the French, who made it chic, called *palle-maille.* In England it was taken up with enthusiasm by James I, who called it "pell mell" and passed it down the royal line, until Charles II had a new road laid out for it in 1661. Needless to say, Catherine Street, as Pall Mall was officially named (after Charles's queen, Catherine of Braganza), was *very* fashionable. No. 79 must have been one of its livelier addresses, since Charles's gregarious mistress, Nell Gwyn, lived there. The king gave her the house when she complained about being a mere leaseholder, protesting that she had "always conveyed free under the Crown" (as it were); it remains, to this day, the only privately owned bit of Pall Mall's south side. Stroll slowly, the better to appreciate the creamy facades and perfect proportions along this showcase of 18th- and 19th-century British architecture.

Notable examples are two James Barry–designed buildings, the **Travellers' Club** and the **Reform Club,** both representatives of the upper-class gentleman's retreat that made St. James's the club land of London. The Reform is the most famous club of all, thanks partly to Jules Verne's Phileas Fogg, who accepted the around-the-world-in-80-days bet in its smoking room, and was thus soon qualified to join the Travellers'. And—hallelujah—women can join the Reform. The RAC Club (for Royal Automobile Club, but it's never known as that), with its marble swimming pool, and the Oxford and Cambridge Club complete the Pall Mall quota; there are other, even older, establishments—Brooks's, the Carlton, Boodles, and White's (founded in 1736, the oldest of all)—in St. James's Street around the corner, alongside *the* gentlemen's bespoke (custom) shoemaker, Lobb's, and, at No. 6, *the* hatter, James Lock, which has one of the most historic store facades in the city—you half expect Lord Byron or Anthony Trollope to walk out the door.

❽ Piccadilly Circus. New York has its Times Square, in Venice it's Piazza San Marco, and London has Piccadilly Circus. As natives say, if you stand here long enough, you will meet everyone you know. The name got stuck during the early 17th century, when a humble tailor on the Strand named Robert Baker sold an awful lot of picadils—a collar ruff all the rage in courtly circles—and built a house with the proceeds. Snobs dubbed his new-money mansion Piccadilly Hall, and the name stuck. As for "Circus," that refers not to the menagerie of backpackers and camera-clickers clustered around the steps of **Eros,** but to the circular junction of five major roads.

Eros, London's favorite statue and symbol of the *Evening Standard* newspaper, is not in fact the Greek god of erotic love at all, but the angel of Christian charity, commissioned in 1893 from the young sculptor Alfred Gilbert as a memorial to the philanthropic Earl of Shaftesbury (the angel's bow and arrow are a sweet allusion to the earl's name). It cost Gilbert £7,000 to cast the statue he called his "missile of kindness" in the novel medium of aluminum, and because he was paid only £3,000, he promptly went bankrupt and fled the country. (Not to worry—he was knighted in the end.) Eros has lately done his best to bankrupt Westminster Council, too, owing to some urgent leg surgery and a new coat of protective microcrystalline synthetic wax. Around

Eros, London roars on—this hub is home to a very large branch of Tower Records, the tawdry Trocadero Centre (video arcades, food courts, chain stores, the Guinness World of Records), a SegaWorld, and a perpetual traffic jam. Beneath the blight, however, is beauty: just behind the modern bank of neon advertisements are some of the most elegant Edwardian-era buildings in town.

Portland Place. The elegant throughway to Regent's Park was London's widest street during the 1780s, when brothers Robert and James Adam designed it. The first sight to greet you here, drawing the eye around the awkward corner, is the curvaceous portico and pointy Gothic spire of **All Souls Church,** one part of Nash's Regent Street plan that remains. It is now the venue for innumerable concerts and Anglican services broadcast to the nation by the British Broadcasting Corporation. The 1931 block of Broadcasting House next door is home to the BBC's five radio stations and the new ☞ **BBC Experience,** *above.* It curves, too, if less beautifully, and features an Eric Gill sculpture of Shakespeare's Ariel (aerial—get it?) over the entrance, from which the playful sculptor was obliged to excise a portion of phallus lest it offend public decency—which the modified model did in any case.

Regent Street. This curvaceous thoroughfare was conceived by John Nash and his patron, the Prince Regent—the future George IV—as a kind of ultra-catwalk from the Prince's palace, Carlton House, to Regent's Park (then called Marylebone Park). The section between Piccadilly and Oxford Street was to be called the Quadrant and lined with colonnaded purveyors of "articles of fashion and taste," in a big PR exercise to improve London's image as the provincial cousin of smarter European capitals. The scheme was never fully implemented, and what there was fell into such disrepair that, early this century, Aston Webb (of the Mall route) collaborated on the redesign you see today. It is still a major shopping street. Hamleys, the gigantic toy emporium, is fun; and since 1875 there has been Liberty, which originally imported silks from the East, then diversified to other Asian goods, and is now best known for its "Liberty print" cottons, its jewelry department, and—still—its high-class Asian imports. The stained-glass–lighted mock-Tudor interior, with beams made from battleships, is worth a look.

❼ Royal Academy of Arts. Burlington House was built in the Palladian style for the Earl of Burlington around 1720, and it is one of the few surviving mansions from that period. The chief occupant today is the Royal Academy of Arts, which mounts major art exhibitions, usually years in the planning. Old Masters are the basic bill of fare, but in 1997 the academy mounted a show of Britain's leading enfants terribles, called "Sensation," which caused just that. One can only imagine what Sir Joshua Reynolds—whose statue is in the academy courtyard—would have made of Damien Hirst's formaldehyde-preserved tiger-shark sculpture or Marcus Harvey's 10-ft-tall portrait of infamous child killer Myra Hindley. The academy's own fabled collection has unfortunately been dispersed to other museums, notably the Tate and the National Gallery; the latter got the prize—the *Taddeo Tondo* (a sculpted disk) by Michelangelo of the Madonna and Child. Every June, the RA mounts the **Summer Exhibition,** a mishmash of sculpture and painting, with about 1,000 things crammed into every cranny. Art-weary now? Try the shop; it's one of the best museum stores in town. The White Card is accepted. ⊠ *Burlington House, Piccadilly, W1,* ☎ *0171/ 439–7438 or 0171/439–4996.* ☞ *Admission varies according to exhibition, usually 10–5:30.* ☉ *Daily 10–6. Tube: Piccadilly Circus.*

❻ St. James's Church. Recessed from the street behind a courtyard, filled most days with a crafts market, and completed in 1684, this was the last of Sir Christopher Wren's London churches and his own favorite. It contains one of Grinling Gibbons's finest works, an ornate limewood reredos (the screen behind the altar). A 1940 bomb scored a direct hit here, but the church was completely restored, albeit with a fiberglass spire. It's a lively place, offering all manner of lecture series—many on incongruously New Age themes—and concerts, mostly baroque, as well as a brass-rubbing center.

NEED A BREAK?

The Wren at St. James's, attached to the church, has not the faintest whiff of godliness, as the cake display proves. Hot dishes at lunchtime are vegetarian, very good, and very inexpensive. There are tables outside in spring and summer.

❷ St. James's Palace. With its solitary sentry posted at the gate, this surprisingly small palace of Tudor brick was once home to many British sovereigns, including the first Elizabeth and Charles II, who spent his last night here before his execution. Today, it is the residence of another Charles—the future King Charles III (that is, if the current Prince of Wales makes it to Westminster Abbey). His front door actually debouches right onto the street, but he always uses a back entrance. Matters to ponder as you look (you can't go in): the palace was named after a hospital for women lepers, which stood here during the 11th century; Henry VIII had it built; foreign ambassadors to Britain are still accredited to the Court of St. James's even though it has rarely been a primary royal residence; and the present queen made her first speech here. Friary Court out front is a splendid setting for Trooping the Colour, part of the Changing of the Guard ceremony (☞ Buckingham Palace, *above*). Everyone loves to take a snap of the scarlet-coated guardsman standing sentinel outside the imposing Tudor gateway. ⊠ *Friary Court, SW1. Tube: Green Park.*

❹ St. James's Square. One of London's oldest and leafiest squares was also the most snobbish address of all when it was laid out around 1670, with 14 resident dukes and earls installed by 1720. Since 1841, No. 14—one of the several 18th-century residences spared by World War II bombs—has housed the **London Library,** which, with its million or so volumes, is the best private humanities library in the land. You can go in and read the famous authors' complaints in the comments book—but not the famous authors' books, unless you join, at £100 a year.

⑬ Selfridges. With its row of massive Ionic columns, this huge store was opened three years after Harry Gordon Selfridge came to London from Chicago in 1906. Now British run, Selfridges rivals Harrods (☞ Knightsbridge, Kensington, and Holland Park, *below*) in size and stock, and it is finally rivaling its glamour, too, since investing in major face-lift operations. It stands toward the Marble Arch end of Oxford Street, close by the flagship branch of everyone's favorite chain store, **Marks & Spencer** (usually known by its pet names M&S or Marks & Sparks)—supplier of England's underwear, purveyor of woollies (sweaters, that is), producer of dishes passed off as homemade at dinner parties. This place has by far the highest turnover of stock of any shop in the land, so expect crowds at all times.

Shepherd Market. Though it looks like a quaint and villagelike tangle of streetlets, this was anything *but* quaint when Edward Shepherd laid it out in 1735 on the site of the orgiastic, two-week-long May Fair (which gave the whole district its name). Now there are sandwich bars, pubs and restaurants, boutiques and nightclubs, and a (fading) red-light reputation in the narrow lanes.

⑭ Speakers' Corner. This corner harbors a late-20th-century public spectacle. Here, on Sunday afternoons, anyone is welcome to mount a soapbox and declaim upon any topic. It's an irresistible showcase of eccentricity, though sadly diminished since the death in 1994 of the "Protein Man," who thought the eating of meat, cheese, and peanuts led to uncontrollable acts of passion that would destroy Western civilization. The pamphlets he sold for four decades down Oxford Street are now collector's items.

★ **③ Spencer House.** Ancestral abode of the Spencers—Diana's family—this great mansion is perhaps the finest example of 18th-century elegance, on a domestic scale, extant in London. Superlatively restored by Lord Rothschild, the house was built in 1766 for the first Earl Spencer, heir to the first Duchess of Marlborough. A gorgeous Doric facade, complete with pediment adorned with classical statues, announces at once Earl Spencer's passion for the Grand Tour and the classical antiquities of the past. Inside, James "Athenian" Stuart decorated the gilded State Rooms, including the Painted Room, the first completely neoclassic room in Europe. The most ostentatious part of the house (and the Spencers—witness the £40,000 diamond shoe buckles the first countess proudly wore—could be given to ostentation) is the florid bow window of the Palm Room: covered with stucco palm trees, it conjures up both ancient Palmyra and modern Miami Beach. ✉ *27 St. James's Pl., SW1,* ☎ *0171/499–8620.* ▣ *£6.* ☉ *Guided tour Sun. 10:45 AM–4:45 (tickets on sale Sun. at 10:30). Closed Aug. and Jan. Tube: Green Park.*

★ **⑯ Wallace Collection.** Assembled by four generations of Marquesses of Hertford and given to the nation by the widow of Sir Richard Wallace, bastard son of the fourth, this collection of art and artifacts is important, exciting, under visited—and free. As at the Frick Collection in New York, the setting here, Hertford House, is part of the show—a fine late-18th-century mansion, built for the Duke of Manchester and completely renovated during the late 1970s.

The first marquess was a patron of Sir Joshua Reynolds, the second bought Hertford House, the third—a flamboyant socialite—favored Sèvres porcelain and 17th-century Dutch painting; but it was the eccentric fourth marquess who, from his self-imposed exile in Paris, really built the collection, snapping up Bouchers, Fragonards, Watteaus, and Lancrets for a song (the French Revolution having rendered them dangerously unfashionable), augmenting these with furniture and sculpture, and sending his son Richard out to do the deals. With 30 years of practice behind him, Richard Wallace continued acquiring treasures after his father's death, scouring Italy for majolica and Renaissance gold, then moving most of it to London. Look for Rembrandt's portrait of his son, the Rubens landscape, the Van Dycks and Canalettos, the French rooms, and of course the porcelain. The highlight is Fragonard's *The Swing,* which conjures up the 18th century's let-them-eat-cake *frivolité* better than any other painting around. Don't forget to smile back at Frans Hals's *Laughing Cavalier* in the Big Gallery or say hello to Thomas Sully's enchanting *Queen Victoria,* which resides in a rouge-pink salon (just to the right of the main entrance) that is probably the prettiest room in town. ✉ *Hertford House, Manchester Sq., W1,* ☎ *0171/935–0687.* ▣ *Free.* ☉ *Mon.–Sat. 10–5, Sun. 2–5.*

Waterloo Place. This is a long rectangle off Pall Mall, punctuated by the Duke of York Memorial Column atop the Duke of York Steps, and littered with statues, among them Florence Nightingale, the "Lady with the Lamp" nurse-heroine of the Crimean War; Captain R. F. Scott, who led a disastrous Antarctic expedition in 1911–12 and is here frozen in a bronze by his wife; Edward VII, mounted; George VI; and, as usual, Victoria, here in terra-cotta. Flanking Waterloo Place looking onto Pall Mall are two of the gentlemen's clubs for which St. James's came to be known as Clubland: the **Athenaeum** and the former United Service Club, now the **Institute of Directors.** The latter was built by John Nash in 1827–28 but was given a face-lift by Decimus Burton 30 years later to match it up with the Athenaeum across the way, which he had designed. It's fitting that you gaze on the Athenaeum first, since it was— and is—the most elite of all the societies. (It called itself "the Society" until 1830 just to rub it in.) Most prime ministers and cabinet ministers, archbishops, and bishops have belonged; the founder, John Wilson Croker (the first to call the British right-wingers "Conservatives"), decreed it the club for artists and writers, and so literary types (Sir Arthur Conan Doyle, Rudyard Kipling, J. M. Barrie—the posh ones) have graced its lists, too. Women are barred. Most clubs will tolerate female guests these days, but few admit women members, and anyway, even if your anatomy is correct, it's almost impossible to become a member unless you have the connections—which, of course, is the whole point.

SOHO AND COVENT GARDEN

A quadrilateral delineated by Regent Street, Coventry/Cranbourn streets, Charing Cross Road, and the eastern half of Oxford Street encloses Soho, the most fun part of the West End. This appellation, unlike the New York neighborhood's similar one, is not an elision of anything, but a blast from the past—derived (as far as we know) from the shouts of "So-ho!" that royal huntsmen in Whitehall Palace's parklands were once heard to cry. One of Charles II's illegitimate sons, the Duke of Monmouth, was an early resident, his dubious pedigree setting the tone for the future: For many years, Soho was London's strip show/peep show/clip joint/sex shop/brothel center. The mid-'80s brought legislation that granted expensive licenses to a few such establishments and closed down the rest; most prostitution had already been ousted by the 1959 Street Offences Act. Only a cosmetic smear of red-light activity remains now, plus a shop called "Condomania" and one or two purveyors of couture fetish wear for trendy club goers.

These clubs, which cluster around the Soho grid, are the diametric opposite of the St. James's gentlemen's museums—they cater to youth, change soundtracks every month, and post tyrannical fashion police at the door. Another breed of Soho club is the strictly members-only media haunts (the Groucho, the Soho House, Fred's, Brown's, Black's), salons for carefully segregated strata of high-income hipsters. The same crowd populates the astonishing selection of restaurants, but then so does the rest of London and all its visitors—because Soho is gourmet country.

It was after the First World War, when London households relinquished their resident cooks en masse, that Soho's gastronomic reputation was established. It had been a cosmopolitan area since the first immigrant wave of French Huguenots arrived in the 1680s. More French came fleeing the revolution during the late 18th century, then the Paris Commune of 1870, followed by Germans, Russians, Poles, Greeks, and (especially) Italians and, much later, Chinese. Pedestrianized Gerrard Street, south of Shaftsbury Avenue, is the hub of London's compact Chinatown, which boasts restaurants, dim sum houses, Chinese supermarkets, and annual February New Year's celebrations, plus a brace of scarlet pagoda-style archways and a pair of phone booths with pictogram dialing instructions.

Soho and Covent Garden

Adelphi, **14**
Bow Street
Magistrates'
Court, **10**
Carnaby Street, **1**
Cleopatra's
Needle, **13**
Courtauld Institute
Galleries, **12**

Covent Garden
Piazza, **4**
Garrick Club, **8**
Leicester Square, **3**
London Transport
Museum, **6**
Royal Opera
House, **9**

St. Paul's Church, **5**
Soho Square, **2**
Theatre Museum, **7**
Theatre Royal, Drury
Lane **11**

The former Covent Garden Market became the Piazza in 1980, and it still functions as the center of a neighborhood—one that has always been alluded to as "colorful." It was originally the "convent garden" belonging to the Abbey of St. Peter at Westminster (later Westminster Abbey). The land was given to the first Earl of Bedford by the Crown after the Dissolution of the Monasteries in 1536. The Earls—later promoted to Dukes—of Bedford held on to the place right up until 1918, when the eleventh Duke managed to off-load what had by then become a liability. In between, the area enclosed by Long Acre, St. Martin's Lane, Drury Lane, and assorted streets north of the Strand had gone from the height of fashion (until the snobs moved west to brand-new St. James's) to a period of arty-literary bohemia during the 18th century, followed by an era of vice and mayhem, to once more become vegetable provisioner to London when the market building went up in the 1830s, followed by the Flower Market in 1870 (Eliza Dolittle's alma mater in Shaw's *Pygmalion* and Lerner and Loewe's musical version, *My Fair Lady*).

Still, it was no Mayfair, what with 1,000-odd market porters spending their 40 shillings a week in the alehouses, brothels, and gambling dens that had never quite disappeared. By the time the Covent Garden Estate Company took over the running of the market from the 11th Duke, it seemed as if seediness had set in for good, and when the fruit-and-veg trade moved out to the bigger, better Nine Elms Market in Vauxhall in 1974, it left behind a decrepit wasteland. But this is one of London's success stories: The Greater London Council (now sadly defunct) stepped in with a dream of a rehabilitation plan—not unlike the one that was tried, though less successfully, in the Parisian equivalent, Les Halles. By 1980 the transformation was complete.

Numbers in the text below correspond to numbers in the margin and on the Soho and Covent Garden map.

A Good Walk

Soho, being small, is easy to explore, though it's also easy to mistake one narrow, crowded street for another, and even Londoners go astray here. Enter from the northwest corner, Oxford Circus, and head south for about 200 yards down Regent Street, turn left into Great Marlborough Street, and head to the top of **Carnaby Street** ①. Turn right off Broadwick Street into Berwick (pronounced Berrick) Street, famed as central London's best fruit and vegetable market. Then step through tiny Walker's Court (ignoring the notorious hookers' bulletin board), cross Brewer Street, named for two extinct 18th-century breweries, and you'll have arrived at Soho's hip hangout, Old Compton Street. From here, Wardour, Dean, Frith, and Greek streets lead north, all of them bursting with restaurants and clubs. Either of the latter two lead north to **Soho Square** ②, but head one block south instead, to Shaftesbury Avenue, heart of theater land, across which you'll find Chinatown's main drag, Gerrard Street. Below Gerrard Street is **Leicester Square** ③, and running along its west side is Charing Cross Road, the bibliophile's dream. You'll find some of the best of the specialist bookshops in little Cecil Court, running east just before Trafalgar Square.

The easiest way to find the **Covent Garden Piazza** ④ and market building is to walk down Cranbourn Street, next to the Leicester Square tube, then down Long Acre, and turn right at James Street. Around here, are **St. Paul's Church** ⑤—the actors' church—the **London Transport Museum** ⑥, and the **Theatre Museum** ⑦, as well as plenty of shops and cafés. (If your aim is to shop, **Neal Street,** Floral Street, the streets around Seven Dials, and the Thomas Neale's mall all reward exploration.) From Seven Dials, veer 45 degrees south into Mercer Street, turning right on

Long Acre, then left into Garrick Street, past the **Garrick Club** ⑧, left into Rose Street, and right into Floral Street. At the other end you'll emerge onto Bow Street, right next to the **Royal Opera House** ⑨ and the **Bow Street Magistrates' Court** ⑩. Continuing on and turning left into Russell Street, you reach Drury Lane and the **Theatre Royal** ⑪.

At the end of Drury Lane is the Aldwych, a great big croissant of a potential traffic accident, with a central island on which stand three hulking monoliths: India House, Melbourne House, and the handsome 1935 neoclassic Bush House, headquarters of the BBC World Service. Stranded on traffic islands to the west are the 1717 St. Mary-le-Strand, James Gibbs's (of St. Martin-in-the-Fields fame; ☞ Westminster and Royal London, *above*) first public building, inspired by the baroque churches of Rome, and Wren's St. Clement Danes (with a tower appended by Gibbs), whose 10 bells peal the tune of the nursery rhyme "Oranges and lemons, Say the bells of St. Clements . . ." even though the bells in the rhyme belong to the St. Clements in Eastcheap. Inside is a book listing 1,900 American airmen who were killed during World War II. Heading west, perhaps stopping at the **Courtauld Institute Galleries** ⑫, walk the ¾-mi traffic-clogged **Strand** to the southern end, where you take Villiers Street down to the Thames. See the historic York Watergate and **Cleopatra's Needle** ⑬ by Victoria Embankment Gardens, cross the gardens northwest to the **Adelphi** ⑭, circumnavigating the Strand by sticking to the embankment walk, and you'll soon reach Waterloo Bridge, where (weather permitting) you can catch some of London's most glamorous views, toward both the City and Westminster around the Thames bend.

TIMING

The distance covered here is around 5 mi if you include the lengthy walk down the Strand and riverside stroll back. Skip that, and it's barely a couple of miles, but you will almost certainly get lost, because the streets in both Covent Garden and Soho are winding and chaotic and not logically disposed. Although getting lost is half the fun, it does make it hard to predict how long this walk will take. You can whiz round both neighborhoods in an hour, but if the area appeals at all, you'll want all day—for shopping, lunch, the Theatre and Transport museums, and the Courtauld Galleries. One way to do it is to start at Leicester Square at 2 PM, when the Half Price Theatre Booth opens, pick up tickets for later, and then walk, shop, and eat in between.

HOW TO GET THERE

A popular way to get to Soho is to hop on the Northern Line to Tottenham Court Road and walk south down Charing Cross Road, then west along Old Compton Street into the district proper, or eastward, by turning left at Shaftsbury Avenue, over to the Covent Garden area. The Covent Garden tube stop is on the Piccadilly Line; Leicester Square—the nearest tube to Soho—is on the Northern Line. The best Soho buses are the Nos. 14, 19, 24, 29, 38, or 176 to Charing Cross Road/Shaftsbury Avenue; for Covent Garden, get those listed above or the ones that stop along the Strand: Nos. 1, 4, 11, 15, 23, 26, 68, 76, 91, 168, 171, and 188.

Sights to See

⑭ **Adelphi.** A regal riverfront row of houses that was the work of London's Scottish architects—all four of them. John, Robert, James, and William Adam, being brothers, gave rise to the name, from the Greek *adelphoi,* meaning brothers. All the late-18th-century design stars were roped in to beautify the interiors, but the grandeur gradually eroded, and today very few of the 24 houses remain; 7 Adam Street is the best.

⑩ Bow Street Magistrates' Court. This was where the prototype of the modern police force first operated. Known as the Bow Street Runners (because they chased thieves on foot), they were the brainchild of the second Bow Street magistrate—none other than Henry Fielding, the author of *Tom Jones* and *Joseph Andrews*. The late-19th-century edifice on the site went up during one of the market improvement drives. It now houses three courts, including that of the Metropolitan Chief Magistrate, who hears all extradition applications.

❶ Carnaby Street. The '60s synonym for swinging London fell into a post-party depression, reemerging sometime during the '80s as the main drag of a public-relations invention called West Soho. Blank stares would greet anyone asking directions to such a place, but it is geographically logical, and the tangle of streets—Foubert's Place, Broadwick Street, Marshall Street—do cohere, at least in type of merchandise (youth accessories, mostly, with a smattering of designer boutiques). Broadwick Street is also notable as the birthplace, at No. 74, in 1758, of the great visionary poet and painter William Blake. At age 26 he came back for a year to sell prints next door, at No. 72 (now an ugly tower block), and then remained a Soho resident in Poland Street.

⑬ Cleopatra's Needle. Off the triangular-handkerchief Victoria Embankment Gardens, where office sandwich-eaters and people who call it home coexist, is London's *very oldest thing,* predating its arbitrary namesake, and London itself, by centuries. The 60-ft pink granite obelisk was erected at Heliopolis, in lower Egypt, in about 1475 BC, then moved to Alexandria, where in 1819 Mohammed Ali, the Turkish Viceroy of Egypt, rescued it from its fallen state and presented it to the British. The British, though grateful, had not the faintest idea how to get the 186-ton gift home, so they left it there for years until an expatriate English engineer contrived an iron pontoon to float it to London via Spain. Future archaeologists will find an 1878 "time capsule" underneath, containing the morning papers, several bibles, a railway timetable, some pins, a razor, and a dozen photos of Victorian pinup girls.

⑫ Courtauld Institute Galleries. One of London's most beloved art collections, the Courtauld has been closed for a complete renovation but is scheduled to reopen in fall 1998. Normally, the Galleries are found in grand 18th-century classical Somerset House, alongside a vast compilation of civil servants (conjure up the red-tape-bestrewn Circumlocution Offices in Dickens's *Little Dorrit*) who still lurk inside. Founded in 1931 by the textile maven Samuel Courtauld, this is London's finest Impressionist and Postimpressionist collection (Manet's *Bar at the Follies-Bergère* is the star), with bonus post-Renaissance works thrown in. Botticelli, Breughel, Tiepolo, and Rubens are also represented, thanks to the exquisite bequest of Count Antoine Seilern's Princes Gate collection. The gala reopening of the galleries will be celebrated with a special exhibition of the Courtauld's Impressionist drawings, rarely on display. ⊠ *The Strand, WC2,* ☎ *0171/873–2526. Tube: Temple.*

❹ Covent Garden Piazza. The restored 1840 market building around which Covent Garden pivots is known as the Piazza. Inside, the shops are mostly higher-class clothing chains, plus a couple of cafés and some knickknack stores that are good for gifts. There's a superior crafts market on most days, too. If you turn right, you'll reach the indoor **Jubilee Market,** with stalls selling clothing, army surplus gear, more crafts, and more knickknacks. At yet another market off to the left (on the way back to the tube), the leather goods, antiques, and secondhand clothing stalls are a little more exciting. In summer it may seem that everyone you see around the Piazza (and the crowds are legion) is a fellow tourist, but there is still plenty of office life in the area, and Londoners continue to flock here.

❽ Garrick Club. Named for the 18th-century actor and theater manager David Garrick, this club is, because of its literary-theatrical bent, more louche than its St. James's brothers, and famous actors, from Sir Laurence Olivier down, have always been proud to join—along with Dickens, Thackeray, and Trollope, in their time. Find the **Lamb and Flag** down teeny Rose Street to the left. Dickens drank in this pub, better known in its 17th-century youth as the Bucket of Blood, owing to the bare-knuckle boxing matches held upstairs. (You'll find that many London pubs claim Dickens as an habitué, and it's unclear whether they lie or the author was the city's premier sot.)

❸ Leicester Square. This square (pronounced Lester) is showing no sign of its great age. Looking at the neon of the major movie houses, the fast-food outlets (plus a useful Häagen-Dazs café), and the disco entrances, you'd never guess it was laid out around 1630. By the 19th century it was already bustling and disreputable, and now it's usually one of the only places crowded after midnight—with suburban teenagers, Belgian backpackers, and London's swelling ranks of the homeless. That said, it is not a threatening place, and the liveliness can be quite cheering. In the middle is a statue of a sulking Shakespeare, clearly wishing he were somewhere else and perhaps remembering the days when the cinemas were live theaters—burlesque houses, but live all the same. Here, too, are figures of Hogarth, Reynolds, and Charlie Chaplin, and underneath is an invisible new £22 million electrical substation. One landmark certainly worth visiting is the **Society of London Theatre ticket kiosk,** on the southwest corner, which sells half-price tickets for many of that evening's performances (☞ Theater *in* Chapter 5). On the northeast corner, in Leicester Place, stands **Notre Dame de France,** with a wonderful mural by Jean Cocteau in one of its side chapels.

🕊 ❻ London Transport Museum. Housed in the old Flower Market at the southeastern corner of the Covent Garden Piazza, this museum tells the story of mass transportation in the capital, and it is much better than it sounds. It is particularly child-friendly, with lots of touchscreen interactive material; live actors in costume (including a Victorian horse-dung collector), though you should go early to see them); old rolling stock; period smells and sounds; and best of all, a tube-driving simulator. There's also a café and a shop selling the wonderful old London Transport posters, plus mugs, socks, bow ties, and so on, printed with that elegant London tube map, designed by Harry Beck in 1933 and still in use today. The White Card is accepted. ✉ *Piazza, WC2,* ☎ *0171/379–6344.* 🎟 *£4.50.* ☽ *Sat.–Thurs. 10–6, Fri. 11–6. Tube: Covent Garden.*

Neal Street. One of Covent Garden's most intriguing shopping streets begins north of Long Acre, catercorner to the tube station, and is closed to traffic halfway down. Here you can buy everything you never knew you needed—apricot tea, sitars, vintage aviators' jackets, silk kimonos, Alvar Aalto vases, halogen desk lamps, shoes with heel lower than toe, collapsible top hats, and so on. To the left off Neal Street, on Earlham Street, is Thomas Neal's—a new, upmarket, designerish clothing and housewares mall named after the founder (in 1693) of the star-shape cobbled junction of tiny streets just past there, called Seven Dials—a surprisingly residential enclave, with lots going on behind the tenement-style warehouse facades. Turning left into the next street off Neal Street, Shorts Gardens, you come to Neal's Yard (note the comical, water-operated wooden clock), originally just a whole-foods wholesaler and now an entire holistic village, with therapy rooms, an organic bakery and dairy, a great vegetarian café, and a medical herbalist's shop reminiscent of a medieval apothecary.

🕐 **Rock Circus.** This shamelessly touristy offshoot of Madame Tussaud's waxworks (☞ Regent's Park and Hampstead, *below*) features animatronic and wax pop stars miming to their hits or frozen in time, chronologically displayed to give the impression of a museum of popular music. As some might imagine, this is strictly for younger teens. ✉ *London Pavilion, Piccadilly Circus, W1,* ☎ *0171/734–7203.* ☒ *£7.95.* ☉ *Sun., Mon., Wed., and Thurs. 11–9, Tues. noon–9; Fri. and Sat. 11–10. Tube: Piccadilly Circus.*

❾ Royal Opera House. The fabled home of the Royal Ballet and Britain's finest opera company is now closed until 2001—mammoth renovations will try to bring this 19th-century treasure into the 21st. Here, in days of yore, Joan Sutherland brought down the house as Lucia di Lammermoor, and Rudolf Nureyev and Margot Fonteyn became the greatest ballet duo of all time. For such delights, seats were top dollar—nearly £100—or just 1/20 of that lordly amount. Whatever the price, it was worth it if you loved red-and-gold Victorian decor, which always managed to give a very special feel to the hush that precedes the start of a performance. London's premier opera venue was designed in 1858 by E. .M Barry, son of Sir Charles, the House of Commons architect. This is actually the third theater on the site. The first opened in 1732 and burned down in 1808; the second opened a year later under the aegis of one John Anderson, only to succumb to fire in 1856 (Anderson, who had lost two theaters already, had an appalling record when it came to keeping the limelights apart from the curtains). Once the house reopens, tickets will probably be more pricey than ever (despite government subsidies)—let's hope they remember riots broke out in 1763, 1792, and 1809, when the cost of rebuilding inflated the price of admission. But top prices are almost worth it if you can enjoy the house's Crush Bar, which adds opulence to the pastime of people-watching during an intermission. Call for current updates on the gypsylike schedules of the Royal Opera and the Royal Ballet; for further information, ☞ Chapter 5. ✉ *Bow St.,* ☎ *0171/240–1066 or 0171/304–4000. Tube: Covent Garden.*

❺ St. Paul's Church. If you want to commune with the spirits of Vivien Leigh, Noël Coward, Edith Evans, and Charlie Chaplin, this might be the place. Memorials to them and many other theater greats are found in this 1633 work of the great Inigo Jones, which has always been known as "the actors' church," thanks to the neighboring theater district and St. Paul's prominent parishioners (well-known actors often read the lessons at services). Fittingly, its portico was the setting for *Pygmalion*'s opening scene. St. Paul's Church (the great cathedral is eastward in the City) is across the Covent Garden Piazza, often picturesquely punctuated with street entertainers—those who have passed auditions for this most coveted of London's street venues.

❷ Soho Square. Laid out about 1680, this square was fashionable during the 18th century. Only two of the original houses still stand plus the 19th-century central garden. It's now a place of peace and offices (among them Paul McCartney's music publishers and Bloomsbury Publishing). That isn't a Tudor landmark in the center, but a Tudor-style thatch-and-daub Victorian gardener's hut—an almost fairy-tale sight to enjoy during a take-out munch in the park.

NEED A
BREAK?
Take any excuse you can think of to visit either of Soho's wonderful rival patisseries: **Maison Bertaux** (⊠ 28 Greek St.) or **Pâtisserie Valerie** (⊠ 44 Old Compton St.). Both serve divine gâteaux, milles-feuilles, croissants, éclairs, and more, the former in an upstairs salon, the latter in a darkish room behind the cake counters.

Strand. Remember Judy Garland doing Burlington Bertie in Chaplin drag, walking down the Strand with gloves in hand, in *A Star Is Born*? William Hargreaves's song was a popular number in the Strand music halls that put the street on the map afresh during the early 1900s. Now its presence on maps is about all that the characterless Strand has to recommend it.

❼ Theatre Museum. This mostly below-ground museum aims to re-create the excitement of theater itself. There are usually programs in progress allowing children to get in a mess with makeup or have a giant dressing-up session. Permanent exhibits paint a history of the English stage from the 16th century to Mick Jagger's jumpsuit, with tens of thousands of theater playbills and sections on such topics as Hamlet through the ages and pantomime—the peculiar British theatrical tradition whereby men dress as ugly women (as distinct from RuPaul), and girls wear tights and play princes. There's a little theater in the bowels of the museum and a ticket desk for "real" theaters around town, plus an archive holding video recordings and audiotapes of significant British theatrical productions. ⊠ *7 Russell St., WC2,* ☎ *0171/836–7891.* 🖃 *£3.50.* ☉ *Tues.–Sun. 11–7. Tube: Covent Garden.*

⓫ Theatre Royal, Drury Lane. This is London's best-known auditorium and almost its largest. Since World War II, its forte has been musicals (*Miss Saigon* is the current resident; past ones have included *The King and I, My Fair Lady, South Pacific, Hello, Dolly!* and *A Chorus Line*)—though David Garrick, who managed it from 1747 to 1776, made its name by reviving the works of the by-then-obscure William Shakespeare. It enjoys all the romantic accessories of a London theater—a history of fires (it burned down three times, once in a Wren-built incarnation), rioting (in 1737, when a posse of footmen demanded free admission), attempted regicides (George II in 1716 and his grandson George III in 1800), and even sightings of the most famous phantom of theater land, the Man in Grey (in the Circle, matinees). The entrance is on Catherine Street.

BLOOMSBURY AND LEGAL LONDON

The character of an area of London can change visibly from one street to the next. Nowhere is this so clear as in the contrast between fun-loving Soho and intellectual Bloomsbury, a mere 100 yards to the northeast, or between arty, trendy Covent Garden and—on the other side of Kingsway—sober Holborn. Both Bloomsbury and Holborn are almost purely residential and should be seen by day. The first district is best known for its famous flowering of literary-arty bohemia, personified by the clique known as the Bloomsbury Group during this century's first three decades, and for the British Museum and the University of London, which dominate it now. The second sounds as exciting as, say, a center for accountants or dentists, but don't be put off—filled with magnificently ancient buildings, it's more interesting and beautiful than you might suppose.

Let's get the Bloomsbury Group out of the way since you can't visit them, and nothing exists to mark its territory beyond a sprinkling of Blue Plaques. (London has about 400 of these government-sponsored tablets commemorating persons who enhanced "human welfare or happiness" and have been dead for at least 20 years.) There's also a plaque in Bloomsbury Square saying nothing about this elite core of writers and artists except that they lived around here. The chief Bloomsburies were Virginia Woolf, E. M. Forster, Vanessa and Clive Bell, Duncan Grant, Dora Carrington, Roger Fry, John Maynard Keynes, and Lytton Strachey, with satellites including Rupert Brooke and Christopher Isherwood. They agreed with G. E. Moore's philosophical notion that "the pleasures of human intercourse and the enjoyment of beautiful objects . . . form the rational ultimate end of social progress." True to their beliefs, when they weren't producing beautiful objects, the friends enjoyed much human intercourse, as has been exhaustively documented, not least in Virginia Woolf's own diaries. All you need do to find out more about them is to read the "Review" supplements of the Sunday broadsheets, which are forever running Bloomsbury exposés as if they were fresh gossip.

More clearly visible than those literary salons is the time-warp territory of interlocking alleys, gardens and cobbled courts, and town houses and halls where London's legal profession grew up. The Great Fire of 1666 razed most of the city but spared the buildings of legal London, and the whole neighborhood oozes history. What is best about the area is that it lacks the commercial veneer of other historic sites, mostly because it still is very much the center of London's legal profession. Barristers, berobed and bewigged, may add an anachronistic frisson to your sightseeing, but they're only on their way to work.

They are headed for one of the four "Inns of Court": Gray's Inn, Lincoln's Inn, Middle Temple, and Inner Temple. Those arcane names are simply explained. The inns were just that: lodging houses for the lawyers who, back in the 14th century, clustered together here so everyone knew where to find them and presently took over the running of the inns themselves. The temples were built on land owned by the Knights Templar, a chivalric order founded during the First Crusade during the 11th century; their 12th-century Temple Church still stands here. Few barristers (British for trial lawyers) still live in the inns, but nearly all keep chambers (British for barristers' offices) here, and all are still obliged to eat a requisite number of meals in the hall of "their" inn during training—no dinner, no career. They take exams, too.

Numbers in the text correspond to numbers in the margin and on the Bloomsbury and Legal London map.

A Good Walk

From Russell Square tube, walk south down Southampton Row and west on Great Russell Street, passing **Bloomsbury Square** on the left, en route to London's biggest and most important collection of antiquities, the **British Museum** ①. Leaving this via the back exit leads you to Montague Place, which you should cross to Malet Street, straight ahead, to reach the **University of London** ②. On the left after you pass the university buildings is the back of the Royal Academy of Dramatic Art, or RADA (its entrance is on Gower Street), where at least half of the most stellar British thespians got their training, with **University College** ③ following at the top of Malet Place. For a delightful detour, head west over to Scala Street (just one block west from the Goodge Street tube stop, then one block north on Charlotte Street) to find the delightful Victorian-era wonders of **Pollock's Toy Museum** ④. Back around the university, head over to Gordon Street to reach Gordon Square. If you're interested in Asian art, stop in at the **Percival David Foundation of Chinese Art** ⑤; if you want to stop in at the spectacular new **British Library** ⑥, head north up to Euston Road. Otherwise, continue south down busy Woburn Place, veering left down Guilford Street to reach Coram's Fields, home of the **Thomas Coram Foundation** ⑦; then turn left south of there on Guilford Place, then right to Doughty Street and the **Dickens House Museum** ⑧. Two streets west, parallel to Doughty Street, is pretty Lamb's Conduit Street (whose pretty pub, the Lamb, Dickens inevitably frequented).

At the bottom of Lamb's Conduit Street you reach Theobald's Road, where you enter the first of the Inns of Court, **Gray's Inn** ⑨, emerging from here onto High Holburn (pronounced Hoe-bunbun)—heavy with traffic, as (with the Strand) it is the main route from the City to the West End and Westminster—and Hatton Garden, running north from Holburn Circus and still the center of London's diamond and jewelry trade. Pass another ghost of former trading, **Staple Inn** ⑩, and turn left down tiny Great Turnstile Row to reach **Lincoln's Inn** ⑪, where you pass the Hall and continue around the west side of New Square to Carey Street, which leads you round into Portugal Street. Here you'll find the Old Curiosity Shop, probably one of the rare places in London Dickens did *not* frequent. Recross to the north side of Lincoln's Inn Fields to **Sir John Soane's Museum** ⑫ or walk the other way on Carey Street to reach the **Royal Courts of Justice** ⑬, which run through to the Strand. Off to the left is Fleet Street and the 1610 **Prince Henry's Room** ⑭. Cross the Strand to **Temple** ⑮ and pass through the elaborate stone arch to Middle Temple Lane, which you follow past **Temple Church** ⑯ to the Thames.

TIMING

This is a substantial walk of 3 to 4 mi, and it has two distinct halves. The first half, around Bloomsbury, is not so interesting on the surface, but it features a major highlight of London, the British Museum, where you could easily add 1 mi to your total and certainly at least two hours. The Dickens House is also worth a stop. The second half, legal London, is a real walker's walk, with most of the highlights in the architecture and atmosphere of the buildings and streets. The exception is Sir John Soane's Museum, which will absorb an extra hour. The walk alone can be done comfortably in two hours and is best on a sunny day.

HOW TO GET THERE

The best tube stops for the Inns of Court are Holborn on the Central and Piccadilly lines (surface and walk east up High Holborn, then south), or Chancery Lane on the Central Line. For the British Museum, Tottenham Court Road (Northern and Central lines) or Russell Square (Piccadilly Line) are equidistant. The No. 7 is the best bus for the BM; for the Inns of Court, get the Nos. 8, 17, 25, 45, 46, or 243 to High Holborn, or the Nos. 17, 19, 38, 45, 46, 55, or 243 to Theobalds Road.

Sights to See

Bloomsbury Square. This was laid out in 1660, making it the earliest of the Bloomsbury squares, although none of the original houses remain; what is most remarkable about it now is that you can always find a parking spot in the huge underground garage. You'll find it by exiting the tube at Tottenham Court Road—a straight, very ugly street where London buys its electrical appliances, hi-fi equipment, and computer accessories—and taking Great Russell Street east. Bloomsbury is dotted with squares—Gordon, Tavistock, Bedford, and Brunswick squares are the names of some of the more picturesque.

❻ **British Library.** Since 1759, the British Library had always been housed in the British Museum on Gordon Square. But as Britain's greatest library was entitled to a free copy of every single book, periodical, newspaper, and map published in the United Kingdom—a gift of George II, along with his Royal Library (all this translated into 2 mi of additional shelf space per year)—room at the old library, needless to say, ran out long ago. A grand new edifice was commissioned, to rise a few blocks north of the British Museum, between Euston and St. Pancras stations. After many years and delays—first the building wasn't finished and the funding ran out, and then there were problems with the new stacks— the year 1991 was the intended moving date for the innumerable (somewhere around 18 million, actually) volumes. As it turns out, the great exodus of books has only just begun, a mass migration that won't be completed until the millennium. Until then, part by part, the new library is welcoming researchers and visitors—call the special numbers to see if the wing you need is open yet. The general public, of course, is interested in seeing the library's treasures on view: happily, the Magna Carta, Gutenberg Bibles, Captain Cook journals, and Charlotte Brontë letters should all be on show in the Rare Books Room. ⊠ 96 Euston Rd., ☏ 0171/412–7000.☎ Free. ☼ Mon.–Sat. 10–5, Sun. 2:30–6 PM. Tube: Holborn or Tottenham Court Rd.

★ ❶ **British Museum.** With a facade like a great temple, this celebrated treasure house—filled with plunder of incalculable value and beauty from around the globe—is housed in a ponderously dignified Greco-Victorian building that makes a suitably grand impression. This is only appropriate, for inside you'll find some of the greatest relics of humankind: the Elgin Marbles, the Rosetta Stone, the Magna Carta, the Ur Treasure—everything, it seems, but the Ark of the Covenant. The place is vast—there are 2½ mi of floor space inside, split into nearly 100 galleries—so arm yourself with a free floor plan directly as you go in, or they'll have to send out search parties to rescue you.

The collection began in 1753, when Sir Hans Sloane, physician to Queen Anne and George II, bequeathed his personal collection of curiosities and antiquities to the nation. It then quickly grew, thanks to enthusiastic kleptomaniacs after the Napoleonic Wars—most notoriously the seventh Earl of Elgin, who lifted marbles from the Parthenon and Erechtheum while on a Greek vacation between 1801 and 1804. Although Lord Elgin did a great thing in saving the marbles for posterity, their continuing presence in the British Museum is a source of embarrassment to many British subjects, who believe the Greeks should now have their "Elgin Marbles" back, as, indeed, do the Greeks.

The enormous building, with its Classical Greek–style facade featuring figures representing the Progress of Civilization, was finished in 1847, the work of Sir Robert Smirke. Ascending the steps, you go straight into the main entrance hall (get your floor plan here). Wherever you go, there are marvels, but certain objects and collections are more important, rarer, older, or downright unique, and because you may wish to include these in your wanderings, here follows a highly edited résumé (in order of encounter) of the BM's greatest hits:

Close to the entrance hall, in the south end of Room 25, is the **Rosetta Stone,** found in 1799, and carved in 196 BC with a decree of Ptolemy V in Egyptian hieroglyphics, demotic, and Greek. It was this multilingual inscription that provided the French Egyptologist Jean-François Champollion with the key to deciphering hieroglyphics.

Maybe the **Elgin Marbles** oughtn't to be here, but since they are—and they are, after all, among the most graceful and heartbreakingly beautiful sculptures on earth—you can find them in Room 8, west of the entrance. The best part is what remains of the Parthenon frieze that girdled the interior of Athena's temple on the Acropolis, carved around

60

Bloomsbury and Legal London

440 BC (the handless, footless Dionysus who used to recline along its east pediment is especially well known). While you're in the west wing, you can see one of the Seven Wonders of the Ancient World—in fragment form, unfortunately—in Room 12: the **Mausoleum of Halicarnassus.** This 4th-century tomb of Mausolus, King of Caria, was the original "mausoleum."

Also close to the entrance, but east, in Rooms 30 and 31 in the part of the British Library open to the public, are two of the four existing copies of that prototype census and manual of early British law, King John's 1215 charter, the **Magna Carta,** as well as the spectacularly illuminated 7th-century **Lindisfarne Gospels,** the work of a monk called Eadfrith. Also on display are handwritten manuscripts by, among others, Jane Austen, William Wordsworth, and John Lennon.

Upstairs are some of the most perennially popular galleries, especially beloved by children: Rooms 60 and 61, where the **Egyptian Mummies** live. You'll find here the preserved corpses not only of humans but also of a menagerie of animal companions discovered alongside them.

Proceeding clockwise, you'll come to Room 40, above the main entrance, where the **Mildenhall Treasure** glitters. This haul of 4th-century Roman silver tableware was found beneath the sod of a Suffolk field in 1942. Next door, in Room 41, is the equally splendid **Sutton Hoo Treasure,** including swords and helmets, bowls and buckles, all encrusted with jewels—which was buried at sea with (they think) Redwald, King of the Angles, during the 7th century and excavated from a Suffolk field in 1938–39.

In Room 37 lies Pete Marsh, so named by the archaeologists who unearthed the **Lindow Man** from a Cheshire peat marsh. He was ritually slain, probably as a human sacrifice, during the 1st century and lay perfectly pickled in his bog until 1984. During 1998, the museum will also be a temporary home to some of the ethnographic treasures of the Museum of Mankind (whose collections are on the move to its New Oxford Street branch). For the millennium, the British Museum plans to unveil a spectacular domed cultural complex in its Great Court. ⊠ *Great Russell St., WC1, ☎ 0171/636–1555 or 0171/580–1788. ⊠ Free, 1½-hr guided tour £6. ☉ Mon.–Sat. 10–5, Sun. 2:30–6; tour twice daily in winter, 4 times daily in summer (call for times). Tube: Tottenham Court Rd., Holburn, Russell Sq.*

NEED A BREAK? The **museum's self-service** restaurant and café get very crowded but serve a reasonable selection of not overly mass-produced meals beneath a plaster cast of a part of the Parthenon frieze that Lord Elgin didn't remove. ☉ *Mon.–Sat. noon–4:15, Sun. 2:45–5:15; café, Mon.–Sat. 10–3.*

8 **Dickens House Museum.** This is the only one of the many London houses Charles Dickens (1812–1870) inhabited that's still standing, and it would have had a real claim to his fame in any case because he wrote *Oliver Twist* and *Nicholas Nickleby* and finished *Pickwick Papers,* here between 1837 and 1839. The house looks exactly as it would have in Dickens's day, complete with first editions, letters, and tall clerk's desk (where the master wrote standing up, often chatting with visiting friends and relatives), plus a treat for Lionel Bart fans—his score of *Oliver!* Down in the basement is a replica of the Dingley Dell kitchen from *Pickwick Papers.* ⊠ *48 Doughty St., WC1, ☎ 0171/405–2127. ⊠ £3.50. ☉ Mon.–Sat. 10–5. Tube: Russell Sq.*

❾ Gray's Inn. Although the least architecturally interesting of the four Inns of Court and the one most damaged by German bombs during the '40s, this still has its romantic associations. In 1594, Shakespeare's *Comedy of Errors* was performed for the first time in its hall—which was lovingly restored after World War II and has a fine Elizabethan screen of carved oak. You must make advance arrangements to view Gray's Inn's hall, but you can stroll around the secluded and spacious gardens, first planted by Francis Bacon in 1606. You may visit only after applying in writing, in advance, to the librarian. ⊠ *Holborn,* ☎ *0171/405–8164.* ☉ *Chapel weekdays 10–4. Tube: Holburn, Temple.*

★ ⓫ Lincoln's Inn. There's plenty to see at one of the oldest, best preserved, and most comely of the Inns of Court—from the Chancery Lane Tudor brick gatehouse to the wide-open, tree-lined, atmospheric Lincoln's Inn Fields and the 15th-century Chapel remodeled by Inigo Jones in 1620. The wisteria-clad New Square, London's only complete 17th-century square, is not the newest part of the complex; the oldest-looking buildings are—the 1845 Hall and Library, which you must obtain the porter's permission to enter. Pass the Hall and continue around the west side of New Square, and you'll see an archway leading to Carey Street. You have just headed "straight for Queer Street." Since the bankruptcy courts used to stand here, you can divine what the old expression means. A guided tour is available. ⊠ *Chancery La., WC1,* ☎ *0171/405–1393.* ☉ *Gardens and chapel weekdays 12:30–2:30; public may also attend Sun. service at 11:30 in chapel during legal terms. Tube: Chancery Lane.*

❺ Percival David Foundation of Chinese Art. This collection, belonging to the University of London, is dominated by ceramics from the Sung to Qing dynasties—from the 10th to the 19th centuries, in other words. It's on **Gordon Square**, which Virginia Woolf, the Bells, John Maynard Keynes (all, severally, at No. 46), and Lytton Strachey (at No. 51) called home for a while. ⊠ *53 Gordon Sq., WC1,* ☎ *0171/387–3909.* ☒ *Free.* ☉ *Weekdays 10:30–5 (sometimes closed 1–2 for lunch). Tube: Russell Sq.*

☝ ❹ Pollock's Toy Museum. For some, this will merit a visit whether they have children or not! A charming treasure trove of a small museum in a warren of rooms in an 18th-century town house, Pollock's is crammed with antique dolls, dolls' houses, and teddy bears. Best of all are the fabulous little toy theaters that Pollock made famous during the Victorian era: more than a few of England's most famous actors grew up playing with these cardboard delights. Even better: you can still buy reproductions of these cut-and-paste theater kits in the toy store on the premises. (Bring lots of money if you want to purchase some of the antique kits still for sale.) ⊠ *1 Scala St., W1,* ☎ *0171/636–3452.* ☒ *£2.50.* ☉ *Mon.–Sat. 10–5. Tube: Goodge St.*

⓮ Prince Henry's Room. This is the Jacobean half-timber house built in 1610 to celebrate the investiture of Henry, James I's eldest son, as Prince of Wales; it's marked with his coat of arms and a a PH on the ceiling. It's an entrance to the lawyers' sanctum, Temple, where the Strand becomes Fleet Street, and you can go in to visit the small Samuel Pepys exhibition. ⊠ *17 Fleet St., EC4,* ☎ *0171/936–2710.* ☉ *Mon.–Sat. 11–2. Tube: Temple.*

⓭ Royal Courts of Justice. Here is the vast Victorian Gothic pile containing the nation's principal Law Courts, with 1,000-odd rooms running off 3½ mi of corridor. And here are heard the most important civil law cases—that's everything from divorce to fraud, with libel in between—and you can sit in the viewing gallery to watch any trial you like, for a live version of *Court TV.* The more dramatic criminal cases are heard at the

Old Bailey. Other sights to witness include the 238-ft-long main hall and the compact exhibition of judges' robes. ⊠ *The Strand, WC2,* ☎ *0171/936–6000.* ☞ *Free.* ⊙ *Weekdays 9–4:30. Closed Aug. and Sept. Tube: Temple.*

★ ⑫ **Sir John Soane's Museum.** Guaranteed to raise a smile from the most blasé and footsore tourist, this museum hardly deserves the burden of its dry name. Sir John (1753–1837), architect of the Bank of England, bequeathed his house to the nation on the condition that nothing be changed. We owe him our thanks because he obviously had enormous fun with his home, having had the means to finance great experiments in perspective and scale and to fill the space with some wonderful pieces. In the Picture Room, for instance, two of Hogarth's *Rake's Progress* series are among the paintings on panels that swing away to reveal secret gallery pockets with more paintings. Everywhere mirrors and colors play tricks with light and space, and split-level floors worthy of a fairground fun house disorient you. In a basement chamber sits the vast 1300 BC Sarcophagus of Seti I, lighted by a domed skylight two stories above. When Sir John acquired this priceless object for £2,000, he celebrated with a three-day party. ⊠ *13 Lincoln's Inn Fields, WC2,* ☎ *0171/405–2107.* ☞ *Free.* ⊙ *Tues.–Sat. 10–5. Tube: Holburn, Temple.*

⑩ **Staple Inn.** Despite its name, this is not an inn of court, but the former wool staple, where wool was weighed and traded and its merchants were lodged. It is central London's oldest surviving Elizabethan half-timber building and, thanks to extensive restoration, with its overhanging upper stories, oriel windows, and black gables striping the white walls, looks the same as it must have in 1586 when it was brand-new.

⑮ **Temple.** The entrance to Temple—the collective name for **Inner Temple** and **Middle Temple**, and the exact point of entry into the City—is marked by a young (1880) bronze griffin, the **Temple Bar Memorial.** He is the symbol of the City, having replaced (sadly) a Wren gateway (though you can't deny he makes a splendidly heraldic snapshot). In the buildings opposite is an elaborate stone arch through which you pass into Middle Temple Lane, past a row of 17th-century timber-frame houses, and on into Fountain Court. This lane runs all the way to the Thames, more or less separating the two Temples, past the sloping lawns of Middle Temple Gardens, on the east border of which is the Elizabethan **Middle Temple Hall.** If it's open, don't miss that hammerbeam roof, among the finest in the land. ☎ *0171/353–4355.* ⊙ *Weekdays 10–noon and (when not in use) 3–4. Tube: Temple.*

⑯ **Temple Church.** Featuring "the Round"—a rare circular nave—this church was built by the Knights Templar during the 12th century. The Red Knights (so called after the red crosses they wore—you can see them in effigy around the nave) held their secret initiation rites in the crypt here. Having started poor, holy, and dedicated to the protection of pilgrims, they grew rich from showers of kingly gifts, until during the 14th century they were accused of heresy, blasphemy, and sodomy, thrown into the Tower, and stripped of their wealth. You might suppose the church to be thickly atmospheric, but Victorian and postwar restorers have tamed its air of antique mystery. Still, it's a very fine Gothic-Romanesque church, whose 1240 chancel ("the Oblong") has been accused of perfection. ⊠ *The Temple, EC4,* ☎ *0171/353–8462.* ⊙ *Daily 10–4. Tube: Temple.*

❼ **Thomas Coram Foundation.** Captain Thomas Coram devoted half his life to setting up a sanctuary and hospital, which he called the Foundling Hospital, for London's street orphans. He was a remarkable man, a master mariner and shipbuilder, who, having played a major role in the colonization of Massachusetts, returned to London in 1732 to encounter sights he could not endure—babies and children "left to die on dung hills." Petitioning the lunching ladies of his day and their lords, he raised the necessary funds to set up what became the most celebrated Good Cause around, thanks partly to the sparkling benefactors he attracted. Handel donated an organ to the chapel, which he played himself at fund-raising performances of his *Messiah,* and the chapel in turn became *the* place to be seen worshiping on a Sunday. Coram's great friend William Hogarth was one of several famous hospital governors, and his portrait of the founder hangs alongside other works of art (including paintings by Reynolds and Gainsborough) and mementos in the museum, which now stands on the site of the hospital. Sadly, until the governors manage to find a fresh crop of volunteers to man the front of the house, the museum will probably remain off-limits to the public. ⊠ *40 Brunswick Sq., WC2,* ☎ *0171/278–2424. Currently closed to visitors; call to determine if museum has reopened. Tube: Russell Sq.*

❸ **University College.** Set in a satisfyingly classical edifice designed by the architect of the National Gallery, William Wilkins, the college has within its portals the **Slade School of Fine Art,** which did for many of Britain's artists what the nearby (on Gower Street) Royal Academy of Dramatic Art did for its actors. There is a fine collection of sculpture by one of the alumni, John Flaxman, on view inside. You can also see more Egyptology, if you didn't get enough at the neighboring British Museum (☞ *above*), in the **Petrie Museum** (accessed from Malet Place), which contains one of London's weirder treasures: the clothed skeleton of one of the university's founders, Jeremy Bentham, who bequeathed himself to the college.

❷ **University of London.** This relatively youthful institution grew out of the need for a nondenominational center for higher education (Oxford and Cambridge both demanded religious conformity to the Church of England). It was founded by Dissenters in 1826, with its first examinations held 12 years later. Jews and Roman Catholics were not the only people admitted for the first time to an English university— women were, too, though they had to wait 50 years (until 1878) to sit for a degree.

Wig and Pen Club. This—another of those St. James's–style affairs, this time for "men of justice, journalists, and businessmen of the City" (plus former U.S. presidents Nixon and Reagan)—has its home in the only Strand building to have survived the Great Fire of 1666. Its Legal Tours allow access to the gorgeous gardens of the Inner and Middle Temples, plus other secret sights, and include meals, refreshments, honorary membership for the day (even for women), and expert tour guides. ⊠ *229 Strand, WC2,* ☎ *0171/583-7255.* ☜ *½-day Legal Tour £50, full day £70.50.*

THE CITY

You may have assumed you had entered the City of London when your plane touched down at Heathrow, but note that capital letter: the City of London is not the same as the city of London. The "capital-C" City is an autonomous district, separately governed since William the Conqueror's time, and despite its compact size (it's known as the Square Mile), it remains the financial engine of Britain and one of the world's leading centers of trade. The City, however, is more than just London's Wall Street: it is also home to two of London's most notable sights, the Tower of London and St. Paul's, one of the world's greatest cathedrals—truly, a case of the money changers encompassing the temple! Temple Bar marks the western edge of the district, which does cover 677 acres, though not in a remotely straight-sided fashion. The curvy shape described by its boundaries—Smithfield in the north, Aldgate and Tower Hill in the east, and the Thames on the south—resembles nothing so much as an armadillo, with Temple Bar at snout level.

The City is London's most ancient part, although there is little remaining to remind you of that beyond a scattering of Roman stones. It was Aulus Plautius, Roman ruler of Britain under Claudius, who established the Romans' first stronghold on the Thames halfway through the 1st century AD. The name "Londinium," though, probably derives from the Celtic *Lyn-dun,* meaning "fortified town on the lake," which suggests far earlier settlement. It was really only after Edward the Confessor moved his court to Westminster in 1060 that the City gathered momentum. As Westminster took over the administrative role, the City was free to develop the commercial heart that still beats strong.

The Romans had already found Londinium's position handy for trade—the river being navigable yet far enough inland to allow for its defense—but it was the establishment of crafts guilds in the Middle Ages, followed in Tudor and Stuart times by the proliferation of great trading companies (the Honourable East India Company, founded in 1600, was the star), that really started the cash flowing.

Three times the City has faced devastation—and that's not counting the "Black Monday" of 1992, when the pound sterling crashed. The Great Fire of 1666 spared practically none of the labyrinthine medieval streets—a blessing in disguise, actually, because the Great Plague of the year before had wiped (or driven) out most of the population and left a terrible mess in the cramped, downright sordid houses. With the wind in the west, they said, you could smell London from Tilbury. The fire necessitated a total reconstruction, in which Sir Christopher Wren had a big hand, contributing not only his masterpiece, St. Paul's Cathedral, but 49 other parish churches.

The third wave of destruction, after the plague and the fire, was, of course, dealt by the German bombers of the Second World War, who blitzed the City with 57 days and nights of special attention, wreaking as much havoc as the Great Fire had managed. The ruins were rebuilt, but slowly and with no overall plan, creating an awkward patchwork of the old and the new, the interesting and the flagrantly awful. The City's colorful past can be hard to visualize among today's gray reality, but there are clues. Wander through its maze of streets and you will come across ancient coats of arms and street names redolent of life in the Middle Ages: Ropemaker Street, Pudding Lane, Jewry Street, and Fish Street. During the week, the place is overrun with people—but since a mere 8,000 or so people call it home today, the City is deserted on weekends, with most restaurants shuttered and streets forlorn and windswept. It's this schizophrenic quality, swinging from hectic activity to near total silence, that accounts for much of the City's unique atmosphere. Where else do outsize skyscrapers tower over tiny parish churches? Where else does the Lord Mayor, clad in ceremonial robes and chain of office and escorted by foot soldiers in 17th-century garb bearing pikes and muskets, ride in an 18th-century coach—during the Lord Mayor's Show, the procession held every November to celebrate the installation of a new Lord Mayor—past buildings in which satellite communications have long since become routine?

Numbers in the text correspond to numbers in the margin and on the City map.

A Good Walk

Begin at the gateway to the City—and we mean that literally. Until the 18th century there were eight such gates, of which only one survives; the others exist in name only (Cripplegate, Ludgate, Bishopsgate, Moorgate, and so on). The surviving one is Temple Bar, a bronze griffin on the Strand opposite the Royal Courts of Justice, at which the sovereign has to ask the Lord Mayor's permission to enter the City. Walk east to **Fleet Street** and turn left on Bolt Court to Gough Square and **Dr. Johnson's House** ①, passing **Ye Olde Cheshire Cheese** ② on Wine Office Courte en route back to Fleet Street and the journalists' church, **St. Bride's** ③. The end of Fleet Street is marked by the messy traffic intersection called Ludgate Circus, which you should cross to Ludgate Hill to reach **Old Bailey** ④ and the Central Criminal Courts.

Continuing along Ludgate Hill, you come to **St. Paul's Cathedral** ⑤, Wren's masterpiece. There's not much else to see around here, though plans are pending for the reinstallation of Sir Christopher Wren's 1672 Temple Bar gateway close to its original site, which will serve as the City's western entry. Instead, retrace your steps to Newgate Street, detouring up King Edward Street to the **National Postal Museum** ⑥ and to the road called Little Britain, where you'll see the archway to **St. Bartholomew the Great Church** ⑦ on the left and will come to London's meat market, Smithfield, at the end. Cross Aldersgate Street and take the right fork to London Wall, named for the Roman rampart that stood along it. It's a dismal street, now dominated by postmodern architect Terry Farrell's late-'80s follies, but about halfway along you can see a section of 2nd- to 4th-century wall at St. Alphege Garden. There's another bit in an appropriate spot back at the start of London Wall, outside the **Museum of London** ⑧; and behind that is the important arts mecca of gray concrete, the **Barbican Centre** ⑨, and **St. Giles Without Cripplegate** ⑩. You can walk all around there without touching the ground (well, ground level).

Back on London Wall, turn south into Coleman Street, then right onto Masons Avenue to reach Basinghall Street and the **Guildhall** ⑪, then follow Milk Street south to Cheapside ("chep" is Middle English); it was on this street that the bakers of Bread Street, the cobblers of Cordwainers Street, the goldsmiths of Goldsmith Street, and all their brothers gathered to sell their wares. Here is another symbolic center of London, the church of **St. Mary-le-Bow** ⑫. Walk to the east end of Cheapside, where seven roads meet, and you will be facing the **Bank of England** ⑬. Turn your back on the Bank, and there's the Lord Mayor's Palladian-style abode, the Mansion House, with Wren's **St. Stephen Walbrook Church** ⑭ behind it and the **Royal Exchange** ⑮ in between Threadneedle Street and Cornhill. Farther down Cornhill to Lime Street is **Lloyd's of London** ⑯.

Now head down Queen Victoria Street, where you'll pass the remains of the Roman **Temple of Mithras** ⑰, then, after a sharp left turn into Cannon Street, you'll come upon **Monument** ⑱, Wren's memorial to the Great Fire of London. Just south of there is **London Bridge** ⑲. Turn left onto Lower Thames Street, for just under a mile's walk—passing Billingsgate, London's principal fish market (until 1982) for 900 years, and the Custom House, built early in the last century—to the **Tower of London** ⑳, which may be the single most unmissable of London's sights. **Tower Bridge** ㉑, just outside it isn't bad either.

TIMING

This is a marathon. Unless you want to be walking all day without a chance to do justice to London's most famous sights, the Tower of London and St. Paul's Cathedral—not to mention the Museum of London,

Tower Bridge, and the Barbican Centre—you should consider splitting the walk into segments. Conversely, if you're not planning to go inside, this walk makes for a great day out, with lots of surprising vistas, river views, and history. The City is a wasteland on weekends and after dark, so choose your time. There's a certain romantic charm to the streets when they're deserted, but it's hard to find lunch.

HOW TO GET THERE

This is a big and confusing area, with, however, several tube stops that will deposit you within walking distance of most of the sights. These are: on the Central Line, the Bank and St. Paul's stops; on the District and Circle lines, the Monument, Cannon Street, and Mansion House stops (plus Blackfriars, which is a little off-center). The Moorgate and Barbican stops (Circle, Metropolitan, Hammersmith, and City lines) are the nearest to the theaters of the Barbican Centre, while the next stop west, Farringdon, is best for exploring Clerkenwell. Finally, the only sensible way to get to the Tower of London is via the District and Circle lines to the Tower Hill stop. As for buses, Nos. 4, 8, 25, 56, or 172 deposit you centrally, by St. Paul's. For the Barbican Centre, Nos. 21, 43, 76, 133, 141, 172, 214, and 271 to Moorgate are best.

Sights to See

⑬ **Bank of England.** Known familiarly for the past couple of centuries as "The Old Lady of Threadneedle Street," after someone's parliamentary quip, the bank, which has been central to the British economy since 1694, manages the national debt and the foreign exchange reserves, issues banknotes, sets interest rates, looks after England's gold, and regulates its banking system. Sir John Soane designed the Neoclassic hulk in 1788, wrapping it in windowless walls (which are all that survives of his building) to suggest a stability that the ailing economy of the post-Thatcher years tends to belie. It is ironic that an executive of so sober an institution should have been Kenneth Grahame, author of *The Wind in the Willows*. This and other facets of the bank's history are traced in the Bank of England Museum. ✉ *Bartholomew La., EC4*, ☎ *0171/601–5545.* 🎫 *Free.* ☉ *Easter–Sept., weekdays 10–5, Sun. 11–5; Oct.–Easter, weekdays 10–6. Tube: Bank, Monument.*

⑨ **Barbican Centre.** Home to the Royal Shakespeare Company and its two theaters, the London Symphony Orchestra and its auditorium, the Guildhall School of Music and Drama, a major gallery for touring exhibitions, two cinemas, a convention center, and apartments for a hapless two-thirds of the City's residents (most part-time), the Barbican is an enormous concrete maze Londoners love to hate. The name comes from a defensive fortification of the City, and defensive is what Barbican apologists (including architects Chamberlain, Powell, and Bon) became when the complex was finally revealed in 1982, after 20 years as a construction site. There ensued an epidemic of jokes about getting lost forever in the Barbican bowels. A hasty rethinking of the contradictory signposts and nonsensical "levels" was performed, and navigatory yellow lines materialized, Oz-like, on the floors, but it didn't help much—the Barbican remains difficult to navigate. Time has mellowed the gray concrete into a darker blotchy brownish-gray, and Londoners have come to accept, if not exactly love the place, because of its contents. Actors rate the theater acoustics especially high, and the steep bank of the seating makes for a good stage view. The visiting exhibitions are often worth a trek, as are the free ones in the foyer.

Negotiating the winding walkways of the deserted residential section, then descending in elusive elevators to the lower depths of the Centre (where the studio auditorium, the aptly named Pit, lives), spotting stray sculptures and water gardens, receiving electric shocks from the

The City

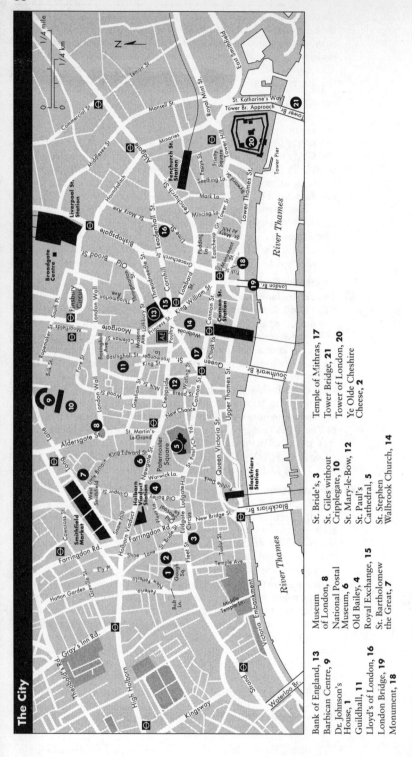

Bank of England, **13**
Barbican Centre, **9**
Dr. Johnson's
House, **1**
Guildhall, **11**
Lloyd's of London, **16**
London Bridge, **19**
Monument, **18**

Museum
of London, **8**
National Postal
Museum, **6**
Old Bailey, **4**
Royal Exchange, **15**
St. Bartholomew
the Great, **7**

St. Bride's, **3**
St. Giles without
Cripplegate, **10**
St. Mary-le-Bow, **12**
St. Paul's
Cathedral, **5**
St. Stephen
Walbrook Church, **14**

Temple of Mithras, **17**
Tower Bridge, **21**
Tower of London, **20**
Ye Olde Cheshire
Cheese, **2**

brass rails—all this has its perverse charm, but there is one unadulterated success in the Barbican, though unfortunately it's not often open to the public. Secreted on an upper floor is an enormous, lush conservatory in a towering glass palace, spacious enough for full-grown trees to flourish. Tours are conducted for a minimum of 10 people and must be booked in advance. The White Card is accepted. ⊠ *Silk St., EC2,* ☎ *0171/638–4141, 0171/628–0183 tour reservations, 0171/628–3351 RSC backstage tour.* ✉ *Barbican Centre free, gallery £5, conservatory £1.* ☉ *Barbican Centre Mon.–Sat. 9 AM–11 PM, Sun. noon–11 PM; gallery Mon.–Sat. 10–7:30, Sun. noon–7:30; conservatory weekends noon–5:30 when not in use for private function (call first). Tube: Moorgate, Barbican.*

NEED A BREAK?
The Barbican Centre's **Waterside Café** has salads, sandwiches, and pastries; they're unremarkable but are served in a tranquil, enclosed concrete (naturally) waterside terrace. Sometimes customers are serenaded by practice sessions of the Guildhall School of Music and Drama's orchestra next door.

❶ Dr. Johnson's House. This is where Samuel Johnson lived between 1746 and 1759, while in the worst of health, compiling his famous dictionary in the attic. Like Dickens, he lived all over town, but like Dickens's House, this is the only one of Johnson's abodes remaining today. It is an appropriately 17th-century house, exactly the kind of place you would expect the Great Bear, as Johnson was nicknamed, to live in. It is a shrine to the man possibly more attached to London than anyone else ever, and it includes a first edition of his dictionary among the Johnson and Boswell mementos. After soaking up the atmosphere, repair around the corner in Wine Office Court to the famed Ye Olde Cheshire Cheese pub, once Johnson and Boswell's favorite watering hole. ⊠ *17 Gough Sq., EC4,* ☎ *0171/353–3745.* ✉ *£3.* ☉ *May–Sept., Mon.–Sat. 11–5:30; Oct.–Apr., Mon.–Sat. 11–5. Tube: Chancery Lane, Temple.*

Fleet Street. This famous street follows the course of, and is named after, one of London's ghost rivers. The Fleet, so called by the Anglo-Saxons, spent most of its centuries above ground as an open sewer, offending local nostrils until banished below in 1766. It still flows underfoot, now a sanctioned section of London's sewer system. The street's sometime nickname, "Street of Shame," has nothing to do with the stench. It refers to the trade that made it famous: the press. Since the end of the 15th century, when Wynkyn de Worde set up England's first printing press here, and especially after 1702, when the first newspaper, the *Daily Courant,* moved in, followed by (literally) all the rest, "Fleet Street" has been synonymous with newspaper journalism. The papers themselves all moved out during the 1980s, but the British press is still collectively known as "Fleet Street." To find a relic from the old days, check out the black-glass-and-chrome Art Deco *Daily Mirror* building.

⓫ Guildhall. In the symbolic nerve center of the City, the Corporation of London ceremonially elects and installs its Lord Mayor as it has done for 800 years. The Guildhall was built in 1411, and though it failed to avoid either the 1666 or 1940 flames, its core survived, with a new roof sensitively appended during the 1950s and further cosmetic embellishments added during the '70s. The fabulous hall is a psychedelic patchwork of coats of arms and banners of the City Livery Companies, which inherited the mantle of the medieval trade guilds, to which we actually owe the invention of the City in the first place. Actually, this honor really belongs to two giants, Gog and Magog, the pair of mythical beings who founded ancient Albion, and who glower upon the Prime Minister's annual November banquet from their west gallery grandstand in 9-ft-high painted lime-wood form. The 1970s west wing houses the **Guildhall Library**—mainly City-related books and documents, plus a collection belonging to one of the Livery Companies, the Worshipful Company of Clockmakers, with more than 600 timepieces on show, including a skull-faced watch that belonged to Mary, Queen of Scots. ⊠ *Gresham St., EC2,* ☎ *0171/606–3030.* 🖭 *Free.* ☻ *Mon.– Sat. 10–5 (library closed Sat.). Tube: St. Paul's, Moorgate, Bank, Mansion House.*

⑯ Lloyd's of London. Richard Rogers's (of Paris Pompidou Centre fame) fantastical steel-and-glass medium-rise of six towers around a vast atrium, with his trademark inside-out ventilation shafts, stairwells, and gantries, may be the most exciting recent structure erected in London. The building is best seen at night, when cobalt and lime spotlights make it leap out of the deeply boring gray skyline as though it were Carmen Miranda at a wake. The institution that commissioned this fabulous £163 million funhouse has been trading in insurance for two centuries and is famous the world over for several reasons: (1) having started in a coffeehouse; (2) insuring Betty Grable's legs; (3) accepting no corporate responsibility for losses, which are carried by its investors; (4) having its "Names"—the rich people who underwrite Lloyd's losses; (5) seeming unassailable for a very long time . . .; (6) until 1990, when it lost £2.9 billion; (7) which caused the financial ruination, and worse, of many Names. Appropriately, the viewing galleries over the trading floor and the museum of Lloyd's history, containing the Lutine Bell, which heralds important announcements (one ring for bad news), remain closed to the public. ⊠ *1 Lime St., EC3,* ☎ *0171/623–7100.*

⑲ London Bridge. Dating from only 1972, this bridge replaced the 1831 Sir John Rennie number that now graces Lake Havasu City, Arizona, the impulse purchase of someone at the McCulloch Oil Corporation, who (rumor has it) was under the impression that he'd bought the far more picturesque Tower Bridge. The version before that one, the first in stone and the most renowned of all, stood for 600 years after it was built in 1176, the focus of many a gathering thanks to the shops and houses crammed along its length, not to mention the boiled and tar-dipped heads of traitors that decorated its gatehouse after being removed in the Tower of London. Before *that* the Saxons had put up a wooden bridge; it collapsed in 1014, which was probably the origin of the refrain "London Bridge is falling down." Nobody is sure of the exact location of the very earliest London Bridge—the Roman version around whose focus London grew—but it was certainly very close to the 100-ft-wide, three-span, pre-stressed concrete cantilever one that you see today.

⑱ Monument. Commemorating the "dreadful visitation" of the Great Fire of 1666, this is the world's tallest isolated stone column. It is the work of Wren, who was asked to erect it "On or as neere unto the place where the said Fire soe unhappily began as conveniently may be." And so here it is—at 202 ft, exactly as tall as the distance it stands from Farriner's baking house in Pudding Lane, where the fire started. Above the viewing gallery (311 steps up—a better workout than any StairMaster) is a flaming bronze urn, and around it a cage for the prevention of suicide, which was a trend for a while during the 19th century. ⊠ *Monument St., EC3,* ☎ *0171/626–2717.* 🖭 *£1.* ☻ *Apr.–Sept., weekdays 9–5:30, weekends 2–5:30; Oct.–Mar., Mon.–Sat. 9–3:30. Tube: Monument.*

⑧ Museum of London. If there's one place to get the history of London sorted out, it's here—although there's a great deal to sort out: Oliver Cromwell's death mask, Queen Victoria's crinolined gowns, Selfridge's

Art Deco elevators, and the Lord Mayor's Coach are just some of the goodies here. The museum appropriately shelters a section of the 2nd- to 4th-century London wall, which you can view from a window inside, near to the Roman monumental arch the museum's archaeologists reconstructed a mere two decades ago. Anyone with the least interest in how this city evolved will adore this museum, especially said reconstructions and the dioramas—like one of the Great Fire (flickering flames! sound effects!), a 1940s air-raid shelter, a Georgian prison cell, and a Victorian street complete with fully stocked shops—as well as the Catwalk, which guides you interactively through the ages. Galleries proceed chronologically for easy comprehension right up to the new "London Now" gallery. The White Card is accepted, and all tickets allow unlimited return visits for three months. ⊠ *London Wall, EC2,* ☎ *0171/600–3699.* ⊡ *£4, free 4:30–5:50.* ⊘ *Tues.–Sat. 10–6, Sun. noon–6.*

❻ **National Postal Museum.** An important landmark for philatelists, this was founded in 1965, but the collection is as old as the postal service itself and is one of the world's best—everything from the Penny Black, the world's first adhesive stamp, to lovely Victorian valentines are on show here. ⊠ *King Edward Bldg., King Edward St., EC1 ,* ☎ *0171/ 239–5420.* ⊡ *Free.* ⊘ *Mon.–Thurs. 9:30–4:30, Fri. 9:30–4. Tube: St. Paul's.*

❹ **Old Bailey.** This, the present-day **Central Criminal Court,** is where Newgate Prison stood from the 12th century right until the beginning of this one. Few survived for long in the version pulled down in 1770. Those who didn't starve were hanged, or pressed to death in the Press Yard, or they succumbed to the virulent gaol (the archaic British spelling of "jail") fever—any of which must have been preferable to a life in the stinking, subterranean, lightless Stone Hold or to suffering the robberies, beatings, and general victimization endemic in what the novelist Henry Fielding called the "prototype of hell." The next model lasted only a couple of years before being torn down by raving mobs during the anti-Catholic Gordon Riots of 1780, to be replaced by the Newgate that Dickens visited several times (obviously in between pubs) and described in several novels. In fact, Fagin ended up in the Condemned Hold here in *Oliver Twist,* from which he would have been taken to the public scaffold that replaced the Tyburn Tree (☞ St. James's and Mayfair, *above*) and stood outside the prison until 1868. The Central Criminal Court replaced Newgate in 1907. The most famous and most interesting feature of the solid Edwardian building is the gilded statue of blind Justice perched on top, scales in her left hand, sword in her right. Ask the doorman which current trial is likely to prove juicy, if you're that kind of ghoul—you may catch the conviction of the next Crippen or Christie (England's most notorious wife-murderers, both tried here). Cameras are not allowed in the court. Check the day's hearings on the sign outside. ⊠ *Newgate St., EC4.* ⊘ *Public Gallery weekdays 10–1 and 2–4 (line forms at Newgate St. entrance). Tube: Blackfriars.*

⓯ **Royal Exchange.** Inhabiting the isosceles triangle between Threadneedle Street and Cornhill, this is the third version to have stood here, but the first to have been blessed by Queen Victoria—at its 1844 opening. Sir William Tite designed the massive templelike building—its pediment featuring 17 limestone figures (Commerce, plus merchants) supported by eight sizable Corinthian columns—to house the then-thriving futures market. The market has now moved on, leaving the Royal Exchange, which you may no longer enter, as a monument to money.

❼ St. Bartholomew the Great Church. Reached via a perfect half-timbered gatehouse atop a 13th-century stone archway, this is one of London's oldest churches. Along with its namesake on the other side of the road, St. Bartholomew's Hospital, the Norman church was founded by Rahere, Henry I's court jester. At the Dissolution of the Monasteries, Henry VIII had most of it torn down; the Romanesque choir loft is all that survives from the 12th century.

❸ St. Bride's. From afar, study the extraordinary steeple of this church—its uniquely tiered shape gave rise, legend has it, to the traditional wedding cake. This, the first of Wren's city churches, did not escape wartime bomb damage, and was reconsecrated only in 1960 after a 17-year-long restoration. As St. Paul's (in Covent Garden) is the actors' church, so St. Bride's belongs to journalists, many of whom have been buried or memorialized here, as reading the wall plaques will tell you. Even before the press moved in, it was a popular place to take the final rest. By 1664 the crypts were so crowded that diarist Samuel Pepys had to bribe the grave digger to "justle together" some bodies to make room for his deceased brother. Now the crypts house a museum of the church's rich history, and a bit of Roman sidewalk. ✉ *Fleet St., EC4,* ☎ *0171/353–1301.* 🎟 *Free.* 🕙 *Mon.–Sat. 9–5, Sun. between services at 11 and 6:30. Tube: Chancery Lane.*

❿ St. Giles Without Cripplegate. Standing south of the Barbican complex, this is one of the only City churches to have withstood the Great Fire, only to succumb to the Blitz bombs three centuries later. The tower and a few walls survived; the rest was rebuilt to the 16th-century plan during the 1950s, and now the little church struggles hopelessly for attention among the Barbican towers, whose parishioners it tends. Past parishioners include Oliver Cromwell, married here in 1620, and John Milton, buried here in 1674.

⓬ St. Mary-le-Bow. Wren's 1673 church has one of the most famous sets of bells around—a Londoner must be born within the sound of Bow Bells to be a true cockney. The origin of that idea was probably the curfew rung on the Bow Bells during the 14th century, even though "cockney" only came to mean Londoner three centuries later, and then it was an insult.

NEED A
BREAK?
The **Place Below** is literally below the church, in St. Mary-le-Bow's crypt, and gets packed with City workers weekday lunchtime—the self-service soup and quiche are particularly good. It's also open for breakfast, and Thursday and Friday evenings it features a posh and sophisticated vegetarian set dinner.

★ **❺ St. Paul's Cathedral.** The symbolic heart of London, St. Paul's will take your breath away. In fact, its dome—the world's third largest—will already be familiar, since you see it peeping through on the skyline from many an angle, riding high (although now nudged by skyscrapers) over the rooftops of the City, just as it does in Canaletto's 18th-century views of the Thames. The cathedral is, of course, the masterpiece of Sir Christopher Wren (1632–1723), completed in 1710 after 35 years of building and much argument with the Royal Commission, then, much later, miraculously (mostly) spared by the World War II bombs. Wren had originally been commissioned to restore Old St. Paul's, the Norman cathedral that had replaced, in its turn, three earlier versions, but the Great Fire left so little of it standing that a new cathedral was deemed necessary.

Wren's first plan, known as the New Model, did not make it past the drawing board, while the second, known as the Great Model, got as far as the 20-ft oak rendering you can see here today before it, too, was rejected, whereupon Wren is said to have burst into tears. The third, however, known as the Warrant Design (because it received the royal warrant), was accepted, with the fortunate coda that the architect be allowed to make changes as he saw fit. Without that, there would be no dome, because the approved design had featured a steeple. Parliament felt that building was proceeding too slowly (in fact, 35 years is lightning speed, as cathedrals go) and withheld half of Wren's pay for the last 13 years of work. He was pushing 80 when Queen Anne finally coughed up the arrears.

When you enter and see the dome from the inside, you may find that it seems smaller than you expected. You aren't imagining things—it *is* smaller, and 60 ft lower, than the lead-covered outer dome. Between the inner and outer domes is a brick cone, which supports the familiar 850-ton lantern, surmounted by its golden ball and cross. Nobody can resist making a beeline for the dome, so we'll start beneath it, standing dead center, on top of Wren's memorial, which his son composed and had set into the pavement, and which reads succinctly: LECTOR, SI MONUMENTUM REQUIRIS, CIRCUMSPICE, (READER, IF YOU SEEK HIS MONUMENT, LOOK AROUND YOU.

Now climb the 259 spiral steps to the **Whispering Gallery.** This is the part of the cathedral with which you bribe children, who are fascinated by the acoustic phenomenon: Whisper something to the wall on one side, and a second later it transmits clearly to the other side, 107 ft away. The only problem is identifying "your" whisper from the cacophony of everyone else's, since this is a popular game. Look down onto the nave from here, and up to the frescoes of St. Paul by Sir James Thornhill (who nearly fell off while painting them), before ascending farther to the Stone Gallery, which encircles the outside of the dome and affords a spectacular panorama of London. Up again (careful—you will have tackled 627 steps altogether), and you reach the Golden Gallery, from which you can view the lantern through a circular opening called the oculus.

Back downstairs there are the inevitable monuments and memorials to see, though fewer than one might expect because Wren didn't want his masterpiece cluttered up. The poet John Donne, who had been Dean of St. Paul's for his final 10 years (he died in 1631), lies in the south choir aisle; his is the only monument remaining from Old St. Paul's. The vivacious choir stall carvings nearby are the work of Grinling Gibbons, as is the organ, which Wren designed and Handel played. The painters Sir Joshua Reynolds and J. M. W. Turner are commemorated, as is George Washington. The American connection continues behind the high altar in the **American Memorial Chapel,** dedicated in 1958 to the 28,000 GIs stationed here who lost their lives in World War II.

A visit to the **crypt** brings you to Wren's tomb, the black marble sarcophagus containing Admiral Nelson (who was pickled in alcohol for his final voyage here from Trafalgar), and an equestrian statue of the Duke of Wellington on top of his grandiose tomb. Finally, to catch Wren's facade and dome at its most splendid, remember to make a return trip to see St. Paul's at night. ⊠ *St. Paul's Churchyard, EC4,* ☎ *0171/236–4128.* 🎫 *Cathedral, ambulatory (American Chapel), crypt, and treasury £4; galleries £3.50; combined ticket £6.* ☉ *Cathedral Mon.–Sat. 8:30–4:30 (closed occasionally for special services); ambulatory, crypt, and galleries Mon.–Sat. 9:30–4:15. Tube: St. Paul's.*

⓮ St. Stephen Walbrook Church. This is the parish church many think is Wren's best, by virtue of its practice dome, which predates the Big One at St. Paul's by some 30 years. Two inside sights warrant investigation: Henry Moore's 1987 central stone altar, which sits beneath the dome ("like a lump of Camembert," say critics), and, well, a telephone—an eloquent tribute to that genuine savior of souls, Rector Chad Varah, who founded the Samaritans, givers of phone aid to the suicidal, here in 1953.

⓱ Temple of Mithras. This minor place of pilgrimage in the Roman City was unearthed on a building site in 1954 and was taken, at first, for an early Christian church. In fact, worshipers here favored Christ's chief rival during the 3rd and 4th centuries: Mithras, the Persian god of light. Mithraists aimed for all the big virtues but still were not appreciated by early Christians, from whom their sculptures and treasures had to be concealed. These devotional objects are now on display back at the Museum of London, while here, on Queen Victoria Street, not far from the Bank of England, you can see the foundations of the temple itself.

★ ☜ ㉑ **Tower Bridge.** Despite its venerable, nay, medieval, appearance, this is a Victorian youngster that celebrated its centenary in June 1994. Constructed of steel, then clothed in Portland stone, it was deliberately styled in the Gothic persuasion to complement the Tower next door, and it is famous for its enormous bascules—the "arms," which open to allow large ships through. Nowadays this rarely happens, but when river traffic was dense, the bascules were raised about five times a day.

The bridge's 100th-birthday gift was a new exhibition, one of London's most imaginative and fun. You are conducted back in time in the company of "Harry Stoner," an animatronic bridge construction worker worthy of Disneyland, to witness the birth of the Thames's last downstream bridge. History and engineering lessons are painlessly absorbed as you meet the ghost of the bridge's architect, Sir Horace Jones, see the bascules work, and wander the walkways with their grand upstream–downstream views annotated by interactive video displays. Be sure to hang onto your ticket and follow the signs to the Engine Rooms for part two; here the original steam-driven hydraulic engines gleam, and a cute rococo theater is the setting for an Edwardian-style music-hall production of the bridge's story. ☎ 0171/403–3761.⬚ £5.70. ☉ Apr.–Oct., daily 10–6:30; Nov.–Mar., daily 10–5:15 (last entry 1¼ hrs before closing). Tube: Tower Hill.

Tower Hill Pageant. This is London's first "dark-ride" museum, where automated cars take you past mock-ups of scenes from most periods of London's past, complete with "people," sound effects, and even smells. The Museum of London has set up an adjoining archaeological display with finds from the Thames. ✉ Tower Hill Terr., EC3N, ☎ 0171/709–0081. ⬚ £6.95, combined ticket with Tower Bridge £8.75. ☉ Apr.–Oct., daily 9:30–5:30; Nov.–Mar., daily 9:30–4:30. Tube: Tower Hill.

★ ⑳ **Tower of London.** This has top billing on many tourist itineraries for good reason. Nowhere else does London's history come to life so vividly as in this minicity of melodramatic towers stuffed to bursting with heraldry and treasure, the intimate details of lords and dukes and princes and sovereigns etched in the walls (literally in some places, as you'll see), and quite a few pints of royal blood spilled on the stones. Be warned that visitor traffic at the sight of sights is copious, meaning not only lines for the best bits, but a certain dilution of atmosphere, which can be disappointing if you've been fantasizing scenes from Elizabeth and Essex. At least you need no longer spend all day in line for the prize exhibit, the Crown Jewels, since they have been transplanted to a new home where moving walkways hasten progress at the busiest times.

The reason the Tower holds the royal gems is that it is still one of the royal palaces, although no monarch since Henry VIII has called it home. It has also housed the Royal Mint, the Public Records, the Royal Menagerie, and the Royal Observatory, although its most renowned and titillating function has been, of course, as a jail and place of torture and execution.

A person was mighty privileged to be beheaded in the peace and seclusion of **Tower Green** instead of before the mob at Tower Hill. In fact, only seven people were ever important enough—among them Anne Boleyn and Catherine Howard, wives two and five of Henry VIII's six; Elizabeth I's friend Robert Devereux, the Earl of Essex; and the nine day queen, Lady Jane Grey, aged 17. Tower Green's other function was as a corpse dumping ground when the chapel just got too full. You can see the executioner's block, with its bathetic forehead-size dent, and his axe—along with the equally famous rack, where victims were stretched, and the more obscure scavenger's daughter, which pressed a body nearly to death, plus assorted thumbscrews, iron maidens, and so forth—in the **Martin Tower,** which stands in the northeast corner.

Before we go any farther, you should know about the excellent free and fact-packed tours that depart every half hour or so from the Middle Tower. They are conducted by the 42 Yeoman Warders, better known as Beefeaters—ex-servicemen dressed in resplendent navy-and-red (scarlet-and-gold on special occasions) Tudor outfits. Beefeaters have been guarding the Tower since Henry VII appointed them in 1485. One of them, the Yeoman Ravenmaster, is responsible for making life comfortable for Larry, Hardy, George, Hugin, Mumia, and Rhys—the Tower Ravens. This used to be a delicate duty, since if they were to desert the Tower (goes the legend), the kingdom would fall. Today, the Tower takes no chances: the ravens' wings are clipped.

In prime position stands the oldest part of the Tower and the most conspicuous of its buildings, the **White Tower.** This central keep was begun in 1078 by William the Conqueror; by the time it was completed, in 1097, it was the tallest building in London, underlining the might of those victorious Normans. Henry III (1207–1272) had it whitewashed, which is where the name comes from, then used it to house his menagerie, including the polar bear the King of Norway had given him.

The spiral staircase—winding clockwise to help the right-handed swordsman defend it—is the only way up, and here you'll find the **Royal Armouries,** Britain's national museum of arms and armor, with about 40,000 pieces on display. One of the Tower's original functions was as arsenal, supplying armor and weapons to the kings and their armies. Henry VIII started the collection in earnest, founding a workshop at Greenwich as a kind of bespoke tailor of armor to the gentry, but the public didn't get to see it until the second half of the 17th century, during Charles II's reign—which makes the Tower Armouries Britain's oldest public museum.

Here you can see weapons and armor from Britain and the Continent, dating from Saxon and Viking times right up to our own. Among the highlights are four of those armors Henry VIII commissioned to fit his ever-increasing bulk, plus one for his horse. The medieval warhorse was nothing without his *shaffron,* or head protector, and here you'll find a 500-year-old example, one of the oldest pieces of horse armor in the world. Don't miss the tiny armors on the third floor—one belonging to Henry's son (who survived in it to become Edward VI), and another just a bit more than 3 ft tall. In the **New Armouries,** added during the 17th century, are examples of almost every weapon made for the British soldier from the 17th to 19th centuries.

Most of the interior of the White Tower has been much altered over the centuries, but the **Chapel of St. John,** downstairs from the armouries, is unadulterated 11th-century Norman—very rare, very simple, and very beautiful. Underneath it is a particularly nasty cell, "Little Ease," an ironic name, as the unfortunate inmate (Guy Fawkes was one of those brought here) couldn't stand, sit, or lie down—a replica is on view at the London Dungeon (☞ The South Bank, *below*). The other fortifications and buildings surrounding the White Tower date from the 11th to 19th centuries. Starting from the main entrance, you can't miss the **moat.** Until the Duke of Wellington had it drained in 1843, this was a stinking, stagnant mush, obstinately resisting all attempts to flush it with water from the Thames. Now there's a little raven graveyard in the grassed-over channel, with touching memorials to some

The Tower

of the old birds (who are not known for their kind natures, by the way, and you risk a savage pecking if you try to befriend them).

Across the moat, the **Middle Tower** and the **Byward Tower** form the principal landward entrance, with **Traitors' Gate** a little farther on to the right. This London equivalent of Venice's Bridge of Sighs was where the boats delivered prisoners to their cells, and so it was where those condemned to death got their last look at the outside world. During the period when the Thames was London's chief thoroughfare, this was the main entrance to the Tower.

Immediately opposite Traitors' Gate is the former Garden Tower, better known since about 1570 as the **Bloody Tower**. Its name comes from one of the most famous unsolved murders in history, the saga of the "little princes in the Tower." In 1483 the boy king, Edward V, and his brother Richard were left here by their uncle, Richard of Gloucester, after the death of their father, Edward I. They were never seen again, Gloucester was crowned Richard III, and in 1674 two little skeletons were found under the stairs to St. John's Chapel. The obvious conclusions have always been drawn—and were, in fact, even before the skeletons were discovered.

Another famous inmate was Sir Walter Raleigh, who was kept here from 1603 to 1616. It wasn't such an ordeal, as you'll see when you visit his spacious rooms, where he kept two servants, had his wife and two sons live with him (the younger boy was christened in the Tower chapel), and amused himself by writing his *History of the World*. Unfortunately, he was less lucky on his second visit in 1618, which terminated in his execution at Whitehall.

Next to the Bloody Tower is the circular **Wakefield Tower**, which dates from the 13th century and once contained the king's private apartments. It was the scene of another royal murder in 1471, when Henry VI was killed in mid-prayer. Henry founded Eton College and King's College, Cambridge, and they haven't forgotten: Every May 21, envoys from both institutions mark the anniversary of his murder by laying white lilies on the site.

The shiniest, the most expensive, and absolutely the most famous exhibits here are, of course, the **Crown Jewels,** now housed in the **Duke of Wellington's Barracks.** In their new setting you get so close that you could lick the gems (if it weren't for the wafers of bulletproof glass), and they are enhanced by laser lighting, which hurts the eyes with sparkle. Before you meet them in person, you are given a high-definition-film preview along with a few scenes from Elizabeth's 1953 coronation.

It's a commonplace to call these baubles priceless, but it's impossible not to drop your jaw at the notion of their worth. They were, in fact, lifted once—by Colonel Thomas Blood, in 1671—though only as far as a nearby wharf. The colonel was given a royal pension instead of a beating, fueling speculation that Charles II, short of ready cash as usual, had had his hand in the escapade somewhere. These days security is as fiendish as you'd expect, since the jewels—even though they would be literally impossible for thieves to sell—are *so* priceless that they're not insured. However, they are polished every February by Garrard, the royal jewelers.

A brief résumé of the top jewels: Finest of all is the **Royal Sceptre,** containing the earth's largest cut diamond, the 530-carat Star of Africa. This is also known as Cullinan I, having been cut from the South African Cullinan, which weighed 20 ounces when dug up from a De Beers mine at the beginning of the century. Another chip off the block, Cullinan II, lives on the **Imperial Crown of State** that Prince Charles is due to wear at his coronation—the same one that Elizabeth II wore in her coronation procession; it was made for Victoria's coronation in 1838. Aside from its 2,800 diamonds, it features the Black Prince's ruby, which Henry V was supposed to have worn at Agincourt, and which is actually an imposter—it's no ruby, it's a semiprecious spinel. The other most famous gem is the Koh-i-noor, or "Mountain of Light," which adorns the **Queen Mother's crown.** When Victoria was presented with this gift horse in 1850, she looked it in the mouth, found it lacking in glitter, and had it chopped down to almost half its weight.

An addendum to the major jewels in the Martin Tower is accurately called "Crowns and Diamonds." See naked crown frames—the coronation crown of George IV, George I's Imperial State Crown, Victoria's State Crown—surrounded by 12,500 loose diamonds on permanent loan from de Beers. It's a graphic illustration of how the Royals once had to rent the stones that would adorn their headpiece on the big day.

The little chapel of **St. Peter ad Vincula** can be visited only as part of a Yeoman Warder tour. The third church on the site, it conceals the remains of some 2,000 people executed at the Tower, Anne Boleyn and Catherine Howard among them. Being traitors, they were not so much buried as dumped under the flagstones, but the genteel Victorians had the courtesy to rebury their bones during renovations.

One of the more evocative towers is **Beauchamp Tower,** built west of Tower Green by Edward I (1272–1307). It was soon designated as a jail for the higher class of miscreant, including Lady Jane Grey, who is thought to have added her Latin graffiti to the many inscriptions carved by prisoners that you can see here.

Just south of the Beauchamp Tower is an L-shape row of half-timber Tudor houses, with the **Queen's House** at the center. Built for the governor of the Tower in 1530, this place saw the interrogation or incarceration of several of the more celebrated prisoners, including Anne Boleyn and the Gunpowder Plot conspirators. The Queen's House also played host to the Tower's last-ever prisoner, Rudolph Hess, the Nazi who parachuted into London in 1941 to seek asylum.

Don't forget to stroll along the battlements before you leave; from them, you get a wonderful overview of the whole Tower of London. ⊠ *H. M. Tower of London, Tower Hill, EC3N,* ☎ *0171/709–0765.* 🎫 *£9, small additional charge for Fusiliers Museum.* ☉ *Mar.–Oct., Mon.–Sat. 9:30–6:30, Sun. 2–6; Nov.–Feb., Tues.–Sat. 9:30–5, Sun.–Mon. 10–5 (last admission may be sold as early as 4, depending on crowds). For tickets to Ceremony of the Keys (locking of main gates, nightly at 10), write well in advance to the Resident Governor and Keeper of the Jewel House, Queen's House, H. M. Tower of London, EC3. Give your name, the dates you wish to attend (including alternate dates), and number of people (up to 7) in your party, and enclose a self-addressed, stamped envelope. Yeoman Warder guides leave daily from Middle Tower, subject to weather and availability, at no charge (but a tip is always appreciated), about every 30 mins until 3:30 in summer, 2:30 in winter. Tube: Tower Hill.*

❷ **Ye Olde Cheshire Cheese.** This is one of the many places in which that acerbic compiler of the first dictionary, Dr. Johnson, drank (like Dickens, he is claimed by many a pub). This was, in fact, his "local," around the corner from his house. It retains a venerable open-fires-in-tiny-rooms charm when not too packed with tourists. Among 19th-century writers who followed Johnson's footsteps to the bar here were Mark Twain and, yes, Charles Dickens.

THE EAST END

Made famous by Dickens and infamous by Jack the Ripper, the East End remains one of London's most hauntingly evocative neighborhoods. There is a good argument for considering it the real London, since East Enders are born "within the sound of Bow Bells," and are therefore cockneys through and through (not to mention models for the characters of England's favorite soap opera, *Eastenders*). The district began as separate villages—Whitechapel and Spitalfields, Shoreditch, Mile End, and Bethnal Green—melding together during the population boom of the 19th century, a boom that was shaped by French Huguenot and Jewish refugees, by poverty, and, in the past several decades, by a growing Bengali community. Whitechapel is where the Salvation Army was founded and the original Liberty Bell was forged, but, of course, what everyone remembers about it is that its Victorian slum streets were stalked by the most infamous serial killer of all, Jack the Ripper. (Many outfitters offer walking tours of "Jack's London": the most popular is run by Original London Walks ☎ 0171/624–3978, but the best may be led by Paul, ☎ 0181/558–9446, who leaves from Aldgate East.) Two centuries earlier, neighboring Spitalfields provided sanctuary for the French Huguenots. They had fled here after the Edict of Nantes (which had allowed them religious freedom in Catholic France) was revoked in 1685, and had found work in the nascent silk industry, many of them becoming prosperous master weavers. Today, as it turns out, Spitalfields is one of London's most cutting-edge neighborhoods, with stylish boutiques and artists (Gilbert and George, among them) setting up shop. All in all, prosperous is not really the word for the East End of today, but what the area lacks in tourist attractions it makes up for in history and urban romance of a sublime sort.

Numbers in the text correspond to numbers in the margin and on the East End map.

A Good Walk

The easiest way to reach Whitechapel High Street is via the District Line to Aldgate East tube. Turn left out of the tube station. Behind 90 Whitechapel High Street once stood George Yard Buildings, where Jack the Ripper's first victim, Martha Turner, was discovered in August 1888. Nowadays you'll find the **Whitechapel Gallery** ① instead. Continue east until you reach Fieldgate Street on the right, where you'll find the **Whitechapel Bell Foundry** ②, then, retracing your steps, turn right into Osborn Street, which soon becomes **Brick Lane,** ③.

Brick Lane itself and the narrow streets running off it offer a paradigm of the East End's development. Its population has always been in flux, with some moving in to find refuge here as others were escaping its poverty. Just before the start of Brick Lane you can take a short detour (turn left, then right) to see the birthplace of one who did just that. Flower and Dean streets, past the ugly 1970s housing project on Thrawl Street and once the most disreputable street in London, was where Abe Sapperstein, founder of the *Harlem Globetrotters,* was born in 1908. On the west end of **Fournier Street** ④, see Nicholas Hawkesmoor's masterpiece, **Christ Church, Spitalfields** ⑤, and some fine early Georgian houses, then follow Wilkes Street north of the church, where you'll find more 1720s Huguenot houses (one has been turned into the **Spitalfields Heritage Centre** ⑥), and turn right into Princelet Street, once important to the Jewish settlers. Where No. 6 stands now, the first of several thriving Yiddish theaters opened in 1886, playing to packed houses until the following year, when a false fire alarm, rung during a January performance, ended with 17 people being crushed to death, and so demoralized the theater's actor-founder, Jacob Adler, that he moved his troupe to New York. Adler played a major role in founding that city's great Yiddish theater tradition—which, in turn, had a significant effect on Hollywood.

Now you reach Brick Lane again and the **Black Eagle Brewery** ⑦. Turn left at Hanbury Street, where, in 1888, behind a seedy lodging house at No. 29, Jack the Ripper left his third mutilated murderee, "Dark" Annie Chapman. A double murder followed, and then, after a month's lull, came the death on this street of Marie Kelly, the Ripper's last victim and his most revolting murder of all. He had been able to work indoors this time, and Kelly, a young widow, was found strewn all over the room, charred remains of her clothing in the fire grate. (Of course, Jack the Ripper's identity never has been discovered, although to this day theories are still bandied about.)

Now turn onto Lamb Street and the two northern entrances to **Spitalfields Market** ⑧, or turn left on Commercial Street to Folgate Street and **Dennis Sever's House** ⑨. (If you have kids, they might have fun—and learn something, too—going to **Spitalfields City Farm** ⑩ a few blocks away.) Go back west through Folgate Street to reach Shoreditch High Street, where you can catch Bus 22A, 22B, or 149 north to Kingsland Road, or get there across Bethnal Green Road, left, then right onto Club Row, to **Arnold Circus** ⑪ and then two streets north, to **Columbia Road** ⑫. Cross Hackney Road and slip up Waterson Street—that's about a half-mile walk. On Kingsland Road, you'll come to the row of early 18th-century almshouses that are the **Geffrye Museum** ⑬. Head east about 500 yards on Hackney Road (Cremer Street, south of the museum, gets you there), and you come to the **Hackney City Farm** ⑭. Going south down Warner Place (across Hackney Road opposite the farm entrance), you come to Old Bethnal Green Road, at the end of which a right turn brings you to the **Bethnal Green Museum of Childhood** ⑮.

Now you can catch either Bus 106 or 253 or walk south about a half mile down Cambridge Heath Road as far as the Mile End Road. Turning left, you'll pass several historical landmarks that provide more food for thought than thrills for the senses. On the north side of the street are the former **Trinity Almshouses** ⑯, with the statue of William Booth on the very spot where the first Salvation Army meetings were held. Behind you, on the northwest corner of Cambridge Heath Road is the **Blind Beggar** ⑰ pub, with the **Royal London Hospital** ⑱ a few yards to the left, and its Archives behind.

TIMING

This is a long walk, and not for everyone. The East End isn't picturesque, and the sights are anything but world famous. However, those who get pleasure from discovery and an adventurous route will enjoy these hidden corners. If you visit on a Sunday morning, the East End has a festive air: About half the neighborhood sprouts hundreds of market stalls (especially in and around Middlesex Street, Brick Lane, and Columbia Road). After shopping, you could go on to take brunch among cows and sheep on a farm, then play at being Georgians in a restored, candlelighted 18th-century town house. You would miss out on a few weekday-only sights, but—as a Victorian peep-show barker might say— yer pays yer money and yer takes yer choice. A weekday focus for your jaunt might well be the excellent Whitechapel Gallery, the Geffrye Museum, or the Bethnal Green Museum of Childhood, any of which will take an hour or two. Aside from visits, the walk alone is a three-hour marathon, done at a brisk pace. The suggested bus links might be appealing since the in-between parts aren't going to win tourism awards.

HOW TO GET THERE

The best tubes to start from are Whitechapel or Aldgate East on the District/Hammersmith and City lines, or Aldgate on the Metropolitan and Circle lines. Buses include Nos. 8, 22A, 22B, 26, 35, 47, 48, and 78. To continue up into the northern part of the area, around Shoreditch and Spitalfields, including the Geffrye Museum (get the 22A or B or the 67 for that), get Nos. 8, 22A, 22B, 26, 35, 47, 48, 55, 67, 78, and 243 to the junction of Shoreditch High Street and Bishopsgate.

Sights to See

❶ **Arnold Circus.** A perfect circle of arts-and-crafts–style houses around a central raised bandstand, this is the core of the Boundary Estate— "model" housing built by Victorian philanthropists and do-gooders for the slum-dwelling locals, and completed as the century began. It's of special interest to architecture buffs.

⑮ **Bethnal Green Museum of Childhood.** This is the East End outpost of the Victoria and Albert Museum—in fact, this entire iron, glass, and brown-brick building was transported here from South Kensington in 1875. Since then, believe it or not, its contents have grown into the biggest toy collection in the world. The central hall is a bit like the Geffrye Museum zapped into miniature: Here are doll's houses (some royal) of every period. Each genre of plaything has its own enclosure, so if teddy bears are your weakness, you need waste no time with the train sets. The museum's title is justified upstairs, in the recently opened, fascinating—and possibly unique—social-history-of-childhood galleries. Free art workshops are given for children over the age of 3. ⊠ *Cambridge Heath Rd., E2,* ☎ *0181/980–4315.* ▣ *Free.* ☾ *Mon.–Thurs. and Sat. 10–5:50, Sun. 2:30–5:50; art workshop Sat. at 11 and 2. Tube: Bethnal Green.*

The East End

➐ Black Eagle Brewery. This is the only one of the former East End breweries still standing. It is a very handsome example of Georgian and 19th-century industrial architecture, too, along with its mirrored 1977 extension. It belonged to Truman, Hanbury, Buxton & Co., which in 1873 was the largest brewery in the world (the English always did like their bitters). The building now houses the East End Tourism Trust offices and the present Truman brewery's administration. You can't go in except to look at the old stables and vat house on the east side. Opposite, however, the old brewery canteen has been turned into the little **Brick Lane Music Hall** (⊠ 152 Brick La.), a cute and shabby theater serving up an *echt* East End dinner (latkes—potato pancakes—are a feature on most menus) and an old-fashioned laugh-a-minute cabaret show. ⊠ *91 Brick La., E1,* ☎ *0171/377–8787.* 🎟 *Dinner and show £20.* ☼ *Wed., Fri, and Sat. at 7:30. Tube: Aldgate East, Shoreditch.*

⓱ The Blind Beggar. This is the Victorian den of iniquity where Salvation Army founder William Booth preached his first sermon. Also, on the south side of the street stands a stone inscribed, HERE WILLIAM BOOTH COMMENCED THE WORK OF THE SALVATION ARMY, JULY 1865, marking the position of the first Sally Army platform, while back by the pub, a statue of William Booth stands where the first meetings were held. Booth didn't supply the pub's main claim to fame, though. The Blind Beggar's real notoriety dates only from March 1966, when Ronnie Kray—one of the Kray twins, the former gangster kings of London's East End underworld—shot dead rival "godfather" George Cornell in the saloon bar.

➌ Brick Lane. This street has, in its time, seen the manufacture of bricks (during the 16th century, when it was named), beer, and bagels, but nowadays it is the center of the East End's Bengali community. (You can still get the bagels, though, at No. 159, the 24-hour **Beigel Bake.**) All along here you'll see shops selling psychedelic saris and stacks of sticky Indian sweets, video stores renting Indian movies, and Bengali, Bangladeshi, and Pakistani restaurants, popular among Londoners for the most authentic and least expensive curries in town. On Sunday morning the entire street is packed with stalls in a companion market to the nearby Petticoat Lane.

➎ Christ Church, Spitalfields. This is the 1729 masterpiece of Wren's associate, Nicholas Hawksmoor. Hawksmoor built only six London churches; this one was commissioned as part of Parliament's 1711 "Fifty New Churches Act." The idea was to score points for the Church of England against such nonconformists as the Protestant Huguenots. (It must have worked; in the churchyard, you can still see some of their gravestones, with epitaphs in French.) The Spitalfields district once flourished thanks to the silk-weaving trade of its émigré population, but as the silk industry declined (19th-century machinery had made hand weaving redundant), the church fell into disrepair and its gardens even acquired a reputation as a tramps' ground (and the sobriquet "Itchy Park"). By 1958 the structure was crumbling to bits and had to be closed. It was saved from demolition—but only just—and reopened in 1987, though restoration work won't be complete until 1999. Until then, opening hours are restricted, but there are occasional evening concerts (and a music festival in June); there is always a fine view of the colonnaded portico and tall spire from Brushfield Street to the west. ⊠ *Commercial St., E1,* ☎ *0171/377–0287.* 🎟 *Free, charge for concerts.* ☼ *Weekdays noon–2:30, Sun. services. Tube: Aldgate East.*

⓬ Columbia Road. On Sundays, this narrow street gets buried under forests of potted palms, azaleas, ivy, ficus, freesia, tiger lilies, carnations, roses, and hosts of daffodils in London's main plant and flower market. Prices are ultralow, and lots of the Victorian shop windows around the stalls are filled with wares—terra-cotta pots, vases, gardening tools, hats, and antiques. ⊙ *Sun. 7–2. Tube: Old St.*

★ ❾ **Dennis Sever's House.** Ever want to feel what Ebenezer Scrooge felt like when the three ghosts visited him? Enter this extraordinary time machine of a house—a Georgian terrace belonging to the eponymous performer/designer/scholar from Escondido, California, who has dedicated his life not only to the restoration of his house but also to raising the ghosts of a fictitious Jervis family that might have inhabited it over two centuries. Sever himself lives a replica of Georgian life, without electricity, but with a butler in full 18th-century livery to light the candles and lay the fires—for the Jervises. The rooms are shadowy set pieces of rose-laden Victorian wallpapers, Jacobean paneling, Georgian wing chairs, baroque carved ornaments, "Protestant" colors (upstairs), and "Catholic" shades (downstairs). Three evenings a week he stages a performance, or a "time travel experience," of philosophical bent, trailing the Jervises through 10 rooms and five generations (from 1724 to 1919, to be precise), always missing them by moments; these unforgettable candlelight tours run almost three hours, and reservations are imperative. Sever's stunning house is also open the first Sunday and Monday of the month for an open house—reservations are essential on Mondays. ⊠ *18 Folgate St., E1,* ☎ *0171/247–4013.* 🎟 *£5 Sun., £7 Mon., £30 evenings.* ⊙ *1st Sun. of month 2–5, 3 performances per wk (days vary) 7:30–10:20. Tube: Liverpool St.*

❹ **Fournier Street.** This contains fine examples of the neighborhood's characteristic Georgian terraced houses, many of them built by the richest of the early 18th-century Huguenot silk weavers (see the enlarged windows on the upper floors). Most of those along the north side of Fournier Street have now been restored by conservationists; others still contain textile sweatshops—only now the workers are Bengali. On the Brick Lane corner is the **Jamme Masjid,** where local Muslims worship. UMBRA SUMMUS (WE ARE SHADOWS), announces the inscription above the entrance, an apt epitaph for the successive communities that have had temporary claim on the building. Built in 1742 as a Huguenot chapel, it converted to Methodism in 1809, only to become the Spitalfields Great Synagogue when the Orthodox Machzikei Hadath sect bought it in 1897.

★ ⓭ **Geffrye Museum.** This is a small and perfectly formed museum that re-creates domestic English interiors of every period from Elizabethan through postwar '50s utility, all in sequence, so that you walk through time. The best thing about the Geffrye (named after the 17th-century Lord Mayor of London whose land this was) is that its rooms are not the grand parlors of the gentry one normally sees in historic houses but copies of real family homes, as if talented movie-set designers had been let loose instead of academic museum curators. There's also a walled, scented herb garden and a full program of accessible lectures, including regular "bring a room to life" talks. A new group of 20th-century rooms is in the offing. ⊠ *Kingsland Rd., E2,* ☎ *0171/739–9893.* 🎟 *Free.* ⊙ *Tues.–Sat. 10–5, Sun. 2–5; period-room talks Sat. at 2 and 3:30. Tube: Liverpool St., then Bus 2A, 22B, 67, 149, or 243.*

☙ ⓮ **Hackney City Farm.** This one is smaller than the city farm at Spitalfields (☞ *below*), and so are its animals. Bees and butterflies are the stars here, along with the kinds of wildflowers they like, as well as an ecologically sound pond. If you're walking this route, drop in and buy a pot of London honey. ⊠ *1A Goldsmiths Row, E2,* ☎ *0171/729–6381.* 🎟 *Free.* ⊙ *Tues.–Sun. 10–4:30.*

LONDON DOCKLANDS VISITORS CENTRE – This is the jumping-off place for exploring London's most rapidly changing neighborhood. Docklands has emerged from what only a decade ago was a wasteland—partly low-cost residential, partly working docks, partly nothing. Now it houses national newspaper offices, a brand-new riverside business community containing Britain's tallest building, sports facilities, and even a farm. Its boundaries are roughly defined by **Tower Bridge** and the **Design Museum** to the west and **London City Airport** and the **Royal Docks** to the east, though the area inside a loop of the Thames called the **Isle of Dogs** is of most interest. Here is **Canary Wharf,** which, with its 50-story Cesar Pelli Tower (⊠ 1 Canada Sq.), is the most notorious development project Britain has seen in years. Olympia & York, the Canadian developers, went bust; bomb scares closed the observation deck; the arts funding ran out; shops stayed vacant; jokes were made. But here are waterfront promenades and pubs, a new London piazza called **Cabot Square,** a large shopping mall, and even a concert hall. Take the high-tech **Docklands Light Railway** (DLR) to Crossharbour (change at Bank) and pick up a free map. An exhibition, information desk, and film introduce the area. ⊠ *3 Limehouse, E14,* ☎ *0171/512–1111.* ⊙ *Weekdays 9–6, weekends and holidays 10–4:30; bus tour of area departs Tues. at 2, Thurs. at 10:30, and Sun. at 11:30.*

⓲ Royal London Hospital. Founded in 1740, the early days of the Royal London were as nasty as its then-neighborhood near the Tower of London. Waste was carried out in buckets and dumped in the street; bed-bugs and alcoholic nurses were problems, but according to hospital records patients didn't die—they were "relieved." Anyone who lived but refused to give thanks to both the hospital committee and God went on a blacklist, to be banned from further treatment. In 1759, the hospital moved to a new building, the core of the one you see today. By then it had become the best hospital in London, and it was enhanced further by the addition of a small medical school in 1785, and then, 70 years later, an entire state-of-the-art medical college. Thomas John Barnado, who went on to found the famous Dr. Barnado's Homes for Orphans, came to train here in 1866. Ten years later, with the opening of a new wing, the hospital became the largest in the United Kingdom, and now, though mostly rebuilt since World War II, it remains one of London's most capacious. Behind it, the **Royal London Hospital Archives** have displays of medical paraphernalia, objects, and documentation to illustrate the 250-year history of this East London institution. ⊠ *Crypt of St. Augustine with St. Philip's Church, Newark St., E1,* ☎ *0171/377–7000, Ext. 3364.* 🖾 *Free.* ⊙ *Weekdays 10–4:30. Tube: Whitechapel.*

⓾ Spitalfields City Farm. This is just what it sounds like—a sliver of rural England squashed between housing projects. It's one of about a dozen such places in London, which exist to educate city kids in country matters. Available are pony rides, local history tours by horse and cart, a Sunday brunch, summer barbecues—an altogether surreal experience. ⊠ *Pedley St., E1,* ☎ *0171/247–8762.* 🖾 *Free, horse and cart tour starting at £3.* ⊙ *Tues.–Sun. 9:30–5:30; Sun. brunch 11–3; barbecue June–Sept., Wed. at 7 (call to confirm); horse and cart tour Sun. at 11 and 2:30 (weather permitting). Tube: Shoreditch, Liverpool St..*

➅ Spitalfields Heritage Centre. This modest institution is dedicated to research into local immigrant communities and the preservation of the neighborhood's historic buildings. Huguenots rented the 1720 house—it still has their silk-weaving attic—but in 1870 the little **United Friends Synagogue** was grafted onto the back. You can still see its wooden ark, pulpit, seats, and boards listing benefactors, complete with errors in

Hebrew. London's third-oldest (purpose-built) synagogue sometimes houses exhibitions and presents videos about the Jewish East End; otherwise, the Heritage Centre remains rather erratic as a museum, since it is in the process of (underfinanced) restoration. ⊠ *19 Princelet St., E1,* ☎ *0171/377–6901.* ▣ *Free.* ⊙ *Normally open weekdays 10–5, but call first. Tube: Aldgate East.*

❽ **Spitalfields Market.** There's been a market here since the mid-17th century, but the current version is overflowing with crafts and design shops and stalls, a sports hall, restaurants and bars, and different-purpose markets every day of the week. The nearer the weekend, the busier it all gets, culminating in the Sunday arts-and-crafts and green market. The latest additions are an opera house and a swimming pool, and events are being staged all the time. ⊠ *65 Brushfield St., E1,* ☎ *0171/247–6590.* ▣ *Free.* ⊙ *Daily 10–7; market stalls weekdays 11–2, weekends 9–4. Tube: Liverpool St.*

⓰ **Trinity Almshouses.** This is just a redbrick student hostel, but it has interesting origins, having been built (possibly with Wren's help) in 1695 for "28 decayed Masters and Commanders of Ships or ye widows of such," bombed during World War II, and restored by the London County Council. Behind, even better concealed, is the oldest Jewish cemetery in Britain, founded by the Sephardic community in 1657 after Cromwell allowed them back into the country. (If you would like to view the cemetery, call the United Synagogues Cemetery Maintenance Department, ☎ 0171/790–1445.)

❷ **Whitechapel Bell Foundry.** It may be off the beaten track, but this working foundry was responsible for some of the world's better-known chimes. Before moving to this site in 1738, the foundry cast Westminster Abbey's bells (in the 1580s), but its biggest work, in every sense, was the 13-ton Big Ben, cast in 1858 by George Mears, and requiring 16 horses to transport it from here to Westminster. Its other important work was casting the original Liberty Bell (now in Philadelphia) in 1752, and both it and Big Ben can be seen in pictures, along with exhibits about bell making, in a little museum in the shop. You can even buy a small table bell (for about £36) if they have them in stock. Note, however, that the actual foundry is off-limits. ⊠ *34 Whitechapel Rd., E1,* ☎ *0171/247–2599.* ▣ *Free.* ⊙ *Weekdays 8:30–5:30. Tube: Aldgate East.*

❶ **Whitechapel Gallery.** Housed in a spacious 1901 Art Nouveau building, this has an international reputation for its shows, which are often on the cutting edge of contemporary art. The American painter Jackson Pollock exhibited here in the '50s, as did the pop artist Robert Rauschenberg in the '60s, and David Hockney had his first solo show here in the '70s. More recently, the Tate Gallery visited the Whitechapel and bought American Bill Viola's powerful video installation, the *Nantes Triptych,* which shows Viola submerged underwater, his wife giving birth on one side, his mother dying in a hospital on the other. Other exhibitions highlight the local community and culture, and there are programs of lectures, too. The Whitechapel Café serves remarkably inexpensive, home-cooked, whole-food hot meals, soups, and cakes. ⊠ *Whitechapel High St., E1,* ☎ *0171/377–0107.* ▣ *Free (fee for some exhibitions).* ⊙ *Tues.–Sun. 11–5, Wed. 11–8. Tube: Aldgate East.*

OFF THE   **WILLIAM MORRIS GALLERY –** An 18th-century house in northeast London
BEATEN PATH   where the artistic polymath William Morris (1834–1896)—craftsman, painter, and writer—lived for eight years, this gallery contains many examples of his work and that of his fellow artisans in the Arts and Crafts

Movement. ⊠ *Water House, Lloyd Park, Forest Rd.,* ☎ *0181/527–3782.* ☉ *Tues.–Sat. 10–1 and 2–5, 1st Sun. of each month 10–noon and 2–5. Tube: Walthamstow Central, then 15-min walk down Hoe St., turn left at Forest Rd.*

THE SOUTH BANK

That old and snide North London dig about needing a passport to cross the Thames is no longer heard now. For decades, natives never ventured beyond the watery curtain that divides the city in half; tourists, too, rarely troubled the area unless they were departing from Waterloo Station. Starting with the 1976 creation of the South Bank Centre, however, the South Bank—the riverside stretch between Waterloo Bridge and Hungerford Bridge—has been taken over by Culture with a capital and emphatically illuminated C. Today, developers and local authorities have expanded the South Bank's potential farther east with an explosion of attractions that is turning this once-neglected district into London's most happening new neighborhood. The '80s brought renovations and innovations such as Gabriel's Wharf, London Bridge City, Hay's Galleria, and Butler's Wharf; the '90s arrived, and so did such headline-making sights as the spectacular reconstruction of Shakespeare's Globe—the most famous theater in the world—the OXO Tower, and the London Aquarium. These will again be augmented in the lead-up to the millennium by the new Tate Gallery, a giant Ferris wheel, and a new look for the South Bank Centre itself. Clearly, the South Bank has become a dazzling perch for culture vultures.

Actually, it is fitting that so much of London's artistic life should once again be centered here on the South Bank—back in the days of Ye Olde London Towne, **Southwark** was the city's oldest "suburb": though just across the river from London Bridge, it was conveniently outside the City walls and laws, and therefore the ideal location for the theaters, taverns, and cock-fighting arenas that served as after-hours entertainment in the Middle Ages. The Globe Theatre, in which Shakespeare acted and held shares, was one of several established here after theaters were banished from the City in 1574 for encouraging truancy in young apprentices, and for being generally rowdy. In truth, the Globe was as likely to stage a few bouts of bearbaiting as the latest interpretations of Shakespeare. Today, at the reconstructed "Wooden O," of course, you can just see the latter.

Numbers in the text correspond to numbers in the margin and on the South Bank map.

A Good Walk

Start scenically at the south end of Tower Bridge, finding the steps on the east (left) side, which descend to the start of a pedestrians-only street, Shad Thames. Now turn your back on the bridge and follow this quaint path between cliffs of the good-as-new warehouses, which are now **Butler's Wharf** ①, but were once the seedy, dingy, dangerous shadow lands where Dickens killed off evil Bill Sikes in *Oliver Twist.* See the foodies' center, the Gastrodrome, and the **Design Museum** ②; then, just before you get back to Tower Bridge, turn away from the river, along Horsleydown Lane, follow Tooley Street, take the right, follow Tooley Street, and take either the right turn at Morgan Lane to **HMS *Belfast*** ③ or continue to **Hay's Galleria** ④, with London Bridge and the **London Dungeon** ⑤ beyond. Next, turn left into Joiner Street underneath the arches of London's first (1836) railway, then right onto St. Thomas Street, where you'll find the **Old St. Thomas's Operating Theatre** ⑥ and Herb Garret, with **Southwark Cathedral** ⑦ just across Borough High Street, and another of the South Bank's recent office developments, St. Mary Overie Dock, down Cathedral Street. See the west wall, with a rose window outline of Winchester House, the palace of the Bishops of Winchester until 1626, built into it, and take a tour of the little **Golden Hinde** ⑧ and the **Clink** ⑨ next door. Continue to the end of Clink Street onto Bankside, detouring left up Rose Alley, where in 1989 the remains of a famous Jacobean theater, the Rose Theatre, were unearthed, though because of office development surrounding the preserved foundations, there's not much to see. The next little alley is New Globe Walk, where there is much to see: the reconstruction of that most famous of Jacobean theaters, **Shakespeare's Globe** ⑩. Next along Bankside is the 17th-century Cardinal's Wharf, where, as a plaque explains, Wren lived while St. Paul's Cathedral was being built; then Bankside Power Station, which is to become the new Tate Gallery by the year 2000; and **Bankside Gallery** ⑪.

Now you reach your fourth bridge on this walk, Blackfriars Bridge, which you pass beneath to join the street called Upper Ground, spending some time in the Coin Street Community Builders' fast-emerging neighborhood, which features the **OXO Tower** ⑫ and Gabriel's Wharf, a marketplace of shops and cafés. Farther along Upper Ground, you reach the South Bank Centre, with the **Royal National Theatre** ⑬ first, followed by the **Museum of the Moving Image (MOMI)** ⑭, the **Royal Festival Hall** ⑮, and the **Hayward Gallery** ⑯. You'll find distractions all over this section of the walk, especially in summer—secondhand bookstalls, entertainers, and a series of plaques annotating the buildings opposite. When you've passed the South Bank Centre, look across the river for the quintessential postcard vista of the Houses of Parliament, which continues past Westminster Bridge to St. Thomas's Hospital. Jubilee Gardens has now been razed in preparation for the 500-ft Ferris wheel that's coming in 1999. Next, you reach the former County Hall, which is now the **London Aquarium** ⑰, and farther along the river, beyond the **Florence Nightingale Museum** ⑱, **Lambeth Palace** ⑲ stands by Lambeth Bridge, with the **Museum of Garden History** ⑳ in St. Mary's next door. Now if you take a detour to the right off Lambeth Road, you could be "doing the Lambeth Walk" down the street of the same name. A cockney tradition ever since the 17th century, when there was a spa here, the Sunday stroll was immortalized in a song from the 1937 musical *Me and My Girl*, which recently proved a hit all over again in the West End and on New York City's Broadway. A little farther east along Lambeth Road you reach the **Imperial War Museum** ㉑.

TIMING

On a fine day, this 2- to 3-mi walk makes a very scenic wander, since you're following the south bank of the great Thames nearly all the way. Fabulous views across to the north bank take you past St. Paul's and the Houses of Parliament, and you pass—under, over, or around—no fewer than seven bridges. It's bound to take far longer than a couple of hours because the sightseeing is heavy. The Imperial War Museum, MOMI, Shakespeare's Globe, the Hayward Gallery, the Design Museum, and the Aquarium are major events, needing much more than an hour apiece (depending on your interests), while the London Dungeon doesn't take long, unless you have kids in tow—which is why you'd go in at all. The other museums on this route—the Clink, Garden History, Old Operating Theatre, Florence Nightingale, the South Bank Centre foyers, and the Bankside Gallery—are compact enough to squeeze together en route to your main event. And that's the nicest thing to do with this walk: have tickets waiting at the end. The National Theatres, the NFT, or Shakespeare's Globe can all oblige, but remember the theaters stay dark on Sundays. Dinner or a riverside drink at the OXO

Tower Brasserie, the Gastrodrome restaurants, or the People's Palace is another idea for a big finish. Public transportation is thin on the ground here, so pick a day when you're feeling energetic; there are no short-cuts once you're under way.

HOW TO GET THERE

The tube stop to use is Waterloo on the Northern and Bakerloo lines, though you could also go to the Embankment stop (same lines, plus District and Circle) or Charing Cross (same, plus Northern), and walk across the Charing Cross pedestrian bridge. Buses that take you into the rather confusing territory behind the South Bank Centre include Nos. 1, 68, 76, 168, 171, 176, 178, and 188. For farther downstream, near Shakespeare's Globe, get the 21, 35, 40, 47, or 133 to Tooley Street, or get the tube to Blackfriars and walk across that bridge (offering a particularly scenic walk), or to Mansion House, and walk across Southwark Bridge. The latter is the best way to the OXO Tower.

Sights to See

⓫ Bankside Gallery. In this modern building, two artistic societies—the Royal Society of Painter-Printmakers and the Royal Watercolour Society—have their headquarters. Together they mount exhibitions of current members' work, usually for sale, alongside artists' materials and books. Next door is **Bankside Power Station,** which is to become the new Tate Gallery by the year 2000. ⊠ *48 Hopton St., SE1,* ☎ *0171/928–7521.* ☞ *£3.50.* ☉ *Tues.–Sat. 10–5, Sun. 1–5. Tube: Blackfriars, then walk across bridge.*

❶ Butler's Wharf. An '80s development that is maturing gracefully, this is full of deluxe loft-style warehouse conversions and swanky new blocks. People flock here thanks partly to London's saint of the stomach, Sir Terence Conran (also responsible for high-profile central London restaurants Bibendum, Mezzo, and Quaglino's). He has given it his "Gastrodrome" of four restaurants, a vintner's, a deli, a bakery, and who knows what else by now.

❾ The Clink. Originally the prison attached to Winchester House, palace of the Bishops of Winchester until 1626, "the clink" still serves as a general term for jail. One of five Southwark prisons, it was the first to detain women, most of whom were "Winchester Geese"—another euphemism meaning prostitutes, the bishops donated to the language. The oldest profession was endemic in Southwark, especially around the bishops' area of jurisdiction, known as "the Liberty of the Clink." Their graces' sensible solution was to license prostitution rather than ban it, but a Winchester goose who flouted the rules ended up, of course, in the Clink. Now there is a museum tracing the history of prostitution in "the Liberty" and showing what the Clink was like during its 16th-century prime. ⊠ *1 Clink St., SE1,* ☎ *0171/403–6515.* ☞ *£4.* ☉ *Daily 10–6. Tube: London Bridge.*

❷ Design Museum. The first museum in the world to elevate the everyday design we take for granted to the status of art exhibit, placing it in its social and cultural context, opened in 1989. On the top floor, the Collection traces the evolution of mass-produced goods, with showcases full of telephones and washing machines, plates and hi-fi equipment, computers and Coke bottles, and plenty of backup material, from ads to films. Alongside the Collection, the regularly revamped Review looks deeply into a particular aspect of the consumer durable. Special exhibitions are held downstairs on the first floor, and there's also a program of lectures and events, as well as the very good Blueprint Café, with its own river terrace. ⊠ *Butler's Wharf, SE1,* ☎ *0171/403–6933.* ☞ *£5.* ☉ *Daily 10:30–5:30. Tube: Tower Hill, then walk across river.*

The South Bank

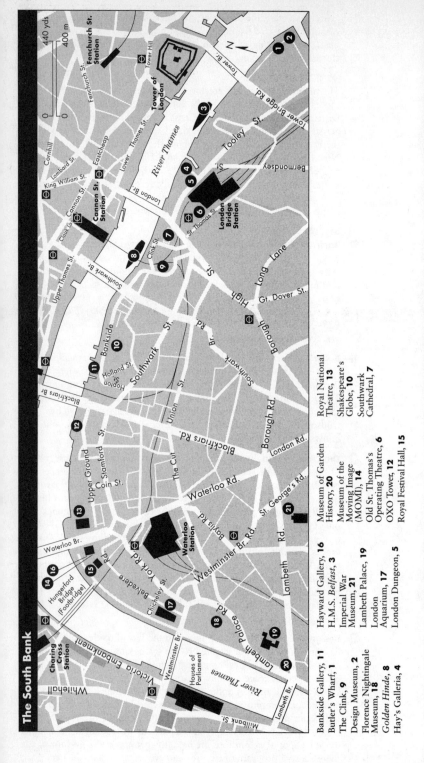

Bankside Gallery, **11**
Butler's Wharf, **1**
The Clink, **9**
Design Museum, **2**
Florence Nightingale
Museum, **18**
Golden Hinde, **8**
Hay's Galleria, **4**

Hayward Gallery, **16**
H.M.S. *Belfast,* **3**
Imperial War
Museum, **21**
Lambeth Palace, **19**
London
Aquarium, **17**
London Dungeon, **5**

Museum of Garden
History, **20**
Museum of the
Moving Image
(MOMI), **14**
Old St. Thomas's
Operating Theatre, **6**
OXO Tower, **12**
Royal Festival Hall, **15**

Royal National
Theatre, **13**
Shakespeare's
Globe, **10**
Southwark
Cathedral, **7**

OFF THE
BEATEN PATH

DULWICH PICTURE GALLERY – A really distinguished and lovable small gallery, the Dulwich has important works by Rembrandt, Van Dyck, Rubens, Poussin, and Gainsborough, among others. Anyone who fell in love with Sir John Soane's house (☞ Bloomsbury and Legal London, *above*) may wish to make the trek out here, since this gallery was designed by the same architect. If you do come all this way, you'll be happy to know that Dulwich Village is pleasant for wandering about, with its handsome 18th-century houses strung out along its main street. Most of the land around here belongs to the local, famous school, the Dulwich College Estate, founded during the early 17th century by the actor Edward Alleyn, and this keeps strict control of modern development. Opposite the Gallery, Dulwich Park is a well-kept municipal park with a particularly fine display of rhododendrons in late May. ⊠ *College Rd.*, ☎ *0181/693-8000.* ☜ *£3, free Fri.* ☉ *Tues.–Fri. 10–1 and 2–5, Sat. 11–5, Sun. 2–5. British Rail: Dulwich (from Victoria or London Bridge).*

⑱ Florence Nightingale Museum. Here you can learn all about the founder of the first school of nursing, that most famous of health-care reformers, "the Lady with the Lamp." See the reconstruction of the barracks ward at Scutari (Turkey), where she tended soldiers during the Crimean War (1854–56) and earned her nickname; here also is a Victorian East End slum cottage showing what she did to improve living conditions among the poor; and here is the Lamp. The museum is in **St. Thomas's Hospital,** which was built in 1868 to the specifications of Florence Nightingale. Most of it was bombed to bits in the Blitz then rebuilt to become one of London's teaching hospitals. ⊠ *2 Lambeth Palace Rd., SE1,* ☎ *0171/620-0374.* ☜ *£2.50.* ☉ *Tues.–Sun. 10–4. Tube: Waterloo, or Westminster and walk over bridge.*

⑧ Golden Hinde. Sir Francis Drake circumnavigated the globe in this little galleon, or one just like it. This exact replica has now finished *its* 23-year round-the-world voyage—much of it spent along U.S. coasts both Pacific and Atlantic—and has settled here to continue its educational purpose. ⊠ *St. Mary Overie Dock, Southwark, SE1,* ☎ *0171/403-0123.* ☜ *£2.30.* ☉ *Daily 10–5. Tube: Mansion House.*

④ Hay's Galleria. Hay's Wharf was built by Thomas Cubitt in 1857 on the spot where the port of London's oldest wharf had stood since 1651. It was known as "London's larder" on account of the edibles landed here until it wound down gradually, then closed in 1970. In 1987 it was reborn as this Covent Gardenesque parade of bars and restaurants, offices, and shops, all weatherproofed by an arched glass atrium roof supported by tall iron columns. The centerpiece is a fanciful kinetic sculpture by David Kemp, *The Navigators,* which looks like the skeleton of a pirate schooner crossed with a dragon and spouts water from various orifices. Inevitably, jugglers, string quartets, and crafts stalls abound. This courtyard hub of the developing London Bridge City needed all the help it could get in its early days, but it has settled in nicely now with its captive crowd of office workers from the adjacent new developments.

⑯ Hayward Gallery. This is one of the city's major art-exhibition spaces, its bias fixed firmly in this century. This stained and windowless bunker tucked behind the South Bank Centre concert halls has come in for the most flak of all the Thames-side buildings, enduring constant threats to flatten it and start again, but it's still here, topped by its multicolor neon tube sculpture, the most familiar feature on the South Bank skyline. ⊠ *South Bank Complex, SE1,* ☎ *0171/928-3144.* ☜ *Admission varies according to exhibition.* ☉ *Thurs.–Mon. 10–6, Tues.–Wed. 10–8. Tube: Waterloo.*

⟲ ❸ **HMS *Belfast*.** At 656 ft, this is one of the largest and most powerful cruisers the Royal Navy has ever had. It played a role in the D-day landings off Normandy, left for the Far East after the war, and has been becalmed here since 1971. On board there's an outpost of the Imperial War Museum, which tells the Royal Navy's story from 1914 to the present and shows you what life on board a World War II battleship was like, from mess decks and bakery to punishment cells, and from operations room to engine room and armaments. ✉ *Morgan's La., Tooley St., SE1,* ☎ *0171/407–6434.* 🎟 *£4.40.* ☉ *Mid-Mar.–Oct., daily 10–5:30; Nov.–mid-Mar., daily 10–4. Tube: London Bridge.*

OFF THE
BEATEN PATH

HORNIMAN MUSEUM – This educational museum of anthropology that manages to be fun, too, is set in 16 acres of gardens in south London with well-displayed ethnographic and natural history collections, a Music Gallery, and a colony of honey bees visibly at work in their glass-fronted hive. Other highlights are the aquarium stocked with endangered species and the new educationally oriented Centre for Understanding the Environment. ✉ *100 London Rd., Forest Hill,* ☎ *0181/699–1872 or 0181/699–2339.* 🎟 *Free.* ☉ *Mon.–Sat. 10:30–6, Sun. 2–6. British Rail: Forest Hill.*

㉑ **Imperial War Museum.** Despite its title, this museum of 20th-century warfare does not glorify bloodshed but attempts to evoke what it was like to live through the two world wars. Of course, there is hardware for martial-minded children—a Battle of Britain Spitfire, a German V2 rocket, tanks, guns, submarines—but there is an equal amount of war art (David Bomberg, Henry Moore, John Singer Sargent, Graham Sutherland, to name a few), poetry, photography, and documentary film footage. One very affecting exhibit is *The Blitz Experience*, which is what it sounds like—a 10-minute taste of an air raid in a street of acrid smoke with sirens blaring and searchlights glaring. More recent wars attended by British forces are thoughtfully commemorated, too, right up to the Gulf War of 1991.

The museum is housed in an elegant domed and colonnaded building, erected during the early 19th century to house the Bethlehem Hospital for the Insane, better known as the infamous Bedlam. By 1816, when the patients were moved here, they were no longer kept in cages to be taunted by tourists (see the final scene of Hogarth's *Rake's Progress* at Sir John Soane's Museum [☞ Bloomsbury and Legal London, *above*] for some sense of how horrific it was), since reformers—and George III's madness—had effected more humane standards of confinement. Bedlam moved to Surrey in 1930.

✉ *Lambeth Rd., SE1,* ☎ *0171/416–5000.* 🎟 *£4.70.* ☉ *Daily 10–6. Tube: Lambeth North.*

⓳ **Lambeth Palace.** This has, for 800 years, been the London base of the Archbishop of Canterbury, top man in the Church of England. Much of the palace is hidden behind great walls, and even the Tudor gatehouse, visible from the street, is closed to the public, but you can stand here and absorb the historical vibrations echoing from such momentous events as the 1381 storming of the palace during the Peasants' Revolt against the poll tax (a modern version of which Thatcher recently reinstated, whereupon riots ensued, and the tax was sheepishly repealed) and the 1534 clash of wills when Thomas More refused to sign the Oath of Supremacy claiming Henry VIII (and not the pope) as leader of the English Church, for which he was sent to the Tower and executed for treason the following year. Adjacent to this house is the Museum of Garden History (☞ *below*). ✉ *Lambeth Palace Rd., SE1. Tube: Waterloo.*

⑰ London Aquarium. Until recently, County Hall was the name of this curved, colonnaded neoclassic hulk, which, with the interference of two world wars, took 46 years (1912–1958) to build. It was home to London's local government, the Greater London Council (GLC), which mutated out of the London County Council in 1965, and disbanded in 1986. Now, after a £25 million injection, a three-level aquarium (full of incongruous sharks and stingrays) has been installed; there are also educational exhibits and piscine sights previously unseen on these shores. It is not the biggest aquarium you've ever seen—especially if you've been to SeaWorld—but the exhibit is arranged on several subterranean levels, with areas for different oceans and water environments. The rain forest is a highlight—it's almost like the real thing. Between here and the South Bank Centre is the former **Jubilee Gardens,** which is the site of the millennium Ferris wheel to be installed next year. Even without the 500-ft rotating elevation, views of the Houses of Parliament and Westminster Bridge are fine from here. ⊠ *County Hall, Riverside Building, Westminster Bridge Rd., SE1,* ☎ *0171/967–8000.* ⊡ *£6.50.* ☉ *Sept.–May, daily 10–6; June–Aug., daily 9:30 AM–7:30 PM. Tube: Westminster*

☝ ➎ The London Dungeon. Here's the most gory, grisly, gruesome museum in town, where realistic waxwork people are subjected in graphic detail to all the historical horrors the Tower of London merely suggests. Tableaux depict famous bloody moments—like Anne Boleyn's decapitation, or the martyrdom of St. George—alongside the torture, murder, and ritual slaughter of more anonymous victims, all to a soundtrack of screaming, wailing, and agonized moaning. London's times of deepest terror—the Great Fire and the Great Plague—are brought to life, too, and so are its public hangings. And did you ever wonder what a disembowelment actually looks like? See it here. Naturally, children absolutely adore this place, which is among London's top tourist attractions; expect long lines. ⊠ *28–34 Tooley St., SE1,* ☎ *0171/403–0606.* ⊡ *£8.95.* ☉ *Apr.–Sept., daily 10–5:30; Oct.–Mar., daily 10–4:30. Tube: London Bridge.*

⑳ Museum of Garden History. Housed in St. Mary's Church, next to Lambeth Palace, this museum was founded in 1977 (when the church was deconsecrated), by the Tradescant Trust. The Trust is named after John Tradescant (circa 1575–1638), botanist extraordinaire, who brought to these shores the lilac, larch, jasmine, and spiderwort, named Tradescantia in his honor. In the nave are changing horticultural exhibitions, supplemented by a reconstructed—or regrown—17th-century knot garden. Tradescant's tomb in the graveyard is carved with scenes from his worldwide plant-discovery tours and surrounded with the plants he discovered. Near it, William Bligh, captain of the *Bounty,* is buried, which suits the theme—the *Bounty* was on a breadfruit-gathering mission in 1787 when the crew mutinied. ⊠ *Lambeth Palace Rd., SE1,* ☎ *0171/261–1891.* ⊡ *Donations welcome.* ☉ *Weekdays 11–3, Sun. 10:30–5. Closed mid–Dec.–early Mar. Tube: Waterloo.*

☝ ⑭ Museum of the Moving Image (MOMI). MOMI may be the most fun of all London's museums, and many will linger for a couple of hours minimum. This popular attraction is attached to the **National Film Theatre** (or NFT), underneath Waterloo Bridge, whose two movie theaters boast easily the best repertory programming in London, favoring obscure, foreign, silent, forgotten, classic, noir, and short films over blockbusters. There's a third theater in MOMI, but if you reckon you'll just have a quick look around before you catch a movie here, think again. The main feature is a history of cinema from 4,000-year-old Javanese shadow puppets to Spielbergian special effects, and very good the displays are, too, but the supporting program is even better, and it stars *you*. Actors dressed as John Wayne or Mae West or usherettes or chorus girls pluck you out of obscurity to read the TV news or audition for the chorus line or fly like Superman over the Thames. They also perform, mime, improvise, and generally bring celluloid to life, while all around, various screens show clips from such epoch-making giants as Hitchcock and Eisenstein, plus newsreels and ads. Techies can learn focus-pulling and satellite beaming; artists can try animation; eggheads can explore such ethical issues as censorship and documentary objectivity. Needless to say, this is always a big hit with kids. The White Card is accepted. ⊠ *South Bank Centre, SE1,* ☎ *0171/401–2636.* ▥ *£6.25.* ☉ *Daily 10–6, last admission at 5. Tube: Waterloo.*

NEED A BREAK?	The **NFT restaurant and cafeteria**—especially the big wooden tables outside—are popular for lunch or supper. You don't have to buy a membership.

❻ Old St. Thomas's Operating Theatre. All that remains of one of England's oldest hospitals, which stood here from the 12th century until the railway forced it to move in 1862, this was where women went under the knife. The theater was bricked up and forgotten for a century but has now been restored into an exhibition of early 19th-century medical practices: the operating table onto which the gagged and blindfolded patients were roped, the box of sawdust underneath for catching their blood, the knives, pliers, and handsaws the surgeons wielded, and—this was a theater in the round—the spectators' seats. Next door is a sweeter show: the **Herb Garret,** with displays of medicinal herbs used during the same period. ⊠ *9A St. Thomas St., SE1,* ☎ *0171/955–4791.* ▥ *£2.50.* ☉ *Tues.–Sun. 10–4. Closed Dec. 15–Jan. 5. Tube: London Bridge.*

⓬ OXO Tower. This might very well turn out to be the 21st-century version of Big Ben—a wonderful Art Deco tower, filled with designers' workshops overlooking the Thames. Long a London landmark to the cognoscenti, the OXO has graduated from its former incarnations as a power-generating station and warehouse into a vibrant community of artists' and designers' workshops, a pair of restaurants and cafés, as well as five floors of the best low-income housing in the city, via a £20 million plan by Coin Street Community Builders. There's a rooftop viewing gallery for the latest river vista in town, and a performance area on the first floor, which comes alive all summer long—as does the entire surrounding neighborhood. All the designers/makers have been selected by totally non-democratic methods, meaning the work is of incredibly high standard. They all rely on you to disturb them any time they're open. Don't be shy—they really mean it; visitors are most welcome, whether buying, commissioning, or just browsing. The biggest draw remains the OXO Tower Restaurant extravaganza (☞ Chapter 3). ⊠ *Bargehouse St., SE1,* ☎ *0171/401–3610.* ▥ *Free.* ☉ *Studios and shops Tues.–Sun. 11–6. Tube: Blackfriars or Waterloo.*

⓯ Royal Festival Hall. This is the largest auditorium of the South Bank Centre, with superb acoustics and a 3,000-plus capacity. It is the oldest of the riverside blocks, raised as the centerpiece of the 1951 Festival of Britain, a postwar morale-boosting exercise. The London Philharmonic resides here, symphony orchestras from the world over like to visit, and choral works, ballet, serious jazz and pop, and even film with live accompaniment are also staged. There is a multiplicity of foyers, with free rotating exhibitions, a good, independently run restaurant, the People's Palace, and a very good bookstore. The next building you come to also contains concert halls, one medium and one small, the **Queen Elizabeth Hall** and the **Purcell Room,** respectively. Both offer

BONUS MILES MAKE GREAT SOUVENIRS.

Earn Miles With Your MCI Card.

Take the MCI Card along on this trip and start earning miles for the next one. You'll earn frequent flyer miles on all your calls and save with the low rates you've come to expect from MCI. Before you know it, you'll be on your way to some other international destination.

Sign up for MCI by calling 1-800-FLY-FREE

Earn Frequent Flyer Miles.

Is this a great time, or what? :-)

Easy To Call Home.

1. To use your MCI Card, just dial the WorldPhone access number of the country you're calling from.
2. Dial or give the operator your MCI Card number.
3. Dial or give the number you're calling.

# Austria (CC) ♦	022-903-012
# Belarus (CC)	
From Brest, Vitebsk, Grodno, Minsk	8-800-103
From Gomel and Mogilev regions	8-10-800-103
# Belgium (CC) ♦	0800-10012
# Bulgaria	00800-0001
# Croatia (CC) ★	0800-22-0112
# Czech Republic (CC) ♦	00-42-000112
# Denmark (CC) ♦	8001-0022
# Finland (CC) ♦	08001-102-80
# France (CC) ♦	0-800-99-0019
# Germany (CC)	0800-888-8000
# Greece (CC) ♦	00-800-1211
# Hungary (CC) ♦	00▼800-01411
# Iceland (CC) ♦	800-9002
# Ireland (CC)	1-800-55-1001
# Italy (CC) ♦	172-1022
# Kazakhstan (CC)	8-800-131-4321
# Liechtenstein (CC) ♦	0800-89-0222
# Luxembourg	0800-0112
# Monaco (CC) ♦	800-90-019
# Netherlands (CC) ♦	0800-022-9122
# Norway (CC) ♦	800-19912
# Poland (CC) ÷	00-800-111-21-22
# Portugal (CC) ÷	05-017-1234
Romania (CC) ÷	01-800-1800
# Russia (CC) ÷ ♦	
To call using ROSTELCOM ■	747-3322
For a Russian-speaking operator	747-3320
To call using SOVINTEL ■	960-2222
# San Marino (CC) ♦	172-1022
# Slovak Republic (CC)	00-421-00112
# Slovenia	080-8808
# Spain (CC)	900-99-0014
# Sweden (CC) ♦	020-795-922
# Switzerland (CC) ♦	0800-89-0222
# Turkey (CC) ♦	00-8001-1177
# Ukraine (CC) ÷	8▼10-013
# United Kingdom (CC)	
To call using BT ■	0800-89-0222
To call using C&W ■	0500-89-0222
# Vatican City (CC)	172-1022

CHASE

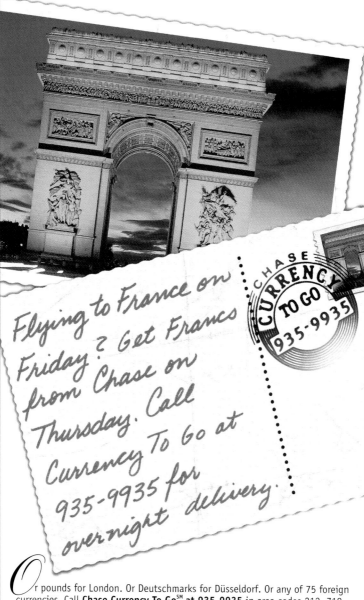

Flying to France on Friday? Get Francs from Chase on Thursday. Call Currency To Go at 935-9935 for overnight delivery.

CHASE CURRENCY TO GO 935-9935

$\mathcal{O}$r pounds for London. Or Deutschmarks for Düsseldorf. Or any of 75 foreign currencies. Call **Chase Currency To Go**℠ **at 935-9935** in area codes 212, 718, 914, 516 and Rochester, N.Y.; all other area codes call 1-800-935-9935. We'll deliver directly to your door.* Overnight. And there are no exchange fees. Let Chase make your trip an easier one.

CHASE. The right relationship is everything.℠

predominantly classical recitals of international caliber, with due respect paid to 20th-century composers and the more established jazz and vocal artists.

⓭ Royal National Theatre. When it opened in 1976, Londoners generally felt the same way about this low-slung, multilayered block the color of heavy storm clouds, designed by Sir Denys Lasdun, that they would feel a decade later about the far nastier Barbican (☞ The City, *above*). But whatever its merits or demerits as a landscape feature (and architects have subsequently given it an overall thumbs-up, while rejecting the derogatory-sounding term "brutalist"), the Royal National Theatre—still abbreviated colloquially to the preroyal warrant "NT"—has wonderful insides.

There are three auditoriums in the complex. The biggest one, the **Olivier,** is named after Sir Laurence, chairman of the first building commission and first artistic director of the National Theatre Company, formed in 1962. (In between the first proposal of a national theater for Britain and the 1949 formation of that building commission, an entire century passed.) The **Lyttleton** theater, unlike the Olivier, has a traditional proscenium arch, while the little **Cottesloe** mounts studio productions and new work in the round. Interspersed with the theaters are various levels of the foyer, where exhibitions are shown, bars and restaurants are frequented, and free entertainment is provided, and the whole place is lively six days a week. The Royal National Theatre Company does not rest on its laurels. It attracts many of the nation's top actors (Anthony Hopkins, for one, does time here) in addition to launching future stars. Because it is a repertory company, you'll have several plays to choose from even if your London sojourn is short, but, tickets or not, wander around and catch the buzz. ⊠ *South Bank, SE1,* ☎ *0171/ 928–2252 box office.* 🎫 *Tour £3.50.* ☺ *1-hr tour of theater backstage Mon.–Sat. at 10:15, 12:30, and 5:30; foyer Mon.–Sat. 10 AM–11 PM. Tube: Waterloo.*

★ ⓾ Shakespeare's Globe. Three decades ago, Sam Wanamaker—then an aspiring actor—pulled up in Southwark in a cab and was amazed to find that the fabled Shakespeare's fabled Globe Theatre didn't actually exist. Worse: a tiny plaque was the only sign on the former site of the world's most legendary theater. So appalled was he that London lacked a center for the study and worship of the Bard of Bards, Wanamaker worked ceaselessly, until his death in 1993, to raise funds for his dream—a full-scale reconstruction of the theater. The dream was realized in 1996 when an exact replica of Shakespeare's open-roof Globe Playhouse (built in 1599; incinerated in 1613) was created, using authentic Elizabethan materials and craft techniques—green oak timbers joined only with wooden pegs and mortise and tenon joints; plaster made of lime, sand, and goat's hair; and the first thatched roof in London since the Great Fire. In addition, a second, indoor theater is now being built to a design of the 17th-century architect Inigo Jones. The whole complex stands 200 yards from the original Globe on the appropriate site of the 17th-century Davies Amphitheatre, admittedly more a bullbaiting, prizefighting sort of venue than a temple to the legitimate stage, but at least Samuel Pepys immortalized it in his diaries.

The Globe is a celebration of the great Bard's life (1564–1616) and work, an actual rebirth of his "Great Wooden O" (see *Henry V*), where his plays are presented in natural light (and sometimes rain) to 1,000 people on wooden benches in the "bays," plus 500 "groundlings," who stand on a carpet of filbert shells and clinker, just as they did nearly four centuries ago. For any theater buff, this stunning project is unmissable. Although the open-air Globe Theatre is only open for per-

SHAKESPEARE LIVES!

REBIRTH OF THE GLOBE THEATRE

AS IT IS SAID ABOUT THE ONE true church, Britain's theater is also founded on a rock—the enduring Shakespeare. Stratford-upon-Avon remains the primary shrine, but 1997 has welcomed the opening of the cathedral—London's new Globe Theatre. More than three centuries ago, the Puritans closed the first "Wooden O," for which venue Shakespeare wrote *Hamlet, King Lear,* and *Julius Caesar,* among other peerless dramas. Now, 350 years later, the most famous playhouse in the world has been lovingly re-created, down to its Norfolk-reed roof. The theater has been reconstructed just 200 yards from its original site—ground as holy to Shakespeare's followers as Bayreuth's is to Wagner-philes.

For sheer drama—literally—few things can top the memorable jolt of walking into the new Globe. Enter, and some Wellsian genie transports you back to Elizabethan England. Step past the entrance into a soaring 45-ft-high arena, made surprisingly intimate by three half-timber galleries picturesquely encircling the stage. Ahead of you is the "pit," or orchestra level, filling up with 500 standees—"groundlings," to use the historic term—massed in front of the high stage. Soaring overhead is a twin-gabled stage canopy—the "heavens"—framed by exquisitely painted trompe l'oeil marble columns and a "lords' gallery," all fretted with gilded bosses, painted planets, and celestial bodies. Above you is the lowering London sky, which may at any time provide an authentic mid-performance drenching!

Of course, the new Globe is not a perfect time capsule. Occasionally, Juliet's wherefores will have to compete with the roar of jets. Ladies no longer proffer oranges or stools, and yesteryear's magpie hats have been superseded by Ray-Bans and baseball caps. Some ground rules have also changed. Most performances begin in the afternoon and, while floodlighting will be used to illuminate the theater at dusk, there will be no spotlights to focus the action on stage. The audience, on view at all times, becomes as much a part of the theatrical proceedings as the actors. Elizabethans made theatergoing almost as blood-and-thunder an experience as a football match of today. You've heard of the Super Bowl: view this as the Shakespeare Bowl—go ahead and boo Iago or hiss at Macbeth; you'll have plenty of company.

THE GLOBE THEATRE is but one facet of the entire complex, which, when completed in 1999, will include the 300-seat Inigo Jones indoor theater (to be used year-round, unlike the open-air Globe, which will be open only from June to September), a restaurant, an education center (with wonderful classes and lectures year-round), a library and shop, and the largest Shakespearean exhibition in the world. The plan is to present four plays each season. Happily, even when the Globe is not open for performances, a guided tour will always include its interior—a perfect opportunity to try out your "Friends, Romans, Countrymen!"

formances during the summer season, it can be viewed year-round if you take the helpful tour provided by the Shakespeare's Globe Exhibition Centre, an adjacent museum that provides fascinating background material on both the Elizabethan theater and the actual construction of the new Globe. Kids and theater lovers can purchase one of the bricks in the ongoing construction in their name—the certificate might make a great show-and-tell back home! For further information, *see* the Close-Up box, "Shakespeare Lives!" ⊠ *New Globe Walk, Bankside, SE1,* ☎ *0171/928–6406,* ⅎ⅏ *0171/401–8261.* ☞ *Exhibition £5.* ☉ *Daily 10–5; call for performance schedule. Tube: Mansion House, then walk across Southwark Bridge; or Blackfriars, then walk across Blackfriars Bridge.*

❼ **Southwark Cathedral.** Pronounced *Suth*-uck, this is the second-oldest Gothic church in London, after Westminster Abbey, with parts dating from the 12th century. Although it houses some remarkable memorials, not to mention a program of lunchtime concerts, it is little visited. It was promoted to cathedral status only in 1905, before that having been the priory church of **St. Mary Overie** (as in "over the water"— on the South Bank). Look for the gaudily renovated 1408 tomb of the poet John Gower, friend of Chaucer, and for the Harvard Chapel. Another notable buried here is Edmund Shakespeare, brother of William.

CHELSEA AND BELGRAVIA

Chelsea is where J. M. W. Turner painted his sunsets, John Singer Sargent his society portraits, where Oscar Wilde wrote *The Importance of Being Earnest*, and where Mary Quant cut her first miniskirt. Today, Chelsea is a neighborhood as handsome as its real estate is costly. Strolling its streets you will often notice gigantic windows adorning otherwise ordinary houses. They are remnants of Chelsea's 19th-century bohemian days, when they served to bring light into artists' studios; now they are mostly used to hike property values a few notches higher. This is the place—especially King's Road—that gave birth to Swinging '60s London, then to '70s punk youth culture. The '90s version of this colorful thoroughfare is not really the center of anything, but it's hard not to like walking it.

Chelsea's next-door neighborhood is aristocratic Belgravia, with King's Road and Knightsbridge its southern and northern borders, Sloane Street and Grosvenor Place its western and eastern ones, and vast Belgrave Square, home to many embassies, in the middle. Diagonally across the square, Belgrave Place will lead past grand mansions (all painted Wedgwood-white to denote that they, as every other house in this district, are the property of England's richest landowners, the Dukes of Westminster) through to Eaton Square, the aptly chosen locale for the TV series *Upstairs, Downstairs*. It is no accident that this whole neighborhood of wealth and splendor is grouped around the back of Buckingham Palace—many titled peers wished to live adjacent to the Court. Belgravia is relatively young: It was built between the 1820s and the 1850s by the builder-developer-entrepreneur Thomas Cubitt (who had as great an influence on the look of London in his day as Wren and Nash had in theirs), under the patronage of Lord Grosvenor, and was intended to rival Mayfair for spectacular snob value and expense. Today it still does.

Numbers in the text correspond to numbers in the margin and on the Chelsea and Belgravia map.

A Good Walk

Start at **Cheyne Walk** ①, stretching in both directions from Albert Bridge, going all the way west to see the statue of Thomas More, then doubling back for a left turn into Cheyne Row to reach **Carlyle's House** ②. Where the east end of Cheyne Walk runs into Royal Hospital Road, you'll find the **Chelsea Physic Garden** ③, while a right after the garden on Royal Hospital Road brings you to the **National Army Museum** ④. Royal Hospital Road takes its name from the institution next door to the museum, the magnificent **Royal Hospital** ⑤. A left turn from here up Franklin's Row and Cheltenham Terrace brings you to famous **King's Road** ⑥, which you could follow east until you reach the beginning of Belgravia: Sloane Square, named after Sir Hans Sloane, whose collection founded the British Museum (☞ Bloomsbury and Legal London, *above*), and who bought the manor of Chelsea in 1712. Cross the square more or less in a straight line, and follow Cliveden Place for a taste of Belgravia. The grand, white-stucco houses have changed not at all since the mid-19th century, and Eaton Square, which you'll soon come upon, remains such a desirable address that the rare event of one of its houses coming on the market makes all the property pages. Its most famous residents were fictional, of course, as the enduringly popular period soap, *Upstairs, Downstairs* was set here. A left turn on **Belgrave Place** ⑦ brings you to Belgrave Square, dense with embassies, but the best thing to do around here is follow your nose. Other than Palladian-perfect mansions, chic alleys, and magnificent Georgian squares—in addition to Belgrave and Eaton, the smaller Lowndes, Cadogan, Trevor, Brompton, and Montpelier—there are no particular Belgravia sights. After taking in Belgrave Place and the picturesque mews next to Eaton Place, however, you might continue eastward on Belgrave Place, walk south several blocks on Eaton Place and head for the lovely warren of streets and alleys around Chester Row and Minerva Mews.

TIMING

This may read like a short hop, but the walk above covers a good 2 to 3 mi. If you explore side streets, you could double the figure—and if you don't explore side streets, you'll be missing the best aspect of these neighborhoods, which are primarily, expensively, residential. The sights along the way will probably detain you less than the shops; even though King's Road isn't what it used to be, it's still fruitful. In summer you'll want to spend time in the Physic Garden or around the Royal Hospital, so make sure you're heading out on one of the opening days. If you're dead set on the Physic Garden, that means Wednesday or Sunday afternoon from April to October.

HOW TO GET THERE

Chelsea is notoriously ill served by tube stops. The best, and really the only, way into the area is to get the District and Circle lines to Sloane Square, then strike out by foot along King's Road. Or catch a bus—Nos. 11, 19, 22, 137, or 211. Farther down toward the river, around World's End and Fulham, the 19, 49, 239, 249, 319, and 345 are the buses to look for. The edge of Belgravia farthest from Chelsea is accessible from Hyde Park Corner on the Piccadilly Line. Nos. 2, 8, 9, 10, 14, 16, 19, 22, 36, 38, 52, 73, 74, 82, and 137 buses also stop there. Choose a bus that appears on both lists for travel between the two neighborhoods.

Sights to See

❼ **Belgrave Place.** One of the main arteries of Belgravia—London's swankiest neighborhood—Belgrave Place is lined with grand, imposing Regency-era mansions (now mostly embassies). Walk down this street toward Eaton Place to pass two of Belgravia's most beautiful mews—Eaton Mews North and Eccleston Mews, both fronted by grand Westminster-white rusticated entrances right out of a 19th-century engraving:

Chelsea and Belgravia

Belgrave Place, **7**
Carlyle's House, **2**
Chelsea Physic
Garden, **3**
Cheyne Walk, **1**
King's Road, **6**
National Army
Museum, **4**
Royal Hospital, **5**

There are few other places where London is both so picturesque and elegant.

② **Carlyle's House.** Carlyle's house was a thriving salon of 19th-century authors attracted by the fame of Thomas Carlyle (1795–1881), who wrote a blockbuster, an all-but-since-forgotten history of the French Revolution, and founded the London Library, and by the wit of his wife, the poet Jane Carlyle. Dickens, Thackeray, Tennyson, and Browning were regular visitors, and you can see the second-floor drawing room where they met just as they saw it, complete with leather armchair, decoupage screen, fireplace, and oil lamps, all in ruddy Victorian hues. ⊠ *24 Cheyne Row, SW3,* ☎ *0171/352–7087.* ☞ *£3.* ۞ *Apr.–Oct., Wed.–Sun. 11–5 (last admission 4:30). Tube: Sloane Sq., then walk down King's Rd., or take Bus 11, 19, 22, 49, 219, or 249.*

③ **Chelsea Physic Garden.** First planted by the Society of Apothecaries in 1673 for the study of medicinal plants, these gardens are still in use for the same purpose today. The herbs and shrubs and flowers, planted to a strict plan but tumbling rurally over the paths nevertheless, are interspersed with woodland areas, England's first rock garden, and ancient trees, some of which were tragically uprooted in a 1987 hurricane. In the middle stands a statue of Sir Hans Sloane, physician to Queen Anne and George II, whose collection formed the basis of the British Museum, and who saved the garden from closing in 1722, making sure nobody would ever be allowed to build over it. ⊠ *Swan Walk, 66 Royal Hospital Rd., SW3,* ☎ *0171/352–5646.* ☞ *£3.50.* ۞ *Apr.–Oct., Sun. and Wed. 2–5; daily noon–5 during Chelsea Flower Show (3rd wk of May). Tube: Sloane Sq., then walk down King's Rd., or take Bus 11, 19, 22, 49, 219, or 249.*

★ ① **Cheyne Walk.** Rhyming with "rainy," this street features some beautiful Queen Anne houses (particularly Norman Shaw's ornamental 1876 Cheyne House, to the right off Albert Bridge) and a storm of Blue Plaques marking famous ex-residents' abodes. George Eliot died at No. 4 in 1880; Dante Gabriel Rossetti annoyed the neighbors of No. 16 with his peacock collection (there's still a clause in the lease banning the birds); at Carlyle Mansions (after the King's Head and Eight Bells pub), Henry James died, and T. S. Eliot and Ian Fleming lived. The western reaches were painters' territory, most notably of James McNeill Whistler, who lived at No. 96 and then No. 101, and J. M. W. Turner, who used No. 119 as a retreat, shielding his identity behind the name Admiral "Puggy" Booth. Also toward the western end, outside the Church of All Saints, is a golden-faced statue of **Thomas More** (who wouldn't sign the Oath of Supremacy at Lambeth Palace in 1534 and was executed as a traitor), looking pensive and beatific on a throne facing the river, in a 1969 addition to the Walk.

⑥ **King's Road.** This was where the miniskirt strutted its stuff in the '60s and where Vivienne Westwood and Malcolm McLaren clothed the Sex Pistols in bondage trousers from their shop, Sex, in 1975, thus spawning punk rock. Westwood, one of Britain's most innovative fashion stars, still has her shop at No. 430, where the road, fittingly, kinks. Both boutique and neighborhood are called **World's End,** possibly because Chelsea-ites believe that's what it does here. The Fulham district begins around this stretch, full of yuppie singles, and ever more shopping opportunities. The other end of King's Road, leading into Sloane Square, has various fashion stores (no longer style-setters, on the whole) and some rather good antiques shops and markets along the way. The **Pheasantry,** at No. 152, is recognizable by some over-the-top Grecian statuary in a fancy portico. Named in its mid-19th-century pheasant-breeding days, it had a phase from 1916 to 1934 as a ballet school where Margot Fonteyn and Alicia Markova learned first position. Now it's a club-restaurant haunted by the braying breed of Chelsea yuppie dubbed "Sloane Rangers" by '80s style-watchers. The Peter Jones department store marks the exit from the north of Chelsea and the beginning of Belgravia: Sloane Square.

❹ **National Army Museum.** This museum covers the history of British land forces from the Yeoman of the Guard (the first professional army, founded 1485 and ancestors of the Tower's Beefeaters) to the present. It is best explained in its current exhibit, entitled *The Rise of the Redcoat,* which takes you from Henry V (1413–1422) all the way to George III (1760–1820). A great deal of effort is made to convey the experience of those who lived through the wars, and a visit should enhance anyone's grasp of London's history and its personages. ⊠ *Royal Hospital Rd., SW3,* ☎ *0171/730–0717.* 🖃 *Free.* ☉ *Mon.–Sat. 10– 5:30, Sun. 2–5:30. Tube: Sloane Sq.*

❺ **Royal Hospital.** The hospice for elderly and infirm soldiers was founded by Charles II in 1682—some say after a badgering from his softhearted, high-profile mistress, Nell Gwyn, but more probably as an act of expedience. His troops had hitherto enjoyed not so much as a meager pension and were growing restive after the civil wars of 1642–46 and 1648. Charles wisely appointed the great architect of burned-out City churches, Sir Christopher Wren, to design this small village of redbrick and Portland stone, set in manicured gardens (which you can visit) surrounding the "Figure Court" —named after the 1692 bronze figure of Charles II dressed up as a Roman soldier—and the Great Hall (dining room) and chapel. The latter is enhanced by the choir stalls of Grinling Gibbons (who did the bronze of Charles, too), the former by a vast oil of Charles on horseback by Antonio Verrio, and both are open to inspection.

No doubt you will run into some of the 400-odd residents. Despite their advancing years, these "Chelsea Pensioners" are no shrinking violets. In summer and for special occasions they sport dandy scarlet frock coats with gold buttons, medals, and natty tricorne hats, and, being of proven good character (a condition of entry, along with old age and loyal service), might offer to show you around—in which case you may wish to supplement their daily beer and tobacco allowance with a tip.

May is the big month at the Royal Hospital. The 29th is Oak Apple Day, when the pensioners celebrate Charles II's birthday by draping oak leaves on his statue and parading around it in memory of a hollow oak tree that expedited the king's miraculous escape from the 1651 Battle of Worcester. In the same month, the Chelsea Flower Show, the year's highlight for thousands of garden-obsessed Brits, is also held here. ⊠ *Royal Hospital Rd., SW3,* ☎ *0171/730–0161.* 🖃 *Free.* ☉ *Apr.– Sept., Mon.–Sat. 10–noon and 2–4, Sun. 2–4; Oct.–Mar., Mon.–Sat. 10–noon and 2–4. Tube: Sloane Sq.*

KNIGHTSBRIDGE, KENSINGTON, AND HOLLAND PARK

Even in these supposedly democratic days, you still sometimes hear people say that the *only* place to live in London is in the grand residential area of the Royal Borough of Kensington. True, the district is an endless cavalcade of streets lined with splendid houses redolent of stuccoed wealth and pillared porches, but there are other fetching attractions here—some of the most fascinating museums in London, stylish squares, elegant antiques shops, and Kensington Palace, the home of Diana,

Princess of Wales, until her death, and Queen Victoria when she was a girl—which put the district literally on the map. South and west of this historic edifice, you'll find the stamping grounds of the Sloane Rangers—a quintessentially London type of gilded youth whose upper-class accents make English sound like a foreign language. They tend to haunt salubrious Knightsbridge, east of Belgravia and north of Chelsea, offering as it does about equal doses of elite residential streets and ultra-shopping opportunities. To *its* east is one of the highest concentrations of important artifacts anywhere, the Museum Mile of South Kensington, with the rest of Kensington offering peaceful strolls and a noisy main street. The Holland Park neighborhood is worth visiting for its big, fancy, tree-shaded houses and its exquisite and unexpected park.

Kensington first became the *Royal* Borough of Kensington (and Chelsea) by virtue of a king's asthma. William III, who suffered terribly from the Thames mists over Whitehall, decided in 1689 to buy Nottingham House in the rural village of Kensington so that he could breathe more easily; besides, his wife and co-monarch, Mary II, felt confined by water and wall at Whitehall. Courtiers and functionaries and society folk soon followed where the crowns led, and by the time Queen Anne was on the throne (1702–14), Kensington was overflowing. In a way, it still is, because most of its grand houses, and the Victorian ones of Holland Park, have been divided into apartments, or else are serving as foreign embassies.

Numbers in the text correspond to numbers in the margin and on the Knightsbridge, Kensington, and Holland Park map.

A Good Walk

This is an all-weather walk—museums and shops for rainy days, grass and strolls for sunshine. When you surface from the Knightsbridge tube station—one of London's deepest—you are immediately engulfed by the manic drivers, professional shoppers, and ladies-who-lunch who make up the local population. If you're in a shopping mood, start with Harvey Nichols—right at the tube—and its six floors of total fashion. Sloane Street, leading south, is strung with the boutiques of big-name European designers, while **Harrods** ① is found to the west down Brompton Road—then continue west down this road, pausing at Beauchamp (pronounced *Bee*-chum) Place and Walton Street if shopping is your intention. Presently, at the junction of Brompton and Cromwell roads, you'll come to the pale, Italianate **Brompton Oratory** ②, which marks the beginning of museum territory, with the **Victoria and Albert Museum** ③ first, at the start of Cromwell Road, the **Natural History Museum** ④ next, and the **Science Museum** ⑤ behind it. (The neighborhood's three large museums, incidentally, can also be reached via a long underground passage from the South Kensington tube.) Turn left to continue north up Exhibition Road, a kind of unfinished cultural main drag that was Prince Albert's conception (the **National Sound Archive** ⑥ is here, among others), toward the road after which British moviemakers named their fake blood, Kensington Gore, to reach the giant, round Wedgwood china–box of the **Royal Albert Hall** ⑦, the scaffolding-shrouded **Albert Memorial** ⑧ opposite, and the **Royal College of Art** ⑨ next door.

Now follow **Kensington Gardens** (which is what this western neighbor of Hyde Park is called) west to its end, and a little farther, perhaps detouring into the park to see **Kensington Palace** ⑩ and, behind it, one of London's rare, private "Millionaires' Row" sanctuaries, **Kensington Palace Gardens** ⑪. Turn off Kensington High Street down little Derry Street, with the offices of London's local paper, the *Evening Standard,* on the left, and what was once Derry and Tom's department store—

it closed down in the '70s—on the right. (The best feature of the store was its magical roof garden, complete with palm trees, ponds, and flamingos; it's still there, now part of a nightclub owned by Richard Branson, the high-profile London figure also responsible for the Virgin Megastores, Virgin Atlantic Airways, etc.) Take a turn around peaceful **Kensington Square** ⑫, then, returning to High Street, either follow Kensington Church Street up to Notting Hill Gate—with the little 1870 St. Mary Abbots Church on its southwest corner and a cornucopia of expensive antiques in its shops all along the way—or take the longer, scenic route.

Turn left off Kensington Church Street into Holland Street, admiring the sweet 18th-century houses (Nos. 10, 12–13, and 18–26 remain). As you cross Hornton Street you'll see to your left an orange-brick 1970s building, the Kensington Civic Centre (donor of parking permits, home of the local council), and Holland Street becomes the leafy Duchess of Bedford's Walk, with Queen Elizabeth College, part of London University, on the right. Turn left before Holland Park into Phillimore Gardens (perhaps detouring east into Phillimore Place to see No. 44, where Kenneth Grahame, author of *The Wind in the Willows,* lived from 1901 to 1908), then left again into Stafford Terrace to reach **Linley Sambourne House** ⑬. Step back to High Street, and turn right. Past the gates of the park is the **Commonwealth Experience** ⑭, which you could explore before entering **Holland Park** ⑮. Exit the park at the gate by the tennis courts (near the Orangery) onto Ilchester Place, follow Melbury Road a few yards, and turn right onto Holland Park Road to reach **Leighton House** ⑯. Late last century, Melbury Road was a veritable colony of artists, though the Victorian muse they followed failed to appeal to later sensibilities, and they're now an obscure bunch—except for Dickens's illustrator, Marcus Stone, who had No. 8 built in 1876. From here you could turn right onto Addison Road to see the Technicolor tiles rioting over Sir Ernest Debenham's Peacock House at No. 8 (he founded the eponymous Oxford Street department store). If you continue north, you reach plane tree–lined Holland Park Avenue, main thoroughfare of an expensive residential neighborhood that provides more pleasant strolling territory, if you feel you haven't walked enough.

TIMING

This walk is at least 4 mi long and is almost impossible to achieve without going inside somewhere. The best way to approach these neighborhoods is to treat Knightsbridge shopping and the South Kensington museums at one go. The rest of the tour works as a scenic walk on a fine day, because the places to see—Leighton and Linley Sambourne houses, the Commonwealth Institute, and Kensington Palace—are less time-consuming than the V&A, Natural History, and Science museums. During "term time," these are populated by more or less orderly school parties during the week, while weekends and school vacations see them fill up with more random arrangements of children. The parks are best in the growing seasons—from the crocuses and daffodils of early spring through the tulips to the roses—and during fall, when the foliage show easily rivals New England's. Kensington Gardens closes its gates at sundown, though you can get into Holland Park later during the summer, thanks to the restaurant and the Open Air Theatre.

HOW TO GET THERE

There are many tubes here, but which you choose will depend on which part you want. As a rule of thumb, the eponymous tube stop will be your best bet—Knightsbridge on the Piccadilly Line, Kensington High Street on District and Circle, and Holland Park on the Central Line. The best buses between Kensington High Street and

Knightsbridge, Kensington, and Holland Park

Knightsbridge are Nos. 9, 10, and 52. From Kensington to Holland Park, get the 9, 27, 28, or 31.

Sights to See

8 **Albert Memorial.** Seemingly permanently shrouded in the world's tallest freestanding web of scaffolding, the intricate structure housing this 14-ft bronze statue of Albert is undergoing a £14 million million renovation (including a pure gold-leaf coat donated by an anonymous benefactor). The work is not due to be finished until the year 2000. Albert's grieving widow, Queen Victoria, had this elaborate confection erected on the spot where his Great Exhibition had stood a mere decade before his early death from typhoid fever in 1861.

2 **Brompton Oratory.** This is a product of the English Roman Catholic revival of the late 19th century led by John Henry Cardinal Newman (1801–1890), who established this oratory in 1884 and whose statue you see outside. A then-unknown 29-year-old architect, Herbert Gribble, won the competition to design the place, an honor that you may conclude went to his head when you see the vast, incredibly ornate interior. It is punctuated by treasures far older than the church itself, like the giant Twelve Apostles in the nave, carved from Carrara marble by Giuseppe Mazzuoli during the 1680s and brought here from Siena's cathedral.

14 **The Commonwealth Experience.** With its swimming-pool-blue walls and asymmetric copper tent roof, this museum is one of London's more eccentric structures. A tour of the interior is like a trip around the world, or at least around the 50 Commonwealth nations, with lifestyles and histories of other continents displayed. Education is an important part of the work done at this vibrant institute, which hosts a lot of music, art, and film events and the Disneyland-like simulator ride called "Wonders of the World." ⊠ *230 Kensington High St., W14,* ☎ *0171/603–4535.* ⊡ *£4.45.* ☉ *Daily 10–5. Closed Dec. 18–25. Tube: High Street Kensington.*

1 **Harrods.** In case you didn't notice it, this well-known shopping mecca has its domed terra-cotta Edwardian bulk outlined in thousands of white lights at night. The 15-acre Egyptian-owned store's sales weeks are world class, and the environment is as frenetic as a stock market floor; its motto, *Omnia, omnibus, ubique* (everything, for everyone, everywhere), is not too far from the truth. Visit the pet department, a highlight for children, and don't miss the extravagant Food Hall, with its stunning Art Nouveau tiling in the neighborhood of meat and poultry and continuing on in the fishmongers' territory, where its glory is rivaled by displays of the sea produce itself. This is the place to acquire your green-and-gold souvenir Harrods bag, as food prices are surprisingly competitive. ⊠ *87–135 Brompton Rd., SW1,* ☎ *0171/730–1234. Tube: Knightsbridge.*

NEED A BREAK? **Patisserie Valerie** (⊠ 215 Brompton Rd., ☎ 0171/832-9971), just down the road from Harrods, offers light meals and a gorgeous array of pastries. It's perfect for breakfast, lunch, or tea.

15 **Holland Park.** The former grounds of the Jacobean Holland House opened to the public only in 1952. Since then, many treats have been laid on within its 22 hectares. Holland House itself was nearly flattened by World War II bombs, but the east wing remains, now incorporated into a youth hostel and providing a fantastical stage for the April–September **Open Air Theatre** (☎ 0171/602–7856 box office). The glass-walled Orangery also survived to host art exhibitions and wedding receptions, while next door, the former Garden Ballroom has become the Belvedere restaurant; nearby is a lovely café. From the Belvedere's terrace you see the formal Dutch Garden, planted by Lady Holland in the 1790s with the first English dahlias. North of that are woodland walks, lawns populated by peacocks and guinea fowl and the odd, awkward emu, a fragrant rose garden, great banks of rhododendrons and azaleas (which bloom profusely in May), a well-supervised children's Adventure Playground, and even a Japanese water garden, legacy of the 1991 London Festival of Japan. If that's not enough, you can watch cricket on the Cricket Lawn on the south side, or tennis on the several courts.

OFF THE
BEATEN PATH

KENSAL GREEN CEMETERY – Heralding itself as "London's first Necropolis," this west London cemetery was established in 1832 and beats the more famous Highgate for atmosphere, if only because it is less populous with the living. Within its 77 acres are more freestanding mausoleums than in any other cemetery in Britain, some of them almost the size of small churches, and most of them constructed while their future occupants were still alive. Those who balked at burial but couldn't afford a mausoleum of their own could opt for a position in the catacombs, and these, with their stacks of moldering caskets, are a definite highlight for seekers of the macabre, though they can only be seen as part of a tour. In the cemetery, you will find the final resting places of the novelists Trollope, Thackeray, and Wilkie Collins; of the great engineer Isambard Kingdom Brunel (1806–1859); and of Decimus Burton, Victorian architect of the Athenaeum Club, the Wellington Arch, the Kew Gardens greenhouses, and many other bits of London you'll have just seen. ⊠ *Harrow Rd., W10,* ☎ *0181/969–0152; tours 0171/402–2749.* ▱ *Suggested donation £2.* ◷ *Mon.–Sat. 9–5:30, Sun. 10–5:30 (times may vary Nov.–Feb., so call first); 2-hr guided tour (including catacombs) Mar.–Oct., weekends at 2:30, and Oct.–Feb., Sun. at 2; catacomb tour 1st Sun. of month (call for times). Tube: Kensal Green.*

★ ❿ **Kensington Palace.** Kensington was put, socially speaking, on the map when King William III, "much incommoded by the Smoak of the Coal Fires of London," decided in the 17th century to vacate Whitehall and relocate to a new palace outside the center city in the "village" of Kensington. The new palace did enjoy a smooth passage as royal residence. Twelve years of renovation were needed before William and Mary could move in; and it continued to undergo all manner of refurbishment during the successive three monarchs' reigns. By coincidence, these monarchs happened to suffer rather ignominious deaths. First, William III fell off his horse when it stumbled on a molehill and succumbed to pleurisy in 1702. Then, in 1714, Queen Anne (who, you may recall, was fond of brandy) suffered an apoplectic fit thought to have been brought on by overeating. Next, George I, the first of the Hanoverian Georges, had a stroke said to have been caused by "a surfeit of melons"—admittedly not at Kensington, but in a coach to Hanover in 1727. Worst of all, in 1760, poor George II burst a blood vessel while on the toilet (the official line was, presumably, that he was on the throne).

But the royal curtain here always rang up on a remarkable new cast of characters, no more so than when the 18-year-old Princess Victoria of Kent was called from her bed in June 1837 by the Archbishop of Canterbury and the Lord Chamberlain. Her uncle, William IV, was dead, they told her, and she was to be queen. The state rooms where Victoria had her ultrastrict upbringing have recently been renovated, a process which still continues, gradually restoring more of the fabulous Court Dress Collection to our sight. Meantime, the King's Apartments are the best part of the (compulsory) guided tour. Look out for

Tintorettos and Van Dycks among the canvases; see the Mortlake tapestries commissioned by Charles I, and look at that ceiling in the cupola room: It appears domed but is actually as flat as a ceiling. This palace is an essential stop for royalty vultures because it's the only one where you may actually catch a glimpse of the real thing. Princess Margaret, the Duke and Duchess of Gloucester, and Prince and Princess Michael of Kent all have apartments here, as did, of course, Diana, Princess of Wales, until her tragic death. A highlight of a visit here is the celebrated Court Dress Collection. At press time there was some discussion as to what manner of permanent memorial to the beloved "people's princess" should be installed here, if any. For a consoling (and expensive) cup of tea, repair to the palace's Orangery—surely one of London's most civilized settings and the festive hall where many Windsor birthday parties and weddings were held (a good number of which Princess Diana attended). ⊠ *The Broad Walk, Kensington Gardens, W8,* ☎ *0171/937–9561.* ▣ *£6.* ⊙ *May–Dec., daily 10–3:30 (last admission 1 hr before closing). Tube: High Street Kensington.*

⓫ **Kensington Palace Gardens.** Starting behind Kensington Palace, this is one of London's rare private roads, guarded and gated both here and at the Notting Hill Gate end. If you walk it, you will see why it earned the nickname "Millionaires' Row"—it is lined with palatial white-stucco houses designed by a selection of the best architects of the mid-19th century. The novelist William Makepeace Thackeray, author of *Vanity Fair,* died in 1863 at No. 2—a building that now houses an embassy (Israel's), as do most of the others.

⓬ **Kensington Square.** Having been laid out around the time William moved to Kensington Palace up the road, this is one of London's most venerable squares. A few early 18th-century houses remain, with Nos. 11 and 12 the oldest.

NEED A
BREAK?

In Wright's Lane you'll find **The Muffin Man,** a cozy anachronism of a tea shop. Here waitresses in floral aprons serve toasted sandwiches, cream teas, and, yes, English muffins.

⓰ **Leighton House.** This was the home of Frederic Leighton (1830–1896)—painter, sculptor, president of the Royal Academy. Endowed with a peerage by Queen Victoria, he unfortunately expired a month later. The prize room here is the incredible Arab Hall. George Aitchison designed this Moorish fantasy in 1879 to show off Leighton's valuable 13th- to 17th-century Islamic tile collection, and, adorned with marble columns, dome, and fountain, it is exotic beyond belief. The rest of the rooms are more conventionally, stuffily Victorian, but they do feature many paintings by Leighton, plus those of Edward Burne-Jones, John Millais, and other leading Pre-Raphaelites. ⊠ *12 Holland Park Rd., W14,* ☎ *0171/602–3316.* ▣ *Free.* ⊙ *Mon.–Sat. 11–5. Tube: Holland Park.*

★ ⓭ **Linley Sambourne House.** Stuffed with delightful Victorian and Edwardian antiques, fabrics, and paintings, this is one of the most charming 19th-century London houses extant—little wonder it was filmed for Merchant/Ivory's *A Room with A View.* During the 1870s, it was home to the political cartoonist Edward Linley Sambourne. It has been renovated by the Victorian Society to look as it did then, complete with William Morris wallpapers and illustrations from the (now defunct) satirical magazine *Punch,* including many of Sambourne's own, adorning the walls. ⊠ *18 Stafford Terr., W8,* ☎ *0181/994–1019.* ▣ *£3.* ⊙ *Mar.–Oct., Wed. 10–4, Sun. 2–5. Tube: High Street Kensington.*

☺ **London Toy & Model Museum.** Here are five floors of—yes—toys and models of all vintages, from practically prehistoric (okay, Year One) to not yet born, in the case of the Whatever Next? gallery's displays. Two highlights are the minutely detailed working coal mine and the fairground, both with moving parts, though the entire museum is a delight in its domestic-scale setting. Don't miss the tea garden in summertime. ✉ *21–23 Craven Hill, W2,* ☎ *0171/706–8000.* ✇ *£4.95.* ⊙ *Tues.–Sat. 10–5:30, Sun. 11–5:30.*

❻ **National Sound Archive.** In this aural outpost of the British Library, you may listen to the Queen who made this neighborhood possible: The million recordings held here include one of Victoria speaking sometime in the 1880s, but you have to book in advance to hear her, or anyone else. There's a small exhibit of early recording equipment and ephemera, too. ✉ *29 Exhibition Rd., SW7,* ☎ *0171/589–6603.* ✇ *Free.* ⊙ *Weekdays 10–5 (Thurs. 10–9). Tube: South Kensington.*

☺ ❹ **Natural History Museum.** Architect Alfred Waterhouse had relief panels scattered across the outrageously ornate French Romanesque–style terra-cotta facade of this museum, depicting extant creatures to the left of the entrance, extinct ones to the right. Inside, that categorization is sort of continued in reverse, with Dinosaurs on the left and the Ecology Gallery on the right. Both these renovated exhibits (the former with life-size moving dinosaurs, the latter complete with moonlit "rain forest") make essential viewing in a museum that, realizing it was becoming crusty, has subsequently invested millions overhauling itself in recent years.

The Creepy Crawlies Gallery features a nightmarish superenlarged scorpion, yet ends up making tarantulas cute (8 out of 10 animal species, one learns here, are arthropods). Other wonderful bits include the Human Biology Hall, which you arrive at through a birth-simulation chamber; the full-size blue whale; and the moving dinosaur diorama (which is a bit too bloody for toddlers). The Earth Galleries are also unmissable, with ambitious exhibits about the structure of our planet: "The Power Within," "Restless Surface," and "Visions of the Earth." Understandably, this place usually resembles grade-school recess. The White Card is accepted. ✉ *Cromwell Rd., SW7,* ☎ *0171/938–9123.* ✇ *£6, free weekdays 4:30–5:50 and weekends 5–5:50.* ⊙ *Mon.–Sat. 10–5:50, Sun. 11–5:50. Tube: South Kensington.*

❼ **Royal Albert Hall.** This domed, circular 8,000-seat auditorium (as well as the Albert Memorial, opposite) was made possible by the Victorian public, who donated funds for it. More money was raised, however, by selling 1,300 future seats at £100 apiece—not for the first night, but for every night for 999 years. (Some descendants of purchasers still use the seats.) The Albert Hall is best-known for its annual July–September Henry Wood Promenade Concerts (the "Proms"), with bargain-price standing (or promenading, or sitting-on-the-floor) tickets sold on the night of the world-class classical concerts. London also enjoys the "Erics," when the rock guitarist Eric Clapton services adoring fans for 10 days here every February. ✉ *Kensington Gore, SW7,* ☎ *0171/589–3203.* ✇ *Fee varies according to event. Tube: South Kensington.*

❾ **Royal College of Art.** Housed in a glass-dominated building designed by Sir Hugh Casson in 1973, the RCA provides great contrast with the Victoriana surrounding it, including the Albert Hall next door. Famous in the '50s and '60s for processing David Hockney, Peter Blake, and Eduardo Paolozzi, the college is still one of the country's foremost art schools, and there's usually an exhibition, lecture, or event here that's open to the public. ✉ *Kensington Gore, SW7,* ☎ *0171/584–5020.* 🎟 *Free.* ☉ *Weekdays 10–6 (call to check times). Tube: South Kensington.*

⑤ **Science Museum.** This, the third of the great South Kensington museums, stands behind the Natural History Museum in a far plainer building. It features loads of hands-on exhibits, with entire schools of children apparently decanted inside to interact with them; but it is, after all, painlessly educational. Highlights include the Launch Pad gallery, which demonstrates basic scientific principles (try the beautiful plasma ball, where your hands attract "lightning"—if you can get them on it); *Computing The and Now* show, which gets the most crowded of all; *Puffing Billy,* the oldest train in the world; and the actual *Apollo 10* capsule. The White Card is accepted. ✉ *Exhibition Rd., SW7,* ☎ *0171/938–8000.* 🎟 *£5.95.* ☉ *Mon.–Sat. 10–6, Sun. 11–6. Tube: South Kensington.*

★ ③ **Victoria and Albert Museum.** Recognizable by the copy of Victoria's Imperial Crown it wears on the lantern above the central cupola, this institution is always referred to as the V&A. It is a huge museum, showcasing the applied arts of all disciplines, all periods, all nationalities, and all tastes, and it is a wonderful, generous place to get lost in, full of innovation and completely devoid of pretension. The collections are *so* catholic that confusion is a hazard—one minute you're gazing on the Jacobean oak 12-ft-square four-poster Great Bed of Ware (one of the V&A's most prized possessions, given that Shakespeare immortalized it in *Twelfth Night*); the next, you're in the 20th-century end of the equally celebrated Dress Collection, coveting a Jean Muir frock you could actually buy at nearby Harrods.

Prince Albert, Victoria's adored consort, was responsible for the genesis of this permanent version of the 1851 Great Exhibition, and his queen laid its foundation stone in her final public London appearance in 1899. From the start, the V & A had an important role as a research institution, and that role continues today, with many resources available to scholars, designers, artists, and conservators. Two of the latest are the Textiles and Dress 20th Century Reference Centre, with ingenious space-saving storage systems for thousands of bolts of cloth, and the Textile Study Galleries, which perform the same function for 2,000 years' worth of the past.

Follow your own whims around the 7 mi of gallery space, but try to reach the new and spectacular Glass Gallery, where a collection spanning four millennia is reflected between room-size mirrors under young designer Danny Lane's breathtaking glass balustrade. The latest additions are the Raphael Galleries, where seven massive cartoons the painter completed in 1516 for his Sistine Chapel tapestries are housed, and the Silver Galleries, displaying six centuries of English silver. On Wednesdays, Late View continues—a kind of museum salon, with lectures and a wine bar. The White Card is accepted. ✉ *Cromwell Rd., SW7,* ☎ *0171/938–8500.* 🎟 *£5, free Thurs.–Tues. after 4:30.* ☉ *Mon. noon–5:50, Tues.–Sun. 10–5:50, Wed. Late View 4:30–9:30. Tube: South Kensington.*

NEED A BREAK?   Rest your overstimulated eyes in the brick-walled **V&A café**, where full meals and small snacks are available, and where the Sunday Jazz Brunch (11–5), accompanied by live music and Sunday papers, is fast becoming a London institution.

HYDE PARK, KENSINGTON GARDENS, BAYSWATER, AND NOTTING HILL

The Royal Parks of Hyde Park and Kensington Gardens are among London's unique features: Great swaths of green in the middle of the city, where it really is possible to decelerate from London's fast lane. The description "royal" is somewhat paradoxical, for today, these are the most democratic of places, where Londoners from all walks of life come to relax (and let off steam as soapbox orators). Although it's probably been centuries since any major royal had a casual stroll here, these parks remain the property of the Crown, and it was the Crown that saved them from being devoured by the city's late-18th-century growth spurt. North of the pair of parks—which are separate entities, although the boundary is virtually invisible—lies Bayswater. The main drag, Queensway, expresses Bayswater's nature quite aptly: This is a neighborhood that looks fancy, with its grand white-stucco terraced houses and leafy squares, but is somewhat disreputable, as demonstrated by the 1963 Profumo sex scandal—involving a government minister, a teenage showgirl, and a Soviet naval attaché—which unfurled behind closed Bayswater doors and toppled a government (see the movie *Scandal* for the whole story). Farther northwest lies Notting Hill, a trendsetting square mile of multiethnicity, music, and markets, with lots of see-and-be-seen-in restaurants and younger, more egalitarian, and more adventurous versions of the Cork Street commercial modern-art galleries. The style-watching media has dubbed the musician/novelist/film-biz/drug-dealer/fashion-victim local residents and hangers-out Notting Hillbillies. The whole thing has mushroomed around one of the world's great antiques markets, Portobello Road.

Numbers in the text correspond to numbers in the margin and on the Hyde Park, Kensington, and Notting Hill map.

A Good Walk

Where else would you enter Hyde Park but at **Hyde Park Corner.** The most impressive of the many entrances is the Hyde Park Screen by Apsley House, usually called **Decimus Burton's Gateway** because it was he who designed this triple-arched monument in 1828. The next gate along to the north, a gaudy unicorns-and-lions-rampant number wrought in scarlet-, cobalt-white-, and gold-painted metal, was a 90th-birthday gift to Elizabeth the Queen Mother and is therefore the **Queen Mother's Gate.** Follow the southern perimeter along the sand track called **Rotten Row,** now used by the Household Cavalry, which lives at the **Knightsbridge Barracks** to the left.

Follow Rotten Row west to the **Serpentine.** When you pass its **Bridge,** you leave Hyde Park, enter **Kensington Gardens,** and come to the **Serpentine Gallery.** En route to the formal garden at the end of the Long Water, **The Fountains,** you pass the statues of **Peter Pan,** and the horse and rider called **Physical Energy.** Continuing westward you reach the **Round Pond,** and **Kensington Palace.** Follow the Broad Walk north past the playground on the left, Bayswater Road, leaving the park by Black Lion Gate, and you are almost opposite Queensway, a rather peculiar, cosmopolitan street of ethnic confusion, late-night cafés and restaurants, a skating rink, and the Whiteleys shopping-and-movie mall. Turn left at the end into Westbourne Grove, however, and you've entered Notting Hill, and you'll reach the famous **Portobello Road** after a few blocks. Turn left for the Saturday antiques market and shops, right to reach the Westway and the flea market. For Notting Hill's grandest houses, stroll over to Lansdowne Road, Crescent, and Square.

Hyde Park, Kensington Gardens, and Notting Hill

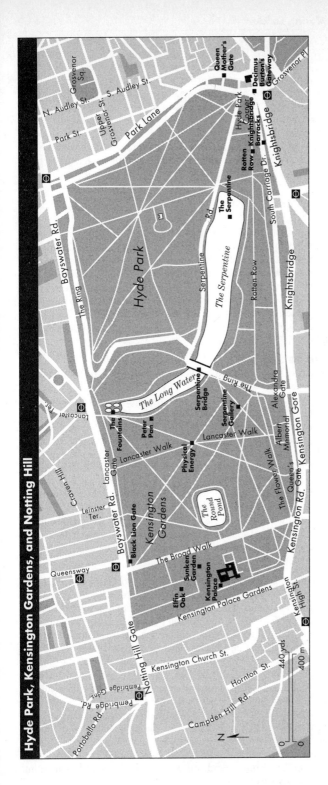

This is a route that changes vastly on weekends. Saturday is Portobello Road's most fun day, so you may prefer to start at the end and work backward, using the parks for "R and R" from your shopping exertions. Do the same on Fridays if you're a flea-market fan. Sundays, the Hyde Park and Kensington Gardens railings all along Bayswater Road are hung with very bad art, which may slow your progress; this is also prime perambulation day for locals. Whatever your priorities, this is a long walk if you explore every corner, with the perimeter of the two parks alone covering a good 4 mi, and about half as far again around the remainder of the route. You could cut out a lot of park without missing out on essential sights, and walk the whole thing in a brisk three hours.

For Hyde Park and Kensington Gardens, get off the Central Line at Queensway or Lancaster Gate, or enter the park from Hyde Park Corner on the Piccadilly Line. If you want Portobello Market and environs, the best tube stops are Ladbroke Grove or Westbourne Park (Hammersmith and City lines), then ask directions; the Notting Hill stop on the District, Circle, and Central lines is also an option. Buses for the area include Nos. 12, 70, and 94 for anything off Bayswater Road, or Nos. 27, 28, 31, and 52 for penetrating the depths of Notting Hill.

Sights to See

Ⓢ **Hyde Park.** Along with the smaller St. James's and Green Parks to the east, Hyde Park started as Henry VIII's hunting grounds. He had no altruistic intent but more or less stole the land, for his pleasure, from the monks at Westminster at the 1536 Dissolution of the Monasteries. James I was more generous and allowed the public in at the beginning of the 17th century, as long as they were "respectably dressed." Nowadays, as summer visitors can see, you may wear whatever you like—a bathing suit will do. Along its south side runs **Rotten Row**. It was Henry VIII's royal path to the hunt—hence the name, a corruption of *route du roi*. It's still used by the Household Cavalry, who live at the **Knightsbridge Barracks**—a high-rise and a long, low, ugly red block—to the left. This is the brigade that mounts the guard at Buckingham Palace, and you can see them leave to perform this duty in full regalia, plumed helmet and all, at around 10:30, or await the return of the exhausted ex-guard about noon.

Ⓢ **Kensington Gardens.** More formal than neighboring Hyde Park, Kensington Gardens was first laid out as palace grounds. The paved Italian garden at the top of the Long Water, **The Fountains,** is a reminder of this, though of course **Kensington Palace** itself is the main clue to the gardens' royal status, with its early 19th-century Sunken Garden north of the palace complex, complete with a living tunnel of lime trees and golden laburnum. Several statues are worth looking out for: George Frampton's 1912 *Peter Pan* is a bronze of the boy who lived on an island in the Serpentine and never grew up, and whose creator, J. M. Barrie, lived at 100 Bayswater Road, not 500 yards from here. Southwest of Peter at the intersection of several paths is George Frederick Watts's 1904 bronze of a muscle-bound horse and rider, entitled *Physical Energy*. By the playground close to the Round Pond is the remains of a tree carved with scores of tiny woodland creatures, Ivor Innes's *Elfin Oak*. The **Round Pond** acts as a magnet for model-boat enthusiasts and duck feeders.

NEED A
BREAK? About halfway down Queensway (No. 127), **Maison Pechon** is a patisserie, but one that serves full English breakfasts, omelets, jacket potatoes, and salads alongside its French tarts, brioches, cream cakes, and
cookies.

Portobello Road. Tempted by tassels, looking for a 19th-century snuff
spoon or dashingly Deco frock (just don't believe the dealer when he
says the Vionnet label just fell off), or hunting for a gracefully Georgian silhouette of the Earl of Chesterfield? Head to Portobello Road,
world famous for its Saturday antiques market (arrive at about 9 AM
to find the real treasures-in-the-trash; after 10, the crowds pack in wall
to wall. Actually, the Portobello Market is three markets: Antiques, "fruit
and veg," and a flea market. The street begins at Notting Hill Gate,
though the antiques stalls start a couple of blocks north, around Chepstow Villas. Lining the sloping street are also dozens of antiques shops
and indoor markets, open most days—in fact, serious collectors will
want to do Portobello on a weekday, when they can explore the 90-
some antiques and art stores in relative peace. Where the road levels
off, around Elgin Crescent, youth culture and a vibrant neighborhood
life kicks in, with all manner of interesting small stores and restaurants
interspersed with the fruit and vegetable market. This continues to the
Westway overpass ("flyover" in British), where London's best flea
market (high-class, vintage, antique, and secondhand clothing; jewelry;
and junk) happens Fridays and Saturdays, then on up to Goldbourne
Road. There's a strong West Indian flavor to Notting Hill, with a
Trinidad-style Carnival centered along Portobello Road on the August
bank-holiday weekend. *Tube: Notting Hill Gate, Ladbroke Grove.*

Serpentine Gallery. Influential on the trendy art circuit, this gallery hangs
several exhibitions of modern work a year, often very avant-garde indeed, and always worth a look. It overlooks the west bank of the **Serpentine**, a beloved lake, much frequented in summer, when the south
shore Lido resembles a beach and the water is dotted with hired row-
boats. Walk the bank, and you will soon reach the picturesque, stone
Serpentine Bridge built in 1826 by George Rennie, which marks the
boundary between Hyde Park and Kensington Gardens. ⊠ *Kensington Gardens, W2,* ☏ *0171/402–6075.* 🎟 *Free.* ☉ *Daily 10–6. Closed
Christmas wk. Tube: Lancaster Gate.*

NEED A
BREAK? The **tearoom** on the Serpentine is constantly changing hands and always
seems rather overpriced, but it does offer tea, coffee, and snacks in an
overwhelmingly green setting.

REGENT'S PARK AND HAMPSTEAD

Regent's Park and Hampstead in north London contain some of the
prettiest and most rural parts of the city, as well as some of the most
aristocratic architecture in the world (thanks to the terraces and town
houses of John Nash, 19th-century design whiz) and some important
historical sights. For the sheer pleasure of idle exploring, these city districts are hard to beat. All told, this section covers a large area. It starts
from the Georgian houses superimposed on medieval Maryburne, continues around John Nash's Regency facades and his park, stretches on
into north London's canal-side youth center, climbs up the hill to the
city's chicest, most expensive "village," and finishes, fittingly, at its most
famous cemetery.

Marylebone Road (pronounced Marra-le-bun) these days is remarkably mostly for its permanent traffic jam, some of it heading to Madame

Tussaud's. At the east end is the first part of John Nash's impressive Regent's Park scheme, the elegantly curvaceous Park Crescent (1812–1818), which Nash planned as a full circus at the northern end of his ceremonial route from St. James's. Like most of the Nash houses around the park, it was wrecked during World War II, reconstructed, and rebuilt behind the repaired facade in the 1960s. Northeast of the park, Camden Town is the neighborhood that houses London's highest concentration of single people in their twenties.

The cliché about Hampstead is that it is just like a pretty little village—albeit one with designer shops, expensive French delicatessens, restaurants, cafés, cinemas, and so on. In fact, like so many London neighborhoods, Hampstead did start as a separate village, when plague-bedeviled medieval Londoners fled the city to this clean hilltop 4 mi away. By the 18th century, its reputation for cleanliness had spread so far that its water was being bottled and sold, as the Perrier of its day, to the hoi polloi down the hill. That was the beginning of Hampstead's heyday as an artistic and literary retreat attracting many famous writers, painters, and musicians to its leafy lanes—as it still does. Just strolling around here is rewarding: Not only are the streets incredibly picturesque, they also harbor some of London's best Georgian buildings.

Numbers in the text correspond to numbers in the margin and on the Regent's Park and Hampstead map.

A Good Walk

Begin at the tube station whose name will thrill the Sherlock Holmes fan: Baker Street—the **Sherlock Holmes Museum** ① is at 221B, of course. Turn left and follow the line of tour buses past **Madame Tussaud's** ② and the **London Planetarium,** then to the end of Harley Street—an English synonym for private (as opposed to state-funded) medicine because it is lined with the consulting rooms of the country's top specialist doctors—to Park Crescent and, across the street, **Regent's Park** ③. Enter along the Outer Circle and turn left on Chester Road. Straight ahead are Queen Mary's Gardens, the lake, and the **Regent's Park Open-Air Theatre** ④. Turn left onto the Broad Walk from Chester Road, look west past the mock-Tudor prefab tearoom for one of London's rare uninterrupted open vistas toward the London Central Mosque, then continue on to the **London Zoo** ⑤. From here, you can take a round-trip detour on the water bus and spy on the back gardens along the **Grand Union Canal** (which everyone calls the Regent's Canal) to Little Venice. Don't get *too* excited—the canal you're on (constructed 1812–1820) is the only one there is, but this peaceful little bit of London does have an atmosphere unique to it, with enormous white wedding-cake houses set back from the banks, and it's a good strolling location.

North of the zoo, cross Prince Albert Road to Primrose Hill, a high point (literally, at 206 ft), and the best place to be on the night of November 5, when London's biggest bonfire burns a Guy Fawkes effigy, and there's a spectacular fireworks display. Heading east from here (the easiest route is Regent's Park Road), then left down Parkway, past the **Jewish Museum** ⑥) brings you to the center of Camden Town. Turn left at the foot of Parkway, and battle your way north along Camden High Street (actually, the crowds are unbearably dense only on the weekend) to **Camden Lock** ⑦. From here you can keep going east, although it's less scenic, to King's Cross, site of one of London's main train stations, the new British Library building, the city's highest concentration of for-hire streetwalkers, and the **London Canal Museum** ⑧.

Back at the Lock, you could walk up Haverstock Hill, or travel three stops on the Northern Line from Camden Town tube (make sure you

Regent's Park and Hampstead

take the Edgware branch) to Hampstead (or 181 ft below it, in London's deepest tube station). Cross High Street to Heath Street and turn right to Church Row, said to be London's most complete Georgian street. At the west end is the 1745 "village" church of St. John's, where the painter John Constable is buried. Just south of the tube, Flask Walk is another pretty street, narrow and shop-lined at the High Street end, then widening after you pass the Flask—the pub it is named for. This place has a pretty courtyard and was once described by Samuel Richardson in his 18th-century novel *Clarissa* as "a place where second-rate persons are to be found, often in a swinish condition." Lunch here, or opt for a bite at Hampstead's chic Cafe Rouge, Al Casbah, Graffiti, or the Coffee Cup. Nearby Well Walk was where the spring surfaced, its place now marked by a dried-up fountain. John Constable lived here, as well as John Keats (in, of course, **Keats House** ⑨, currently closed for renovation) and, later, D. H. Lawrence. Head some blocks north to regal **Fenton House,** a National Trust treasure trove with some lovely gardens, then amble around the corner to Admiral's Walk to gaze at the house with a roof that echoes the quarterdeck of a ship immortalized in *Mary Poppins*; farther along East Heath Road you'll find the Gothic manse (now owned by Boy George) that inspired Hell Hall in *One Hundred and One Dalmations*. You now have two choices: If you've had enough fresh air, walk down Fitzjohn's Avenue and visit the **Freud Museum** ⑩ and then continue down Finchley Road to the impressive **Saatchi Collection** ⑪; Beatles aficionados will head posthaste, instead, to the fabled **Abbey Road Studios** ⑫. If you've been blessed with a clear London day, take advantage and take the long walk northeast up Spaniards Road, traversing **Hampstead Heath** to Hampstead Lane, to the bucolic oasis of **Kenwood House** ⑬, well worth a visit for its setting alone. To the east of Hampstead, and also topping a hill, is the former village of Highgate, which has some fine houses, especially along its Georgian High Street, and retains a peaceful period atmosphere. But it is most famous for **Highgate Cemetery** ⑭.

TIMING

You may well want to divide this tour into segments, using the (notoriously inefficient) Northern Line of the tube to jump between the Regent's Park and Hampstead neighborhoods. It will take you at least three hours to cover on foot the full length of this walk.

There are several approaches, of course. In summer, with children, you might center a north London jaunt around Regent's Park, the zoo, Camden Lock, and a canal trip, a day's worth of sightseeing. If you wanted to add Madame Tussaud's and the planetarium, you'd have a frenetic day, especially in summer, because you might be in line for an hour. A summer's day without children might start at the other end, with Hampstead Heath, Kenwood House, a stroll around Hampstead and a pub or two on the agenda—plenty for one day. Teenagers and youth will spend all day and night in Camden Town, and may as well admit it. They, and anyone else who wants the whole Camden Lock spectacle, should go north on a weekend; those who prefer quiet should do the opposite. Neither Camden nor Hampstead are completely dead during the week, though, because both have residents who tend to go out a lot. Bear in mind that much of this itinerary is washed out by rain, not only because there's a lot of ground to cover, but because many of the pleasures are to be had from strolling.

HOW TO GET THERE

For Regent's Park, Regent's Park tube (on the Bakerloo Line) is obviously an option, though Camden Town on the Northern Line, then a walk up Parkway is almost as close. Hampstead is best accessed from, yes, Hampstead tube. Make sure you get on the right "branch" of the Northern Line—you want the train to Edgware. Buses for Regent's Park include Nos. 18, 27, and 30 along the Marylebone Road or Nos. 13, 82, 113, 139, and 274 to Lord's Cricket Ground. The 274 is the bus for the zoo. For Hampstead, catch the 268.

Sights to See

★ ⑫ **Abbey Road Studios.** The most famous Beatles site in London, this is the fabled studio where the Fab Four recorded their entire output. The studios themselves are closed to the public, but many travelers journey here to see the famous traffic crossing used by the group on the cover of their *Abbey Road* album (☞ Close-Up box "Strawberry Beatles Forever: A Trip to Abbey Road"). ⊠ *3 Abbey Rd., NW8 Tube: St. John's Wood.*

🖐 ⑦ **Camden Lock.** What was once just a pair of locks on the Grand Union Canal has now developed into London's third-most-visited tourist attraction. It's a vast honeycomb of markets that sell just about everything, but mostly crafts, clothing (vintage, ethnic, and young designer), and antiques, and it is a virtual caricature of its neighborhood, Camden Town. Here, especially on a weekend, the crowds are dense, young, and relentless, and you may tire of the identical T-shirts, pants, boots, vintage wear, and cheap leather on their backs and in the shops. Camden definitely has its charms, though. Gentrification has been layered over a once overwhelmingly Irish neighborhood, vestiges of which coexist with the youth culture: Inverness Street fruit-and-vegetable market alongside the Arlington House homeless shelter, architects' offices, and antiques stores. ⊠ *Camden Lock, Camden High St., NW1 ,* ☎ *No phone.* ☉ *Markets weekends. Tube: Camden Town or Chalk Farm.*

NEED A BREAK?

You will not go hungry in Camden Town. Among the countless cafés, bars, pubs, and restaurants, the following stand out for good value and good food: **Marine Ices** (⊠ 8 Haverstock Hill, past lock) has a window dispensing ice cream to strollers, and pasta, pizza, and sundaes inside. **Bar Gansa** (⊠ 2 Inverness St., near tube) offers Spanish tapas—small dishes for sharing. **Cottons Rhum Shop, Bar and Restaurant** (⊠ 55 Chalk Farm Rd., past lock) is a Caribbean island in miniature, with great rum cocktails and jerk chicken.

Fenton House. This is Hampstead's oldest surviving house. Now a National Trust property, it has an interesting collection of antiques and period interiors, along with some 17th-century-style gardens. ⊠ *Hampstead Grove, NW3,* ☎ *0171/435–3471.* 🎟 *£3.* ☉ *Mar., weekends 2– 5:30; Apr.–Oct., Wed.–Fri. 2–5:30, weekends 11–5:30. Tube: Hampstead.*

⑩ **Freud Museum.** The father of psychoanalysis lived here for only a few months, between his escape from Nazi persecution in his native Vienna in 1938 and his death in 1939. Many of his possessions emigrated with him and were set up by his daughter, Anna (herself a pioneer of child psychoanalysis), as a shrine to her father's life and work. Four years after Anna's death in 1982, the house was opened as a museum. It replicates the atmosphere of Freud's famous consulting rooms, particularly through the presence of *the couch.* You'll find Freud-related books, lectures, and study groups here, too. ⊠ *20 Maresfield Gardens, NW3,* ☎ *0171/435–2002.* 🎟 *£3.* ☉ *Wed.–Sun. noon–5. Tube: Swiss Cottage, Finchley Rd.*

🖐 **Hampstead Heath.** However pretty the houses may be, this wild park, which spreads for miles to the north, is actually the nicest thing about Hampstead. On the southwest corner stands the rebuilt version of a

STRAWBERRY BEATLES FOREVER:

A TRIP TO ABBEY ROAD

FOR COUNTLESS BEATLEMANIACS and baby boomers, No. 3 Abbey Road is one of the most beloved spots in London. Here, outside the legendary Abbey Road Studios, is the most famous zebra crossing in the world. Immortalized on the Beatles' *Abbey Road* 1969 album, this footpath became a Mod monument when, on August 8 of that year, John, Paul, George, and Ringo posed— walking symbolically *away* from the recording facility, incidentally—for photographer Iain Macmillan for the famous album shot.

Today, many fans venture to Abbey Road to leave their signature on the white stucco fence that fronts the studio facility. "All You Need is Beatles!", "God is a Beatle!", "Imagine—John coming back!", "John is Gone—What a price to pay for being a genius!", "Why don't you do it in the road?" and "Strawberry Beatles Forever" are a few of the flourishes left (note that these are whitewashed out every three months, by agreement with the neighborhood community, to make room for new graffiti).

The recording facility's Studio 2 is where the Beatles recorded their entire output, from "Love Me Do" onward, including, most momentously, *Sgt. Pepper's Lonely Hearts Club Band* (early 1967). Today, tourists like to Beatle-ize themselves by taking the same sort of photo, but be careful: Rushing cars make Abbey Road a dangerous intersection. Currently, there are few places in London that commemorate the Fab Four (wouldn't it be wonderful if Abbey Road Studios, now closed to the public, could become a Beatles museum one day?), so the best way Beatle-lovers can enjoy the history of the group is to take one of the smashing walking tours offered by the Original London Walks, including "The Beatles In-My-Life Walk" (11 AM at the Baker Street underground on Saturday and Tuesday), and "The Beatles Magical Mystery Tour" (11 AM at Dominion Theater Exit, Tottenham Court Road, on Sunday and Thursday; call ☎ 0171/624–3978).

ABBEY ROAD is in the elegant neighborhood of St. John's Wood, just a 10-minute ride on the tube from central London: Take the Jubilee subway line to the St. John's Wood tube stop, head southwest three blocks down Grove End Road, and—especially if you were one of the 63 million people that tuned in to the *Ed Sullivan Show* February 8, 1964, and grew up with the Beatles—be prepared for a heart-stopping vista right out of Memory Lane.

famous inn, **Jack Straw's Castle** (⊠ North End Way, NW3, ☎ 0171/ 435–8885). It is named after the Peasants' Revolt leader who hid out and was captured here in 1381 after destroying Sir Robert Hales's residence and priory, the Prior of St. John. Hales was hated for enforcing the poll tax, which led to the uprising—and which, when reintroduced in 1990, proved as unpopular the second time around. Another historic pub stands off the northwest edge, on Hampstead Lane. The **Spaniard's Inn** (⊠ Spaniard's Rd., NW3, ☎ 0181/455–3276), in contrast to the above, is little changed since the early 18th century, when (they say) the notorious highwayman Dick Turpin hung out here. Keats also drank here, as did Shelley and Byron—but not Dickens; when his eternal pub crawl brought him up to Hampstead, he preferred Jack Straw's Castle. Today, you'll find it crammed with chic locals and happy tourists. *Tube: Hampstead.*

⓮ Highgate Cemetery. The older, west side of this sprawling early Victorian graveyard, featuring many an overwrought stone memorial, can be visited only by a tour given by the Friends of Highgate Cemetery—a group of volunteers who virtually saved the place from ruin. The shady streets of the dead, Egyptian Avenue and the Circle of Lebanon, are particularly Poe-like, but the famous graves are mostly on the newer, less atmospheric east side, which is still in use and may be wandered freely. No tour is required to explore the newer, east side of Highgate Cemetery, home to some famous permanent residents: Karl Marx's enormous black bust is probably the most visited site, but George Eliot is also buried here. This is not London's oldest cemetery—that distinction belongs to Kensal Green, with its spine-chilling catacombs and Gothic mausoleums. ⊠ *Swains La., Highgate, N6, ☎ 0181/340– 1834. ▨ East side £1, west side tour £2. ۞ East side Apr.–Oct., daily 10–4:45, and Oct.–Mar., daily 10–3:45; west side tour Apr.–Oct., weekdays at 2 and 4, weekends periodically 11–4, and Nov.–Mar., weekdays at noon, 2, and 3, weekends periodically 11–3. Tube: Archway.*

NEED A
BREAK?

> **Lauderdale House** in Waterlow Park, across Swain's Lane from Highgate Cemetery, was built during the 16th century by a master of the Royal Mint and is now a community and arts center, with a great café serving homemade hot meals as well as snacks.

❻ Jewish Museum. This newly located museum tells a potted history of the Jews in London from Norman times, though the bulk of the exhibits date from the end of the 17th century (when Cromwell repealed the laws against Jewish settlement) and later. ⊠ *Raymond Burton House, 129 Albert St., NW1, ☎ 0171/284–1997. ▨ £3. ۞ Sun.–Thurs. 10–4.*

❾ Keats House. Here you can—or will be able to see, as the house and gardens are currently closed for renovations through 1999—see the plum tree under which the young Romantic poet composed "Ode to a Nightingale," many of his original manuscripts, his library, and other possessions he managed to acquire in his short life. It was in February 1820 that Keats coughed blood up into his handkerchief and exclaimed, "I know the color of that blood; it is arterial blood. I cannot be deceived in that color. That drop of blood is my death warrant. I must die." He left this house in September, moved to Rome, and died of consumption there, in early 1821, at age 25. ⊠ *Keats House, Wentworth Pl., Keats Grove, NW3, ☎ 0171/435–2062. ▨ Free. ۞ Apr.– Oct., weekdays 10–6, Sat. 10–5, Sun. 2–5; Nov.–Mar., weekdays 1–5, Sat. 10–5, Sun. 2–5. Closed 1 hr for lunch. Tube: Hampstead.*

NEED A
BREAK? Hampstead is full of eating places, including a few that have been here
forever. Try **The Coffee Cup** (⊠ 74 Hampstead High St.), serving all-day
English breakfasts, pastries, and things-on-toast; or the **Hampstead Tea
Rooms** (⊠ 9 South End Rd.) for its sandwiches, pies, and its great win-
dow full of pastries and cream cakes.

⑬ **Kenwood House.** Perfectly and properly Palladian, this mansion was
first built in 1616 and remodeled by Robert Adam in 1764. Adam refaced
most of the exterior and added the gaudy library, which, with its
curved, painted ceiling, rather garish coloring, and gilded detailing, is
the sole highlight of the house for decor buffs. What is unmissable here
is the **Iveagh Bequest**—a collection of paintings the Earl of Iveagh gave
the nation in 1927, starring a very great Rembrandt self portrait and
works by Reynolds, Van Dyck, Hals, Gainsborough, and Turner. Top
billing goes to Vermeer's *Guitar Player*—one of the most beautiful paintings anywhere. In front of the house, a graceful lawn slopes down to
a little lake crossed by a dinky bridge—all in perfect 18th-century upper-
class taste. Nowadays the lake is dominated by its concert bowl, which
stages a popular summer series of orchestral concerts, including at least
one performance of Handel's *Music for the Royal Fireworks,* complete
with fireworks. There's a handy café in the former stables. ⊠ *Hampstead La., NW3,* ☎ *0181/348–1286.* ⊡ *Free.* ☉ *Mid-Mar.–Sept., daily
10–6; Oct.–Easter, daily 10–4. Tube: Golder's Green, then Bus 210.*

⑧ **London Canal Museum.** Here, in a former ice storage house, you can
learn about the rise and fall of London's once extensive canal network.
Outside, on the Battlebridge Basin, float the gaily painted narrow
boats of modern canal dwellers—a few steps and a world away from
King's Cross, which remains one of London's least salubrious neighborhoods. The quirky little museum is accessible from Camden Lock
if you take the towpath. ⊠ *12–13 New Wharf Rd., N1,* ☎ *0171/713–
0836.* ⊡ *£2.50.* ☉ *Apr.–Sept., Tues.–Sun. 10–4; call for winter hrs.
Tube: King's Cross.*

☾ **London Planetarium.** This domed building stands right next to Madame
Tussaud's (☞ *below*), but it could hardly provide greater contrast
with the waxworks (though you can save a bit of cash by combining
them in a single visit). Inside the dome, exact simulations of the night
sky are projected by the Digistar Mark 2 projector and accompanied
by gosh-wow-fancy-that narration. The shows, which change daily, are
good enough to addict children to astronomy. There are regular laser
shows and rock music extravaganzas. ⊠ *Marylebone Rd., NW1,* ☎
0171/935–6861. ⊡ *£5.65, joint ticket with Madame Tussaud's (☞
below) £11.20.* ☉ *Show every 40 mins weekdays 12:20–5, weekends
10:20–5. Tube: Baker Street.*

☾ ⑤ **London Zoo.** The zoo opened in 1828, peaked in popularity during the
1950s (when more than 3 million visitors passed through its turnstiles
every year), but recently faced the prospect of closing its gates forever.
Its problems started when animal-crazy Brits, apparently anxious
about the morality of caging wild beasts, simply stopped visiting. But
the zoo fought back, pulling heartstrings with a *Save Our Zoo* campaign and tragic predictions of mass euthanasia for homeless polar bears,
and, at the 11th hour, found commercial sponsorship that was generous enough not only to keep the wolves from the door (or, rather, the
wolves indoors) but also to fund a great big modernization program.

Zoo highlights that will not change include the Elephant and Rhino
Pavilion, which closely resembles the South Bank Arts Complex; the
graceful Snowdon Aviary, spacious enough to allow its tenants free flight;
and the 1936 Penguin Pool, where feeding time sends small children

into raptures. New thrills will include the construction of a desert swarm-ing with locusts; a rain forest alive with butterflies, bats, and hum-mingbirds; and a cave lighted by fireflies. This being the headquarters of the Zoological Society of London, much work is done here in wildlife conservation, education, and the breeding of endangered species, and emphasis is being shifted onto these aspects in the exhibits, with more displays to help explain them to visitors. The first step along this road was the Children's Zoo, which shows how people and animals live together, and features domestic animals from around the world. ⊠ *Regent's Park, NW1,* ☎ *0171/722–3333.* ☜ *£8.* ☉ *Sum-mer, daily 9–6; winter, daily 10–4; penguin feed daily 2:30; aquarium feed daily 2:30; reptile feed Fri. 2:30; elephant bath daily 3:45. Tube: Camden Town, and Bus 74.*

🐣 ❷ **Madame Tussaud's.** This—one of London's busiest sights—is nothing more, nothing less than the world's premier exhibition of lifelike wax-work models of celebrities. Madame T. learned her craft while mak-ing death masks of French Revolution victims and in 1835 set up her first show of the famous ones near this spot. Nowadays, "Super Stars" of entertainment, in their own hall of the same name, outrank any aristo in popularity, along with the newest segment, "The Spirit of London," a "time taxi ride" that visits every notable Londoner from Shake-speare to Benny Hill. But top billing still goes to the murderers in the Chamber of Horrors, who stare glassy-eyed at you—this one from the electric chair, that one next to the tin bath where he dissolved several wives in quicklime. What, aside from ghoulish prurience, makes peo-ple stand in line to invest in London's most expensive museum ticket? It must be the thrill of rubbing shoulders with Shakespeare, Martin Luther King Jr., the Queen, and the Beatles—most of them dressed in their own clothes—in a single day. ⊠ *Marylebone Rd., NW1,* ☎ *0171/935–6861.* ☜ *£8.95, joint ticket with planetarium (*☞ *above) £11.20* ☉ *Sept.–June, weekdays 10–5:30, weekends 9:30–5:30; July–Aug., daily 9:30–5:30. Tube: Baker St.*

★ ❸ **Regent's Park.** This, the youngest of London's great parks, was laid out in 1812 by John Nash, working, as ever, for his patron, the Prince Regent (hence the name), who was crowned George IV in 1820. The idea was to re-create the feel of a grand country residence close to the center of town, with all those magnificent white-stucco terraces fac-ing in on the park. As you walk the Outer Circle, you'll see how suc-cessfully Nash's plans were carried out, although the center of it all, a palace for the prince, was never built—George was too busy fiddling with the one he already had, Buckingham Palace. The most famous and impressive of Nash's terraces would have been in the prince's line of vision from the planned palace, so it was extra ornamental. **Cum-berland Terrace** has a central block of Ionic columns surmounted by a triangular Wedgwood blue pediment that is like a giant cameo. Snow-white statuary personifying Britannia and her empire (the work of the on-site architect, James Thomson) further single it out from the pack. The noted architectural historian Sir John Summerson described it thus: "the backcloth as it were to Act III, and easily the most breath-taking architectural panorama in London."

As in all London parks, planting here is planned with the aim of hav-ing something in bloom in all seasons, but if you hit the park in May, June, or July, head first to the Inner Circle. Your nostrils should lead you to **Queen Mary's Gardens,** a fragrant 17-acre circle that riots with roses in summer, and heather, azaleas, and evergreens in other seasons. The **Broad Walk** is a good vantage point from which to glimpse the minaret and golden dome of the **London Central Mosque** on the far west side of the park, or—if it's a summer evening or a Sunday afternoon—witness a remarkable recent phenomenon. Wherever you look, the sport being enthusiastically played (subject to the ritual annual banning by the park authorities) is not cricket but softball, now Britain's fastest-growing participant sport (bring your mitt). Actually, you're likely to see cricket, too.

❹ Regent's Park Open-Air Theatre. This has been mounting mostly Shakespeare productions every summer since 1932—everyone from Vivien Leigh to Jeremy Irons has performed here. *A Midsummer Night's Dream* is the one to catch—never is that enchanted Greek wood more lifelike than it is here, augmented by genuine bird squawks and a rising moon. The park can get chilly, so bring a blanket—and rain stops the play only when heavy, so an umbrella may be wise, too. ⊠ *Open-Air Theatre, Regent's Park, NW1,* ☎ *0171/486–2431.* ⊙ *June–Aug. Tube: Baker St., Regent's Park.*

⓫ Saatchi Collection. This blinding white space is all crisp lines and quietness, the better to contemplate the front lines of contemporary paintings, installations, and sculpture—by the likes of Lucian Freud, Paula Rego, Damian Hirst, Rachel Whiteread, Janine Antoni—collected by the advertising mogul. ⊠ *98A Boundary Rd., NW8,* ☎ *0171/624–8299.* ☞ *Free.* ⊙ *Fri. and Sat. noon–6. Tube: Swiss Cottage.*

❶ Sherlock Holmes Museum. You can tell you've reached this museum when you see the actor dressed as a Victorian policeman outside, and the sign that claims this as 221B Baker Street, the address of Arthur Conan Doyle's fictional detective. Inside, "Holmes's housekeeper" conducts you into a series of Victorian rooms full of Sherlock-abilia. By the way, the 221B, if it existed, would be down the block in the Abbey National Building Society's head office at Abbey House, 215–229 Baker Street. ⊠ *221B Baker St., NW1,* ☎ *0171/935–8866.* ☞ *£5.* ⊙ *Daily 10–6. Tube: Baker St.*

2 Willow Road. Modern Movement master Erno Goldfinger put this house up in the 1930s, and the National Trust has now kindly restored it and filled it with important (and currently very trendy) Modernist furniture and art. Note that there are limited visitor hours with timed tickets because the house is small; call for details. ⊠ *2 Willow Rd., NW1,* ☎ *0171/435–6166.* ☞ *£4.* ⊙ *Spring–fall (call for times). Tube: Hampstead.*

GREENWICH

About 8 mi downstream from central London—which means seaward, to the east—lies a neighborhood you'd think had been conceived to provide the perfect day out. Greenwich is another of London's self-contained "villages," only one with unique sights surrounding the residential portion. The buildings of Greenwich are among the most splendid in Britain: Spreading both grandly and elegantly beside the river, the colonnades and pediments of Sir Christopher Wren's Royal Naval College and Inigo Jones's Queen's House seem to be part of a complex of Grecian temples transported to the Thames. Here, too, is the Old Royal Observatory, which measures time for our entire planet, and the Greenwich Meridian, which divides the world in two—you can stand astride it with one foot in either hemisphere. The National Maritime Museum and the proud clipper ship *Cutty Sark* thrill seafaring types, and landlubbers can stroll the green acres of parkland that surround the buildings, the quaint 19th-century houses, and the weekend crafts and antiques markets.

Numbers in the text correspond to numbers in the margin and on the Greenwich map.

A Good Walk

Before you start to walk, bear in mind that the journey to Greenwich is fun in itself, especially if you approach by river, arriving at the best possible vista of the **Royal Naval College,** with the **Queen's House** behind. On the way, the boat glides past famous sights on the London skyline (there's a guaranteed spine chill on passing the Tower) and the ever-changing docklands, and there's always a cockney navigator enhancing the views with wise-guy commentary. You could also take the Docklands Light Railway (DLR), a high-speed elevated track, which opened in 1987. It connects with the tube network at Bank and brings you to Island Gardens, exactly opposite the Royal Naval College, with the finest possible view, of course. You can't miss the squat little circular brick building with its glass-dome roof; this is the entrance to the Greenwich Foot Tunnel, where an ancient elevator takes you down to a walkway under the Thames that brings you up very close to the **Cutty Sark**① and the *Gipsy Moth IV*②.

By continuing along King William Walk, you come to the wrought-iron gates of the **Royal Naval College** ③, from the south end of which you approach the building that Wren's majestic quadrangles frame, the **Queen's House** ④, followed by the **National Maritime Museum** ⑤. Now head up the hill in Greenwich Park overlooking the Naval College and Maritime Museum to the **Old Royal Observatory** ⑥ and the **Ranger's House** ⑦. Walking back through the park toward the river, you'll enter the pretty streets of Greenwich Village to the west. There are plenty of bookstores and antiques shops for browsing, and, at the foot of Crooms Hill, the modern **Greenwich Theatre** ⑧—a West End theater, despite its location, which mounts well-regarded, often star-spangled productions—and the **Fan Museum** ⑨ opposite. Finish up at the excellent **Greenwich Antique Market** ⑩ (Burney Street near the museum and theater), and the Victorian **Covered Crafts Market** ⑪ by the *Cutty Sark,* on College Approach.

TIMING

First of all, the boat trip takes about an hour from Westminster Pier (next to Big Ben), or 25 minutes from the Tower of London, so figure in enough time for round-trip, unless the weather's really awful, or it's winter and the boats have stopped. Aim for an early start. Although the distance covered in this walk is barely a mile, Greenwich can't be "done" in a day. There are such riches here, especially if the maritime theme is your thing, that whatever time you allow will seem halved. If the weather's good, you'll be tempted to stroll aimlessly around the quaint villagelike streets, too, and maybe take a turn in the park. If you want to take in the markets, you'll need to come on a weekend. The antiques market is open 8–4; the crafts market, 9–5.

HOW TO GET THERE

Thames Passenger Service Federation (☎ 0171/930–4097) runs trips by boat from Westminster Pier every 30 minutes from 10:30 to 4, in April, May, September, and October; 10 to 5, June, July, and August; and less frequently in winter. Buses 188 and 286 are alternatives.

Sights to See

⑪ **Covered Crafts Market.** You'll find this Victorian market by the *Cutty Sark,* on College Approach. As you'd expect, this one features crafts, but there are more of the sort of ceramics, jewelry, knitwear, and leather goods that you might actually want to own than is common in such places, and you get to buy them from the people who made them. ⊙ *Weekends 9–5.*

🐚 ❶ **Cutty Sark.** This romantic tea clipper was built in 1869, one of fleets and fleets of similar wooden tall-masted clippers that during the 19th century plied the seven seas, trading in exotic commodities—tea, in this case. The *Cutty Sark*, the last to survive, was also the fastest, sailing the China–London route in 1871 in only 107 days. Now the photogenic vessel lies in dry dock, a museum of one kind of seafaring life—and not a comfortable kind for the 28-strong crew, as you'll see. The collection of figureheads is amusing, too. ⊠ *King William Walk*, ☎ *0181/858–3445.* ▣ *£3.50.* ☉ *June–Sept., Mon.–Sat. 10–6, Sun. noon–6; Oct.–May, Mon.–Sat. 10–5, Sun. noon–5; last admission 30 mins before closing.*

❾ **Fan Museum.** In two newly restored houses dating from the 1820s, opposite the Greenwich Theatre, is this highly unusual museum. The 2,000 fans here, which date from the 17th century onward, comprise the world's only such collection, and the history and purpose of these often exquisitely crafted objects are explained satisfyingly. It was the personal vision—and fan collection—of Helene Alexander that brought it into being in 1991, and the workshop and conservation and study center that she has also set up ensure that this anachronistic art has a future. ⊠ *10–12 Croom's Hill,* ☎ *0181/858–7879.* ▣ *£5.* ☉ *Tues.–Sat. 11–4:30, Sun. noon–4:30.*

🐚 ❷ **Gipsy Moth IV.** The boat in which Sir Francis Chichester achieved the first single-handed circumnavigation of the globe in 1966 is dry-docked beside the *Cutty Sark*. Inside you'll see the tiny space the sailor endured for 226 days, and the ingenious way everything he needed was installed. The Queen knighted him on board here, using the same sword with which the previous Elizabeth had knighted that other seagoing Francis, Sir Francis Drake, three centuries before. Please note that the *Gipsy Moth* was closed at press time, and no details were available about its reopening, so call ahead. ⊠ *King William Walk,* ☎ *0181/858–3445.* ▣ *50p.* ☉ *Apr.–Oct., Mon.–Sat. 10–6, Sun. noon–6.*

❿ **Greenwich Antique Market.** If you're visiting on the weekend, this market on Burney Street near the Fan Museum and Greenwich Theatre is open for business. It has a lot of bric-a-brac and books, too, and it's well known among the cognoscenti as a good source for vintage clothing.

❽ **Greenwich Theatre.** Officially a West End theater, despite its location, this modern venue mounts well-regarded, often star-spangled productions. ☎ *0181/858–7755.*

🐚 ❺ **National Maritime Museum.** Greenwich's star attraction contains everything to do with the British at sea in the form of paintings, models, maps, globes, sextants, uniforms (including the one Nelson died in at Trafalgar, complete with bloodstained bullet hole), and—best of all—actual boats, including a collection of ornate, gilded royal barges. ⊠ *Romney Rd.,* ☎ *0181/858–4422.* ▣ *£5, including Queen's House and Old Royal Observatory (☞ below).* ☉ *Mon.–Sat. 10–6, Sun. noon–6.*

🐚 ❻ **Old Royal Observatory.** Founded in 1675 by Charles II, this imposing institution was designed the same year by Christopher Wren for John Flamsteed, the first Astronomer Royal. The red ball you see on its roof has been there only since 1833. It drops every day at 1 PM, and you can set your watch by it, as the sailors on the Thames always have. In fact, nearly everyone sets their watch by it: This "Greenwich Timeball," along with the Gate Clock inside the observatory, are the most visible manifestations of Greenwich Mean Time, and since 1884, the ultimate standard for time around the world. Also here is the **Prime Meridian,** a brass line laid on the cobblestones at 0° longitude, one side being the eastern, one the western hemisphere. In 1948 the Old Royal Obser-

Greenwich

Covered Crafts
Market, **11**
Cutty Sark, **1**
Fan Museum, **9**
Gipsy Moth IV, **2**
Greenwich Antique
Market, **10**
Greenwich Theatre, **8**
National Maritime
Museum, **5**
Old Royal
Observatory, **6**
Queen's House, **4**
Ranger's House, **7**
Royal Naval College, **3**

vatory lost its official status: London's glow had grown too intense, and the astronomers moved to Sussex, while the Astronomer Royal decamped to Cambridge. They left various telescopes, chronometers, and clocks for you to view in their absence. ⊠ *Greenwich Park,* ☎ *0181/858–4422.* ⊠ *Joint admission with National Maritime Museum (☞ above).* ⊙ *Daily 10–5.*

★ ❹ **Queen's House.** The queen for whom Inigo Jones began designing the house in 1616 was James I's Anne of Denmark, but she died three years later, and it was Charles I's French wife, Henrietta Maria, who inherited the building when it was completed in 1635. It is no less than Britain's first Classical building—the first, that is, to use the lessons of Italian Renaissance architecture—and is therefore of enormous importance in the history of English architecture. Inside, the Tulip Stair, named for the fleur-de-lys–style pattern on the balustrade, is especially fine, spiraling up, without a central support, to the Great Hall. The Great Hall itself is a perfect cube, exactly 40 ft in all three directions, decorated with paintings of the Muses, the Virtues, and the Liberal Arts. The White Card is accepted. ☎ *0181/858–4422.* ⊠ *£5.50, including National Maritime Museum and Old Royal Observatory (☞ above).* ⊙ *Mon.– Sat. 10–6, Sun. noon–6.*

❼ **Ranger's House.** This handsome early 18th-century mansion, which was the Greenwich Park Ranger's official residence during the 19th century, now houses collections of Jacobean portraits and early musical instruments. Concerts are regularly given here, too. It stands just outside the park boundaries, on the southwest side of **Greenwich Park,** which is one of London's oldest royal parks. It had been in existence for more than 200 years before Charles II commissioned the French landscape artist Le Nôtre (who was responsible for Versailles and for St. James's Park) to redesign it in what was, in the 1660s, the latest French fashion. The flower garden on the southeast side and the deer enclosure nearby are particularly pleasant. Look also for Queen Elizabeth's Oak on the east side, around which Henry VIII and his second queen, Anne Boleyn, Elizabeth I's mother, are said to have danced. ⊠ *Chesterfield Walk, Blackheath,* ☎ *0181/853–0035.* ⊠ *Free.* ⊙ *Apr.– Sept., daily 10–6; Oct.–Mar., daily 10–4; closed 1 hr for lunch.*

★ ❸ **Royal Naval College.** Begun by Christopher Wren in 1694 as a home, or hospital (as in the Chelsea Royal Hospital, not Charing Cross Hospital) for ancient mariners, it became instead a school for young ones in 1873. You'll notice how the structures part to reveal the Queen's House across the central lawns. Wren, with the help of his assistant, Hawksmoor, was at pains to preserve the river vista from the house, and there are few more majestic views in London than the awe-inspiring symmetry he achieved. Behind the college are two buildings you can visit. The **Painted Hall,** the college's dining hall, derives its name from the baroque murals of William and Mary (reigned 1689–95; William alone 1695–1702) and assorted allegorical figures, the whole supported by trompe l'oeil pillars that Sir James Thornhill (who decorated the inside of St. Paul's dome, too) painted between 1707 and 1717. In the opposite building stands the **College Chapel,** which was rebuilt after a fire in 1779 and is altogether lighter, in a more restrained, neo-Grecian style. At Christmas 1805, Admiral Nelson's body was brought from the Battle of Trafalgar to lie in state here. ⊠ *Royal Naval College, King William Walk,* ☎ *0181/858–2154.* ⊠ *Free.* ⊙ *Daily 2:30–4:45.*

In case you want to see the world.

At American Express, we're here to make your journey a
smooth one. So we have over 1,700 travel service locations
in over 120 countries ready to help. What else would you
expect from the world's largest travel agency?

do more ®

AMERICAN
EXPRESS

Travel

In case you want to be welcomed there.

We're here to see that you're always welcomed at establishments everywhere. That's why millions of people carry the American Express® Card – for peace of mind, confidence, and security, around the world or just around the corner.

do more

Cards

In case you're running low.

We're here to help with more than 118,000 Express Cash locations around the world. In order to enroll, just call American Express before you start your vacation.

do more

Express Cash

And just in case.

We're here with American Express® Travelers Cheques
and Cheques *for Two.*® They're the safest way to carry
money on your vacation and the surest way to get a
refund, practically anywhere, anytime.

Another way we help you...

do more®

**Travelers
Cheques**

UPSTREAM FROM LONDON

The Thames is Britain's longest river. It winds its way through the Cotswolds, beyond the "dreaming spires" of Oxford and past majestic Windsor Castle—here far more the lazy, leafy country river than the dark gray urban waterway you see in London. Once you leave the city center, going west, or upstream, you reach a series of former villages—Chiswick, Kew, Richmond, Putney—that, apart from the roar of aircraft coming in to land at Heathrow a few miles farther west, still retain a peaceful, almost rural atmosphere, especially in places where parkland rolls down to the riverbank. In fact, it was really only at the beginning of this century that these villages expanded into London proper. The royal palaces and grand houses that dot the area were built not as town houses but as country residences with easy access to London by river.

TIMING

Each of the places we list here could easily absorb a whole day of your time, and Hampton Court is especially huge. Access is fairly easy: The District Line of the underground runs out to Kew and Richmond, as does Network SouthEast from Waterloo, which also serves Twickenham and Hampton Court. Chiswick House can be reached by tube to Turnham Green, then the E3 bus; or by tube to Hammersmith and Bus 290. A pleasant, if slow, way to go is by river. Boats depart Westminster Pier (just by Big Ben) for Kew (1½ hours), Richmond (2–3 hours), and Hampton Court (4 hours) several times a day in summer, less frequently from October through March. As you can tell from those sailing times, the boat trip is worth taking only if you make it an integral part of your day out, and even then, be aware that it can get very breezy on the water and that the scenery going upstream is by no means constantly fascinating. ✉ *Westminster Pier,* ☎ *0171/930–4097.*

Chiswick and Kew

Chiswick is the nearest Thames-side destination to London, with Kew just a mile or so beyond it. Much of Chiswick today is a nondescript suburb developed at the beginning of this century. But, incongruously stranded among the terraced houses, a number of fine 18th-century houses and a charming little village survive. The village atmosphere of Kew is still distinct, making this one of the most desirable areas of outer London. What makes Kew famous, though, are the Royal Botanic Gardens.

A Good Walk

Chiswick's **Church Street** (reached by an underpass from Hogarth's House) is the nearest thing to a sleepy country village street in all of London, despite its proximity to the Great West Road. Follow it down to the Thames and turn left at its foot to reach the sturdy 18th-century riverfront houses of **Chiswick Mall.** The ½-mi walk along here takes you far away from mainstream London and into a world of elegance and calm. You will pass several riverside pubs as you head along this stretch of the Thames toward Hammersmith Bridge. The **Dove** is the prettiest, if the most crowded, with its terrace hanging over the water, though the food is better at the **Blue Anchor,** which you reach first.

There's a similarly peaceful walk to be had about 1 mi to the west along the 18th-century river frontage of **Strand-on-the-Green,** whose houses look over the narrow towpath to the river, their tidy brick facades covered with wisteria and roses in summer. Strand-on-the-Green ends at Kew Bridge, opposite which is **Kew Green,** where local teams play cricket on summer Sundays. All around it are fine 18th-century houses, and, in the center, a church in which the painters Gainsborough and John Zoffany (1733–1810) are buried.

Sights to See

★ **Chiswick House.** Built circa 1725 by the Earl of Burlington as a country residence in which to entertain friends, and as a kind of temple to the arts, this is the very model of a Palladian villa, inspired by the Villa Capra near Vicenza in northeastern Italy. The house fans out from a central octagonal room in perfect symmetry, guarded by statues of Burlington's heroes, Palladio himself and his disciple, Inigo Jones. Burlington's friends—Pope, Swift, Gay, and Handel among them—were well qualified to adorn a temple to the arts. This is the Lord Burlington of Burlington House, Piccadilly, home of the Royal Academy and, of course, Burlington Arcade. It goes without saying that he was a great connoisseur, and an important patron, of the arts, but he was also an accomplished architect in his own right, fascinated—obsessed even— by the architecture and art of the Italian Renaissance and ancient Rome, with which he'd fallen in love during his Italian grand tour (every well-bred boy's rite of passage). Along with William Kent (1685– 1748), who designed the interiors and the rambling gardens here, Burlington did an awful lot to disseminate the Palladian ideals around Britain: Chiswick House sparked enormous interest, and you'll see these forms reflected in hundreds of subsequent English stately homes both small and large. ⊠ *Burlington La.,* ☎ *0181/995–0508.* ⊠ *£2.50.* ☉ *Apr.–Sept., daily 10–6; Oct.–Mar., daily 10–4; closed 1 hr for lunch. Tube: Turnham Green.*

Hogarth's House. This is where the painter lived from 1749 until his death in 1764. Unprotected from the six-lane Great West Road, which remains a main route to the West Country, the poor house is besieged by the surrounding traffic, but it's worth visiting for its little museum consisting mostly of the amusingly moralistic engravings for which Hogarth is best known, including the most famous of all, *The Rake's Progress* series of 1735. ⊠ *Hogarth La.,* ☎ *0181/994–6757.* ⊠ *Free.* ☉ *Apr.–Sept., Mon.–Sat. 11–6, Sun. 2–6; Oct.–Mar., Mon.–Sat. 11–4, Sun. 2–4. Closed 1st 3 wks of Sept. and last 3 wks of Dec. Tube: Turnham Green.*

★ **Kew Gardens.** The Royal Botanic Gardens at Kew are a spectacular 300 acres of public gardens, containing more than 60,000 species of plants. In addition, this is the country's leading botanical institute, with strong royal associations. Until 1840, when Kew Gardens was handed over to the nation, it had been the grounds of two royal residences: the White House (formerly Kew House) and Richmond Lodge, or the Dutch House. George II and Queen Caroline lived at Richmond Lodge in the 1720s, while their eldest son, Frederick, Prince of Wales, and his wife, Princess Augusta, came to the White House during the 1730s. The royal wives were keen gardeners. Queen Caroline got to work on her grounds, while next door Frederick's pleasure garden was developed as a botanical garden by his widow after his death. She introduced all kinds of "exotics," foreign plants brought back to England by botanists. Caroline was aided by a skilled head gardener and by the architect Sir William Chambers, who built a series of temples and follies, of which the crazy 10-story **Pagoda** (1762), visible for miles around, is the star turn. The celebrated botanist Sir Joseph Banks (1743–1820) then took charge of Kew, which developed rapidly in both its roles—as a beautiful landscaped garden, and as a center of study and research.

The highlights of a visit to Kew are the two great 19th-century greenhouses filled with tropical plants, many of which have been there as long as their housing. Both the **Palm House** and the **Temperate House** were designed by Sir Decimus Burton, the first opening in 1848, the second in 1899 (though it had been begun 40 years earlier); the latter was the biggest greenhouse in the world and today contains the biggest greenhouse plant in the world, a Chilean wine palm rooted in 1846. You can climb the spiral staircase almost to the roof and look down on this and the dense tropical profusion from the walkway. The **Princess of Wales Conservatory,** the latest and the largest plant house at Kew, was opened in 1987 by Princess Diana. Under its bold glass roofs, designed to maximize energy conservation, there are no less than 10 climatic zones, their temperatures all precisely controlled by computer.

The **Centre for Economic Botany** is housed in the newly constructed Joseph Banks Building, the majority of which is devoted to Kew's research collection on economic botany and to its library. But the public can enjoy exhibitions here on the theme of plants in everyday life. (There is no admission charge, and the center is open Monday–Saturday 9:10–4:30 and Sunday 9:30–5:30.) The plant houses make Kew worth visiting even in the depths of winter, but in spring and summer the gardens come into their own. In late spring, the woodland nature reserve of Queen Charlotte's Cottage Gardens is carpeted in bluebells; a little later, the Rhododendron Dell and the Azalea Garden become swathed in brilliant color. High summer features glorious displays of roses and water lilies, while fall is the time to see the heather garden, near the pagoda. Whatever time of year you visit, something is in bloom, and your journey is never wasted. ⊠ *Royal Botanic Gardens,* ☏ *0181/940–1171.* ⌑ *£4.50, including Queen Charlotte's Cottage Apr.–Sept.* ☉ *Gardens daily 9:30–sunset, greenhouses daily 10–sunset. Tube: Kew Gardens.*

Kew Palace. Kew Palace remains to this day quietly domestic and the smallest royal palace in the land. Through spring 1999, the palace is closed for refurbishment, but you can glimpse the little formal gardens to its rear, redeveloped in 1969 as a 17th-century garden. No details about the new opening hours or admission charge were available at press time. ⊠ *Kew Gardens,* ☏ *0181/940–3321.*

NEED A
BREAK? **Maids of Honour** (⊠ 288 Kew Rd.), the most traditional of Old World English tearooms, is named for the famous tarts invented here and still baked by hand on the premises. It's only open for tea Tuesday–Saturday 2:45–5:30.

Richmond

Named after the palace Henry VII built here in 1500, Richmond is still a welcoming and extremely pretty riverside "village" with many handsome (and mountainously expensive) houses, many antiques shops, a Victorian theater, and, best of all, the biggest of London's royal parks.

Sights to See

★ **Ham House.** Ham House stands to the west of Richmond Park, overlooking the Thames and nearly opposite the oddly named Eel Pie Island. The house was built in 1610 by Sir Thomas Vavasour, knight marshal to James I, then refurbished later the same century by the Duke and Duchess of Lauderdale, who, although not particularly nice (a contemporary called the duchess "the coldest friend and the most violent enemy that ever was known"), managed to produce one of the finest houses in Britain at the time. Now that £2 million has been sunk into restoring Ham House—a project overseen by the National Trust—its splendor can be appreciated afresh. The formerly empty library has been filled with 17th- and 18th-century volumes; the original decorations in the Great Hall, Round Gallery, and Great Staircase have been replicated; and all the furniture and fittings, on permanent loan from the V & A, have been cleaned and restored. The 17th-century gardens, too, merit a visit in their own right. You can reach Ham from Richmond on Bus 65 or 371, or by one of Greater London's most pleasant rural walks, along the eastern riverbank south from Richmond Bridge, lasting half an hour or so. ⊠ *Ham St., Richmond,* ☎ *0181/940–1950.* ⌨ *£5, gardens free.* ۞ *Mar.–Oct., Sat.–Wed. 1–5; Nov.–Dec., weekends 1–5. Tube: Richmond.*

Marble Hill House. On the northern bank of the Thames, almost opposite Ham House, stands another mansion, this one a near-perfect example of a Palladian villa. Marble Hill House was built during the 1720s by George II for his mistress, the "exceedingly respectable and respected" Henrietta Howard. Later the house was occupied by Mrs. Fitzherbert, who was secretly married to the Prince Regent (later George IV) in 1785. Marble Hill House was restored in 1901 and opened to the public two years later, looking very much like it did in Georgian times. A ferry service operates during the summer from Ham House across the river; access by foot is a half-hour walk south along the west bank from Richmond Bridge. ⊠ *Richmond Rd., Twickenham,* ☎ *0181/892–5115.* ⌨ *Free.* ۞ *Easter–Sept., daily 10–6; Oct.–Easter, daily 10–4. Tube: Richmond.*

☾ **Richmond Park.** Charles I enclosed this one in 1637 for hunting purposes, as with practically all the parks. Unlike the others, however, Richmond Park still has wild red and fallow deer roaming its 2,470 acres of grassland and heath and the oldest oaks you're likely to see—vestiges of the medieval forests that once encroached on London from all sides. White Lodge, inside the park, was built for George II in 1729. Edward VIII was born here; now it houses the Royal Ballet School. You can walk from the park past the fine 18th-century houses in and around Richmond Hill to the river, admiring first the view from the top. At the Thames, you may notice Quinlan Terry's recent Richmond Riverside development, which met with the approval of England's architectural adviser, Prince Charles, for its classical facades, and was vilified by many others for playing it safe. *Tube: Richmond.*

NEED A   The **Cricketers,** on Richmond Green, serves a good pub lunch. The mod-
BREAK?   ern, partially glass-roofed **Caffè Mamma,** on Hill Street, serves inexpen-
              sive Italian food. **Beeton's,** on Hill Rise, offers a good, traditional English
              breakfast, lunch, and afternoon tea, as well as proper dinners.

★ **Hampton Court Palace.** Some 20 mi from central London, on a loop of the Thames upstream from Richmond, lies one of London's oldest royal palaces, more like a small town in size, and requiring a day of your time to do it justice. The magnificent Tudor brick house was begun in 1514 by Cardinal Wolsey, the ambitious and worldly lord chancellor (roughly, prime minister) of England and archbishop of York. He wanted it to be the absolute best palace in the land, and in this he succeeded so effectively that Henry VIII grew deeply envious, whereupon Wolsey felt obliged to give Hampton Court to the king. Henry moved in in 1525, adding a great hall and chapel, and proceeded to live much of his rambunctious life here. James I made further improvements at the beginning of the 17th century, but by the end of the century the palace was getting rather run-down. Plans were drawn up by the joint monarchs William III and Mary II to demolish the building and replace it with a still larger and more splendid structure, in conscious emulation of the great palace of Versailles outside Paris. However, the royal purse wouldn't stretch quite that far. It was decided to keep the original buildings but add a new complex adjoining them at the rear, for which Wren was commissioned, and his graceful south wing is one of the highlights of the whole palace. (A serious fire badly damaged some of Wren's chambers in 1986, but they were restored and opened again in 1992, with some of the Tudor features he had covered up uncovered again.) William and, especially, Mary loved Hampton Court and left their mark on the place—see their fine collections of Delftware and other porcelain.

The site beside the slow-moving Thames is perfect. The palace itself, steeped in history, hung with priceless paintings, full of echoing cobbled courtyards and cavernous Tudor kitchens, complete with deer pies and cooking pots—not to mention the ghost of Catherine Howard, who is believed to be still abroad, screaming her innocence (of adultery) to an unheeding Henry VIII—is set in a fantastic array of ornamental gardens, lakes, and ponds. Among the horticultural highlights are an Elizabethan Knot Garden, Henry VIII's Pond Garden, the enormous conical yews around the Fountain Garden, and the Great Vine near the Banqueting House, planted in 1768 and still producing black Hamburg grapes, which you can buy in season. Best of all is the celebrated maze, which you enter to the north of the palace. It was planted in 1714 and is truly fiendish.

Royalty ceased living here with George III; poor George preferred the seclusion of Kew, where he was finally confined in his madness. The private apartments that range down one side of the palace are now occupied by pensioners of the Crown. Known as "grace and favor" apartments, they are among the most coveted homes in the country, with a surfeit of peace and history on their doorsteps. ⊠ *East Molesey,* ☎ *0181/977–8441.* 🎫 *Apartments and maze £8.50, maze alone £2, grounds free.* ☉ *State apartments Apr.–Oct., Tues.–Sun. 9:30–6, Mon. 10:15–6; Nov.–Mar., Tues.–Sun. 9:30–4:30, Mon. 10:15–4:30; grounds daily 8–dusk.*

3 Dining

*No longer would Somerset Maugham
be justified in warning, "If you want
to eat well in England, have breakfast
three times a day." London is in the
midst of a restaurant revolution and
the whole city is talking about it.
Nearly everyone has become a foodie—
even Andrew Lloyd Webber, that
obsessional front-runner and composer
of* Cats *and* Phantom *, who has taken
on a second career as dining critic.
After feasting on Mod Brit cuisine,
visit one (or two or three) of London's
fabulous pubs for a nightcap. Hit the
right one on the right night and watch
that legendary British reserve melt away.*

By Kate
Sekules

AS ANYONE WHO READS the Sunday papers knows, London has had a restaurant boom, or rather, a restaurant atomic bomb explosion. The city has fallen head-over-heels in love with its restaurants—all 5,000 of them—from its vast, glamorous eateries to its tiny neighborhood joints, from pubs where young foodniks find their feet to swank boîtes where celebrity chefs launch their ego flights. You, too, might be smitten, since you will be spending, on average, 25% of your travel budget on eating out.

To appreciate London's rise in the culinary firmament, it helps to recall that at one time it was understood that the British ate to live while the French lived to eat. Change was slow in coming after the Second World War, when steamed puddings and overboiled brussels sprouts were still consumed on a daily basis by tweed-and-flannel-wrapped Brits. When people thought of British cuisine, fish-and-chips came to mind. The latter was a grab-and-gulp dish that tasted best wrapped in newspaper (a spoilsport bureaucracy decreed that this wasn't sanitary, so the days of peeping at the latest murder news through a film of oil came to an end). Then there was always shepherd's pie, ubiquitously available in pubs—though not made according to the song from *Sweeney Todd,* "with real shepherd in it." Visitors used to arrive in London and joke that the most compelling reason Britain conquered half the world is that they probably wanted some decent food. Didn't Britons invade Rajasthan just for a good curry?

Today, nearly everything on the culinary front has changed. Menus seem to evolve every five minutes as chefs outdo each other to come up with flavor-of-the-month delights. Excellent new restaurants open every week, offering cuisines from all over the world—and even, be it said in reverent tones, from Britain itself. The recent restaurant renaissance is credited to the new wave of cutting-edge chefs and inspired entrepreneurs. Sir Terence Conran, inventor of Habitat (British precursor to IKEA), began it all with Quaglino's, the first of the megarestaurants that now decorate every corner of town. His 700-seater Mezzo became the biggest restaurant in Europe when it opened in 1995, though he has since topped that with the King's Road Bluebird, complete with grocery store, fishmonger, and produce market. The biggest ego, though, probably belongs to Marco Pierre White, the first British chef to earn three Michelin stars for his eponymous restaurant, which was then in the Hyde Park Hotel, and has now been relocated to the Belle Epoque–flavored Oak Room at the Meridien. Now, he's taking over everywhere: the Criterion, Mirabelle, and—in tandem with Damien Hirst, the award-winning artist—Quo Vadis and the new, at press time, Pharmacy in Notting Hill Gate. Another hip restaurateur is Oliver Peyton, who had his first success when he discovered a hole in the infamous killjoy alcohol licensing laws and brought the late-night Atlantic to a thirsty population.

Lunching ladies, models, and other assorted glitterati are catered to by gossip-column-regular Mogens Tholstrup at his South Kensington eatery, Daphne, at the Collection, in well-heeled Brompton Cross, and—heralding the craze for Moroccan and Moorish cuisine and cushion-on-the-floor lounging-while-you-dine—the West End–based Momo (still so completely impossible to get into we won't bother to review it). Media darlings, actors, and novelists have always, and still, prefer the two perfect restaurants owned by Christopher Corbin and Jeremy King: Le Caprice and the Ivy. There are, of course, many more stars of this new celebrity category (Restaurateurs and Chefs), but you'll

London Dining *(Boxes Refer to Detail Maps)*

Hampstead and Camden Town

Regent's Park

Maida Vale

Abbey Rd.
Abercorn Pl.
Grove End Rd.
Circus Rd.
Wellington Rd.
Prince Albert Rd.
Outer Circle
Chester Rd.
Albany St.
Outer Circle

Inner Circle

Hall Rd.
St. John's Wood Rd.
Liston Grove
Park Rd.
Chester Rd.

Clifton Rd.
Bloomfield Rd.
Edgware Rd.
Marylebone Rd.
Baker St.
Harley St.
Portland Pl.
Gt. Portland St.

Euston Rd.

Eversholt St.
Hampstead Rd.
Euston Station

Harrow Rd.
Marylebone Flyover
Gloucester Pl.
Seymour Pl.

Tottenham Ct.

Mayfair, St. James's, Soho, Covent Garden, and Bloomsbury

Bishop's Br. Rd.

Paddington Station

Sussex Gdns.
Edgware Rd.

Oxford St.
Oxford Circus

Kensington and Notting Hill Gate

Queensway

Bayswater Rd.

Oxford St.
Grosvenor Square
Brook St.
Bond St.
Regent St.
Grosvenor St.

Berkeley Square

Piccadilly Circus

Kensington Gardens

Hyde Park

Park Lane

Jermyn St.

The Serpentine

W. Carriage Dr.

Kensington Rd.
Kensington Gore
S. Carriage Rd.
Kensington Rd.
Knightsbridge

Grosvenor Pl.

Piccadilly

Green Park

Constitution Hill

Bird

Royal Albert Hall

Prince Consort Rd.

Queen's Gate
Exhibition Rd.
Brompton Rd.
Pont St.
Sloane St.
Cadogan Pl.

Belgrave Square

Eaton Square

Gloucester Rd.

Victoria Station

Victoria

Cromwell Rd.
Old Brompton Rd.
Fulham Rd.
Sloane Ave.
Sloane Sq.

Pimlico Rd.

Buckingham Palace Rd.
Wilton Rd.
Warwick Way

Belgr.

Sydney St.
Old Church St.
King's Rd.
Royal Hospital Rd.
Chelsea Br. Rd.

Lupus

South Kensington, Knightsbridge, and Chelsea

Cheyne Walk
Oakley St.
Albert Br.
Chelsea Embankment
River Thames
Battersea Park

Grosvenor

The City and the South Bank

King's Cross Station

St. Pancras Station

Pentonville Rd.

City Rd.

East Road

Hoxton St.

Old Gt. Eastern St.

Judd St.

King's Cross Rd.

Gray's Inn Rd.

Roseberry Ave.

St. John's St.

Goswell Rd.

Coram's Fields

Woburn

Guilford St.

Southampton Row

Theobald's Rd.

Farringdon Rd.

Clerkenwell Rd.

Liverpool St. Station

Court Rd.

New Oxford St.

High Holborn

Kingsway

Dury Ln.

Aldwych

Charing Cross Rd.

Shaftesbury Ave.

Strand

Victoria

Holborn Viaduct

Newgate St.

Old Bailey

Fleet St.

Law Courts

Cheapside

London Wall

Moorgate

Bishopsgate

Cornhill

Leadenhall St.

Gracechurch St.

Fenchurch St.

Queen Victoria St.

Cannon St.

Cannon St. Station

Embankment

Blackfriars Br.

Blackfriars Station

Southwark Br.

Lower Thames St.

London Br.

River Thames

Charing Cross Stn.

Waterloo Br.

South Bank Arts Complex

Stamford St.

Southwark St.

Tooley St.

London Bridge Station

The Mall

St. James's Park

Whitehall

York Rd.

Union St.

Westminster Br.

Waterloo Station

Waterloo Rd.

Blackfriars Rd.

The Cut

Westminster Br. Rd.

Borough Rd.

London Rd.

Borough High St.

New Kent Rd.

e Walk

St.

Horseferry Rd.

Millbank

Lambeth Palace Rd.

Lambeth Rd.

Kennington Rd.

Imperial War Museum

Walworth Rd.

Regency St.

Horseferry Rd.

Lambeth Br.

Tate Gallery

Albert Embankment

Vauxhall Br.

Kennington Ln.

Kennington Park Rd.

N

oll Br.

Rd.

e Elms Ln.

Vauxhall Station

Kennington Oval

0   1 mile

0   1 km

have to read about them when you get here—which you can easily do by picking up any newspaper. To keep up with the onslaught, they have about 15 restaurant reviewers apiece. A favorite topic among all of them is the terrible tendency for tables to be available only for half an evening, as spoiled maître d's of the most sought-after places stack up the reservations. "We have something at 7, but you'll have to be out by 8:30" is a line you may have to get used to if you're determined to dine in the places of the moment. It goes without saying that you should reserve way, way ahead if this is the case—ridiculously, a two or three month wait for a table is not uncommon in the hottest places these days.

Fortunately, London also does a good job of catering to people interested more in satisfying their appetites without breaking the bank than in the latest food fashions. We have tried to strike a balance in our listings between these extremes, and we've included hip and happening places, neighborhood places, ethnic alternatives, and old favorites, plus some completely undemanding burger joints and regular restaurants for when you merely want to be nourished. There are about 50 cuisines on offer in London, and ethnic restaurants have always been a good bet here, especially the thousands of Indian restaurants, since Londoners see a good tandoori as their birthright (don't worry if they've changed from tandoori places to balti houses since you last looked—balti is only a name for a gloopily sauced curry that you scoop up with nan bread). Londoners are busy enlarging their purview to encompass most of the world. You'll see Malaysian, Spanish, and Turkish places, a drove of Thai restaurants, the aforementioned North African pack, and a new wave of Japanese places, including the soba noodle cafés that are emulating the wonderful and popular Wagamama. With all this going on, traditional British food, when you track it down, appears as one more exotic cuisine in the pantheon.

As for cost, the democratization of restaurants does not necessarily mean smaller checks, and London is still not an inexpensive city. Damage-control methods include making lunch your main meal—the very top places often have bargain lunch menus, halving the price of evening à la carte—and ordering a second appetizer instead of an entrée, to which few places should object. (Note that an appetizer, usually known as a "starter" or "first course" is sometimes called an "entrée," as it is in France, and an entrée in England is dubbed "the main course" or simply "mains.") Seek out fixed-price menus, and watch for hidden extras on the check: "cover," bread, or vegetables charged separately, and service. Many restaurants exclude service charges from the menu (which the law obliges them to display outside), then add 10%–15% to the check, or else stamp SERVICE NOT INCLUDED along the bottom, in which case you should add the 10%–15% yourself. Don't pay twice for service—unscrupulous restaurateurs may add service, then leave the total in the credit card slip blank, hoping for more.

Two final caveats: First, is the roast beef of old England going to give you mad cow disease? If you recall, in 1996, there was a major cull of English oxen infected with feed gone bad, with a reprise in late 1997 to early 1998, when beef-on-the-bone was particularly implicated as a health hazard. Now, most restaurants still have some form of disclaimer for the purity of their beef, and you can bet they're not lying if they say it's safe. Second, beware of Sundays. Many restaurants are closed on this day, especially in the evening; likewise public holidays. Over the Christmas period, London shuts down completely—only hotels will be prepared to feed you. When in doubt, call ahead. It's as well to book a table anyway, but you'll have got the idea by now.

CATEGORY	COST*
££££	over £50
£££	£35–£50
££	£20–£35
£	under £20

per person for a three-course meal, excluding drinks, service, and VAT

Mayfair

AMERICAN/CASUAL

££ ✗ **Smollensky's.** This American-style bar-restaurant is useful for those with children in tow, especially on weekends, when the young are fed burgers, fish sticks, and "Kids' Koktails" and are taken off your hands by sundry clowns and magicians. The grown-ups' menu favors (fresh, additive-free) red meat, with several cuts of steak the specialty, all served with fries and a choice of sauces. There are also clam chowder, potato skins, salads, sandwiches, and fish, such as Louisiana catfish, and a couple of vegetarian choices. ✉ *1 Dover St., W1,* ☎ *0171/491–1199. AE, DC, MC, V. Tube: Green Park.*

£ ✗ **Condotti.** In a neighborhood not known for its casual dining options, this elegant pizzeria is like a breath of fresh air. Anyone familiar with Pizza Express will know the menu already—because this also belongs to the founder of that chain. The Veneziana (with onions, pine nuts, sultanas, and capers) is everyone's fave, and a donation goes to the Venice In Peril Fund when you order it. Or try the King Edward, with a potato base instead of bread, and check out the Paolozzis on the walls. ✉ *4 Mill Street St., W1,* ☎ *0171/499–1308. AE, DC, MC, V. Tube: Oxford Circus.*

BRITISH TRADITIONAL

£££ ✗ **The Greenhouse.** Tucked away behind the Mayfair mansions in a cute, cobbled mews is this elegant salon for people who like their food big and strong. You sit among extravagant topiary and men in ties to partake of British menus in the style of the now-departed famous-from-TV-chef Gary Rhodes: *faggots* (a type of meatball, once reviled) and braised oxtails; smoked eel risotto, venison and bacon stewed in red wine; and stodgy, sticky English desserts such as bread-and-butter pudding and steamed syrup sponge. ✉ *27A Hay's Mews, W1,* ☎ *0171/499–3331. Reservations essential. AE, DC, MC, V. No lunch Sat. Tube: Green Park.*

£–££ ✗ **Browns.** Unpretentious, crowd-pleasing, child-friendly English feeding is accomplished here at the former establishment of the bespoke tailors, Messrs. Cooling and Wells, now converted to Edwardian style by the owner of the very successful regional Browns eateries (the Oxford and Cambridge ones have put generations of students through school). Eat an all-day English breakfast, or steak-and-Guinness pie or salmon cakes, then sticky toffee pudding or sherry trifle. ✉ *47 Maddox St., W1,* ☎ *0171/491–4565. AE, MC, V. Tube: Oxford Circus.*

CONTEMPORARY

£££ ✗ **Coast.** This former car showroom is now a posing palace of cool white curves, a piece of art that also draws a mini-version of itself (via computer) on your check. It features a *slightly* pretentious menu that careens all over the world ("sauté of scallops, lettuce hearts with a creamed lemon and vanilla dressing," "roast sea bass, croûte of herb risotto, grilled *ventreche* and piquant velouté"—please don't ask for translations), ending with the signature dessert of tomato jam on vanilla cream. Avoid downstairs, which is like the set of Stanley Kubrick's film *2001.* ✉ *26B Albermarle St., W1,* ☎ *0171/495–5999. AE, MC, V. Tube: Green Park.*

FRENCH

££££ ✗ **Chez Nico at Ninety Park Lane.** Those with refined palates and very deep pockets would be well advised not to miss Nico Ladenis's exquisite cuisine, served in this suitably hushed and plush Louis XV dining room next to the Grosvenor House Hotel. Autodidact Nico is one of the world's great chefs, and he's famous for knowing it. The menu is in French and untranslated; vegetarians and children are not welcome. There is no salt on the table—ask for some at your peril. It's all more affordable in daylight, proffering set menus from £32 for three courses. ✉ *90 Park La., W1,* ☎ *0171/409–1290. Reservations essential. Jacket and tie. AE, DC, MC, V. Closed weekends and 3 wks in Aug. Tube: Marble Arch.*

££££ ✗ **Le Gavroche.** Albert Roux's son, Michel, retains many of his father's
★   "capital C" Classical dishes under the heading "*Hommage à mon père,*" and has added his own style to this place, once considered London's finest restaurant. The basement dining room is comfortable and sedate, pleasing only if your idea of riveting decor is low-ceilinged and accented with potted plants and bland modern paintings. Yet again, the set lunch is relatively affordable at £40 (for canapés and three courses, plus mineral water, a half-bottle of wine, coffee, and petit fours, service *compris*). In fact, it's the only way to eat here if you don't have a generous expense account at your disposal—which most patrons do. You must reserve at least one week in advance. ✉ *43 Upper Brook St., W1,* ☎ *0171/408–0881. Reservations essential. Jacket and tie. AE, DC, MC, V. Closed weekends and 10 days at Christmas. Tube: Marble Arch.*

££££ ✗ **Oak Room** Bad boy Marco Pierre White enjoys Jagger-like fame from
★   his TV appearances and gossip column reports of his complicated love life and random eruptions of fury. He should stick to his pans, say super-chef critics, meaning it literally in some cases. But, hype aside, Marco may be London's greatest chef and now gets to show off in his most spectacular setting yet—all belle epoque soaring ceilings and gilded bits, and palms and paintings, not to mention the crisp napery and batteries of flatware. If you invest in an evening here, know that he will despise you for ordering his Assiette of Chocolate, which he considers low-class. ✉ *Le Meridien, 21 Piccadilly, W1,* ☎ *0171/734–8000. Reservations essential. Jacket and tie. AE, DC, MC, V. Tube: Piccadilly Circus.*

££££ ✗ **The Square.** Young chef Philip Howard's sophisticated set menus
★   are in the French haute tradition, with ideas from all over grafted on. Some examples will give the best idea: roast foie gras with caramelized endive and late-picked muscat grapes or a velouté of truffles with girolles tortellini (wild mushrooms are high on his shopping list); then an herb-crusted saddle of lamb with white bean puree, or a roast cod with creamed potato and truffles—all are arranged carefully and symmetrically, much like the high-ceiling, apricot-colored room. Some desserts—like the fantastic melted chocolate cake—come on square glass plates because of the restaurant's name (which actually refers to its previous home on St. James's Square). The grown-up clientele is heavy on business types who appreciate impeccable service, complete with a friendly (and necessary—the wine list has the heft of a novel) sommelier. ✉ *Bruton St., SW1,* ☎ *0171/495–7100. Reservations essential. AE, MC, V. No lunch weekends. Tube: Green Park.*

£££ ✗ **Criterion.** This spectacular neo-Byzantine mirrored marble hall, which first opened in 1874, is firmly back on the map, with the arrival of a new regime led by Marco Pierre White. He doesn't cook here, but some of his well-known and often copied dishes appear on a menu whose divisions include one headed "Farinaceous Dishes"—where you'll find his black, buttery risotto with squid ink, for instance. The glamour of the soaring golden ceiling, peacock-blue theater-size drapes, oil paintings, and attentive Gallic service adds up to an elegant night out. ⊠ *Piccadilly Circus, W1, ☎ 0171/930–0488. AE, DC, MC, V. Tube: Piccadilly Circus.*

££–£££ ✕ **L'Odéon.** This contribution to London's mania for giant restaurants overlooks Regent Street in a former airline office, its long, low dimensions peculiarly reminiscent of an aircraft, despite the gauzy partitions throughout. Food is elevated French-bistro-style—grilled Dover sole with beurre noisette; wild mushrooms on brioche toast—and is far more affordable in set menu form, available for lunch and before 7 PM. Tables by the huge arched windows are fun for people-watching. ⊠ *65 Regent St., W1, ☎ 0171/287–1400. AE, DC, MC, V. Tube: Piccadilly Circus.*

FRENCH/BRITISH TRADITIONAL

££££ ✕ **The Connaught.** This charming and very grand mahogany-paneled,
★ velvet-upholstered, and crystal-chandeliered dining room belongs to the absolutely exclusive eponymous hotel (☞ Chapter 4). Waiters wear tails, tables must be booked far in advance, and prices are fearsome; but the restaurant remains London's most respected traditional dining room, with famed French chef Michel Bourdin still in charge of the kitchens after many years. This is the place for game—venison, guinea fowl, pigeon (not local birds)—presented with traditional trimmings or perhaps with some confection of wild mushrooms. "Luncheon dishes" change according to the day of the week (if this is Friday, it must be oxtail) and are not as exorbitant as they seem at first, because the price includes a starter and dessert. The Connaught is by no means a fashionable place, but it is never out of fashion. ⊠ *Carlos Pl., W1, ☎ 0171/499–7070. Reservations essential. Jacket and tie. AE, DC, MC, V. Tube: Green Park.*

£–££ ✕ **Villandry.** This foodie's paradise just moved to huge new premises— the food hall here is now even larger than the one at Harrods! French pâtés, Continental cheeses, fruit tarts, biscuits, and breads galore are for sale, and if you must indulge but can't wait to take a bite, there's a tearoom café and dining room that both serve exquisite lunches. Twice a month, dinners are offered, but they are among the hardest reservations to book in London. ⊠ *170 Great Portland St., W1, ☎ 0171/631– 3131. AE, MC, V. Tube: Great Portland St.*

IRISH

££ ✕ **Mulligans.** Mulligans is straight out of Dublin, down to the draught Guinness and copies of *The Irish Times* in the upstairs bar. Downstairs in the upscale restaurant department, order traditional dishes like steak, Guinness and oyster pie, and Irish stew with homey accompaniments like colcannon (buttery mashed potatoes with cabbage), then a big Irish pudding. ⊠ *13–14 Cork St., W1, ☎ 0171/409–1370. AE, MC, V. Closed Sun. No lunch weekends. Tube: Green Park.*

JAPANESE

££££ ✕ **Nobu.** Nobu Matsuhisa already has New York and Los Angeles, and now he's taking London, with the same formula of new style sashimi (such as halibut, ever-so-slightly seared in tangerine-infused oil), plus the famous *omakase* (chef's choice) meals. Nobu is in the Metropolitan, one of London's hippest hotels, with staff, attitude, clientele, and prices to match, and a minimalissimo decor. ⊠ *19 Old Park La., W1. Reservations essential. AE, DC, MC, V. No lunch weekdays. No dinner Sun. Tube: Hyde Park.*

MEXICAN

£ ✕ **Down Mexico Way.** London is not known for its fine Tex-Mex, but here among the usual tortillas and burritos are a few adventurous num-

140

bers, such as fish in almond-chili sauce, with sides of cheese and jalapeño muffins or spiced spinach. Look for the beautiful Spanish ceramic tiles. Avoid evenings here if you want a quiet night out—the place is often taken over by party animals. ⊠ *25 Swallow St., W1,* ☎ *0171/ 437–9895. AE, DC, MC, V. Tube: Piccadilly Circus.*

St. James's

BRITISH TRADITIONAL

£   ✕ **The Fountain.** At the back of Fortnum and Mason's is this old-
★   fashioned restaurant, as frumpy and as popular as a boarding school matron, serving delicious light meals, toasted snacks, sandwiches, and ice-cream sodas. During the day, go for the Welsh rarebit or cold game pie; in the evening, a no-frills fillet steak is a typical option. It's just the place for afternoon tea and ice-cream sundaes after the Royal Academy or Bond Street shopping, and for pretheater meals. ⊠ *181 Piccadilly, W1,* ☎ *0171/734–4938. AE, DC, MC, V. Closed Sun. Tube: Green Park.*

FRENCH

£££   ✕ **L'Oranger.** Reserve weeks in advance because this 1996 offshoot of
★   the impossible-to-get-into Aubergine in Chelsea just gets better and better, and everyone wants in. Marcus Wareing is the chef, and he cooks with gobsmacking precision and perfection: a tartar of mixed fish; a little cylinder of brill on a raft of crisped potato; the perfect plum *tarte fine* (brandied plum tart). The conservatory room with its train of tables up the middle is romantic, plus there's a little courtyard where the last duel in London was fought, and the all-French waiters are courteous and not snobby. ⊠ *5 St. James's St., SW1,* ☎ *0171/839–3774. Reservations essential. AE, DC, MC, V. No lunch Sun. Tube: Green Park.*

££   ✕ **Café Fish.** Just to the east of St. James's proper, this cheerful, bustling restaurant has an encyclopedic selection of fish (shark and turbot join the trout, halibut, salmon, and monkfish, some brought daily from Normandy), arranged on the menu according to cooking method: chargrilled, steamed, meunière; smoked fish pâté is brought with the bread to get you in the mood as you choose your main selection. ⊠ *39 Panton St., SW1,* ☎ *0171/930–3999. AE, DC, MC, V. Closed Sun. Tube: Piccadilly Circus.*

FRENCH/BRITISH TRADITIONAL

££££   ✕ **The Ritz.** Constantly accused of being London's prettiest dining room, this Belle Epoque palace of marble, gilt, and trompe l'oeil would moisten even Marie Antoinette's eye; add the view over Green Park and the Ritz's secret sunken garden, and it seems obsolete to consider eating. But the British/French cuisine stands up to the visual onslaught, with costly morsels (foie gras, lobster, truffles, caviar, etc.) that are super-rich, all served with a flourish. Old retainers still take great pride in this smooth operation and are still here despite the hotel's change of ownership. Englishness is wrested from Louis XVI by a daily roast "from the trolley," and a "British specialty" like Irish stew or braised oxtail. A three-course menu at £23 and a dinner at £29 make the check more bearable, but the wine list is pricey. A Friday and Saturday dinner dance sweetly maintain a dying tradition. ⊠ *Piccadilly, W1,* ☎ *0171/493– 8181. Reservations essential. Jacket and tie. AE, DC, MC, V. Tube: Green Park.*

MODERN BRITISH

£££   ✕ **The Avenue.** Huge and loud, especially since it got permission to ply its City-glitzy clientele with beverages way beyond their bedtime (here that's until midnight Monday–Thursday; 12:30 AM Friday–Saturday), this was London's first restaurant to be owned by committee. Unlike the horse designed by committee (a camel), it has worked out okay, emulating New York singles-heavy dining-as-theater glamour, with a long, acid yellow uplighted glass bar and a very '80s bank of blinking TV screens at the entrance. The food is pretty good generic Euro-Brit (endive *tarte Tatin*; crab and crispy pork salad with chili dressing; chicken pot au feu), though the baked Alaska could feed 10 and tastes like a s'more with a cocktail cherry. ✉ *7–9 St. James's St., SW1,* ☎ *0171/ 321–2111. AE, DC, MC, V. Tube: Green Park.*

£££ ✕ **Le Caprice.** Secreted in a small street behind the Ritz, Caprice may
★ command the deepest loyalty of any restaurant in London because it gets everything right: the glamorous, glossy black Eva Jiricna interior, the perfect pitch of the informal but respectful service, the food, halfway between Euro-peasant and fashion plate. This food—crispy duck and watercress salad; seared scallops with bacon and sorrel; risotto nero; Lincolnshire sausage with bubble-and-squeak (potato-and-cabbage hash); grilled rabbit with black olive polenta; and divine desserts, too—has no business being so good, because the other reason everyone comes here is that everyone else does, which leads to the best people-watching in town (apart from its sister restaurant, the Ivy ☞ Covent Garden, *below*). ✉ *Arlington House, Arlington St., SW1,* ☎ *0171/629–2239. Reservations essential. AE, DC, MC, V. No lunch Sat. Tube: Green Park.*

£££ ✕ **Quaglino's.** Now well into its first decade, Sir Terence Conran's original huge restaurant, "Quags," is *the* out-of-towners' post-theater or celebration destination, while Londoners like its late hours. The gigantic sunken restaurant boasts a glamorous staircase, "Crustacea Altar," large bar, and live jazz music. The food is fashionably pan-European with some Asian trimmings—crab with mirin and soy; noodles with ginger, chili and cilantro; rabbit with prosciutto and herbs; roast crayfish; plateaux de fruits de mer. Desserts come from somewhere between the Paris bistro and the English nursery (raspberry sablé, parkin pudding with butterscotch sauce), and wine from the Old World and the New, some bottles at modest prices. ✉ *16 Bury St., SW1,* ☎ *0171/930–6767. Reservations essential. AE, DC, MC, V. Tube: Green Park.*

Soho

CAFÉS

£ ✕ **Maison Bertaux.** On two floors in central Soho, this French patisserie is not in the least dainty, but it is the kind of place to refuel after a shopping trek with a savory pastry at lunchtime, or a Danish mid-morning, or even an early supper (it closes at 8 PM). The ancient rivalry with Valerie round the corner still obtains. ✉ *28 Greek St., W1,* ☎ *0171/437–6007. No credit cards. Tube: Leicester Sq.*

£ ✕ **Patisserie Valerie.** Beloved of film-biz people, students, shoppers, and just about everyone else, this dark and antique pastry shop with café is cherished because nothing has changed in years. It does better on the savory flans and pastries than its near-neighbor, Bertaux, but it has equally early closing times. ✉ *44 Old Compton St., W1,* ☎ *0171/ 437–3466. No credit cards. Tube: Leicester Sq.*

CHINESE

££ ✕ **Fung Shing.** This comfortable, cool-green restaurant is a cut above
★ the Lisle/Wardour Street crowd in both service and ambience, as well as food. The usual Chinatown options are supplemented by some exciting dishes. Salt-baked chicken, served on or off the bone with an accompanying bowl of intense broth, is essential, and the adventurous might try intestines—deep-fried cigarette-shape morsels, far more delicious than you'd expect. ✉ *15 Lisle St., WC2,* ☎ *0171/437–1539. AE, DC, MC, V. Tube: Leicester Sq.*

FRENCH

£–£££ ✕ **Mezzo.** Sir Terence Conran's 700-seater Mezzo isn't only London's biggest; it's the most gigantic restaurant in all of Europe. Downstairs is the restaurant proper, with its huge glass-walled kitchen, its Allen Jones murals, its grand piano and dance floor, and its typically Conran-style French menu of things like seafood, rabbit stew, steak-frites, and fig tart. Upstairs, the bar overlooks a canteen-style operation called Mezzonine, where bowls of coconut-galangal fish soup and grilled squid salad and red duck curry are Asian style. Finally, a late-night café-/patisserie/newsstand has a separate entrance next door. The place has been a London landmark from day one, with a see-and-be-seen bustle, despite its low celebrity count. ✉ *100 Wardour St., W1,* ☎ *0171/ 314–4000. AE, DC, MC, V. Tube: Leicester Sq.*

ITALIAN

£ ✕ **Pollo** A homey, family-run, boisterous Italian glorified café that's been here forever, and through which all Londoners pass during their student and/or clubbing days, this does very well for a quick feed with a bottle of house plonk pretheater, or for an afternoon spaghetti carbonara. Watch the crowds in the evenings, though—it's no fun unless you're 18 and at art school. ✉ *20 Old Compton St., W1,* ☎ *0171/ 734–5917. No credit cards. Tube: Leicester Sq.*

MEDITERRANEAN

££ ✕ **Soho Soho.** The ground floor is a lively café bar with a (no reservations) rotisserie, while upstairs is a more formal and expensive restaurant. Inspiration comes from Provence, both in the olive-oil cooking style and the decor, with its murals, primary colors, and pale-ocher terra-cotta floor tiles. The rotisserie serves omelets, salads, charcuterie, and cheeses, plus a handful of such bistro dishes as Toulouse sausages with fries; herbed, grilled poussin fish; and tarte Tatin. Or you can stay in the café-bar and have just a kir or a beer. ✉ *11–13 Frith St., W1,* ☎ *0171/494–3491. AE, DC, MC, V. Tube: Leicester Sq.*

MODERN BRITISH

££££ ✕ **Quo Vadis.** When Marco Pierre White, London's most celebrated chef, and Damien Hirst, Britain's most brilliant artist, decide to go into partnership, you can be sure their new restaurant will be at the cutting edge of food fashion—literally. There are two of Hirst's notorious severed cow heads decorating the upstairs bar here (Patsy Kensit, designer stubble, and rock bigwigs sometimes in attendance). Happily, downstairs in the restaurant proper, the kitchen is serious and good: confit of salmon, corn-fed chicken en cocotte with essence of cèpes, cassoulet of monkfish, and passion-fruit meringue. Occupying the former house of Karl Marx, the restaurant's salons range from stark (skeletons and surgical tools as decor) to Technicolor (aubergine collides with cranberry-hued walls). Will this place be a mere flash-in-the-pantheon or a lasting monument to Mod Brit cuisine? Right now, everybody's placing bets. Main dishes at dinner run from £19 to £40, but there is a fine fixed-price lunch to be had at either £14.95 or £17.95. ✉ *26–29 Tottenham Court Rd., W1,* ☎ *0171/439–4809. Reservations essential. AE, MC, V. Tube: Leicester Sq., Tottenham Court Rd.*

£££ ✕ **Alastair Little.** Little is one of London's most original—and most imitated—chefs, drawing inspiration from practically everywhere (Thailand, Japan, Scandinavia, France, but chiefly Italy) and sometimes bringing it off brilliantly. His restaurant is stark and sparse—it's intentional, darling—so all attention focuses on the menu, which changes not once but twice daily in order to take advantage of the best ingredients. There will certainly be fish, but other than that, it's hard to predict. Look out also for his newer, smaller, cheaper version—but with the same name—just by Ladbroke Grove tube. ✉ *49 Frith St., W1,* ☎

0171/734–5183. *No credit cards. Closed Sun., 2 wks at Christmas, and 3 wks in Aug. No lunch Sat. Tube: Leicester Sq.*

££–£££ ✕ **L'Escargot.** This ever-popular media haunt serves Anglo-French food in its ground-floor brasserie and its more formal upstairs restaurant. Reasonably priced wine from a comprehensive list sets off a robust ragout of spiced lamb or a simple, fresh poached or grilled fish. This place is reliable and relaxed. ⊠ *48 Greek St., W1,* ☎ *0171/437–2679. AE, DC, MC, V. Closed Sun. Tube: Leicester Sq.*

MALAYSIAN

£ ✕ **Melati.** What amounts to a Malaysian café featuring wooden tables and, usually, lines at the door is a very useful place when you don't want to spend too much but are looking for a taste thrill. Whole stuffed squid and a tofu omelet, stir-fried vegetables and the inevitable *nasi goreng* (spicy fried rice with tiny dried shrimp, onions, garlic, etc.) are among the dishes. ⊠ *21 Great Windmill St., W1,* ☎ *0171/437–2745. AE, DC, MC, V. Tube: Leicester Sq.*

PAN-ASIAN

£ **Wok Wok.** A bright, primary-color decor, friendly service, and a menu of fresh soups, noodles, stir-fries and rice dishes from all over the Asias—Thailand, Vietnam, Malaysia, China, Japan, and Indonesia—ensure that this central branch of a small chain should run on and on, especially given the reasonable cost. ⊠ *10 Frith St., W1,* ☎ *0171/437–7080. AE, DC, MC, V. Leicester Sq.*

THAI

££ ✕ **Bahn Thai.** Many people find this the best of London's many Thai restaurants (you can see at least four others from the door), better still now that its ancient, gloomy decor has been excised. An immensely long menu features little chili symbols for the tame of palate, plus easy options like char-grilled poussin marinated in honey and spices with a plum dipping sauce. Other Thai dishes are well explained. ⊠ *21A Frith St., W1,* ☎ *0171/437–8504. AE, MC, V. Tube: Leicester Sq.*

THAI/AMERICAN

££ ✕ **Deals West.** Viscount Linley—Princess Margaret's son—and his two partners have hit on a winning formula here (and in the two other Dealses, at Chelsea Harbour and Hammersmith): an unlikely sounding merger between America and Thailand. Off Carnaby Street in a relaxed, barnlike diner with exposed brick walls, wooden floors, and beams, loudish music accompanies ribs, salads, and burgers—as well as Thai curries. Cocktails, extended hours, and live soul and funk on weekends make this popular with a young, after-work crowd. ⊠ *14–16 Fouberts Pl., W1,* ☎ *0171/287–1001. AE, DC, MC, V. Closed Sun. Tube: Oxford Circus.*

VEGETARIAN

£ ✕ **Cranks.** This is a popular vegetarian chain (there are other branches at Covent Garden, Great Newport Street, Adelaide Street, Tottenham Street, and Barrett Street), bought out by the management in 1992, and still serving meatless meals similar to the '60s menu that made their name. They are always crowded and, irritatingly, insist on closing at 8. ⊠ *8 Marshall St., W1,* ☎ *0171/437–9431. Reservations not accepted. AE, DC, MC, V. Closed Sun. Tube: Leicester Sq.*

Covent Garden

AMERICAN

££ ✕ **Joe Allen's.** Long hours (thespians flock here after the curtains fall
★ in Theatreland) and a welcoming, if loud, brick-walled interior mean New York Joe's London branch is still swinging after two decades. The

fun, California-inflected menu helps: roast stuffed poblano chili or black bean soup are typical starters; entrées feature barbecued ribs with black-eyed peas and London's only available corn muffins, or roast monkfish with sun-dried-tomato salsa. There are the perennial egg dishes and huge salads, too, and Yankee desserts such as grilled banana bread with ice cream and hot caramel sauce. ✉ *13 Exeter St., WC2,* ☎ *0171/ 836–0651. Reservations essential. AE, MC, V. Tube: Covent Garden.*

£ ✗ **Maxwell's.** London's first-ever burger joint, now more than a quarter-century old, cloned itself and then grew up. Here's the result, a happy place under the Opera House serving the kind of food you're home-sick for: quesadillas and nachos, Buffalo chicken wings, barbecued ribs, Cajun chicken, chef's salad, a real New York City–style Reuben, and a burger to die for. ✉ *8–9 James St., WC2,* ☎ *0171/836–0303. AE, DC, V. Tube: Covent Garden.*

BELGIAN

£–££ ✗ **Belgo Centraal.** The wackiest dining concept in town started in Camden at Belgo Noord (☞ *below*) and was so adored, it was cloned uptown in a big basement space you have to enter by elevator. Have mussels and fries in vast quantities, served with your choice of 100 Belgian beers (fruit-flavored, Trappist-brewed, white, or light) by people dressed as monks in a hall like a refectory in a Martian monastery. Also eat *stoemp* (mashed potatoes and cabbage) with steak; wild boar sausages; lobster; roast chicken. The luxury index is low, but so is the check. ✉ *50 Earlham St., WC2,* ☎ *0171/813–2233. AE, DC, MC, V. Tube: Covent Garden.*

BRITISH TRADITIONAL

£££ ✗ **Rules.** Come, escape from the 20th century. Almost 200 years old,
★ this gorgeous London institution has welcomed everyone from Dickens to Charlie Chaplin to Lillie Langtry and the Prince of Wales. The menu is historic and good, even if some food critics feel it's "theme-park-y"; try the noted steak and kidney and mushroom pudding for a virtual taste of the 18th century. Happily, the decor is truly delicious: With plush red banquettes and lacquered Regency yellow walls crammed with oils and framed engravings, this is probably the most beautiful dining salon in London (note, however, that the restaurant includes two upstairs floors). For a main dish, try something from the list of daily specials, which will, in season, include game from Rules's own Scottish estate (venison is disconcertingly called "deer"). Rules is more than a little touristy, but that's because it's so quaint. ✉ *35 Maiden La., WC2,* ☎ *0171/836–5314. AE, DC, MC, V. Tube: Covent Garden.*

FRENCH

££ ✗ **Le Palais du Jardin.** This does a fair imitation of a Parisian brasserie, complete with a seafood bar offering lobsters for around a tenner, though there's plenty else—duck confit with apples and prunes; coq au vin; tuna with a black olive-potato cake. It's not quite as chic as it looks, but neither is it as expensive, which accounts for why it is always busy. ✉ *136 Long Acre, WC2,* ☎ *0171/379–5353. AE, DC, MC, V. Tube: Covent Garden.*

£ ✗ **Café Flo.** This useful brasserie serves unpretentious chicken liver terrine, baguette sandwiches, steak frites or *poisson-frites, tartes,* espresso, fresh orange juice, simple set-price weekend menus . . . everything for the Francophile on a budget. There are branches in Hampstead, Islington, Fulham, and Kensington. ✉ *51 St. Martin's La., WC2,* ☎ *0171/836– 8289. MC, V. Tube: Covent Garden.*

FRENCH/BRITISH

££££ ✗ **Savoy Grill.** The grill continues in the first rank of power dining locations. Politicians, newspaper barons, and tycoons like the comforting food and impeccably discreet and attentive service in the low-key, rather dull, yew-paneled salon. On the menu, an omelet Arnold Bennett (with cheese and smoked fish) is perennial, as is beef Wellington on Tuesday and roast Norfolk duck on Friday. Playgoers can split their theater menu, eating part of their meal before the show, the rest after. ⊠ *Strand, WC2,* ☎ *0171/836–4343. Reservations essential. Jacket and tie. AE, DC, MC, V. Closed Sun. No lunch Sat. Tube: Aldwych.*

INTERNATIONAL

£££ ✕ **The Ivy.** This seems to be everybody's favorite restaurant—everybody who works in the media or the arts, that is. In a deco dining room with blinding white tablecloths, and Hodgkins and Paolozzis on the walls, the celebrated and the wanna-bes eat Caesar salad, roast grouse, shrimp gumbo, braised oxtail, and rice pudding with Armagnac prunes or sticky toffee pudding. For star-trekking ("Don't look now, dear, but there's Ralph Fiennes.") this is without a doubt the top place in London. ⊠ *1 West St., WC2,* ☎ *0171/836–4751. Reservations essential. AE, DC, MC, V. Tube: Covent Garden.*

★

£ ✕ **Pret a Manger.** You'll fall over this 10-year-old sandwich chain's cafés wherever you go, and you'll be grateful because the quality and freshness of the chicken breast and avocado on walnut bread, or the lox and cream cheese bagel, or the spinach quiche, lemon cake, banana bread, almond croissant, etc., are tops. There's even sushi. ⊠ *78 St. Martin's La., WC2,* ☎ *0171/379–5335. No credit cards. Tube: Covent Garden.*

ITALIAN

£££ ✕ **Orso.** The Italian brother of Joe Allen's (☞ *above*), this basement restaurant has the same snappy staff and a glitzy clientele of showbiz types and hacks. The Tuscan-style menu changes every day, but it always includes excellent pizza and pasta dishes, plus entrées based perhaps on grilled rabbit or roast sea bass and first courses of *roquette* (arugula) with shaved Parmesan or deep-fried zucchini flowers stuffed with ricotta. Food here is never boring, much like the place itself. ⊠ *27 Wellington St., WC2,* ☎ *0171/240–5269. Reservations essential. AE, MC, V. Tube: Covent Garden.*

££–£££ ✕ **Bertorelli's.** Right across from the stage door of the Royal Opera House, Bertorelli's is quietly chic, the food is tempting, and the menu is just innovative enough: poached *cotechino* (highly spiced) sausage with lentils and monkfish ragout with fennel, tomato, and olives are two typical dishes. A top-to-toe refurbishment has rearranged the casual versus formal options, with a big café-bar downstairs and a restaurant upstairs. ⊠ *44A Floral St., WC2,* ☎ *0171/836–3969. AE, DC, MC, V. Tube: Covent Garden.*

SEAFOOD/CAFÉ

£ ✕ **Rock and Sole Plaice.** The appalling pun announces central London's only fish-and-chips joint, complete with inside seating (i.e., it's not only takeout). As well as rock salmon, sole, and plaice, there's the usual cod and haddock, battered, deep fried and served with chips, ready for the salt and vinegar shakers. ⊠ *47 Endell St., WC2,* ☎ *0171/836–3785. No credit cards. Tube: Covent Garden.*

VEGETARIAN

£ ✕ **Food for Thought.** This simple basement restaurant (no liquor license) seats only 50 and is extremely popular, so you'll almost always find a line of people down the stairs. The menu—stir-fries, casseroles, salads, and desserts—changes every day, and each dish is freshly made; there's no microwave. ⊠ *31 Neal St., WC2,* ☎ *0171/836–0239. Reservations not accepted. No credit cards. Closed 2 wks at Christmas. Tube: Covent Garden.*

Bloomsbury

BRITISH

£   ✗ **Truckles of Pied Bull Yard.** Wine bars were the hits of '70s London, though hardly any survive to tell the tale. This one's fantastic for a post–British Museum glass of something, along with an old-fashioned ham salad with spiced peaches, or a smoked salmon sandwich, or a slice of Stilton and a glass of port. The nicest part is the courtyard with tables galore in summer. ⊠ *Off Bury Pl., WC1,* ☎ *0171/404–5338. AE, DC, MC, V. Closed Sun. No dinner Sat. Tube: Holborn.*

FRENCH

££–£££   ✗ **Elena's L'Etoile.** Elena Salvoni presided for years and years over
★   L'Escargot in Soho, where she made so many friends among happy customers she was rewarded with her name in lights—at 75 years old. This understated century-old place, whose only concession to trendiness of decor is a row of bentwood chairs unaccountably roped to the top of one wall, is one of London's few remaining unreconstructed French bistro restaurants. There's duck braised with red cabbage in an individual casserole, there's sole meunière, and poulet rôti, terrines, crème caramel, lemon tart, and a warm smile from Elena, whether you're one of the politician/journalist/actor regulars, or just you. Upstairs is a table for sharing—useful for single travelers or business trippers. ⊠ *30 Charlotte St., W1,* ☎ *0171/636–7189. AE, DC, MC, V. Closed Sun. No lunch Sat. Tube: Goodge St.*

££   ✗ **Chez Gerard.** One of an excellent chain of steak-frites restaurants, this one has widened the choice on the utterly Gallic menu to include more for non–red meat eaters: brioche filled with wild mushrooms and artichoke hearts, for instance, plus fish dishes and even something for vegetarians, such as stuffed roast onion. Steak, served with shoestring fries and béarnaise sauce, remains the reason to visit, though. ⊠ *8 Charlotte St., W1,* ☎ *0171/636–4975. AE, DC, MC, V. Tube: Goodge St.*

INDIAN VEGETARIAN

£   ✗ **Mandeer.** Buried in a basement, with tile floors, brick walls, and temple lamps, the Mandeer is useful for being central (off Tottenham Court Road, where there's nothing much else) and extremely cheap at lunchtime, when you help yourself to the buffet. ⊠ *21 Hanway Pl., W1,* ☎ *0171/580–3470. Reservations not accepted for lunch. AE, DC, MC, V. Closed Sun. and 2 wks at New Year's. Tube: Tottenham Court Rd.*

JAPANESE

£   ✗ **Wagamama.** London is wild for Japanese noodles in this big base-
★   ment. It's high-tech (your order is taken on a handheld computer), high-volume—there are always crowds, with which you share wooden refectory tables—and high-turnover, with a fast-moving line always at the door. You can choose ramen in or out of soup, topped with sliced meats or tempura; or "raw energy" dishes—rice, curries, tofu, and so on—all at giveaway prices and doggy-bag sizes. So successful has this formula proved that there is now an entire range of clothing, so that grateful diners can *wear* Wagamama. Many of them alternate this Wagamama experience with the newer one at 10A Lexington Street (☎ *0171/292–0990*), near Oxford Circus. ⊠ *4 Streatham St., WC1,* ☎ *0171/323–9223. Reservations not accepted. No credit cards. Tube: Tottenham Court Rd.*

MODERN BRITISH

££   ✗ **Museum Street Café.** This useful and reliable restaurant near the British Museum serves a limited selection of impeccably fresh dishes, intelligently and plainly cooked by the two young owners, and charged prix fixe. The evening menu might feature char-grilled, maize-fed chicken with pesto, followed by a rich chocolate cake; at lunchtime you might choose a sandwich of Stilton on walnut bread and a big bowl of soup. There is an atypical (for London) ban on smoking. ⊠ *47 Museum St., WC1,* ☎ *0171/405–3211. Reservations essential. MC, V. Closed weekends. Tube: Tottenham Court Rd.*

SEAFOOD

£ ✕ **North Sea Fish Restaurant.** This is the place for the British national ★ dish of fish-and-chips—battered and deep-fried whitefish with thick fries shaken with salt and vinegar. It's a bit tricky to find—three blocks south of St. Pancras station, down Judd Street. Only freshly caught fish is served, and you can order it grilled—though that would defeat the purpose. You can take out or eat in. ⊠ *7–8 Leigh St., WC1,* ☎ *0171/ 387–5892. AE, DC, MC, V. Closed Sun. Tube: Russell Sq.*

South Kensington

FRENCH

££££ ✕ **Bibendum.** When it opened a decade ago, this reconverted Michel-★ in showroom, adorned with Art Deco decorations and brilliant stained glass, became one of London's dining showplaces; even though the great original chef (and now well-known food writer) Simon Hopkinson is long gone from the kitchen, it still is. Hopkinson was famous for preparing simple dishes perfectly, and current chef Matthew Harris continues in a similar vein. Thus you can order herring with sour cream, a risotto, leeks vinaigrette followed by steak au poivre or the perfect boeuf bourgignon, or you might try brains or tripe as they ought to be cooked. The £28 set-price menu at lunchtime is money well spent. ⊠ *Michelin House, 81 Fulham Rd., SW3,* ☎ *0171/581–5817. Reservations essential. MC, V. Closed Sun. Tube: South Kensington.*

££ ✕ **Lou Pescadou.** This place is like a little *tranche* of the South of France, ★ with the sea-theme decor and emphatically French staff. The menu changes often and is based on fish—don't miss the *soupe de poisson* with croutons and *rouille* (rose-color, garlicky mayonnaise) if it's on—but there are other dishes, too, from steak-frites to, perhaps, delicate braised *cervelles* (brains). ⊠ *241 Old Brompton Rd., SW5,* ☎ *0171/ 370–1057. Reservations not accepted. AE, DC, MC, V. Closed Aug. Tube: Earl's Court.*

MEDITERRANEAN

£££ ✕ **The Collection.** Enter this former Katharine Hamnett shop through the spotlighted tunnel over the glass drawbridge, and you're immediately engulfed in one of the most fashionable crowds in London. A huge warehouse setting—adorned with industrial wooden beams and steel cables, a vast bar, and a suspended gallery—makes a great theater for people-watching. Around you are well-dressed nobs gawking at the neighboring tables for an Amber Valletta sighting, or hoping owner-doré Mogens Tholstrup will table-hop to theirs, while they pick at Med food seasoned with Japanese and Thai bits and bobs (seared tuna with sesame, soy, and shiitake mushrooms, or sea bream with cilantro). Ah, fashion, fashion, fashion! ⊠ *264 Brompton Rd., SW3,* ☎ *0171/225– 1212. AE, DC, MC, V. No dinner Sun. Tube: South Kensington.*

POLISH

£ ✕ **Daquise.** This venerable and well-loved Polish café by the tube station is incongruous in this neighborhood, as it is neither style-conscious nor expensive. Fill your stomach without emptying your pocketbook (or, it must be said, overstimulating your taste buds) on *bigos* (sauerkraut with garlic sausage and mushrooms), stuffed cabbage, cucumber salad, or just coffee and cake. ⊠ *20 Thurloe St., SW7,* ☎ *0171/589–6117. No credit cards. Tube: South Kensington.*

Knightsbridge

FRENCH

££££   ✕ **The Capital.** This elegant, clublike dining room has chandeliers and greige rag-rolled walls, a grown-up atmosphere, and formal service. Chef Philip Britten keeps his star bright with perhaps a subtle baked mousse of haddock and ginger, an *emincé* of chicken with olives, or pot-roasted pigeon with Armagnac, then a perfect caramel soufflé with butterscotch sauce. Set-price menus both at lunch (£28) and in the evening (£55—for *seven* courses) make it somewhat more affordable, although the best dishes are found à la carte. ✉ *22–24 Basil St., SW3,* ☎ *0171/589–5171. Reservations essential. Jacket and tie. AE, DC, MC, V. Tube: Knightsbridge.*

££   ✕ **St. Quentin.** A very popular slice of Paris, this restaurant is frequented by French expatriates and locals alike. Every inch of the Gallic menu is explored—Gruyère quiche, escargots, cassoulet, lemon tart—in the bourgeois provincial comfort so many London chains (the Dômes, the Cafés Rouges) try for yet fail to achieve. ✉ *243 Brompton Rd., SW3,* ☎ *0171/589–8005. AE, DC, MC, V. Tube: South Kensington.*

INTERNATIONAL

£   ✕ **Stockpot.** You'll find speedy service at this chain of large, jolly restaurants, often packed to the brim with young people and shoppers. The food is filling and wholesome: try the Lancashire hot pot, for example, and the apple crumble. ✉ *6 Basil St., SW3,* ☎ *0171/589–8627. No credit cards. Tube: Knightsbridge;* ✉ *40 Panton St., off Leicester Sq.,* ☎ *0171/839–5142;* ✉ *18 Old Compton St., Soho,* ☎ *0171/ 287–1066;* ✉ *273 King's Rd., Chelsea,* ☎ *0171/823–3175.*

ITALIAN

£££   ✕ **San Lorenzo.** This well-established, well-heeled trattoria has unexceptional decor and is nothing special food-wise, but it's just the ticket if you're keen to spot the occasional celebrity or to gaze into the world of ladies-who-lunch. The usual upscale Italian dishes are here, but they nod to fashion—try wood pigeon with polenta, or any of the veal dishes. ✉ *22 Beauchamp Pl., SW3,* ☎ *0171/584–1074. AE, DC, MC, V. Closed Sun. Tube: South Kensington.*

£££   ✕ **Zafferano.** Princess Margaret, Eric Clapton, Joan Collins (she asked that the lights be turned down), and any number of Cartier-brooch-wearing neighborhood Belgravians have flocked to this place, which, since 1995, has been London's best exponent of *cucina nuova.* The fireworks are in the kitchen, not in the brick-wall-and-saffron-hued decor, but *what* fireworks: pumpkin ravioli with a splash of amaretto, *mondeghini ai crostini di risotto* (minced pork wrapped in Savoy cabbage leaves), and monkfish with walnuts. The desserts are also *delizioso,* especially the Sardinian pecorino pastries served with undersweetened vanilla ice cream. Be sure to book early: even Al Pacino was turned away one night. ✉ *15 Lowndes St., SW1,* ☎ *0171/235–5800. Reservations essential. AE, MC, V. Tube: Knightsbridge.*

MODERN BRITISH

£–££   ✕ **The Enterprise.** One of the new luxury breed of gastro-pubs, this is perhaps the chicest of the lot—near Harrods and Brompton Cross, it's filled with decorative types who complement the decor: paisley-striped wallpaper, Edwardian side tables covered with baskets and farmhouse fruit, vintage books piled up in the windows, white linen and fresh flowers on the tables. The menu isn't overly pretty—char-grilled squid stuffed with almonds, entrecôte steak, salmon with artichoke hearts—but the ambience certainly is. ✉ *35 Walton St., SW3,* ☎ *0171/584–3148. AE, MC, V. No lunch weekends. Tube: South Kensington.*

Dining in South Kensington, Knightsbridge, and Chelsea

Aubergine, **3**

Bibendum, **7**

Bluebird, **5**

The Capital, **16**

Caravela, **14**

Chelsea Bun Diner, **4**

Chutney Mary, **2**

The Collection, **10**

Daquise, **6**

The Enterprise, **13**

La Brasserie, **9**

La Tante Claire, **19**

Lou Pescadou, **1**

Luba's Bistro, **12**

PJ's, **8**

St. Quentin, **11**

San Lorenzo, **15**

Stockpot, **17**

Zafferano, **18**

PORTUGUESE

££ ✗ **Caravela.** This narrow lower-ground-floor place is one of London's few Portuguese restaurants. You can get *Caldo verde* (cabbage soup), *bacalhau* (salt-cured cod), and other typical dishes while listening (on Friday or Saturday) to the national music, fado—desperately sad songs belted out at thrash-metal volume. ⊠ *39 Beauchamp Pl., SW3,* ☎ *0171/ 581–2366. AE, DC, MC, V. No lunch Sun. Tube: South Kensington.*

RUSSIAN

£ ✗ **Luba's Bistro.** This place has been popular for decades. Expect long wooden tables, plain decor, and authentic Russian cooking—chicken Kiev, beef Stroganoff, etc. Bring your own wine. ⊠ *6 Yeoman's Row, SW3,* ☎ *0171/589–2950. Reservations essential. MC, V. Closed Sun. Tube: South Kensington.*

Chelsea

AMERICAN/CASUAL

££ ✗ **PJ's.** The decor here evokes the Bulldog Drummond lifestyle, with wooden floors and stained glass, a vast, slowly revolving propeller from a 1940s Curtis flying boat, and polo memorabilia. A menu of all-American staples (soft-shell crab, chowder, gumbo, steaks, smoked ribs), big salads, pecan pie, brownies, and Häagen-Dazs should please all but vegetarians, and portions are big, but this place is more remarkable for ambience than for food—it's open late, it's relaxed, friendly, and efficient, and it has bartenders who can mix anything. The sister PJ's in Covent Garden (⊠ 30 Wellington St., ☎ 0171/240–7529) is worth remembering for its excellent weekend "Fun Club" for kids. ⊠ *52 Fulham Rd., SW3,* ☎ *0171/581–0025. AE, DC, MC, V. Tube: South Kensington.*

£ ✗ **Chelsea Bun Diner.** Get fed heaps of food for very little money at this hybrid of an American diner and an English greasy spoon. A huge menu of huge portions—burgers, salads, potato skins, many breakfasts, pastas, and pies—is what you get. ⊠ *9A Limerston St., SW10,* ☎ *0171/ 352–3635. Reservations not accepted. MC, V. Tube: Sloane Sq., then Bus 11, 19, 22, or 31.*

ANGLO-INDIAN

£££ ✗ **Chutney Mary.** London's first-and-only Anglo-Indian restaurant provides a fantasy version of the British Raj, all giant wicker armchairs and palms. Dishes like marsala roast lamb (practically a whole leg, marinated and spiced) and "Country Captain" (braised chicken with almonds, raisins, chilies, and spices) alternate with the more familiar north Indian dishes such as *roghan josh* (lamb curry). The best choices are certainly the dishes re-created from the kitchens of Indian chefs cooking for English palates back in the old Raj days. For this reason, the all-you-can-eat Sunday buffet is not such a great idea, because it leaves those out. Service is deferential, and desserts, unheard of in tandoori places, are usually worth leaving room for. ⊠ *535 King's Rd., SW10,* ☎ *0171/351–3113. Reservations essential. AE, DC, MC, V. Tube: Fulham Broadway.*

CONTEMPORARY

££–£££ ✗ **Bluebird.** From Terence Conran, the man who gave England the wok, the Habitat catalog ("one of the 10 books that changed our life," according to the *Sunday Telegraph*), and several of London's largest restaurants, now comes a full-blown "gastrodome"—supermarket, brasserie, fruit stand, butcher shop, boutique, and café-restaurant, all housed in a snappy King's Road former garage. The place is pale blue and white, very light, and not in the least cozy, with food listed in formulae—e.g., steamed mussels, saffron, leeks; or roasted pheasant, creamed cabbage, shallots; then chilled fruits and apple water ice. Go for the synergy and visual excitement—Conran's chefs share a tendency to promise more than they deliver. ✉ *350 King's Rd, SW3,* ☎ *0171/ 559–1000. Reservations essential. AE, DC, MC, V. Tube: Sloane Sq.*

FRENCH

££££ ✕ **La Tante Claire.** Justly famous, this is one of the best restaurants in
★   London. The decor is light and sophisticated, the service impeccable, and the French wine list impressive, but the food is the point. From the *carte,* you might choose hot pâté de foie gras on shredded potatoes with a sweet wine and shallot sauce, roast spiced pigeon, or Pierre Koffmann's famous signature dish of pigs' feet stuffed with mousse of white meat with sweetbreads and wild mushrooms. As every gourmet expense-accounter knows, the set lunch menu (£28) is a genuine bargain. Lunch reservations must be made 2–3 days in advance, dinner reservations 3–4 weeks in advance. ✉ *68 Royal Hospital Rd., SW3,* ☎ *0171/352–6045. Reservations essential weeks in advance. Jacket and tie. AE, DC, MC, V. Closed weekends, 2 wks at Christmas, 10 days at Easter, and 3 wks in Aug.–Sept. Tube: Sloane Sq.*

£££–££££ ✕ **Aubergine** A table at Aubergine (warning: there are only 14) has
★   been London's toughest reservation to score for almost as long as it's been open because soccer star-turned-chef Gordon Ramsay has every table gasping in awe at his famous, witty cappuccino of white beans with sautéed girolles and truffles, followed by—well, anything at all. This man can do no wrong, as those lucky enough to enjoy his Bresse pigeon with fois gras pizza can vouch. The decor is alluring and bathed in the hues of Impressionist Provence. Reserve months ahead; go for lunch (£24) if money is an object. ✉ *11 Park Walk, SW10,* ☎ *0171/ 352–3449. Reservations essential. AE, DC, MC, V. Closed Sun. No lunch Sat. Tube: South Kensington.*

££ ✕ **La Brasserie.** This is a convenient spot for South Ken museum visits, and it has flexible and long opening hours, a menu of entirely French things—from fish soup to tarte Tatin—and a good buzz on a Sunday morning when the entire well-heeled neighborhood sits around reading the papers and sipping cappuccino. You can't do that at peak times, when you must eat, but the food's reliable, if a little overpriced. ✉ *272 Brompton Rd., SW3,* ☎ *0171/584–1668. AE, DC, MC, V. Tube: South Kensington.*

Kensington and Notting Hill Gate

AMERICAN/CASUAL

£   ✕ **Tootsies.** A superior burger place, Tootsies is dark but cheerful, and decorated with vintage advertisements. Vintage rock plays in the background. Alternatives to the burgers, which come with great fries, are big salads, steaks, BLTs, and several variations on chicken breast. The usual ice creams and pies will do for dessert. There are branches in Fulham, Chiswick, and Notting Hill. ✉ *120 Holland Park Ave., W11,* ☎ *0171/229–8567. Reservations not accepted. MC, V. Tube: Holland Park.*

BRITISH TRADITIONAL

£££ ✕ **Julie's.** This sweet '60s throwback has two parts: an upstairs wine bar and a basement restaurant, both decorated with Victorian ecclesiastical furniture. The cooking is sound, old-fashioned English (salmon-and-halibut terrine, roast pheasant with chestnut stuffing and wild rowan jelly). The traditional Sunday lunches are very popular, and in summer there's a garden for outside eating. ✉ *135 Portland Rd., W11,* ☎ *0171/229–8331. MC, V. No lunch Sat. Tube: Holland Park.*

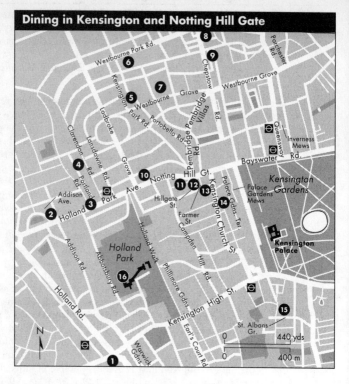

Dining in Kensington and Notting Hill Gate

FRENCH

£££ ✕ **Chez Moi.** Sophisticated French food is served in a warm salmon-pink dining room, which, with the tables widely spaced and the lighting low, demands romantic behavior. There are dishes the menu admits are "traditional" that Chez Moi's fans have depended on for a quarter century—things like rack of lamb with garlic and mint, and beef tournedos with béarnaise—as well as more novel dishes such as the popular "Oursins Chez Moi," ersatz sea urchins made of shrimp and scallop, with fried angel-hair pasta "spines." The desserts are hit-or-miss, but there are ample chocolates brought with the coffee. ⊠ *1 Addison Ave., W11,* ☎ *0171/603–8267. Reservations essential. AE, DC, MC, V. Closed Sun., 2 wks at Christmas, and 2 wks in Aug. No lunch Sat. Tube: Shepherd's Bush.*

CONTEMPORARY

£££ ✕ **Clarke's.** There's no choice on the evening menu at Sally Clarke's award-winning restaurant; her dinners feature ultrafresh ingredients, plainly but perfectly cooked, accompanied by home-baked breads. The plant-and-art-speckled room is similarly home-style, if home is in the big white Kensington houses you see around here. ⊠ *124 Kensington Church St., W8,* ☎ *0171/221–9225. Reservations essential. MC, V. Closed weekends and 2 wks in Aug. Tube: Notting Hill Gate.*

££ ✕ **Pharmacy.** London's latest scene-arena, the Pharmacy is one of those see-and-be seen places where the bar is larger than the restaurant. In this case, the bar seats 180 and is shaped like gigantic aspirin. Yes, this spot looks just like its namesake, the waitstaff is garbed like hospital orderlies, and even the menu looks fab—but then Damien Hirst, artist-provocateur extraordinaire, is involved with the place. The menu highlights "comfort food" and ranges from fisherman's pie and scrambled eggs with black truffles to spit-roast Landes duck, sauce aigre-doux. If you can't snag a table, just have fun at the bar and order the drink called "Cough Syrup." ⊠ *150 Notting Hill Gate, W11,* ☎ *0171/221–2442. AE, MC, V. Tube: Notting Hill Gate.*

££ ✕ **The Sugar Club.** Peter Gordon has been clasped warmly to the Londoner's bosom with his fresh "Australasian" cooking—seared tuna with ginger on cucumber and soba noodles; panfried cod on asparagus, Parmesan and saffron risotto; roast English duck breast on wok-fried black beans with tomato-chili jam; grilled kangaroo—served in two levels of white-walled, serene rooms. It's one of those places so loved by the native glitterati (they're still talking about the night Mick Jagger graced the joint) that you have to reserve way, way ahead. ⊠ *33A All Saints Rd., W11,* ☎ *0171/221–3844. Reservations essential, 2 wks in advance. AE, MC, V. Tube: Westbourne Park.*

GREEK

£ ✕ **Costa's Grill.** Come for good value and such down-to-earth Greek food as grilled fish and *kleftiko* (roast lamb on the bone). The atmosphere is homey and happy, and there's a tiny garden open in summer. ⊠ *14 Hillgate St., W8,* ☎ *0171/229–3794. No credit cards. Closed Sun. and 3 wks in summer. Tube: Notting Hill Gate.*

MEDITERRANEAN

££ ✕ **The Belvedere.** There can be no finer setting for a summer supper or a sunny Sunday brunch than a window table—or a balcony one if you luck out—at this stunning restaurant in the middle of Holland Park. The menu is big on shaved Parmesan, sun-dried tomatoes, and arugula, which suits the conservatorylike room—a favorite of film director and infamously demanding newspaper restaurant critic Michael Winner. ⊠ *Holland Park off Abbotsbury Rd., W8,* ☎ *0171/602–1238. Reservations essential. AE, DC, MC, V. No dinner Sun. Tube: Holland Park.*

MIDDLE EASTERN

£ ✕ **Yas.** Directly opposite Olympia Exhibition Centre, this friendly Persian restaurant with terra-cotta-color walls has a beehive-shape oven
★ by the door, from which lavash bread is brought steaming to your table. Eat this with *panir o sabzi* (soft white cheese with fresh herbs), hummus, *borani-e esfena* (yogurt and spinach), *adasi* (lentils), or any of the 15 dips and salads, then have a simple grilled chicken or lamb dish or the daily special—like Monday's *shirin polow* (chicken and rice with candied orange peel, pistachio and almond). It's open until 5 AM every day. ⊠ *7 Hammersmith Rd., W14,* ☎ *0171/603–9148. DC, MC, V. Tube: Olympia.*

MODERN BRITISH

£££ ✕ **First Floor.** A place for well-off but arty locals, popular both for its inventive food and its ambience—it looks like a bombed church inhabited by distressed nobility. There's a great brunch on weekends; otherwise go for Thai fish cakes, Tuscan lamb stew, or grilled ostrich rump with mango salsa and potato pancake. Sides—coconut mashed potatoes or mustard-apple puree—often hit the heights, as do desserts like pear and almond tart. ⊠ *186 Portobello Rd., W11,* ☎ *0171/243–0072. Reservations essential. AE, MC, V. Tube: Notting Hill Gate.*

£££ ✕ **Kensington Place.** Being a favorite among the local glitterati keeps
★ this place packed and noisy. A huge plate-glass window and mural are backdrops to Rowley Leigh's fashionable food—grilled foie gras with sweet-corn pancake and baked tamarillo with vanilla ice are perennials—but it's the fun buzz that draws the crowds. ⊠ *201 Kensington Church St., W8,* ☎ *0171/727–3184. MC, V. Tube: Notting Hill Gate.*

££ ✕ **The Cow.** Oh, no, not *another* Conran. Yes, this place belongs to Tom, son of Sir Terrence, though it's a million miles from Quag's and Mezzo. Actually a tiny and chic gastro-pub, it comprises a faux-Dublin backroom bar, serving up oysters, crab salad, and pasta with wine; upstairs, a serious chef whips up Tuscan/British specialties—skate poached in minestrone is one temptation. Notting Hillbillies and other stylish folk adore the house special—a half-dozen Irish rock oysters with a pint of Guinness, as well as the mixed grills and steaks that often figure on the menu. ⊠ *89 Westbourne Park Rd., W2,* ☎ *0171/221–0021. Reservations essential. MC, V. No dinner Sun. Tube: Westbourne Park.*

££ ✕ **192.** A noisy, buzzy wine bar/restaurant just off Portobello Road,
★   this is as much a social hangout for the local media mafia as a restaurant, especially on weekends, when you'll feel like you've gate-crashed a party—if you manage to get a table, that is. The chef likes to keep ahead of fashion, and is best on the appetizer list—many people order two of these instead of an entrée. Try the risottos, the seasonal salad (perhaps romanesco, broccoli, anchovy, and gremolata), the fish (sea bass with fennel, lemon, and rosemary; scallop, chickpea, chorizo, and clam casserole), or whatever sounds unusual. ⊠ *192 Kensington Park Rd., W11,* ☎ *0171/229–0482. AE, MC, V. Tube: Notting Hill Gate.*

£–££ ✕ **Prince Bonaparte.** This is one of the new foodie pubs that draws in the crowds. Forget bangers and mash; here you'll get blackened salmon with refried beans, a yummy toffee pudding, and a wide range of interesting beers. Singles take over during the week; young families move in on the weekends. As the night wears on, the place—accented with large windows, church pews, and farmhouse tables—becomes a lively preclub stop (complete with thumping music on weekends). ⊠ *80 Chepstow Rd., W2,* ☎ *0171/229–5912. No credit cards. Tube: Notting Hill Gate, Westbourne Park.*

POLISH

££ ✕ **Wódka.** This smart, modern Polish restaurant is the only one in the
★   world, as far as we know, to serve smart, modern Polish food. It is popular with elegant locals and a sprinkling of celebs and often has the atmosphere of a dinner party. Alongside the smoked salmon, herring, caviar, and eggplant *blinis,* you might also find venison sausages or roast duck with *krupnik* (honey-lemon vodka). From the separate menu, order a carafe of the purest vodka in London (and watch the check inflate); it's encased in a block of ice and is hand-flavored (with bison grass, cherries, rowanberries) by the owner, who, being an actual Polish prince, is uniquely qualified to do this. ⊠ *12 St. Albans Grove, W8,* ☎ *0171/937–6513. Reservations essential. AE, DC, MC, V. No lunch weekends. Tube: High Street Kensington.*

SEAFOOD

£ ✕ **Geales.** This is a cut above your typical fish-and-chips joint. The
★   decor is stark, but the fish will have been swimming just hours beforehand, even the ones from the Caribbean (fried swordfish is a specialty). Geales is popular with the rich and famous, not just loyal locals. ⊠ *2 Farmer St., W8,* ☎ *0171/727–7969. Reservations not accepted. MC. Closed Sun., Mon., 3 wks in Aug., and 2 wks at Christmas. Tube: Notting Hill Gate.*

The City and the South Bank

AMERICAN/CASUAL

£ ✕ **Fatboy's Diner.** One for the kids, this is a 1941 chrome trailer transplanted from the banks of the Susquehanna in Pennsylvania and now secreted, unexpectedly, in a back street, complete with an Astroturf "garden." A '50s jukebox accompanies the dogs, burgers, and fries. ⊠ *296 Bishopsgate, EC2,* ☎ *0171/375–2763. Reservations not accepted. No credit cards. Tube: Liverpool St.*

FRENCH

£££ ✗ **Le Pont de la Tour.** Sir Terence Conran's place across the river, over-
★ looking the bridge that gives it its name, comes into its own in summer, when the outside tables are heaven. Inside there's a vintner and
baker and deli, a seafood bar, a brasserie, and this '30s diner-style restaurant, smart as the captain's table. Fish and seafood (lobster salad;
Baltic herrings in crème fraîche; roast halibut with aioli) and meat and
game (venison fillet with port and blueberry sauce; roast veal with
caramelized endive) feature heavily—vegetarians are out of luck. Prune
and Armagnac tart or chocolate terrine could finish a glamorous—and
expensive—meal. By contrast, an impeccable salade Niçoise in the
brasserie costs about £9. ⊠ *36D Shad Thames, Butler's Wharf, SE1,*
☎ *0171/403–8403. Reservations essential. MC, V. Tube: Tower Hill.*

ITALIAN

£ ✗ **The Eagle.** If the name makes it sound like a pub, that's because it
★ is a pub, albeit a superior one, with wooden floors, a few sofas, and
art on the walls. It does, however, belong in the "Restaurants" section
by virtue of the amazingly good-value nouveau Tuscan food, which
you choose from the blackboard menu (or by pointing) at the bar. There
are about half a dozen dishes, a pasta and/or risotto always among them.
There are currently quite a few places in London charging four times
the price for remarkably similar food; there's also a welcome trend
toward pubs serving good meals—one that the Eagle all but started.
⊠ *159 Farringdon Rd., EC1,* ☎ *0171/837–1353. Reservations not
accepted. No credit cards. No dinner weekends. Tube: Farringdon.*

JAPANESE

£ ✗ **Moshi Moshi Sushi.** London is taking to sushi like New Yorkers did
a decade back, and this wacky glass-walled joint above Platform One
in Liverpool Street station set the ball rolling—or the fish train chug-
ging, since the schtick here is that you pick *tekka* or *kappa maki* (tuna
or cucumber seaweed rolls) or *maguro* (tuna), *sake* (salmon), *saba* (mack-
erel), etc.—in pairs off a conveyor belt that snakes around the counter.
At the end, you count up your color-coded plates to pay. The sushi's
okay, but this is not the place to go for a sophisticated evening. ⊠ *Unit
24 Liverpool St. Station, EC2,* ☎ *0171/247–3227. Reservations not
accepted. No credit cards. Closed weekends. Tube: Liverpool St.*

MODERN BRITISH

££–£££ ✗ **Maison Novelli.** Jean Christophe Novelli is one of the new cult
★ heroes of the Mod Brit cuisine, and his restaurant has drawn foodies
from the day it opened in up-and-coming Clerkenwell, near stylish Islington. The ground floor is a black-and-white hued brasserie, with
cheaper prices; upstairs is the main show—a vaguely Victorian-flavored
room, with walls saturated in violet and adorned with silvered twig
mirrors. Novelli goes where few chefs have gone—he loves to create
new tastes by mixing and matching meat juices, beetroot oils, and other
alchemical elements. Signature dishes are Rabelaisian—confit of goose
neck stuffed with fois gras, four-hour braised oxtail with licorice sauce,
or the famed pig's trotter stuffed "following the mood of the day." All
is not offally, however—you can also come by an elegant roast sea bass
with aubergine caviar or lamb cutlets with Rockford cheese soufflé and
lentils. Finish it all off, if it doesn't finish you first, with a tiramisu Kahlua.
For Novelli's more expensive restaurant, check out Les Saveurs on Curzon Street in Mayfair; for his cheaper place, the wildly popular Nov-

Dining in the City and the South Bank

elli W8, in Kensington. ⌧ *29 Clerkenwell Green, EC1R,* ☎ *0171/251–6606. Reservations essential. AE, MC, V. Tube: Farringdon.*

££–£££ ✕ **OXO Tower Brasserie and Restaurant.** How delightful it is for London finally to get a room with a view—and *such* a view. On the eighth floor of the beautifully revived OXO Tower Wharf building near the South Bank Centre is this elegant space, run by the same people who put the chic Fifth Floor at Harvey Nichols on the map, and featuring Euro food with this year's trendy ingredients (acorn-fed black pig charcuterie with tomato and pear chutney; calves' kidneys with persillade and beetroot jus; Dover sole with sea urchin butter). The ceiling slats turn and change from white to midnight blue, but who on earth notices, with St. Paul's dazzling you across the water? The Brasserie is slightly less expensive than the restaurant, but both have great river views. For food with a view, the terrace tables in summertime are probably the best places in London. ⌧ *Bankside, SE1,* ☎ *0171/803–3888. AE, MC, V. Tube: Waterloo.*

££ ✕ **People's Palace.** Thank goodness for this place—now you can have a civilized meal during your South Bank arts encounter. Run independently from the Royal Festival Hall et al, but by the same owners, it has remarkably low prices considering it has the greatest river view in town (apart from OXO). There are occasional mistakes here, but the more British the dish, the more reliable it proves—roast beef, potted duck, suckling pig sandwich on granary bread, marmalade sponge, sticky toffee pudding—all these are fine. Service is a bit flaky, but the soaring space with its giant windows makes up for everything. ⌧ *Royal Festival Hall, Level 3, South Bank, SE1,* ☎ *0171/928–9999. AE, DC, MC, V. Tube: Waterloo.*

££ ✕ **Quality Chop House.** This was converted from one of the most gor-
★ geous "greasy spoon" cafs in town, retaining the solid Victorian fit-

Three isn't a crowd

when the third is 50% off.

The Party Pass is another great idea from BritRail. Travel in a group and save 50% on the third and fourth person in your party.

It's a great new addition to the range of BritRail passes: the Classic Pass, the Flexipass and the BritRail Senior Pass.

The Party Pass lets you sit back in comfort and style and watch the countryside roll by. And at 50% off, that's something to celebrate.

The BritRail Party Pass is a real crowd pleaser. Call your travel agent or Rail Europe today.

You've read the book. Now book the trip.

For all the best deals on flights, hotels, rental cars, and vacation packages, book them online at www.previewtravel.com. Then click on our Destination Guides featuring content from Fodor's and more. You'll find hotels, restaurants, attractions, and things to do around the globe. There are even interactive maps, videos, and weather forecasts. You'll have everything you need to make your vacation exactly what you want it to be. All it takes is a trip online.

Travel on Your Terms™
www.previewtravel.com
aol keyword: previewtravel

preview travel ℠

tings (including pewlike seats, which you often have to share). It is not
luxurious, but the food is a glorious parody of caf food—bangers and
mash turns out to be homemade herbed veal sausage with rich gravy,
light, fluffy potatoes; egg and chips (fries) are not remotely greasy. There
are also such posh things as salmon fish cakes and steak, and desserts
that change with the seasons. ⊠ *94 Farringdon Rd., EC1,* ☎ *0171/
837–5093. Reservations essential. No credit cards. No lunch Sat., no
dinner Sun. Tube: Farringdon.*

££ ✗ **St. John.** This former smokehouse (ham, not cigars), converted by
★ erstwhile architect owner/chef Fergus Henderson has soaring white walls,
schoolroom lamps, stone floors, iron railings, and plain wooden chairs.
Some find Henderson's chutzpah scary: One infamous appetizer is carrots and egg (a bunch of carrots with green tops intact and a boiled
egg), although the imaginativeness of others—roast bone marrow and
parsley salad; smoked eel, beetroot, and horseradish—excuses this
silliness. Entrées (roast lamb and parsnip; smoked haddock and fennel; deviled crab) can appear shockingly nude on the plate, but they
always have style. An all-French wine list has plenty of affordable bottles, plus lots of Malmseys and ports. Service is efficiently friendly, and
the pastry chef's chocolate slice belongs in the brownie hall of fame.
⊠ *26 St. John St., EC1,* ☎ *0171/251–0848. Reservations essential.
AE, MC, V. No dinner Sun. Tube: Farringdon.*

£ ✗ **Konditor & Cook.** Very useful for theatrical forays over the river, this
caf in the Young Vic theater serves full meals a cut above the tired quiche
and curly sandwiches you might expect. Black ravioli stuffed with
crab or wild mushrooms on toasted brioche are the kind of dishes to
expect, but the pies and cakes—from the eponymous bakery around
the corner, which supplies half of London—are the standout. ⊠ *Young
Vic Theatre, 66 The Cut, SE1,* ☎ *0171/620–2700. MC, V. Closed Sun.
Tube: Waterloo.*

SEAFOOD

££ ✗ **Bill Bentley's.** You can see from the bare walls and the arched ceiling that this once housed a wine merchant's vaults. There are four other
branches in London, all equally old-fashioned in feel, and all serving
old-fashioned boarding school-like fish dishes and seafood platters. ⊠
Swedeland Ct., 202 Bishopsgate, EC2, ☎ *0171/283–1763. Reservations essential. Jacket and tie. MC, V. Closed weekends. No dinner. Tube:
Liverpool St.*

££ ✗ **Livebait.** Perhaps no longer as truly fantastic as when it was independently run, this expanded, plain-looking fish restaurant is still
packing them in, serving English seafood (cockles and mussels alive-
alive-o!) by the pint, home-baked breads (beetroot, garlic, or turmeric,
as well as olive and walnut), and all sorts of fishes: broiled, in pies,
baked, stewed, and generally combined in ways that are never boring.
Note there is also a branch in the Covent Garden area. ⊠ *41–43 The
Cut, SE1,* ☎ *0171/928–7211. Reservations essential. MC, V. Closed
Sun. Tube: Waterloo.*

Camden Town and Hampstead

BELGIAN

££ ✗ **Belgo Noord.** To enter what must be London's least normal restau-
★ rant, you pass the wavy concrete facade and cross the spotlit "drawbridge" over the brushed-steel open kitchen. Inside, waitstaff in maroon
monks' habits sweep over to your refectorylike table to take your
order of *moules-frites* (steamed mussels in various sauces with fries),
waterzooi (a whitefish stew), wild boar sausages, and other authentic
Belgian dishes. Try the Kriek, cherry beer brewed by Trappist monks.

Of course, this is the older, more handsome brother of the Covent Garden Belgo Centraal (☞ *above*). ⊠ *72 Chalk Farm Rd., NW1,* ☎ *0171/267–0718. Reservations essential. AE, MC, V. Tube: Chalk Farm.*

CAFS

£ ✕ **Coffee Cup.** A Hampstead landmark for just about as long as anyone can remember, this smoky, dingy, uncomfortable café is lovable, very cheap, and therefore always packed. You can get anything (beans, eggs, kippers, mushrooms) on toast, grills, sandwiches, cakes, fry-ups, etc.—nothing healthy or fashionable whatsoever. There are tables outside in the summer, but no liquor license. ⊠ *74 Hampstead High St., NW3,* ☎ *0171/435–7565. Reservations not accepted. No credit cards. Tube: Hampstead.*

GREEK

££ ✕ **Lemonia.** On a very pleasant street near Regent's Park is this supe-
★ rior version of London Greek—large and light, friendly, and packed every evening. Besides the usual *mezedes* (appetizers), *souvlaki* (kebabs), *stifado* (beef stewed in wine), and so on, there are interesting specials: quail, perhaps, or *gemista* (stuffed vegetables). ⊠ *89 Regent's Park Rd., NW1,* ☎ *0171/586–7454. Reservations essential. No credit cards. No lunch Sat., no dinner Sun. Tube: Chalk Farm.*

ITALIAN

£ ✕ **Marine Ices.** Although this neighborhood institution is indeed a fine ice cream parlor (which supplies to many restaurants), the name is misleading, because secreted inside the coolly functional marble-floor rooms is a bargain Italian eatery, serving pastas, pizzas, and risottos to fill you up before the irresistible coppas, bombes, cassate, and other ice cream delights. It's at the Chalk Farm end of the markets. ⊠ *8 Haverstock Hill, NW3,* ☎ *0171/485–3132. MC, V. Tube: Chalk Farm.*

VEGETARIAN

£ ✕ **Manna** This place, with its candlelighted chunky pine tables, has fed the local veggies forever, and it still has a whiff of the '60s about it—in a good way. Eat vegetable and tofu tempura; risotto cakes with goat cheese; salads and vegetable tarts, all served up by the friendly staff. ⊠ *4 Erskine Rd., NW3,* ☎ *0171/722–8028. MC, V. No lunch. Tube: Chalk Farm.*

Brunch and Afternoon Tea

It is sometimes suggested that among Londoners, brunch is catching on, while the afternoon ritual (often mistakenly referred to as "high tea") is dying out. Tea, the drink, however, is so ingrained in the national character that tea, the meal, will always have a place in the capital, if only as an occasional celebration, a children's treat, or something you do when your American friends are in town. Reserve for all these, unless otherwise noted.

Brunch

The Belvedere (☞ *above*) in bucolic Holland Park wins hands down for the setting, especially if you bag a rare terrace table on a rare sunny day. There is, admittedly, no official brunch, but you can fake one from the regular menu. ⊠ *Holland Park off Abbotsbury Rd., W8,* ☎ *0171/602–1238. Reservations essential. AE, DC, MC, V. Lunch served weekends noon–3.*

Butler's Wharf Chop House. At this—yet another Terence Conran (Quaglino's, Pont de la Tour, Bibendum . . .) venture—brunch (£13.95 for two courses) is as British as brunch ever gets, with Dublin Bay prawns,

Stilton and celery soup and such, and a fabulous Thames-side setting. ⊠ *36E Shad Thames, SE1, ☏ 0171/403–3403. AE, DC, MC, V. Brunch served Sun. noon–3.*

Christopher's. Imagine you're in Manhattan at this superior Covent Garden purveyor of American food, from pancakes to steak, eggs and fries, via salmon fish cakes and a Caesar salad. Two courses cost £15. ⊠ *18 Wellington St., WC2, ☏ 0171/240–4222. AE, DC, MC, V. Brunch served Sun. noon–4.*

Joe Allen (☞ *above*) is where to take refuge from the lovely British weather and down some Bloody Marys, and maybe a grilled chicken sandwich with Swiss, or a salad of spicy sausage, shrimp, and new potatoes. ⊠ *13 Exeter St., WC2, ☏ 0171/836–0651. Reservations essential. No credit cards. Brunch served Sun. noon–4.*

Room at the Halcyon. For the most romantic brunch in London, check out this elegant room, favored by stars of Hollywood and rock, secreted in the leafy neighborhood of Holland Park. The kitchen is excellent and modern British. ⊠ *129 Holland Park Ave., W11, ☏ 0171/221–5411. AE, DC, MC, V. Brunch served Sun. noon–3:30.*

Afternoon Tea

Note that Claridge's, the Ritz, and the Savoy all require jacket and tie.

Brown's Hotel does rest on its laurels somewhat, with a packaged aura and nobody around but fellow tourists who believe this to be the most famous. Still, everyone swears by the deevy armchairs here. For £16.95 you get sandwiches, a scone with cream and jam, tart, fruitcake, and shortbread. ⊠ *33 Albermarle St., W1, ☏ 0171/493–6020. AE, MC, V. Tea served daily 3–6.*

Claridge's is the real McCoy, with liveried footmen proffering sandwiches, scones, and superior patisseries (£16.50) in the palatial yet genteel Foyer, to the sound of the resident "Hungarian orchestra" (actually a string quartet). ⊠ *Brook St., W1, ☏ 0171/629–8860. AE, DC, MC, V. Tea served daily 3–5.*

Fortnum & Mason. Upstairs at the Queen's grocers, three set teas are ceremoniously offered: standard afternoon tea (sandwiches, scone, cakes, £10.50), old-fashioned high tea (the traditional nursery meal, adding something more robust and savory, £12.25), and Champagne Tea (£15.75). ⊠ *St. James's Restaurant, 4th floor, 181 Piccadilly, W1, ☏ 0171/734–8040. AE, DC, MC, V. Tea served Mon.–Sat. 3–5:20.*

Harrods. For sweet-toothed people, the Georgian Room at this ridiculously well-known department store has a high tea *buffet* that will give you a sugar rush for a week. ⊠ *Brompton Rd., SW3, ☏ 0171/730–1234. AE, DC, MC, V. Tea served Mon.–Sat. 3–5:30.*

The Orangery at Kensington Palace. This Georgian, gorgeous, sunlight-flooded (assuming the sun is out), yes, orangery, is the perfect setting for a light lunch or for tea, serving homemade soups and quiche, cakes, shortbread, pastries, and pots of Earl Grey. ⊠ *Kensington Gardens, W8, ☏ 0171/376–0239. No credit cards. Closed after 4. Tube: High Street Kensington.*

The Ritz. The Ritz's huge, stagey, and sometimes cold Palm Court offers tiered cake stands, silver pots, a harpist, and Louis XVI chaises, plus a great deal of rococo gilt and glitz, all for £21. It's obviously a good excuse for a glass of champagne. Reservations for this extremely popular tea are taken way in advance—months for a Saturday or Sunday. ⊠ *Piccadilly, W1, ☏ 0171/493–8181. Reserve 4 wks ahead; longer for weekends. AE, DC, MC, V. Tea served daily 2–6.*

The Savoy. The glamorous Thames-side hotel does one of the most pleasant teas (£17, or £26 with champagne), its triple-tiered cake stands packed with goodies, its tailcoated waiters thrillingly polite. ⊠ *The Strand, WC2,* ☎ *0171/836–4343. AE, DC, MC, V. Tea served daily 3–5:30.*

Pubs

Even today, when television keeps so many people glued to their own hearth and home, the pub, or public house, or "local"—it has many aliases—is still a vital part of British life. It also should be a part of the tourist experience, as there are few better places to meet the natives in their local habitat. Sit at a table if you want privacy; better, help prop up the bar, where no introductions are needed, and watch that legendary British reserve fade away. There are hundreds of pubs in London, but the best—ever fewer of which still feature original Victorian etched glass, Edwardian panels, and Art Nouveau carvings—are listed below.

As we write, "gastro-pub" fever has hit London. At many places, char grills are being installed in the kitchen out back, while up front the faded wallpapers and the dear ole Mums are being replaced by abstract paintings and food mavens galore (in fact, the best of these new luxe pubs are dealt with in the restaurant reviews above). Some of the following also feature nouveau pub grub, but whether you have Moroccan chicken or the usually dismal ploughman's special, you'll want to order a pint. What Americans call beer, Brits call lager. However, the main Brit pub drink is "bitters"—usually warm. Today, there is a flourishing movement to bring back the traditionally prepared ale that is much less gassy. There's also a vast range of other potations—stouts like Guinness and Murphy's are thick, pitch-black brews you'll either hate or love; ciders, made from apples, are an alcoholic drink in Britain (Bulmer's and Strongbow are the names to remember); shandies are a mix of lager and lemonade or orange sodas; while black and tans are a blend of lager and stout named for the distinctive uniforms worn by turn-of-the-century British troops. Discuss your choices and other arcane details of drink with the barman, turn to your neighbor, raise the glass, and utter that most pleasant of toasts, "Cheers." Note that, in some circles, women are expected to drink out of half-pint, not full-pint, glasses. Be warned if you order a drink that would normally be served with ice in the United States—ice cubes are about as common in pubs as they are in Hades.

Arcane licensing laws forbid the serving of alcohol after 11 PM (10:30 on Sunday; different rules for restaurants) and have created, some argue, a nation of alcoholics, driven to down more pints than is decent in a limited time—a circumstance you see in action at 10 minutes to 11, when the "last orders" bell signals a stampede to the bar. That noted, "lock-ins" are an old tradition—pubs that lock the front door after hours and ask remaining customers to leave by the side door—that bobbies tend to overlook. The list below offers a few pubs selected for central location, historical interest, a pleasant garden, music, or good food, but you might just as happily adopt your own temporary local.

Black Friar. A step from the Blackfriars tube, this spectacular pub has an Arts-and-Crafts interior that is entertainingly, satirically ecclesiastical, with inlaid mother-of-pearl, wood carvings, stained glass, and marble pillars all over the place, and reliefs of monks, fairies, and friars poised above finely lettered temperance tracts, regardless of which, there are six beers on tap. ⊠ *174 Queen Victoria St., EC4,* ☎ *0171/236–5650.*

Bunch of Grapes. A traditional (which means smoky, noisy, and anti-chic) pub, popular since Victoria was on the throne, in the heart of Shepherd Market, the village-within-Mayfair, this place is still home-away-from-home for a full deck of London characters. ⊠ *16 Shepherd Market, W1,* ☎ *0171/629–4989.*

Crown and Goose. This is a sky-blue-walled, art-bedecked Camden Town local, where armchairs augment the tables, coffee and herb tea the beers, and good food (steak in baguettes, smoked chicken salad with honey vinaigrette, baked and stuffed mushrooms) is served to the crowds. ⊠ *100 Arlington Rd., NW1,* ☎ *0171/485–2342.*

Dove Inn. Read the list of famous ex-regulars, from Charles II and Nell Gwyn (mere rumor, but a likely one) to Ernest Hemingway, as you wait for a beer at this very popular, very comely 16th-century riverside pub by Hammersmith Bridge. If it's *too* full, stroll upstream to the Old Ship or the Blue Anchor. ⊠ *19 Upper Mall, W6,* ☎ *0181/748–5405.*

Freemason's Arms. This place is supposed to have the largest pub garden in London, with two terraces, a summerhouse, country-style furniture, and roses everywhere. Try your hand at the 17th-century game of pell mell—a kind of croquet—or at skittles. It's a favorite Hampstead pub, and it's popular with young locals. ⊠ *32 Downshire Hill, NW3,* ☎ *0171/435–2127.*

French House. In the pub where the French Resistance convened during World War II, Soho hipsters and eccentrics rub shoulders now. More than shoulders, actually, because this tiny, *tricolore*-waving, photograph-lined pub is always filled to bursting. ⊠ *49 Dean St., W1,* ☎ *0171/ 437–2799.*

George Inn. The inn sits in a courtyard where Shakespeare's plays were once performed. The present building dates from the late 17th century and is central London's last remaining galleried inn. Dickens was a regular—the inn is featured in *Little Dorrit.* Entertainments include Shakespeare performances, medieval jousts, and morris dancing. ⊠ *77 Borough High St., SE1,* ☎ *0171/407–2056.*

Island Queen. Gigantic caricature pirates leer down at you from the ceiling in this sociable Islington pub, which offers home-cooked food, a busy pool table, and a fab jukebox. The playwright Joe Orton frequented the place; he lived—and died—next door, murdered by his lover. ⊠ *87 Noel Rd., N1,* ☎ *0171/226–0307.*

Jack Straw's Castle. Straw was one of the leaders of the Peasants Revolt of 1381, and he was hanged nearby. In Tudor times this was a favorite hangout for highwaymen, but by the 19th century it had become picturesque and respectable; artists painted charming views from it and Dickens (inevitably) stayed here. Sadly, it was blitzed during World War II, but rebuilt in the 1960s. You can admire the views over Hampstead Heath and drink (weather permitting) in the large and lovely outside courtyard. ⊠ *North End Way, NW3,* ☎ *0171/435–8885.*

The Lamb. Another of Dickens's locals is now a picturesque place for a pint in summer, when you can drink on the patio. ⊠ *94 Lamb's Conduit St., WC1,* ☎ *0171/405–0713.*

Lamb and Flag. This 17th-century pub was once known as "The Bucket of Blood" because the upstairs room was used as a ring for bare-knuckle boxing. Now, it's a trendy, friendly, and entirely bloodless pub, serving food (at lunchtime only) and real ale. It's on the edge of Covent Garden, off Garrick Street. ⊠ *33 Rose St., WC2,* ☎ *0171/836–4108.*

Mayflower. An atmospheric 17th-century riverside inn, with exposed beams and a terrace, this is practically the very place from which the Pilgrims set sail for Plymouth Rock. The inn is licensed to sell American postage stamps. ⊠ *117 Rotherhithe St., SE16,* ☎ *0171/237–4088.*

Museum Tavern. Across the street from the British Museum, this gloriously Victorian pub makes an ideal resting place after the rigors of the culture trail. With lots of fancy glass—etched mirrors and stained-glass panels—gilded pillars, and carvings, the heavily restored hostelry once helped Karl Marx to unwind after a hard day in the Library. He could have spent his *kapital* on any one of six beers available on tap. ⊠ *49 Great Russell St., WC1,* ☎ *0171/242–8987.*

Pheasant and Firkin. David Bruce single-handedly revived the practice of serving beer that's been brewed on the premises and long ago sold the thriving business. The jolly microbrewery/pubs, all named the something and Firkin (a small barrel) are now all over town, all still serving beers called "dogbolter" or "rail ale," and selling T-shirts printed with bon mots like "I had a Pheasant time at the Firkin pub." Students like this a lot. ⊠ *166 Goswell Rd., EC1,* ☎ *0171/235–7429.*

Princess Louise. This fine, popular pub has an over-the-top Victorian interior—glazed terra-cotta, stained and frosted glass, and a glorious painted ceiling. It's not all show, either; the food is a cut above normal pub grub (especially the Thai dishes), and there's a good selection of real ales. ⊠ *208 High Holborn, WC1,* ☎ *0171/405–8816.*

Prospect of Whitby. Named after a ship, this is London's oldest riverside pub, dating to 1520. Once upon a time it was called "The Devil's Tavern" because of the low-life criminals—thieves and smugglers—who congregated here. It's ornamented with pewter ware and nautical memorabilia. ⊠ *57 Wapping Wall, E1,* ☎ *0171/481–1095.*

St. James Tavern. This pretty pub is steps from Piccadilly Circus and five major West End theaters. The decor includes lovely hand-painted Doulton tiles depicting Shakespearean scenes. The kitchen is proud of its fish-and-chips. ⊠ *45 Great Windmill St., W1V,* ☎ *0171/437– 5009.*

Sherlock Holmes. This pub used to be known as the Northumberland Arms, and Arthur Conan Doyle popped in regularly for a pint. It figures in *The Hound of the Baskervilles,* and you can see the hound's head and plaster casts of its huge paws among other Holmes memorabilia in the bar. ⊠ *10 Northumberland St., WC2,* ☎ *0171/930–2644.*

Spaniards Inn. This is another historic, oak-beamed pub on Hampstead Heath, boasting a gorgeous rose garden, scene of the tea party in Dickens's *Pickwick Papers.* Dick Turpin, the highwayman, used to frequent the inn; you can see his pistols on display. Romantic poets—Shelley, Keats, Byron—hung out here, and so, of course, did Dickens. It's extremely popular, especially on Sundays when Londoners take to the heath in search of fresh air. ⊠ *Spaniards Rd., NW3,* ☎ *0171/455– 3276.*

Star Tavern. In the heart of elegant Belgravia, this pub features a postcard-perfect Georgian-era facade. The inside is charming as all get-out; Victorian decor and two roaring fireplaces make this a popular spot. ⊠ *6 Belgrave Mews West, SW1,* ☎ *0171/235–3019.*

Three Greyhounds. Usefully Soho-central, this welcoming, reconditioned mock-Tudor pub serves a great bar meal—homemade Scotch eggs (hard-boiled, wrapped in sausage meat, and deep-fried in bread crumbs), matzo-coated Southern-fried chicken, sandwiches of home-cured ham or herring, oysters by the half dozen. Its other claim to fame is its youthful landlady's name—say hi to Roxy Beaujolais. ⊠ *25 Greek St., W1,* ☎ *0171/734–8799.*

Windsor Castle. This is one to rest at on a Kensington jaunt, saving a large appetite for the food, especially on Sunday, when they do a traditional roast; other days there are oysters and salads, fish cakes and steak sandwiches. In winter there are blazing fires; in summer, an exquisite walled patio garden. ⊠ *114 Campden Hill Rd., W8,* ☎ *0171/ 727–8491.*

Ye Olde Cheshire Cheese. Yes, it is a tourist trap, but this most historic of all London pubs (it dates from 1667) deserves a visit anyway, for its sawdust-covered floors, low wood-beam ceilings, the 14th-century crypt of Whitefriars' monastery under the cellar bar, and the set of 17th-century pornographic tiles upstairs. This was the most regular of Dr. Johnson's and Dickens's *many* locals. ⊠ *145 Fleet St., EC4,* ☎ *0171/353–6170.*

4 Lodging

Queen Elizabeth hasn't invited you this time? No matter. Staying at one of London's grande-dame hotels is the next best thing—some say better— to being a guest at the palace. Royally resplendent decor abounds, and armies of staff are stuck in the pampering mode—the Windsors should have it so good. Even in more affordable choices, inimitable British style brings you a taste of home, with tea makers and Queen Mum pastel wallpaper. Still not cozy enough? Borrow some keys and be a B&B guest.

By Kate
Sekules

STANDING IN THE PARLORLIKE atmosphere of your lobby—burnished oak paneling, time-stained antiques, chintz-softened sofas, the distant tinkle of teacups in the air—a century seems to slip away. The concierge whispers that Queen Victoria used to visit—she, too, probably got willingly lost in the corridors and crannies. In the grand salon sit ancient Chippendale desks that once bore the concentrated energy of the empire's Kiplings and Hardys. Set near a crackling fire, a roomy leather Chesterfield beckons one to approach its quilted field. Yes, our Auld London Towne fantasies may be fading fast in the light of Blair's Britain, but when it comes time to rest your head, the old-fashioned clichés remain very enticing. Who wouldn't want their cream tea served by a frock-coated retainer while lounging in an overstuffed brocade armchair? Or to breakfast on coffee, toast, and croissants in a handmade bed in your powder blue and white Syrie Maugham-esque boudoir, as the Thames flows lazily past your French windows? Choose one of London's heritage-rich hotels—Brown's or Claridge's supply perfect parlors; the Savoy has that river view—and these fantasies can, and always will, be fulfilled.

On the other hand, faster times are bringing more changes to the London hotel scene than there have been in years. There's another hotel on the river now and it makes that coveted bedside view of Big Ben finally available (in fact, there are two new hotels inside the former County Hall, perched on top of the aquarium by Westminster Bridge—one upscale, one affordable). In general, there are more options for budget-watchers than ever before, which is good news for U.S. travelers, long resigned to the unfavorable exchange rate. Chain hotels with cookie-cutter decor, and—as they used to say—all mod cons (modern conveniences), tended to avoid London's center, but they're moving in now, attracted by the big increase in Chunnel travelers and other inter-Europe wayfarers. It adds another option to your vacation planning: You no longer need to blow your entire budget on your bed.

Still, if you want to do just that, London is the place. Prices can soar into the empyrean here, but many of the best hotels are worth it. Take the Connaught, a landmark whose guests wouldn't *dream* of staying anywhere else. Its Edwardian lobby, created in 1897, is unadulterated by things modern; grand and faded, it is filled with oil paintings and antiques in a way interior designers envy but can't really duplicate. In contrast to this dowager aunt–type are hotels such as the Pelham and Covent Garden—most of them renovated town houses, aglitter with sensationally atmospheric Regency-style interiors and richly endowed with stunning furnishings and guests. Designed to be the very epitome of English country housedom, these newer boutique hotels appeal to clientele bent on revisiting the landed gentry culture. Waving the banner SMALL IS BEAUTIFUL, they have stolen a march on the genteel sleeping beauties—the Claridges, the Savoys, and the Dorchesters—who, recently awakened, have launched a broad counterattack. The Sultan of Brunei sank tens of millions into refurbishing the Dorchester; a Hunt heiress sponsored a complete makeover of the Lanesborough, while the Connaught, Savoy, and Claridge's are each being renovated to the tune of a mint. Claridge's was the latest to overhaul itself, having sunk $60 million into renovations and redecorations, some practical (3-inch-thick doors in the guest rooms), some sybaritic (TVs in the bathrooms), others cosmetic (the Queen's nephew, Viscount Linley, redoing the lobby's woodwork). Paying top dollar, of course, does not always mean you'll get stately grandeur—several places have moved away from

London Lodging *(Boxes Refer to Detail Maps)*

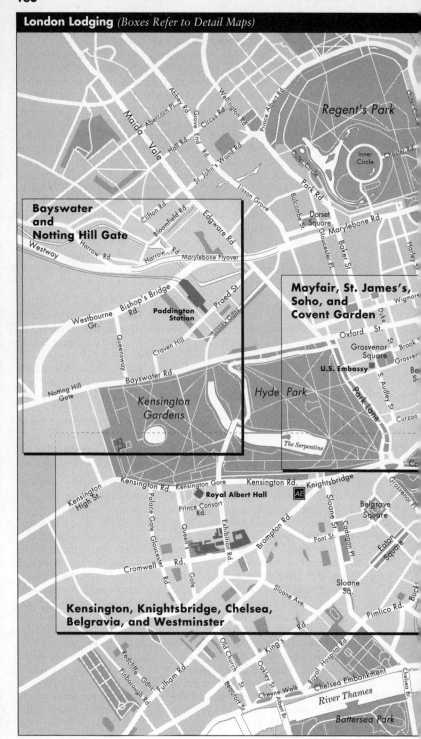

Bayswater and Notting Hill Gate

Regent's Park

Inner Circle

Outer Circle

Chester Rd.

Prince Albert Rd.

Park Rd.

Balcombe St.

Dorset Square

Marylebone Rd.

Gloucester Pl.

Baker St.

Harley St.

Maida Vale

Abbey Rd.

Abercorn Pl.

Grove End Rd.

Circus Rd.

Hall Rd.

St. John's Wood Rd.

Wellington Rd.

Lisson Grove

Clifton Rd.

Bloomfield Rd.

Edgware Rd.

Westway

Harrow Rd.

Harrow Rd.

Marylebone Flyover

Bishop's Bridge Rd.

Praed St.

Paddington Station

Westbourne Gr.

Queensway

Craven Hill

Sussex Gdns.

Bayswater Rd.

Notting Hill Gate

Kensington Gardens

Mayfair, St. James's, Soho, and Covent Garden

Oxford St.

Duke St.

Wigmore

Grosvenor Square

Brook

Grosven

U.S. Embassy

S. Audley St.

Park Lane

Be

Curzon

Hyde Park

The Serpentine

Co

Kensington High St.

Kensington Rd.

Kensington Gore

Kensington Rd.

Knightsbridge

Grosvenor Pl.

Palace Gate

Prince Consort Rd.

Royal Albert Hall

AE

Sloane St.

Belgrave Square

Gloucester Rd.

Queen's Gate

Exhibition Rd.

Brompton Rd.

Pont St.

Cadogan Pl.

Eaton Square

Cromwell Rd.

Sloane Ave.

Sloane Sq.

Pimlico Rd.

Buck

Kensington, Knightsbridge, Chelsea, Belgravia, and Westminster

Redcliffe Gdns.

Finborough Rd.

Fulham Rd.

Old Church St.

King's Rd.

Oakley St.

Beaufort St.

Cheyne Walk

Albert Br.

Royal Hospital Rd.

Chelsea Embankment

Chelsea Br.

River Thames

Battersea Park

Hampstead

King's Cross
Station

Pentonville Rd.

City Rd.

Evershall St.

St. Pancras
Station

King's Cross Rd.

Gray's Inn Rd.

Rosebery Ave.

St. John's St.

Goswell Rd.

East Road

Euston
Station

Coram's
Fields

Farringdon Rd.

City Rd.

Euston Rd.

Judd St.

Woburn Pl.

Guilford St.

Clerkenwell Rd.

London Wall

Moorgate

Gower St.

Tottenham Court Rd.

Bloomsbury

Southampton Row

Theobald's Rd.

High Holborn

Holborn
Viaduct

Newgate St.

Old Bailey

London Wall

Oxford
Circus

Oxford St.

Charing Cross Rd.

Drury Ln.

Kingsway

Aldwych

**Law
Courts**

Fleet St.

Cheapside

Queen Victoria St.

Cannon St.

**Cannon St.
Station**

Regent St.

Brewer St.

Shaftesbury Ave.

**Piccadilly
Circus**

Haymarket

Regent St.

Strand

**Charing
Cross Stn.**

Victoria Embankment

Waterloo Br.

Blackfriars Br.

Blackfriars Rd.

Southwark Br.

Docklands

Piccadilly

Jermyn St.

Pall Mall

The Mall

Whitehall

**South
Bank
Arts
Complex**

Stamford St.

Southwark St.

Park

St. James's
Park

on Hill

Birdcage Walk

York Rd.

Waterloo

The Cut

Union St.

Westminster Br.

**Waterloo
Station**

Waterloo Rd.

Borough Rd.

Borough High St.

**Victoria
Station**

Victoria St.

Westminster Br. Rd.

London Rd.

Willow Rd.

Millbank

Lambeth Palace Rd.

Lambeth Rd.

**Imperial
War
Museum**

New

Kent Rd.

Horseferry Rd.

Lambeth Br.

Kennington Rd.

rwick Way

**Tate
Gallery**

Vauxhall Br.

Vauxhall Br. Rd.

Albert Embankment

Walworth Rd.

Belgrave Rd.

Lupus St.

Grosvenor Rd.

Vauxhall Br.

Kennington Ln.

Kennington Park Rd.

Nine Elms Ln.

**Vauxhall
Station**

Kennington
Oval

N

0   1 mile

0   1 km

Regency flounces and Laura Ashleyisms into pared-down modernity and minimalism. The Halkin was the first frill-free grand hotel; now add the Metropolitan and the ultra-fashionable Hempel. At the other end of the scale, things can be almost as trendy. In design-crazy London, even hostels have become stylish—just look into the future at the Generator.

As the city is the opposite of compact, where you stay can affect your experience significantly. For instance, the West End is equivalent to downtown, but it covers a lot of ground. There's a great deal of difference between, say, posh Park Lane and bustling, touristy Leicester Square, yet both are in the West End. Hotels in Mayfair and St. James's are central, but distant in both mileage and atmosphere from funky, youthful neighborhoods like Notting Hill and Camden Town, and from major tourist sights like the Tower of London, St. Paul's Cathedral, and the large Kensington museums. On the edges of the West End, Soho and Covent Garden feel like the center of the universe these days, with countless restaurants and late-opening bars and clubs.

South Kensington, Kensington, Chelsea, and Knightsbridge are all patrician and peaceful, which will give you a more homey feeling than anything in the West End, while Belgravia is super-elegant, geographically and atmospherically about halfway between the extremes. From Bloomsbury it's a short stroll to the shops and restaurants of Covent Garden, to Theatreland, and to the British Museum. From here, it's a short bus ride to Camden and Regent's Park, too, and Hampstead and Islington are close enough to explore easily. Bayswater is a particularly affordable haven. It's barely considered a real neighborhood by Londoners, but everywhere is accessible from there, and Hyde Park is your backyard. Notting Hill and Holland Park are worth considering as a base if you want something more down-home plus have the antiques of Portobello Road and its surrounding cutting-edge shops and restaurants on your doorstep.

The general custom these days in all but the bottom end of the scale is for rates to be quoted for the room alone (which unless otherwise noted is with bath); breakfast, whether Continental or "full English," comes at extra cost. VAT is usually included, and service, too, in nearly all cases. All the hotels listed here are graded according to their spring 1998 rates, but it's best to check on these figures, which are spiraling ever-upward. Remember, too, that there can be a significant difference off-season. Like hotels in most other European countries, British hotels are obliged by law to display a tariff at the reception desk. If you have not booked ahead, you are strongly advised to study this carefully.

Be sure to make reservations well in advance, as seasonal events, trade shows, or royal occasions can fill hotel rooms for sudden brief periods, and, of course, during highly touristed July and August, too. Thinking ahead also allows you to investigate the various U.S.-based membership programs that offer discounts in Europe, including on London hotel rooms, at a savings of up to 50%. Try **Privilege Card International** (☎ 800/236–9732), Entertainment Publications' **Europe Hotel Directory** (☎ 800/445–4137), or **RMC Travel Centre** (☎ 800/782–2674). Call the **British Tourist Authority** in the U.S. at 800/462–2748. They can give general advice and help you with the next step in booking accommodations, but they can't make individual recommendations—however, you do get a real person, not a recording. Web browsers have two excellent ways to get hotel information: the U.S.'s BTA's site at www.VisitBritain.com has direct links to hotels and much more, while the London Tourist Board's site at www.LondonTown.com facilitates on-line booking for even the smallest B&B. If you do manage to arrive in the capital without a room, the **London Tourist Board Information Centres** at Heathrow and Victoria Station Forecourt can help, and the Visitor Call service provides general advice (☎ 0839/ 123435 (calls cost 49p per minute); or call the **LTB Bookings Hotline** (☎ 0171/932–2020) weekdays 9:30–5:30 for prepaid credit-card bookings (MC, V).

CATEGORY	COST*
££££	over £190
£££	£130–£190
££	£80–£130
£	under £80

All prices are for a double room, VAT included.

Mayfair to Regent's Park

££££ 🏨 **Athenaeum.** The welcome in this independently run baby-grand opposite Green Park is in the details: from Donald, the super-concierge at his door-side desk, to the disposable camera and Japanese rice crackers in the minibar, to the compact health spa. Rooms have distinctive custom-made leather-top mahogany and yew furniture, set against navy-and-cream drapes, Wedgwood green walls, and ultra-thick cream carpets. Without getting out of bed, you can control lighting and temperature, order free videos and CDs, and listen to your voice mail from your two phone lines. In glittering gray marble bathrooms are power showers, mirrors angled to get the back of your head, old-fashioned Bronnley toiletries, and—hallelujah—a real hair dryer; downstairs, there's the cozy Whisky Bar and the not-too-formal Bullochs restaurant. Rooms 201–205 face Green Park; others have a bay that affords a partial, angled view. ✉ *116 Piccadilly, W1V 0BJ,* ☎ *0171/499–3464,* FAX *0171/493–1860. 123 rooms. Restaurant, bar, in-room VCR, health club (no pool). AE, DC, MC, V. Tube: Green Park.*

££££ 🏨 **Brown's.** Founded in 1837 by Lord Byron's "gentleman's gentleman," James Brown, this Victorian country house in central Mayfair comprises 11 Georgian houses and is occupied by many Anglophilic Americans—a habit that was established by the two Roosevelts (Teddy while on honeymoon). Bedrooms feature thick carpets, soft armchairs, brass chandeliers, and brocade wallpapers, as well as air-conditioning, while the public rooms retain their cozy oak-paneled, chintz-laden, grandfather-clock-ticking-in-the-parlor ambience. Right outside the door are the boutiques and art galleries of Bond and Cork streets, while in the lounge, one of London's best-known afternoon teas is served from 3 to 6. ✉ *34 Albemarle St., W1A 4SW,* ☎ *0171/493–6020,* FAX *0171/ 493–9381. 132 rooms. Restaurant, bar. AE, DC, MC, V. Tube: Green Park.*

££££ 🏨 **Claridge's.** Stay here, and you're staying at a hotel legend (founded
★   in 1812), with one of the world's classiest guest lists. The liveried staff is friendly and not in the least condescending, and the rooms are never less than luxurious, thanks to a £40-million refurbishment. Have a drink in the Foyer lounge (24 hours a day) with its Hungarian mini-orchestra, or retreat to the reading room for perfect quiet interrupted only by the sound of pages turning. The bedrooms are spacious, as are the bathrooms, with their enormous shower heads and bells (which still work) to summon either maid or valet from their station on each floor. Beds are handmade and supremely comfortable—the King of Morocco once brought his own, couldn't sleep, and ended up ordering 30 from Claridge's to take home. The grand staircase and magnificent elevator are equally impressive. ✉ *Brook St., W1A 2JQ,* ☎ *0171/629–8860 or 800/ 223–6800,* FAX *0171/499–2210. 200 rooms. 2 restaurants, beauty salon, health club. AE, DC, MC, V. Tube: Bond St.*

££££   🏨 **Connaught.** Make reservations well in advance for this *very* exclu-
★   sive small hotel just off Grosvenor Square—the most understated of
any of London's grand hostelries. The bar and lounges have the air of
an ambassadorial residence, an impression reinforced by the imposing oak staircase and dignified staff. Each bedroom has a foyer, antique furniture (if you don't like the desk, they'll change it), and fresh
flowers, and the management is above such vulgarities as brochure and
tariff—which would be extraneous for guests who inherited the Connaught habit from their great-grandfathers. If you value privacy, discretion, and the kind of luxury that eschews labels, then you have met
your match here. ⊠ *Carlos Pl., W1Y 6AL,* ☎ *0171/499–7070,* 🖷 *0171/
495–3262. 90 rooms. Restaurant, bar. MC. Tube: Bond St.*

££££   🏨 **The Dorchester.** Probably no other hotel this opulent manages to be
★   this charming. A London institution since its 1931 inception, the
Dorchester appears on every "world's best" list. The glamour level is
off the scale: 1,500 square meters of gold leaf and 1,100 of marble gild
this lily, and bedrooms (some not as spacious as you might imagine)
feature Irish linen sheets on canopied beds, brocades and velvets, individual climate control, dual voltage outlets, and Italian marble and
etched glass bathrooms with Floris goodies. Decor throughout is in opulent English country-house style, with more than a hint of Art Deco,
in keeping with the original 1930s building. There's a beauty spa, run
by Elizabeth Arden, a nightclub, a special theater-ticket concierge, the
Oriental and Terrace restaurants, plus the power-dining Grill Room.
Afternoon tea, drinking, lounging, and posing are all accomplished in
the catwalk-shape Promenade lounge, where you may spot one of the
film-star types who will stay nowhere else (Elizabeth Taylor has been
a habitué for decades—in fact, she was sitting in her tub here when
that million-dollar offer to film *Cleopatra* came over the telephone).
⊠ *Park La., W1A 2HJ,* ☎ *0171/629–8888,* 🖷 *0171/409–0114. 197
rooms, 55 suites. 3 restaurants, bar, health club (no pool), nightclub,
business services, meeting rooms. AE, DC, MC, V. Tube: Marble Arch.*

££££   🏨 **47 Park Street.** Secreted back to back with the grand hotels of Park
Lane, this dear (in every sense) little all-suite hotel has the best room
service in town, with 24-hour food direct from the kitchen of Le
Gavroche (☞ Chapter 3). The hotel shares its bar with that poshest-
of-posh dining establishment, too, which means there's a jacket-and-
tie requirement for your quiet nightcap. Bathrooms are on the small
side, but no other drawbacks are apparent in this fabulously discreet,
conventionally decorated, quiet, relaxed, and homey haven, as long as
you can afford it. ⊠ *47 Park St., W1Y 4EB,* ☎ *0171/491–7282,* 🖷
*0171/491–7281. 52 suites with kitchen. Dining room, bar (jacket and
tie required), baby-sitting. AE, DC, MC, V. Tube: Marble Arch.*

££££   🏨 **Four Seasons.** Business travelers, of course, swear by Four Seasons'
standards of luxury and comfort. However, this hotel opened two
decades ago (as Inn on the Park)—do you really want to pull up in front
of a '70s-vintage building in time-burnished London? Still, the discretion and élan of this place (situated opposite Hyde Park, off the end
of Piccadilly, and on the cusp of beautiful Mayfair) inspires more-than-
average loyalty in its guests. ⊠ *Hamilton Pl., Park La., W1A 1AZ,* ☎
0171/499–0888 or 800/223–6800, 🖷 *0171/493–6629. 228 rooms.
2 restaurants, health club. AE, DC, MC, V. Tube: Hyde Park Corner.*

££££   🏨 **Grosvenor House.** "The old lady of Park Lane" has had a recent
overhaul supervised by English Heritage, the people who usually look
after historic museums and stately houses. It's not the kind of place
that encourages hushed whispers or that frowns on trendy Alexander
McQueen outfits, despite the marble floors and wood-paneled library,
open fires, oils, and fine antiques, all inspired by the Earl of Grosvenor's
residence, which occupied the site during the 18th century. The hotel

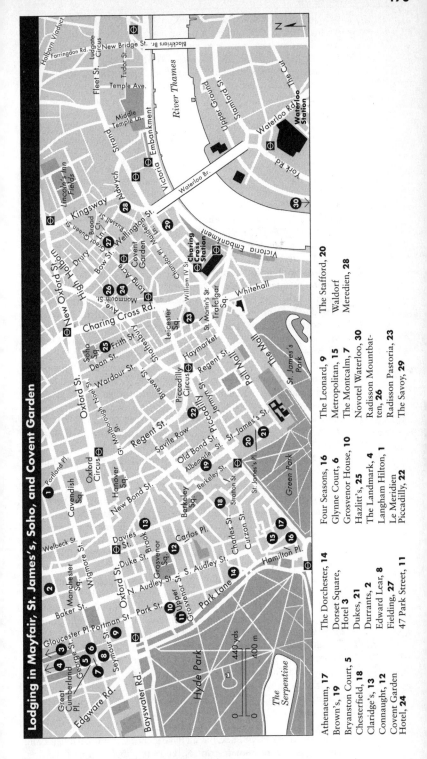

Lodging in Mayfair, St. James's, Soho, and Covent Garden

Athenaeum, **17**
Brown's, **19**
Bryanston Court, **5**
Chesterfield, **18**
Claridge's, **13**
Connaught, **12**
Covent Garden
Hotel, **24**

The Dorchester, **14**
Dorset Square,
Hotel **3**
Dukes, **21**
Durrants, **2**
Edward Lear, **8**
Fielding, **27**
47 Park Street, **11**

Four Seasons, **16**
Glynne Court, **6**
Grosvenor House, **10**
Hazlitt's, **25**
The Landmark, **4**
Langham Hilton, **1**
Le Meridien
Piccadilly, **22**

The Leonard, **9**
Metropolitan, **15**
The Montcalm, **7**
Novotel Waterloo, **30**
Radisson Mountbat-
ten, **26**
Radisson Pastoria, **23**
The Savoy, **29**

The Stafford, **20**
Waldorf
Meredien, **28**

health club is one of the best around, thanks to its good-size pool. Bedrooms are spacious, and most of the marble bathrooms have natural light. Readers have written to say service is decidedly uneven. ⊠ *Park La., W1A 3AA,* ☎ *0171/499–6363,* ⨳ *0171/493–3341. 360 rooms, 70 suites. 3 restaurants, bar, indoor pool, health club. AE, DC, MC, V. Tube: Marble Arch.*

££££ 🔟 **The Landmark.** A year older than the century, the one-time Great Central Hotel and former BritRail HQ was recently renovated to within an glitzy inch of its life. A palm-filled, eight-story glazed atrium "Winter Garden" forms the core, and odd-numbered rooms overlook this. If size matters to you, note that even standard rooms here are among the largest in London and have glamorous bathrooms in marble and chrome outfitted with robe and hair dryer. Despite appearances, this is one of the only London grand hotels that doesn't force you to dress up—even jeans are okay. The Landmark is very near Regent's Park; the West End is a 15-minute walk away. ⊠ *222 Marylebone Rd., NW1 6JQ,* ☎ *0171/631–8000,* ⨳ *0171/631–8080. 309 rooms. Restaurant, 2 bars, indoor pool, health club, business services. AE, DC, MC, V. Tube: Marylebone.*

££££ 🔟 **Langham Hilton.** Opened in 1865 by the Prince of Wales and once London's center of Victorian chic—regular guests included Toscanini, Mark Twain, and Oscar Wilde—the Langham has recently been renovated to become the London flagship of the Hilton chain. All columns and porticoes, its exterior looks very Grand Hotel, especially at night with fairy-tale floodlighting. Inside, the lobby soars to Castle Howard heights—here you find the Chukka Bar, a stately-house salon glowing with daffodil yellow walls, for years a fave watering spot for the BBC brass across the way. Guest rooms are done in soothing Queen Mother pastels, and many have marble-bedecked bathrooms. You're just a few blocks from the Oxford Circus tube stop and many of the big Regent Street stores. ⊠ *1C Portland Pl., W1N 3AA,* ☎ *0171/323–1000.,* ⨳ *0171/323–2340. 400 rooms. 2 restaurants, bar. AE, DC, MC, V. Tube: Oxford Circus.*

££££ 🔟 **Le Meridien Piccadilly.** The massive turn-of-the-century building is fin de siècle elegant, if slightly antiseptic in its white-marble-and-plush-carpet public areas. The vast Oak Room restaurant, however, is exquisite in limed oak paneling and gilt, and it is one of the best hotel restaurants in London, lorded over by famous chef Marco Pierre White. The hotel's second restaurant, far less formal, is a miniature Kew Gardens of arched glass, ferns, and palms. Bedrooms vary in size; a few seventh-floor ones have balconies overlooking Piccadilly. Decor is Edwardian-gent's-club with frills. The health club is the most luxurious and exclusive in London and boasts squash courts, saunas, and billiard tables, as well as a swimming pool. You can't be more central than here. ⊠ *Piccadilly, W1V 0BH,* ☎ *0171/734–8000,* ⨳ *0171/437–3574. 284 rooms. 3 restaurants, bar, indoor pool, health club, library, business services. AE, DC, MC, V. Tube: Piccadilly Circus.*

££££ 🔟 **Metropolitan.** Super-trendy from the moment the DKNY-clad doormen open the gates, this latest Park Lane grand is one of the only addresses for fashion folk, the music biz, and Hollywood youth, just as its bar is the hangout of choice, and its restaurant, leased by Nobu Matsuhisa, of Nobu New York City "new style sashimi" fame, is among the swankiest in town. The lobby is sleek and postmodern (psst. . . didn't the Royalton and other N.Y.C. hotels do this long ago?). The best rooms overlook Hyde Park, but all have identical minimalist beige and white decor, with climate control, bedside panel-operated lighting, U.S./U.K. modem points, ISDN lines, three telephone lines, and satellite and cable TV. The minibar contains the latest alcoholic and health-boosting beverages, and the bathroom's stocked with Kiehl's goodies.

Be here, and pose. ⊠ *Old Park La., W1Y 4LB,* ☎ *0171/447–1000,* ℻ *0171/447–1100. 137 rooms, 18 suites. Restaurant, bar, massage, exercise room, meeting rooms. AE, DC, MC, V. Tube: Hyde Park Corner*

££££ 🏨 **The Montcalm.** Secreted behind Marble Arch in a peaceful Georgian crescent, the Montcalm has kept a low profile since its rock-star days, but it is now back up there with the best of them, thanks to the Japanese owners, Nikko, who have made it an especially efficient, spotless, and calm hotel, with some unusual features. Here is London's only low-allergen bedroom, its only canopied water bed (not in the same room), and one of its few Japanese breakfasts, bathrooms with electronic hair dryers and bidets, and, by the conservatorylike Crescent restaurant, a CD-operated player piano serenading lunchers with a little Brahms. The duplex suites, with their cast iron spiral staircases, are especially winning. ⊠ *Great Cumberland Pl., W1A 2LF,* ☎ *0171/402–4288,* ℻ *0171/724–9180. 116 rooms. Restaurant, bar, meeting rooms. AE, DC, MC, V. Tube: Marble Arch.*

£££–££££ 🏨 **The Leonard.** Four 17th-century buildings were combined to create this property in 1996. Shoppers will particularly appreciate the Mayfair location, just around the corner from Oxford Street. If you stay in a two-bedroom superior suite, you can swing by Marks & Spencer's food halls for provisions, then whip up a dinner in your private kitchen—a plus for families and visitors on longer trips. All the suites have a remarkably residential feel, with sitting and bedroom areas set off by small foyers, and complemented by a judicious mix of lived-in antiques and comfortable reproductions. For more elbow room, try one of the aptly named grand suites, with their palatial sitting rooms and tall windows. The welcoming lobby area is stocked with complimentary newspapers to read by the fire. ⊠ *15 Seymour St., W1H 5AA,* ☎ *0171/935–2010,* ℻ *0171/935–700. 20 suites (3 with kitchenette), 6 rooms. Bar, dining room, room service, exercise room, business services. AE, DC, MC, V.*

£££ 🏨 **Chesterfield.** This former town house of the Earl of Chesterfield is popular with American visitors, many of whom are repeat guests or have links with the English Speaking Union, which has its headquarters next door. It is deep in the heart of Mayfair and has welcoming wood-and-leather public rooms and spacious bedrooms. The staff is outstandingly pleasant and helpful. ⊠ *35 Charles St., W1X 8LX,* ☎ *0171/491–2622,* ℻ *0171/491–4793. 113 rooms. Restaurant. AE, DC, MC, V. Tube: Green Park.*

£££ 🏨 **Dorset Square Hotel.** This special small hotel off Baker Street was
★ the first of four London addresses for husband and wife Tim and Kit Kemp, hoteliers extraordinaire. What they did was decant the English country look into a fine pair of Regency town houses, and then turn up the volume. Everywhere you look are covetable antiques, rich colors, and ideas *House & Garden* subscribers will steal. Naturally, every room is different: The first-floor balconied "Coronet" ones are the largest (two have grand pianos), and a virtue is made of the smallness of the small ones. The marble and mahogany bathrooms have power showers; glossy magazines, a half bottle of claret, and boxes of vitamin C are complimentary. There's a reason for the ubiquitous cricket memorabilia: Dorset Square was the first Lord's grounds. If you want a car rental here, you get a Bentley. ⊠ *39–40 Dorset Sq., NW1 6QN,* ☎ *0171/723–7874,* ℻ *0171/724–3328. 37 rooms. Restaurant, bar. AE, MC, V. Tube: Baker St.*

££ 🏨 **Bryanston Court.** Three Georgian houses have been converted into a hotel in an historic conservation area, a couple of blocks north of Hyde Park and Park Lane. The style is traditional English—open fireplaces, comfortable leather armchairs, oil portraits—though the bedrooms are small and modern, with pink furnishings, creaky floors, and minute bathrooms. Rooms at the back are quieter and face east, so they're bright in the mornings; Room 77 is as big as a suite, but being on the lower ground floor typical of London houses, it's dark. This family-run hotel is an excellent value for the area. ⊠ *56–60 Great Cumberland Pl., W1H 7FD,* ☏ *0171/262–3141,* ﬂ˥ *0171/262–7248. 56 rooms. Restaurant, bar. AE, DC, MC, V. Tube: Marble Arch.*

££ ⊞ **Durrants.** A hotel since the late 18th century, Durrants occupies a quiet corner almost next to the Wallace Collection, a stone's throw from Oxford Street and the smaller, posher shops of Marylebone High Street. It's a good value for the area, and if you like ye wood-paneled, leather-armchaired, dark-red-pattern-carpeted style of olde Englishness, this will suit you. Bedrooms, by way of contrast, are wan and motel-like but perfectly adequate—a few have no bathroom, though this disadvantage has the advantage of saving you £10 a night. Best give the baron of beef–type restaurant a wide berth. ⊠ *George St., W1H 6BH,* ☏ *0171/935–8131,* ﬂ˥ *0171/487–3510. 96 rooms, 85 with bath. Restaurant, bar, dining rooms. AE, MC, V. Tube: Bond St.*

££ ⊞ **Novotel Waterloo.** Looking otherwise precisely like 280 other hotels in 44 countries, this French-owned, inexpensive, reliable chain hotel offers a fitness center and brasserie, conference facilities, in-room satellite TV, tea/coffeemaker, direct-dial phone and hair dryer in very compact rooms, plus—in 40 of them—*that* view. Actually, the view is more a flagrant grandstand spying over Lambeth Palace than a river vista, though you can see from Big Ben to St. Paul's for the £5 supplement the higher-floor rooms command. Mind you, the romance rating does plummet when you can't fling open the window to catch the Thames breeze on account of the guest room climate-control system. ⊠ *113–127 Lambeth Rd., SE1 7JL,* ☏ *0181/748–3433 (central reservations). 189 rooms. Restaurant, bar, health club, meeting rooms. AE, DC, MC, V. Tube: Waterloo.*

£ ⊞ **Edward Lear.** This is a good-value, family-run hotel in a Georgian town house, a minute's walk from Oxford Street, formerly the home of writer/artist Edward Lear (famous for his nonsense verse). Rooms vary enormously in size, with some family rooms very spacious indeed and others barely big enough to get out of bed (avoid Room 14); rooms at the back are quieter. It's a friendly place, but there are no hotel-type facilities (although if you want a jacket pressed you're welcome to borrow the iron). The management is very proud of the English breakfasts—they use the same butcher as the Queen. Recent letters from readers indicate the hotel has seen better days. ⊠ *28–30 Seymour St., W1H 5WD,* ☏ *0171/402–5401,* ﬂ˥ *0171/706–3766. 31 rooms, 15 with shower (no toilet), 4 with full bath. Breakfast room. MC, V. Tube: Marble Arch.*

£ **Glynne Court Hotel.** Despite its location, this is a quiet, small hotel, and so handy for late-night runs to Virgin Records, being just off hectic Marble Arch. It's no luxury joint, but it is a clean and pleasant place, with spacious rooms containing hair dryers, phones, TVs, sinks, and tea/coffeemakers, and the management is friendly. In all, it's a good buy—doubles run about £55—for the area. ⊠ *41 Great Cumberland Pl., W1H 7LG* ☏ *0171/262–4344,* ﬂ˥ *0171/724–2071. 14 rooms. AE, DC, MC, V. Tube: Marble Arch.*

St. James's

££££ ⊞ **The Stafford.** The unique features here in ascending order of importance: The utterly amazing American Bar, where a million ties, baseball caps, and toy planes hang from a ceiling modeled, presumably, on New York's "21" Club, and where Charles (who claims the first dry martini: see the Savoy) has been mixing for 35 years; and the

12 carriage house rooms, installed in the 18th-century stable block, with their own cobbled mews entrances. These havens are very cute and private, with their gas-log fires, black-stained exposed beams, CD players, CNN, and safes, and they're relative bargains. The main hotel has navy-and-gold hallways, rooms with china in cabinets or French doors to the bathrooms, and air-conditioning throughout, but the gorgeous mews remains the Stafford's best profile. ⊠ *St. James's Pl., SW1A 1NJ,* ☏ *0171/493–0111,* ℻ *0171/493–7121. 80 rooms. Restaurant, bar, dining rooms. AE, DC, MC, V. Tube: Green Park.*

£££ 🎬 **Dukes.** This small, exclusive, Edwardian-style hotel, with its lantern-lighted entrance, is central but still quiet, as it is set in its own discreet cul-de-sac, where the Stafford also lies. A small hotel of character, it's suitably filled with squashy sofas, oil paintings of assorted dukes, and muted, rich colors. Its trump cards are that, for such a central location, it offers immense peace and quiet and very reasonable rates, plus personal service (they greet you by name every time), and an especially sweet suite or two, on the top floor, with views over St. James's Park. ⊠ *35 St. James's Pl., SW1A 1NY,* ☏ *0171/491–4840,* ℻ *0171/493–1264. 62 rooms. Restaurant, dining room. AE, DC, MC, V. Tube: Green Park.*

Soho and Covent Garden

££££ 🎬 **Covent Garden Hotel.** Relentlessly chic, theatrically baronial, this
★   is Tim and Kit Kemp's latest extravaganza—a former 1880s-vintage hospital in the midst of the artsy Covent Garden district, now the London home-away-from-home for a mélange of off-duty celebrities, actors, and style mavens. The public salons will keep even the most picky atmosphere-hunter happy: Wallowing in painted silks, *style anglais* ottomans, and 19th-century oils, they are perfect places for a Hollywood star to be interviewed over a glass of sherry. Guest rooms are *World-of-Interiors* stylish, each showcasing matching-but-mixed couture fabrics to stunning effect. Antique-style desks are vast, beds are gargantuan, and modern bathrooms even feature they-*have*-thought-of-everything heated mirrors (steam doesn't stick). Off the lobby, have a nibble in the Brasserie, and you'll agree: For taste, in every sense of the word, the Covent Garden is the top. ⊠ *10 Monmouth St., WC2H 9HB,* ☏ *0171/806–1000,* ℻ *0171/806–1100. 46 rooms, 4 suites. Restaurant, minibars, room service, exercise room, laundry service. AE, MC, V. Tube: Covent Garden.*

££££ 🎬 **The Savoy.** This historic, grand late-Victorian hotel is beloved by
★   wielders of international influence, now as ever. Its celebrated Grill (☞ Chapter 3) has the premier power-lunch tables; it hosted Elizabeth Taylor's first honeymoon in one of its famous river-view rooms; and it poured the world's first martini in its equally famous American Bar—haunted by Hemingway, Fitzgerald, Gershwin, et al. And does it measure up to this high profile? Absolutely. The impeccably maintained, spacious, elegant, bright, and comfortable rooms are furnished with antiques and serviced by valets. A room facing the Thames costs an arm and a leg and requires an early booking, but only the new County Hall Marriott tops that view. Bathrooms have original fittings, with the same sunflower-size shower heads as at Claridge's. Though the Savoy is as grand as they come, the air is tinged with a certain naughtiness, which goes down well with Hollywood types. ⊠ *Strand, WC2R 0EU,* ☏ *0171/836–4343,* ℻ *0171/240–6040. 202 rooms. 3 restaurants, 2 bars, indoor pool, beauty salon, health club. AE, DC, MC, V. Tube: Aldwych.*

££££ 🎬 **Waldorf Meridien.** Close to the Aldwych theaters and Covent Garden, the Waldorf gleams in luscious Edwardiana, with polished marble floors, chandeliers, and cozily comfortable period bedrooms. This is a booking challenge for the wealthy theatergoer (Waldorf or Savoy?) and a suitably glamorous setting for the famous Palm Court tea dances, still going strong every weekend after nearly 90 years. ⊠ *Aldwych, WC2B 4DD,* ☎ *0171/836–2400,* FAX *0171/836–7244. 292 rooms. Restaurant, brasserie, beauty salon. AE, DC, MC, V. Tube: Aldwych.*

£££   🎩 **Hazlitt's.** The solo Soho hotel is in three connected early 18th-
★ century houses, one of which was the last home of essayist William Hazlitt (1778–1830). It's a disarmingly friendly place, full of personality, but devoid of such hotel features as elevators, room service (though if the staff isn't too busy, you can get ad-hoc takeouts), and porter service. Robust antiques are everywhere, assorted prints crowd every wall, plants and stone sculptures appear in odd corners, and every room has a Victorian claw-foot tub in its bathroom. There are tiny sitting rooms, wooden staircases, and more restaurants within strolling distance than you could patronize in a year. Book way ahead—this is the London address of media people, literary types, and antiques dealers. ⊠ *6 Frith St., W1V 5TZ,* ☎ *0171/434–1771,* FAX *0171/439– 1524. 23 rooms. AE, DC, MC, V. Tube: Tottenham Court Rd.*

£££   🎩 **Radisson Mountbatten.** Naming the hotel after the late Lord Mountbatten, last viceroy of India and favorite uncle of Prince Charles, is probably just an excuse to go overboard with the old British Raj theme. The decor reflects Mountbatten's life: photos of the estate where he lived, Indian furnishings, silks, inlaid tables, and screens. It has a good standard of service, bedrooms in various shades of red, with chintz drapes, and bathrooms of Italian marble. A harpist plays in the lounge and a pianist in the comfortable bar, and there are post-theater cabarets in the Centre Stage restaurant three times a week, featuring the very actors you may have just left in the West End theaters. On a somewhat lackluster street, the hotel is a minute's walk to the Covent Garden Piazza. ⊠ *Seven Dials, Covent Garden, WC2H 9HD,* ☎ *0171/836–4300,* FAX *0171/340–3540. 127 rooms. Restaurant, bar. AE, DC, MC, V. Tube: Covent Garden.*

££   🎩 **Fielding.** Tucked away in a quiet alley by the world's first police station (now Bow St. Magistrates' Court), and feeling far from the madding crowds of Covent Garden, this cozy hotel is so adored by its regulars that you'd be wise to book well ahead. A loyal, friendly staff maintains the place as the two founders, now retired, kept it for more than two decades. It is not uneccentric. The bedrooms are all different, shabby-homey rather than chic, and none too spacious, though you can have a suite here for the price of a chain-hotel double. There's no elevator; only one room comes with bath (most have showers); and only breakfast is served in the restaurant. Cute. ⊠ *4 Broad Ct., Bow St., WC2B 5QZ,* ☎ *0171/836–8305,* FAX *0171/497–0064. 26 rooms, 1 with bath, 23 with shower. Bar, breakfast room. AE, DC, MC, V. Tube: Covent Garden.*

££   🎩 **Radisson Pastoria.** A less exorbitant choice for the theatergoer than the Waldorf and the rest (although rates are at the very top of this category), the Pastoria is handily situated just off Leicester Square. The building is about 70 years old, with a suitably modern decor, the bedrooms done in limed oak with light pink walls and navy blue carpets. There's a brasserie-style restaurant to dine in, but Soho, which is restaurant central, is only a few hundred yards away. ⊠ *3–6 St. Martin's St., WC2H 7HL,* ☎ *0171/930–8641,* FAX *0171/925–0551. 58 rooms. Restaurant, bar, coffee shop. AE, DC, MC, V. Tube: Leicester Sq.*

Kensington

££££   🎩 **Blakes.** Blakes is another world—some would say a '70s rock-star
★ era time-warp. It was designed by owner Anouska Hempel (also known

as Lady Weinberg), and each room is a fantasy packed with precious Biedermeier, Murano glass, and modern pieces inside walls of red lacquer and black, or dove-gray moiré, or perhaps—like Room 007, the movie stars' favorite suite—pink. Cinematic mood lighting, featuring recessed halogen spots, compounds the impression that you, too, are a movie star living in a big-budget biopic. The foyer sets the tone with its piles of cushions, Phileas Fogg valises and trunks, black walls, rattan and bamboo, and a noisy parakeet under a gigantic Asian parasol. Downstairs is an equally dramatic, exotic black-and-white restaurant. Stay away if you don't like Hollywood or the music biz. ⊠ *33 Roland Gardens, SW7 3PF,* ☎ *0171/370–6701,* 𝔽𝔸𝕏 *0171/373–0442. 52 rooms. Restaurant. AE, DC, MC, V. Tube: Gloucester Rd.*

£££ 🔟 **The Cranley.** The pedigree of this small Georgian town-house hotel is Ann Arbor, Michigan (where the owners hail from), out of South Ken (where it stands, near the big museums), and it looks the part. Anglo antiques, oils, and etchings are mixed with a lot of U.S.-style swagged drapery in assorted florals and vivid color schemes. Bedrooms have kitchenettes, and many are high-ceilinged and huge-windowed, while two of the apartments have Jacuzzis and patio gardens. The cheaper rooms here and at their nearby 10-room **One Cranley Place** (⊠ SW7 3AB, ☎ 0171/589–7944, 𝔽𝔸𝕏 0171/225–3931), which operates March–October, belong in the ££ category. ⊠ *10–12 Bina Gardens, SW5 0LA,* ☎ *0171/ 373–0123,* 𝔽𝔸𝕏 *0171/373–9497. 26 rooms, 10 apartments. Breakfast room. AE, DC, MC, V. Tube: Gloucester Rd.*

£££ 🔟 **Forte Posthouse Kensington.** This mammoth, fairly utilitarian hotel feels like a smaller one and boasts a few extras you wouldn't expect for the rates, at the low end of this category, and a convenient location in a quiet lane off Kensington High Street. The main attraction is the health club, with a sizable pool, two squash courts, a steam room, and a beauty salon; there's also a secluded little water garden. Standard rooms are on the small side, with plain chain-hotel built-in furniture. Some "executive" rooms are twice the size and are a particularly good value. ⊠ *Wrights La., W8 5SP,* ☎ *0171/937–8170,* 𝔽𝔸𝕏 *0171/ 937–8289. 530 rooms. 2 restaurants, 2 bars, indoor pool, health club, baby-sitting. AE, DC, MC, V. Tube: High Street Kensington.*

£££ 🔟 **The Gore.** Just down the road from the Albert Hall, this very friendly
★ hotel is run by the same people who run Hazlitt's (☞ *above*) and features a similar eclectic selection of prints, etchings, and antiques—the lobby looks like a set from a Luchino Visconti film. Upstairs are spectacular follylike rooms—Room 101 is a Tudor fantasy with minstrel gallery, stained glass, and four-poster bed, and Room 211, done in over-the-top Hollywood style, has a tiled mural of Greek goddesses in the bathroom. The hotel gets a fun, chic, but partying crowd—so don't be shocked if you find some cigarette butts in the hallways. ⊠ *189 Queen's Gate, SW7 5EX,* ☎ *0171/584–6601,* 𝔽𝔸𝕏 *0171/589–8127. 54 rooms. Brasserie. AE, DC, MC, V. Tube: Gloucester Rd.*

£££ 🔟 **Number Sixteen.** A luxury bed-and-breakfast close to South Kensington tube and three blocks or so from the great museums, Number Sixteen stands in a white-portico row of Victorian houses, with not a sign outside to indicate it. There's no uniformity to the bedrooms except for their spaciousness and recently refitted bathrooms, but the decor overall is not so much interior-designed as understated, with new furniture and modern prints juxtaposed with yellowed oils and antiques. There's an elevator, and an enticing garden complete with conservatory and fountain-ette. ⊠ *16 Sumner Pl., SW7 3EG,* ☎ *0171/589– 5232,* 𝔽𝔸𝕏 *0171/584–8615. 36 rooms. Bar. AE, DC, MC, V. Tube: South Kensington.*

££ 🔟 **Hotel 167.** This friendly little bed-and-breakfast is a two-minute walk from the V&A, in a grand white-stucco Victorian corner house. The

Lodging in Kensington, Knightsbridge, Chelsea, Belgravia and Westminster

Abbey House, **2**
Basil Street, **18**
Beaufort, **14**
Berkeley, **20**
Blakes, **8**
Capital, **19**
The Cranley, **6**
Diplomat, **23**

Eden Plaza, **5**
Egerton House, **13**
Eleven Cadogan
Gardens, **25**
Elizabeth, **27**
Forte Posthouse
Kensington Close, **3**
The Franklin, **12**

The Gore, **4**
Goring, **28**
Halkin, **21**
Hotel 167, **7**
Knightsbridge
Green, **17**
Knightsbridge
Hotel, **15**

La Reserve, **9**
L'Hotel, **16**
The
Lanesborough, **22**
London County Hall
Travel Inn
Capital, **32**
London Marriott,
County Hall, **31**

Number Sixteen, **11**
The Pelham, **10**
St. James Court, **29**
The Sloane, **24**
Stakis St. Ermins, **30**
Vicarage, **1**
Wilbraham, **26**

lobby is immediately cheering, with its round marble tables, wrought-iron chairs, palms, and modern paintings; it also does duty as lounge and breakfast room. Bedrooms have a hybrid Victoriana/IKEA decor, with Venetian blinds over double-glazed windows (which you need on this noisy road), plus cable TV and minibars. ⊠ *167 Old Brompton Rd., SW5 0AN,* ☎ *0171/373–0672,* 𝙵𝙰𝚇 *0171/373–3360. 18 rooms with bath. Breakfast room. AE, DC, MC, V. Tube: Gloucester Rd.*

£ ▥ **Abbey House Hotel.** Next door to the Vicarage (☞ below), Abbey House has been voted "Best Value, Best Quality B&B in London" in several surveys, so you'll have to book well in advance for the doubles that go for £60 here. The place occupies a pretty, white-stucco 1860 Victorian town house—once home to a bishop and an MP before World War II—and overlooks a garden square. Rooms are spacious and have color TVs and washbasins, but every room shares a bath with another. An English breakfast is included in the rates, and a cuppa (cup of tea) is complimentary. ⊠ *11 Vicarage Gate, W8,* ☎ *0171/727–2594. 16 rooms, none with bath. No credit cards. Tube: High Street Kensington.*

£ ▥ **Eden Plaza.** When a hotel calls its own rooms "compact," you should imagine a double bed, then add a foot all around, and, yes, that is about the size of a room here. However, like in a cruise ship's stateroom, all you need is creatively secreted—there's a closet, mirror, satellite TV, tea/coffeemaker, and a hair dryer. Rooms are double-glazed against noisy Cromwell Road, though earplugs are useful on account of LOUD color schemes, like purple, kingfisher, and canary. The kids can share free—if you can fit a cot into these rooms—or else they get their own room at half price. The Natural History Museum is just across the street. ⊠ *68–69 Queensgate, London SW7 5JT,* ☎ *0171/370–6111,* 𝙵𝙰𝚇 *0171/370–0932. 62 rooms. Bar. AE, MC, V. Tube: Gloucester Rd.*

£ ▥ **Vicarage.** Spend the cash you save here in the surrounding Kensington antiques shops. This has long been a favorite for the budget-minded: Family-owned, set on a leaf-shaded street just off Kensington Church Street, the Vicarage is set in a large white Victorian house. The decor is sweetly anachronistic, full of heavy, dark-stained wood furniture, patterned carpets, and brass pendant lights, and there's a little conservatory. Many of the bedrooms now have TVs. All in all, this still remains a charmer—but it is beginning to fray around the edges. ⊠ *10 Vicarage Gate, W8 4AG,* ☎ *0171/229–4030. 19 rooms. No credit cards. Tube: High Street Kensington.*

Knightsbridge, Chelsea, Belgravia, Victoria, and Westminster

££££ ▥ **Berkeley.** The Berkeley is a successful mixture of the old and the
★ new—a luxurious, air-conditioned, double-glazed modern building with a splendid penthouse swimming pool that opens to the sky when the weather's good. The bedrooms have swags of William Morris prints or are plain and masculine with little balconies overlooking the street. All have sitting areas and big, tiled bathrooms with bidets. For the ridiculously rich, there are spectacular suites, one with its own conservatory terrace, another with a sauna, but—such is the elegance of this place—you'd feel almost as spoiled in a normal room. Its restaurant is Vong, the Thai/French hybrid cloned from New York; its expensive decor, work-of-art dishes, and exorbitant prices are going down very well with London's big spenders. ⊠ *Wilton Pl., SW1X 7RL,* ☎ *0171/235–6000,* 𝙵𝙰𝚇 *0171/235–4330. 160 rooms. 2 restaurants, indoor and outdoor pool, beauty salon, health club, cinema. AE, DC, MC, V. Tube: Knightsbridge.*

££££ ▥ **Capital.** Reserve well ahead if you want a room here—as you must for a table in the hotel's superb restaurant (☞ Chapter 3). This grand hotel decanted into a private house is the work of David and Margaret Levin, who also own L'Hôtel (☞ *below*), and it exudes their irreproachable taste, with French floral fabrics, fine-grained woods, sober prints, and shelves of books. The 10 rooms of the Edwardian Wing, with its carved wooden staircase, enjoyed the attentions of superstar designer Nina Campbell and were already the height of fashion in the 1920s, when this was the Squires Hotel. ⊠ *22–24 Basil St., SW3 1AT,* ☎ *0171/589–5171,* FAX *0171/225–0011. 48 rooms. Bar. AE, DC, MC, V. Tube: Knightsbridge.*

££££ ⚏ **The Halkin.** If you can't take any more Regency stripes, English-country florals, or Louis XV chaises, this luxurious little place is the antidote. Chill out to the Milanese design: the clean-cut white marble lobby with its royal-blue-leather bucket chairs; the arresting, curved, charcoal-gray corridors; the "diseased mahogany" veneers; and the gray-on-gray bedrooms that light up when you insert your electronic key. Wealthy business and media types frequent the Halkin, so rooms feature fax machines, Reuters, and two phone lines with conference-call capacities, along with two touch-control pads for all the gadgets, cable TV, and VCR. The bathrooms are palaces of shiny chrome. Staying here might be like living in the Design Museum, except that this place employs some of the friendliest staff around—who look pretty good in their white Armani uniforms. ⊠ *Halkin St., SW1X 7DJ,* ☎ *0171/ 333–1000,* FAX *0171/333–1100. 41 rooms. Restaurant, business services. AE, DC, MC, V. Tube: Hyde Park Corner.*

££££ ⚏ **The Lanesborough.** This very grand hotel acts for all the world as
★ though the Prince Regent took a ride through time and is about to resume residence. Royally proportioned public rooms (not lounges but "the Library" and "the Withdrawing Room") lead one off the other like an exquisite giant Chinese box in this multimillion-pound, American-run conversion of the old St. George's Hospital opposite Wellington's house. Everything undulates with richness—brocades and Regency stripes; moiré silks and fleurs-de-lys in the colors of precious stones; magnificent antiques and oil paintings; reproductions of more gilded splendor than the originals; handwoven £250-per-square-yard carpet, as if Liberace and Laura Ashley had collaborated on the design. All you do to register is sign the visitors book, then retire to your room, where you are waited on by a personal butler. Full-size Lanesborough toiletries, umbrellas (take them home), robes (don't), a drinks tray (pay by the inch), and even business cards with your temporary fax (in every room) and phone numbers (two lines) are waiting. If you yearn for a bygone age and are very rich, this is certainly for you. ⊠ *1 Lanesborough Pl., SW1X 7TA,* ☎ *0171/259–5599,* FAX *0171/259–5606. 95 rooms. 2 restaurants, bar. AE, DC, MC, V. Tube: Hyde Park Corner.*

££££ ⚏ **London Marriott Hotel, County Hall.** This exceptionally grand hotel has what visitors to London most often request, and which up until now has not been available—a view of the Houses of Parliament across the Thames (which means, of course, that the hotel is not in Westminster, but on the south side of the river). It's in the former home of the long-defunct local governing body—a mammoth, spectacular, pedimented-and-becolummed affair—and uses the old Members' entrance, with its bronze doors and marble lobby that leads into the former Council Chamber. A Marriott is a reliable thing, and this one has all the expected deluxe accoutrements—from modern, businessy decor to almost-instantly-arriving elevators, and from conference facilities to the use of the fantastic new 24-hour Health & Fitness Spa on the top floors. ⊠ *County Hall, SE1 7PB,* ☎ *0171/928–5200,* FAX *0171/928–5300. 200 rooms. Lounge, bar, indoor pool, health club. AE, DC, MC, V. Tube: Westminster.*

££££ 🏨 **St. James's Court.** You enter this Edwardian pile through a pair of enormous wrought-iron gates, which used to admit carriages into what is now the towering reception. From here, you pass ranks of green leather sofas to reach the pièce de résistance: the landscaped courtyard with its fountain and ceramic frieze of scenes from Shakespeare. Some bedrooms are disproportionately large but cost the same as standards—the reverse is also true, so beware the expensive shoe boxes—and all are plainly decorated in pallid shades with a smattering of antiques and the odd (and some *are* very odd) painting. There are two good restaurants and a business center, and many apartments offer good deals for weekly and longer stays, but unless you have business at Buckingham Palace or around Victoria, the location isn't central enough to warrant the rates. ⊠ *Buckingham Gate, SW1E 6AF,* ☎ *0171/834–6655,* FAX *0171/630–7587. 400 rooms. 2 restaurants, coffee shop, health club, business services. AE, DC, MC, V. Tube: St. James's Park.*

£££ 🏨 **Basil Street.** This gracious Edwardian hotel is on a quiet street behind busy Brompton Road and off (rich) shoppers' heaven, Sloane Street. It has been family-run for three quarters of a century, and it has always been popular with lone women travelers, who get automatic membership at the Parrot Club—an enormous lounge, with copies of *The Lady* and *Country Life* among the coffee cups. All the bedrooms are different; many are like grandma's guest room, with overstuffed counterpanes and a random selection of furniture. You can write letters home in the peaceful gallery, which has polished wooden floors and fine Turkish carpets underneath a higgledy-piggledy wealth of antiques. Americans with a taste for period charm favor this place; some come back often enough to merit the title "Basilite"—a privileged regular offered a 15% discount. ⊠ *Basil St., SW3 1AH,* ☎ *0171/581–3311,* FAX *0171/581–3693. 92 rooms, 72 with bath. Restaurant, wine bar. AE, DC, MC, V. Tube: Knightsbridge.*

£££ 🏨 **Beaufort.** You can practically hear the jingle of Harrods' cash reg-
★ isters from a room at the Beaufort, the brainchild of ex–TV announcer Diana Wallis, who employs an all-woman team to run the hotel. Actually, "hotel" is a misnomer for this elegant pair of Victorian houses. There's a sitting room instead of reception; guests have a front door key, the run of the drinks cabinet, and even their own phone number. The high-ceilinged, generously proportioned rooms are decorated in muted, sophisticated shades to suit the muted, sophisticated atmosphere—but don't worry, you're encouraged by the incredibly sweet staff to feel at home. The rates are higher than the top range for this category but include unlimited drinks, breakfast, and membership at a local health club. ⊠ *33 Beaufort Gardens, SW3 1PP,* ☎ *0171/584–5252,* FAX *0171/589–2834. 29 rooms. AE, DC, MC, V. Tube: Knightsbridge.*

£££ 🏨 **Egerton House.** This absolutely peaceful, private-house-style small hotel was the first in the stable that includes the Franklin and Dukes, and it remains many people's favorite, appealing especially, for some reason, to bankers. Many chintzy, floral, or Regency-stripe bedrooms overlook the gorgeous gardens in back; some have quirky shapes, others have four-poster beds, still others are extra-well-endowed with closet space—in other words, all are different. The staff here is especially personable—and the manager would love to know what you thought of the selections in his handwritten local restaurant guide. ⊠ *Egerton Terr., SW3 2BX,* ☎ *0171/589–2412,* FAX *0171/584–6540. 30 rooms. AE, DC, MC, V. Tube: Knightsbridge.*

£££ 🏨 **Eleven Cadogan Gardens.** This aristocratic, late-Victorian gabled town house is the perfect spot for a pampered honeymoon, but it's very difficult to get into—and we're not referring to the lack of a sign or a reception desk. Fine period furniture and antiques, books and magazines on the tables, landscape paintings and portraits, coupled with some of that solid, no-nonsense furniture that *real* English country houses have in unaesthetic abundance make for a family-home ambience; you might be borrowing the house and servants of some wealthy friends while they're away. Take the elevator or walk up the fine oak staircase to your room, which will have mahogany furniture, a restful color scheme, and pretty bedspreads and drapes. The best rooms are at the back, overlooking a private garden. If you wish to hire a chauffeur-driven car, they have one on standby order. ⊠ *11 Cadogan Gardens, Sloane Sq., SW3 2RJ,* ☎ *0171/730–3426,* ℻ *0171/730–5217. 62 rooms. AE, MC, V. Tube: Sloane Sq.*

£££   ⊞ **The Franklin.** It's hard to imagine, while taking tea in this pretty hotel overlooking a quiet, grassy square, that you're an amble away from busy Brompton and Cromwell roads and the splendors of the V&A. A few of the rooms are small, but the marble bathrooms—in which Floris toiletries and heated towel racks are standard issue—are not; the large garden rooms and suites (which fall into the ££££ category) are romantic indeed. Tea is served daily in the lounge, and there's also a self-service bar. The staff is friendly and accommodating. ⊠ *28 Egerton Gardens, SW3 2DB,* ☎ *0171/584–5533,* ℻ *0171/584–5449. 40 rooms. Bar, parking (fee). AE, DC, MC, V. Tube: South Kensington.*

£££   ⊞ **Goring.** Readers love this hotel—after all, where else does the concierge offer to pack up some bread crumbs for the ducks if you're heading for a stroll in Hyde Park? This hotel is useful if you have to drop in at Buckingham Palace, just around the corner. In fact, visiting VIPs use it regularly as a conveniently close, and suitably dignified, base for royal occasions. The hotel was built by Mr. Goring in 1910 and is now run by third-generation Gorings. The atmosphere remains Edwardian: Bathrooms are marble-fitted, and some of the bedrooms have brass bedsteads and the original built-in closets; many have been opulently redecorated. The bar/lounge looks onto a well-tended garden. ⊠ *15 Beeston Pl., Grosvenor Gardens, SW1W 0JW,* ☎ *0171/834–8211,* ℻ *0171/834–8211. 87 rooms. Restaurant, bar. AE, DC, MC, V. Tube: Victoria.*

£££   ⊞ **L'Hôtel.** An upscale bed-and-breakfast run by the same Levins who
★   own the Capital next door, L'Hôtel is a plainer alternative—less pampering, unfussy decor. There's an air of provincial France, with white wrought-iron bedsteads, pine furniture, and delicious breakfast croissants and baguettes (included in the room rate) served on chunky dark green and gold Parisian café china in the Le Metro cellar wine bar (also open to nonguests). This really is like a house—you're given your own front door key, there's no elevator, and the staff leaves in the evening. Reserve ahead—it's very popular. ⊠ *28 Basil St., SW3 1AT,* ☎ *0171/ 589–6286,* ℻ *0171/225–0011. 12 rooms. Restaurant, wine bar. AE, V. Tube: Knightsbridge.*

£££   ⊞ **The Pelham.** The second of Tim and Kit Kemp's gorgeous hotels,
★   they opened it in 1989 and run it along exactly the same lines as the Dorset Square (☞ Mayfair to Regent's Park, *above*), except that this one looks more like the country house to end all country houses. There's 18th-century pine paneling in the drawing room—one of the most ravishingly elegant hotel salons anywhere—flowers galore, quite a bit of glazed chintz and antique lace bed linen, and the odd four-poster and bedroom fireplace. The first floor (American second floor) suites are extra-spacious with their high ceilings and chandeliers, while some of the top-floor rooms under the eaves have adorable sloping ceilings and casement windows. The Pelham stands opposite the South Kensington tube stop, by the big museums, and close to the shops of Brompton Cross and Knightsbridge. ⊠ *15 Cromwell Pl., SW7 2LA,* ☎ *0171/589–8288,* ℻ *0171/584–8444. 37 rooms. Restaurant, outdoor pool. AE, MC, V. Tube: South Kensington.*

£££ ⊞ **Stakis St. Ermins.** Smack-dab in the middle of Westminster, this hotel is just a short stroll from Westminster Abbey and minutes from Buckingham Palace and the Houses of Parliament. An Edwardian anomaly in the shadow of modern skyscrapers, the hotel is set on a tiny cul-de-sac courtyard fronted with beasts-rampant gates. The lobby is an extravaganza of Victorian Baroque—all cake-frosting stucco work in shades of baby blue and creamy white. The less costly of the two restaurants, the Cloisters, features one of the most magnificent (and overlooked) dining decors in London: a 19th-century Jacobean-style salon. Guest rooms are tastefully decorated; some have snug dimensions—but are all the cozier for it. ⊠ *Caxton St., SW1H 0QW,* ☎ *0171/222–7888,* FAX *0171/222–6914. 290 rooms, 7 suites. 2 restaurants, bar, minibars, room service, laundry service. AE, DC, MC, V. Tube: St. James's Park.*

££–£££ ⊞ **The Diplomat.** From its aristocratically elegant exterior, this hotel looks like a Cecil Beaton stage set: A Wedgwood-white "palazzo" terrace house built by the 19th-century architect Thomas Cubitt, flatiron-shape (it stands at the confluence of two streets), and often decked out with hanging flowerpots of geraniums, it is the very picture of Belgravian chic. Inside, the tiny reception area gives way to a circular staircase lighted by a Regency-era chandelier and topped by a winter-garden dome. Rooms are pleasantly decorated, some with Victorian touches; in the basement is a breakfast nook (a buffet is included in the daily rates). This hotel truly comes into its own once you step out the doorway and find yourself in the heart of Belgravia's beautiful 19th-century mansions (Baroness Thatcher is a block away) and mews. ⊠ *2 Chesham St., SW1X 3DT,* ☎ *0171/235–1544,* FAX *0171/259–6153. 27 rooms. Business services. AE, DC, MC, V. Tube: Sloane Sq., Knightsbridge.*

££–£££ ⊞ **The Sloane.** Many hotels abuse the word "unique" to describe their identical canopied beds or garden views, but the tiny Sloane really *is* unique. It is the only hotel we know of in which you can lie in your canopied bed, pick up the phone, and buy the bed. You could buy the phone, too, but it's the covetable, tasty antiques that you might actually be tempted to take home, and these are also for sale. Nothing so tacky as a price tag besmirches the gorgeous decor—which doesn't stint on strong hues to show off the ever-changing collection of Regency armoires and occasional tables, Victorian desk lamps and crystal decanters—instead, the sweet, young, Euro staff harbors a book of price lists at the desk. Room service is not 24-hour, but there's an aerie of a secret roof terrace, with upholstered garden furniture and a panorama over Chelsea, where lunch and dinner are served to guests. ⊠ *29 Draycott Pl., SW3 2SH,* ☎ *0171/581–5757,* FAX *0171/584–1348. 12 rooms. AE, DC, MC, V. Tube: Sloane Sq.*

££ ⊞ **Knightsbridge Green.** There are more suites than bedrooms at this Georgian hotel that's a two-minute walk from Harrods. One floor is French style, with white furniture; another English, in beech. Costing only £15 more than a double room, the suites are not overpriced, and all the rooms have trouser presses and tea/coffeemakers. There's no restaurant, but there are plenty in the area; or if you ask, they'll send the porter out to find you a sandwich. There's also coffee and cake left out in the lounge—a detail that exemplifies the friendliness of this place. ⊠ *159 Knightsbridge, SW1X 7PD,* ☎ *0171/584–6274,* FAX *0171/ 225–1635. 13 rooms, 12 suites. AE, MC, V. Closed 5 days over Christmas. Tube: Knightsbridge.*

££ ⊞ **Knightsbridge Hotel.** When it comes to measuring location versus value, this could be considered an ideal stopping place. On a tree-lined, quiet, stately square, the Knightsbridge is just a moment from Harrods and a few blocks from the chic boutiques and restaurants of Beauchamp Place. A family-run hotel, it's set in a town house built in the early 1800s. Guest rooms are unassuming yet well furnished, and there's even an exercise room on the premises. ⊠ *12 Beaufort Gardens, SW3 1PT,* ☎ *0171/589–9271,* FAX *0171/823–9672. 40 rooms with bath. Exercise room. AE, MC, V. Tube: Knightsbridge.*

££ 🏠 **La Reserve.** You'll find this unusual small hotel in the lively, classy residential neighborhood of Fulham. The varnished floorboards, black Venetian blinds, works of art (for sale), and primary-color upholstery in the public areas are contemporary and sophisticated. Bedrooms are cluttered only with the minibars, hair dryers, trouser presses, and tea/coffeemakers of more expensive places. Fulham is not within walking distance of central London, but it is two minutes from the Fulham Broadway tube, near Chelsea Football (soccer) Grounds and plenty of restaurants; there's also an in-house brasserie. ⊠ *422–428 Fulham Rd., SW6 1DU,* ☎ *0171/385–8561,* FAX *0171/385–7662. 37 rooms. Restaurant, bar. AE, DC, MC, V. Tube: Fulham Broadway.*

£ 🏠 **Elizabeth Hotel.** This elegant hotel near Victoria Station once served as the private home of aristocrats (including relatives of Edward VII). These days it offers luxuriously (for the price) appointed rooms overlooking an attractive garden below. Rooms come with a bath and/or shower, TV, and a knockout English breakfast. A less luxurious, shared-bath single and double are also available, at a rock-bottom rate. ⊠ *37 Eccleston Sq., SW1V 1PB,* ☎ *0171/828–6812,* FAX *0171/828–6814. 38 rooms. Lounge. No credit cards. Tube: Victoria.*

£ 🏠 **London County Hall Travel Inn Capital.** Don't get too excited—this neighbor of the fancy new Marriott lacks the river view (it's at the back of the grand former seat of local government). Still, you get an incredible value, with the standard facilities of the cookie-cutter rooms of this chain (the phone number's the central reservation line), viz: TV, tea/coffeemaker, en suite bath/shower and—best of all for families on a budget—foldout beds that let you accommodate two kids at no extra charge. You're looking at £50/night for a family of four, in the shadow of Big Ben. *That's* a bargain. ⊠ *Belvedere Rd., SE1 7PB,* ☎ *01582/414341,* FAX *01582/400024. 312 rooms. Restaurant. AE, MC, V. Tube: Westminster.*

£ 🏠 **Wilbraham.** A lovely grandmother of a hotel, this place is as British as tea and crumpets. It's set not far from swanky Sloane Square, comprises three 19th-century row houses, and is decorated in the best shabby-genteel Brit fashion, right down to floral wallpapers (some of those roses could use a bit of watering) and Victorian bric-a-brac. Guest rooms don't have many frills, but there's a pleasant lounge and a restaurant—handy for meeting friends over a glass of sherry. An English breakfast is included in the rates. ⊠ *1–5 Wilbraham Pl., SW1,* ☎ *0171/730–8296,* FAX *0171/730–6815. 53 rooms. Restaurant, lounge. No credit cards. Tube: Sloane Sq.*

Bayswater and Notting Hill Gate

££££ 🏠 **Halcyon.** Discretion, decadent decor, and disco divas (everyone
★   from RuPaul to Snoop Doggy Dogg) make this expensive, enormous, wedding-cake Edwardian on Holland Park Avenue desperately desirable. You want film stars? They've got Johnny Depp, William Hurt, and Julia Roberts, and there are usually local residents like Sting, John Cleese, and *Absolutely Fabulous's* Joanna Lumley haunting the absolutely excellent restaurant. But it's for perfect service and gorgeous rooms you'd follow them here. The Blue Room has moons and stars, the Egyptian Suite is canopied like a bedouin tent, one room has heraldic motifs, and the Halcyon Suite has its own conservatory. All rooms are very large, with the high ceilings and big windows typical of the grand houses here—a 10-minute tube ride to the West End, and steps from London's most exquisite park. ⊠ *81 Holland Park, W11 3RZ,* ☎ *0171/727–*

7288, FAX *0171/229–8516. 44 rooms. Restaurant. AE, DC, MC, V. Tube: Holland Park.*

££££ 🏨 **The Hempel.** This is a prime contender for the "most glamorous hostelry" in London prize. Anouska Hempel did the lush and lavish Blakes, then did a 180-degree turn into these stunning, crisp, clean, white-on-white-on-white-on-white spaces—and we do mean spaces. There's nothing jarring, nothing extraneous, and no visible means of support beneath the furniture. Of course, the Hempel appeals greatly to show-bizzy style hounds. Elton John (remember when he went Zen and sold all his gewgaws?) was one of the first party-throwers in the restaurant here. But beware: the minimalist decor is not for everyone. ✉ *31–35 Craven Hill Gardens, W2 3EA,* ☎ *0171/298–9000,* FAX *0171/472–4666. 43 rooms. Restaurant, bar. AE, DC, MC, V. Tube: Lancaster Gate.*

£££ 🏨 **Abbey Court.** This is a very elegant little hotel that is more like a private home—albeit one with a resident designer. It's in a gracious white Victorian mansion in a quiet streetlet off Notting Hill Gate, which gives easy access to most of London. Inside, the era of Victoria is reflected in deep-red wallpapers (downstairs), Murano glass and gilt-framed mirrors, framed prints, mahogany, and plenty of antiques. Bathrooms look the part but are entirely modern in gray Italian marble, with brass fittings and whirlpool baths. There's 24-hour room service instead of a restaurant (there are plenty around here, though), and guests can relax in the sitting room or the pretty conservatory. ✉ *20 Pembridge Gardens, W2 4DU,* ☎ *0171/221–7518,* FAX *0171/792–0858. 22 rooms. AE, DC, MC, V. Tube: Notting Hill.*

££–£££ 🏨 **Pembridge Court.** A few doors down from the Abbey Court (☞ *above*), in a similar colonnaded white-stucco Victorian row house, is this sweet home-away-from-home of a hotel, cozy with scatter cushions and books, quirky Victoriana, and framed fans from the neighboring Portobello Market. Bedrooms have a great deal of swagged floral drapery, direct-dial phones, and satellite TV, and there's an elevator to the upper floors. Rates include English breakfast—take that into account when doing your sums, since only the half-size small twin rooms fall into the category; larger ones are £10–£30 more. ✉ *34 Pembridge Gardens, W2 4DX,* ☎ *0171/229–9977,* FAX *0171/727–4982. 25 rooms. Restaurant. AE, DC, MC, V. Tube: Notting Hill.*

££–£££ 🏨 **Portobello.** This small, eccentric place has long been a favorite of high-style mavens in the music and design worlds, and it must be said that a tinge of the groovy early '70s still adheres to the corners, and also to the Victorian/Chinoiserie decor (which has turned a bit shabby in a few rooms, enhancing the louche and laid-back effect). The hotel consists of two adjoining Victorian houses that (as is common around here) back onto a beautiful large garden that is shared with the neighbors. The "Cabin Rooms" are minute, with everything you need accessible by reaching out your hand from bed. Many bigger rooms have freestanding Victorian claw-foot bathtubs, though the famous round-bed suite has the *pièce de résistance* of the bath world—an Edwardian "bathing machine," all knobs and shiny brass pipes. Rates include breakfast, and there's a 24-hour bar/restaurant in the basement, though there are a hundred other options in this very happening area. ✉ *22 Stanley Gardens, W11 2NG,* ☎ *0171/727–2777,* FAX *0171/ 792–9641. 25 rooms. Restaurant, bar. AE, DC, MC, V. Closed 10 days over Christmas. Tube: Ladbroke Grove.*

££ 🏨 **London Elizabeth.** Steps from Hyde Park and the Lancaster Gate tube
★ (and from rows of depressing, cheap hotels) is this family-owned gem. The facade is one of the most charming in London, and the charm continues inside—foyer and lounge are crammed with coffee tables and chintz drapery, lace antimacassars, and little chandeliers. This coun-

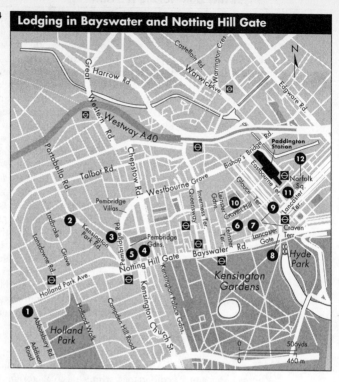

Lodging in Bayswater and Notting Hill Gate

try sensibility persists through the bedrooms done out in palest blue-striped walls, wooden picture rails and Welsh wool bedspreads, or in pink cabbage rose prints and mahogany furniture. Although rooms vary in size, there's a thoughtful tendency here to make sure that what you lose on the swings (small wedge-shape room), you gain on the round-abouts (bigger, brand-new bathroom, or a small balcony), and all have TV, direct-dial phone, and hair dryer. The exceptionally charming Anglo-Irish staff is on call around the clock, and there's a restaurant, the Rose Garden, handy in this culinary wasteland. ⊠ *Lancaster Terr., W2 3PF,* ☎ *0171/402–6641,* FAX *0171/224–8900. 55 rooms. Restaurant, bar. AE, DC, MC, V. Tube: Lancaster Gate.*

£ 🖬 **Adare House.** This is one of the most popular choices among the many B&B options in the Sussex Gardens area—not surprisingly so, since the friendly prices come with some ritzy extras: private baths (in nine rooms), Regency-style wallpapers in the rooms, and Anne O'Neill, who's been welcoming guests here for a quarter of a century. Note that half the rooms only have a shower. ⊠ *153 Sussex Gardens, W2 2RY,* ☎ *0171/ 262–0633,* FAX *0171/706–1859. 16 rooms with bath. No credit cards. Tube: Paddington.*

£ 🖬 **Camelot.** This is an affordable hotel, just around the corner from Paddington Station, with bedrooms featuring utility pine furniture, TVs, tea/coffeemakers, and attractive bathrooms. There's a sitting room and a very pretty breakfast area. Everyone here is friendly beyond the call of duty. The few single rooms without baths are great bargains; the normal rate just busts the top of this category, but includes a break-fast of anything you want—full English, or organic muesli, fruit, and herb tea. ⊠ *45–47 Norfolk Sq., W2 1RX,* ☎ *0171/723–9118,* FAX *0171/ 402–3412. 44 rooms, 36 with bath. MC, V. Tube: Paddington.*

£ 🖬 **Columbia.** If you're a sucker for '70s kitsch and like to stay out late, or alternatively, if you're a family on a tight budget, this unique paradox of a bargain hotel is worth a try. The public rooms in these five joined-up Victorians are as big as museum halls. During the day, at one end they contain the most hip band du jour drinking alcohol; at the other, there are sightseers sipping coffee. However, the place is big enough and the walls thick enough that you'd not even know they were shooting sleazy club wear for *The Face* magazine in Room 100 while you sip tea (provided) in Room 101. Rooms are clean and some are very large, with park views and balconies. It's just a shame that teak veneer, khaki-beige-brown color schemes, and avocado bathroom suites haven't made it back into the style bible yet. ⊠ *95–99 Lancaster Gate, W2 3NS,* ☎ *0171/402–0021,* 𝔽𝔸𝕏 *0171/706–4691. 103 rooms. Restaurant, bar, meeting rooms. AE, MC, V. Tube: Lancaster Gate.*

£   **Commodore.** This peaceful hotel of three converted Victorians is close to the Columbia, but deeper in the big leafy square known as Lancaster Gate. It's another find of a very different stripe, as you'll notice on entering the cozy, carpeted lounge. Try your best to get one of the amazing rooms—as superior to the regular ones as Harrods is to Kmart, but priced the same. Twenty of these are split-level rooms, with sleeping gallery, all large, all different, all with something special—like a walk-in closet with its own stained-glass window. One (No. 11) is a duplex, entered through a secret mirrored door off a lemon-yellow hallway with palms and Greek statuary, with a thick-carpeted, *very* quiet bedroom upstairs and its toilet below. It's getting very popular here, so book ahead. ⊠ *50 Lancaster Gate, W2 3NA,* ☎ *0171/402–5291,* 𝔽𝔸𝕏 *0171/262–1088. 90 rooms. Bar, business services. AE, MC, V. Tube: Lancaster Gate.*

£   ▦ **The Gate.** It's absolutely teeny—just a normal house at the very top of Portobello Road, off Notting Hill Gate. The plain bedrooms have refrigerators, TVs, direct-dial phones, and tea/coffee facilities, plus bath (unless you opt for a smaller, £10 cheaper, shower-only room), and you can have the inclusive Continental breakfast brought up to you, or take it in the first-floor lounge. ⊠ *6 Portobello Rd., W11 3DG,* ☎ *0171/221–2403,* 𝔽𝔸𝕏 *0171/221–9128. 6 rooms with bath. AE, MC, V. Tube: Notting Hill.*

£   ▦ **Lancaster Hall Hotel.** This modest hotel is owned by the German YMCA, which guarantees efficiency and spotlessness. There's a bargain 20-room "youth annex" offering basic rooms with shared baths. ⊠ *35 Craven Terr., W2 3EL,* ☎ *0171/723–9276,* 𝔽𝔸𝕏 *0171/224–8343. 100 rooms, 80 with bath or shower. Restaurant, bar. MC, V. Tube: Lancaster Gate.*

Bloomsbury, Holborn, and Euston

££–£££   ▦ **The Kingsley.** On the main street, steps from the British Museum, this is one Edwardian-style hotel that really does feel sweetly old-fashioned, while avoiding shabbiness or stuffiness—especially since last year's $6 million refurbishment of this former temperance house (tea/coffeemakers and free in-house movies are now among the facilities). The rooms in the turret on the southwest corner, with their curved, six-window wall, are worth asking for, while executive suites have four-posters and Jacuzzis at a rate falling about halfway down the £££ category. ⊠ *Bloomsbury Way, WC1A 2SD,* ☎ *0171/242–5881,* 𝔽𝔸𝕏 *0171/831–0225. 137 rooms. Restaurant, bar, meeting rooms. AE, DC, MC, V. Tube: Holborn.*

££   ▦ **Academy.** These three joined-up Georgian houses, boasting a little patio garden and a fashion-conscious mirrored and wood-floor basement bar/brasserie, supply the most sophisticated and hotel-like facilities in the Gower Street "hotel row." The comfortable bedrooms have a TV (with no extra channels), direct-dial phones, and tea/coffeemakers,

Lodging in Bloomsbury

and the two without en-suite bathrooms are £30/night cheaper. Like most of the hotels in this section, the Academy neighbors the British Museum and University of London, a circumstance that appeals to culture vultures on a budget and affluent students. ✉ *17–21 Gower St., WC1E 6HG,* ☎ *0171/631–4115,* ℻ *0171/636–3442. 33 rooms, 25 with bath/shower. Restaurant, bar. AE, DC, MC, V. Tube: Russell Sq.*

£ 🖼 **Alhambra Hotel.** One of the best bargains in Bloomsbury, this place features singles as low as £30 and doubles as low as £35. The rooms, painted a refreshing blue or red instead of the tired B&B norm of faded rose and cream, are spotless, and have TVs, though most of them lack private bathrooms. Quad rooms just bust this category, but they do have en-suite shower rooms, and are worth considering for a family. ✉ *17–19 Argyle St., WC1,* ☎ *0171/837–9575,* ℻ *0171/916–2476. 52 rooms. AE, MC, V. Tube: King's Cross.*

£ 🖼 **Arosfa Hotel** The friendly owners, Mr. and Mrs. Dorta, mark this B&B directly opposite Dillons bookstore apart from the Gower Street pack—that, and the fact that this was once the home of Pre-Raphaelite painter Sir John Everett Millais. Rooms are simple and spotless, and they're equipped with TVs and sinks, but not necessarily with their own en suite shower (it's about £12 extra for this; still easily within the £ category); those at the back are far quieter. ✉ *83 Gower St., WC1,* ☎ *0171/636–2115,* ℻ *0171/636–2115. 15 rooms. No credit cards. Tube: Goodge St.*

£ **The Generator.** This four-year-old youth hostel is easily the grooviest in town, with a friendly, funky vibe, and vibrant decor—blue neon and brushed steel downstairs, and upstairs dorm rooms painted in bright blue and orange. The Generator Bar has cheap drinks, and the Fuel Stop cafeteria provides inexpensive meals. Rooms are simple, but clean—singles run about £38, doubles about £24 per person, with prices dropping very low for the ones with multiple beds in them. From October to March are bargain-rate months, too. There are no bathrooms en-suite. ✉ *MacNaghten House, Compton Pl. WC1H 9SD,* ☎ *0171/388–7666,* FAX *0171/388–7644. 213 rooms. Restaurant, bar. MC, V. Tube: Russell Sq.*

£ 🔟 **Morgan.** This is a Georgian row-house hotel, family run with charm
★ and panache. Rooms are small and functionally furnished, yet friendly and cheerful overall, with phones and TVs. The five newish apartments are particularly pleasing: three times the size of normal rooms (and an extra £15/night, placing them in the ££ category), complete with eat-in kitchens (gourmet cooking sessions are discouraged) and private phone lines. The tiny, paneled breakfast room (rates include the meal) is straight out of a doll's house. The back rooms overlook the British Museum. ✉ *24 Bloomsbury St., WC1B 3QJ,* ☎ *0171/636–3735. 15 rooms with bath or shower, 5 apartments. Breakfast room. No credit cards. Tube: Russell Sq.*

£ 🔟 **Ridgemount.** The kindly owners, Mr. and Mrs. Rees, make you feel at home. The public areas, especially the family-style breakfast room, have a friendly, cluttered Victorian feel. Some rooms overlook a leafy garden, and two have an en-suite bathroom, for an extra £10/night. ✉ *65 Gower St., WC1E 6HJ,* ☎ *0171/636–1141. 34 rooms, 2 with bath. No credit cards. Tube: Russell Sq.*

£ 🔟 **Ruskin.** Immediately opposite the British Museum, the family-owned Ruskin is both convenient and quiet—all front windows are double-glazed. The bedrooms are clean, though readers say several are very lackluster and depressing; the back ones overlook a pretty garden. Note the bucolic mural (circa 1808) in the sitting room. All in all, the Ruskin remains a very popular option. ✉ *23–24 Montague St., WC1B 5BN,* ☎ *0171/636–7388,* FAX *0171/323–1662. 35 rooms, 7 with shower. AE, DC, MC, V. Tube: Russell Sq.*

£ 🔟 **St. Margaret's.** This guest house on a tree-lined Georgian street has been run for many years by a friendly Italian family. You'll find spacious rooms and towering ceilings, and a wonderful location close to Russell Square. The back rooms have a garden view. ✉ *24 Bedford Pl., WC1B 5JL,* ☎ *0171/636–4277. 64 rooms, 10 with bath. No credit cards. Tube: Goodge St.*

Hampstead and Islington

££ 🔟 **Stakis Islington** This brand new, purpose-built hotel next door to the Islington Business Design Centre has a madly colored, soaring lobby and its own neighborhood to explore, as well as easy access to central London via the tube stop a minute's walk away. One of a reliable, small, Scottish chain, these ultramodern rooms have climate control, satellite TV, and trouser presses, plus, in many of them, panoramic skyline views. ✉ *53 Upper St., N1 0UY,* ☎ *0171/354–7700,* FAX *0171/354–7711. 177 rooms, 6 suites. Restaurant, bar, meeting rooms. AE, DC, MC, V. Tube: Angel.*

££ 🔟 **Swiss Cottage Hotel.** It's a little out of the way on a peaceful street behind the Swiss Cottage tube stop, but this charming hotel will suit those who like to stay in a residential district, save a little on the check, and still have their home comforts. The lounge and reception area are stuffed with antiques and reproductions and smilingly staffed. In summer, French windows open from the bar and the restaurant—which serves an old-fashioned Anglo-French menu—onto the garden. Bedrooms are in Victorian style, most are good-size, and all come with full English breakfast, meaning the rate actually falls in the £ category. ✉ *4 Adamson Rd., NW3 3HP,* ☎ *0171/722–2281,* FAX *0171/483–4588. 80 rooms. Restaurant, bar. AE, DC, MC, V. Tube: Swiss Cottage.*

£ ⊡ **La Gaffe.** Another find, this is a short walk from the Hampstead tube stop. Italian Bernardo Stella has been welcoming the same guests back to these early 18th-century shepherds' cottages for more than a decade. Make no mistake, rooms are tiny, with showers only, and the predominantly pink and beige decor isn't luxurious, but the popular wine bar and restaurant, which (naturally) serve Italian food, are yours to lounge around in at all hours. Between the two "wings" is a raised patio for summer, and each room has TV and phone. You'll love the place if you're a fan of quaint. ⊠ *107–111 Heath St., NW3 6SS,* ☎ *0171/435–8965,* ℻ *0171/794–7592. 14 rooms with shower. Restaurant, wine bar/café. AE, MC, V. Tube: Hampstead.*

Bed-and-Breakfast and Apartment Agencies

££ ⊡ **Bulldog Club.** Once the most exclusive B&B club in Britain, this has recently come under new ownership, which promises the same luxe, chic, and delightful accommodations that made the Bulldog the darling of magazine editors everywhere. In days of yore, you actually got to book rooms in some of London's poshest houses, where grown-up children's rooms were converted for guests. Annual membership is around £25, with most properties available for around £100 a night. A full British breakfast, as well as other goodies are often provided. ⊠ *14 Dewhurst Rd., W14 0ET,* ☎ *0171/371–3202,* ℻ *0171/371–2015. AE, MC, V.*

££ ⊡ **Uptown Reservations.** As the name implies, this B&B booking service accepts only the tonier addresses and specializes in finding hosted apartments and homes for Americans, often executives of small corporations. Nearly all the 50 or so homes on their register are in Knightsbridge, Belgravia, Kensington, and Chelsea, with a few lying farther west in Holland Park and Maida Vale. The private homes vary, of course, but all are good-looking and have private en-suite bathrooms for guests. ⊠ *50 Christchurch St., SW3 4AR,* ☎ *0171/351–3445,* ℻ *0171/351–9383. Facilities vary. Payment by bank transfer or U.S. check; 20% deposit required. No credit cards.*

£–££ ⊡ **US B&B** This long-established family-run agency has some truly spectacular—and some more modest—London homes that host guests, in practically all neighborhoods of the city. Check many of them out before making a commitment via its Web site: www.londonbandb.com. The staff here is most personable and helpful. ⊠ *Box 124859, San Diego, CA 92112,* ☎ *800/872–2632. 50–100 rooms. 30% deposit required.*

£ ⊡ **Primrose Hill B&B.** A small, friendly bed-and-breakfast agency genuinely "committed to the idea that traveling shouldn't be a rip-off." Expatriate American Gail O'Farrell has family homes (to which guests get their own latchkeys) in or near villagey Hampstead, and all are comfortable or more than comfortable. So far this has been one of those word-of-mouth secrets, but now that everyone knows, book well ahead. ⊠ *14 Edis St., NW1 8LG,* ☎ *0171/722–6869. 15 rooms with varying facilities. No credit cards.*

5 Nightlife and the Arts

"Ladies and Gentlemen, the curtain is about to rise" on London's artful pleasures: Bussell at the ballet, Domingo at the Royal Albert Hall, and the best theater in the world—perhaps Ralph Fiennes and Vanessa Redgrave doing star turns, Oliver! *in a West End revival, and unparalleled servings of* Shakespeare. Now you can see, say, The Winter's Tale *at the reconstructed Globe Theatre, where the interaction between player and audience often goes beyond polite applause. Finish off the night at a club sizzling with comedy, cabaret, or all that jazz.*

By Kate
Sekules

AFTER DARK, LONDON is a wonderful place to play. Shakespearean theater and Handel oratorios, chart-friendly discos and post-industrial techno-rock raves, Andrew Lloyd Webber-ish extravaganzas, the roof-rattling Proms concerts, magnificent opera and ballet—if you're into the arts and after-hours scenes, you'll be quickly whirling to a pounding beat. Clearly, there are so many things to see that you can wind up frustrated. This year, however, you'll be *more* frustrated than ever, thanks to the current seismic upheaval on the performing arts scene. Several of the city's leading cultural institutions have been reduced to gypsies, thanks to ongoing multimillion-dollar renovations of their permanent homes. The Royal Opera House is shuttered for the next few years, which means both the Royal Opera and the Royal Ballet will be operating out of a number of second-tier theaters for the foreseeable future. The theater scene has also been hard hit: The Royal Shakespeare Company recently announced it would be touring Britain from May through November—leaving height-of-season London visitors Shakespeare-less (well, not quite: the brand-new Globe Theatre on the Thames continues to pack them in). The final maraschino cherry on the sundae was the news that the Old Vic—long known as one of the most innovative theaters around—was being sold and its troupe evicted. So, for the next two years, chances are you'll have to shuttle madly around to catch the Royal Ballet's *Giselle* or Royal Opera's *La Boheme*. Of course, for these troupes—Britain's best—it will be worth it.

NIGHTLIFE

Nighttime London has rejuvenated itself in the past few years, with a tangible new spirit of fun abroad on the streets, and new hangouts opening at an unprecedented rate. Whatever your pleasure, there's somewhere to go. Are you a club animal? London's boîtes are famously hip, hot, and happening. Music? From indie bands to resident orchestras, free jazz to opera, it's everywhere. Cabaret of the traditional torch-song sort is undergoing a little revival, while comedy, which never slowed down in the first place, remains one of the city's favorite ways to wind down. The gay listing is small, but gives you all you need to find the scene, and there is a fabulous scene. All you need to remember when you hit the town at night is that regular bars (those without special extended licenses) stop serving alcohol at 11 PM (10:30 on Sundays), and the tubes stop running around midnight.

Both those facts do inhibit the free flow of enjoyment, it has to be said. Although there's been a lot of hype about swinging London in recent years, it is no less depressing than it ever was to be thrown out of your warm and fuzzy pub corner at the sound of the bell to try to find a bar with a late license. On the whole, the club scene is for under-30s. If you don't have your ear to the ground in the youth culture department, you will feel out of place in nearly all venues listed under "Clubs" in *Time Out*, the weekly magazine that updates everything to do in London. But if you must put on the glad rags and boogie, we do list a couple of places for swingers nostalgic for that action. The jazz and world music (we used to call it folk) scenes are a different matter. Live music makes for a popular night out for all ages and types. A general rule of thumb: If you like the music, you'll like the crowd.

No doubt you've heard a lot about Britpop in the past couple of years. The bands that made it big are playing the stadium venues now, of course

(Wembley, principally), but one of the joys of the London music scene is discovering your own "indie" bands (short for "independent" and refers to their record label, more than their state of mind), and catching the latest hype before it's hyped. Again, read between the lines in the listings magazines to find your comfort level. Another, completely weird, trend you may choose to follow has been for imitation, or "tribute," bands—Utter Madness, Björn Again, Abba Gold, Ludwig Beatles, YMCA Village People, Below Average White Band, and so on—that perform to party-animal crowds. On the opposite end of the authenticity scale, Latin and flamenco sounds are growing, and you can sometimes learn the dances in a free class before the band comes on.

Bars

The places below are stylish and perfect for martinis and munching hors d'oeuvres. Londoners, however, truly come into their own at their neighborhood pubs—for a listing of the best of these, *see* Chapter 3, Dining.

The American Bar. Festooned with a chin-dropping array of collegiate ties, bric-a-brac, and antique toys, this is one of London's most sensational, funhouse interiors. Even if you're not feeling homesick for the other side of the pond, be sure to check out this dazzler. ⊠ *Stafford Hotel, St. James's Pl., SW1A,* ☎ *0171/493–0111.* ☯ *Daily 11:30–3, 5:30–12. AE, MC, V. Tube: Green Park.*

The Atlantic. This vast, glamorous, wood-floored basement caused a revolution when, in early 1994, it became the first central London bar to be granted a late-late alcohol license. Although there are now others, it's still popular, so that the only way to get a table on a weekend night is to book it for dinner—luckily the food's fine. ⊠ *20 Glasshouse St., W1,* ☎ *0171/734–4888.* ☯ *Mon.–Sat. noon–3 AM, Sun. noon–11. AE, MC, V. Tube: Piccadilly Circus.*

Beach Blanket Babylon. In Notting Hill, close to Portobello Market, this always packed singles bar is distinguishable by its fanciful decor—like a fairy-tale grotto, or a medieval dungeon, visited by the gargoyles of Notre Dame. ⊠ *45 Ledbury Rd., W11,* ☎ *0171/229–2907.* ☯ *Daily noon–11 . AE, MC, V. Tube: Notting Hill Gate.*

Cadogan Hotel Bar. One step beyond the door here and you're back in the Edwardian era. You half expect Lillie Langtry, the famed actress and mistress of King Edward VII, to waltz in the door—but then she used to live upstairs at this stylish hotel. If you feel like toasting Oscar Wilde with his favorite drink, a Hock and Seltzer, you'd better do it elsewhere—poor Oscar was arrested in this very bar that fateful day. ⊠ *Cadogan Hotel, Sloane St., SW1,* ☎ *0171/235–7141.* ☯ *Daily 11–11.AE, MC, V. Tube: Sloane Sq.*

Café Royal Cocktail Bar. Under one of London's most ravishing frescoed ceilings, enjoy a Café Royal cocktail while drinking in the lush 19th-century decor. After all, Oscar Wilde, James McNeill Whistler, and Aubrey Beardsley enjoyed doing just that back when. ⊠ *68 Regent St., W1,* ☎ *0171/437–9090.* ☯ *Daily 11–11. AE, V. Tube: Piccadilly Circus.*

The Library. In this very comfortable, dress code–free but self-consciously "period" (doesn't matter which one as long as it looks old) bar at the swanky Lanesborough Hotel, Salvatore Calabrese offers his completely eccentric collection of ancient cognacs, made in years when something important happened. A shot of this "liquid history" can set you back £500. Don't ask for a brandy Alexander. ⊠ *Hyde Park Corner, SW1,* ☎ *0171/259–5599.* ☯ *Mon.–Sat. 11–11, Sun. noon–2:30 PM and 7–10:30. AE, DC, MC, V. Tube: Hyde Park Corner.*

Cabaret

Comedy Café. Talent nights, jazz, and video karaoke, but mostly stand-up comedy, take place at this popular dive in the City. Admission charges are occasionally waived. There's food available in the evening and usually a late license (for alcohol). ⊠ *66 Rivington St., EC2,* ☎ *0171/739–5706.* ◻ *Free–£8.* ⊙ *Wed.– Thurs. 7:30–1, Fri. and Sat. 7:30–2. MC, V. Tube: Old St.*

Comedy Store. This is the improv factory where the United Kingdom's funniest stand-ups cut their teeth, now relocated to a bigger and better space. The name performers and new talent you'll see may be strangers to you, but you're guaranteed to laugh. ⊠ *Haymarket House, Oxendon St., SW1,* ☎ *0171/344–4444 or 01426/914433.* ◻ *£10– £12.* ⊙ *Shows Tues.–Thurs. and Sun. at 8, Fri. and Sat. at 8 and midnight. AE, MC, V. Tube: Piccadilly Circus.*

Casinos

The 1968 Gaming Act states that any person wishing to gamble *must* make a declaration of intent to gamble at the gaming house in question and *must* apply for membership in person. Membership usually takes about two days. In many cases, clubs prefer for the applicant's membership to be proposed by an existing member. Personal guests of existing members are, however, allowed to participate.

Crockford's. This is a civilized club, established 150 years ago, with none of the jostling for tables that mars many of the flashier clubs. It has attracted a large international clientele since its move from St. James's to Mayfair. The club offers American roulette, Punto Banco, and blackjack. ⊠ *30 Curzon St., W1,* ☎ *0171/493–7771.* ◻ *Membership £150 per yr.* ⊙ *Daily 2 PM–4 AM. Jacket and tie. Tube: Green Park.*

Golden Nugget. This large casino just off Piccadilly has blackjack, roulette, and Punto Banco. ⊠ *22 Shaftesbury Ave., W1,* ☎ *0171/ 439–0099.* ◻ *Membership £3.50 for life.* ⊙ *Daily 2 PM–4 AM. Jacket required. Tube: Piccadilly Circus.*

Palm Beach Casino. In what used to be the old ballroom of the May-fair Hotel, this is a fast-moving and exciting club attracting a large international membership. It has a red-and-gold interior, with a plush restaurant and bar. You can choose from American roulette, blackjack, and Punto Banco. ⊠ *30 Berkeley St., W1,* ☎ *0171/493–6585.* ◻ *Membership £10.* ⊙ *Daily 2 PM–4 AM. Jacket and tie. Tube: Green Park.*

Sportsman Club. This one has a dice table as well as Punto Banco, American roulette, and blackjack. ⊠ *3 Tottenham Court Rd., W1,* ☎ *0171/ 637–5464.* ◻ *Membership £3.45 per yr.* ⊙ *Daily 2 PM–4 AM. Jacket and tie. Tube: Tottenham Court Rd..*

Clubs

Always call ahead, especially to the dance and youth-oriented places, because the club scene is constantly changing. One-nighters (theme nights that take place at particular clubs on the same night every week, or move around from club to club) are very popular but tend to confuse matters with erratic opening and closing times—always check the daily listings in *Time Out* for current info. Unfortunately, the A-list crowd tends to stick to the members-only nightspots London snobbily still believes in—if you want to see Noel Gallagher or Keanu Reeves, chances are the only place you'll see them is at the entrance to Groucho's at 44 Dean Street.

Bagley's Studio. Possibly the largest club in town, Bagley's is notable for getting in the big DJs for one-night blitzes. It doesn't come cheap, though. After surfacing at King's Cross, walk north on York Way, and turn left on Goods Way. ⊠ *King's Cross Freight Depot, off York Way, N1,* ☎ *0171/278–2777.* ☒ *£10–£15.* ☉ *Sat. 10–6, with other raves usually (but not always) scheduled for Thurs., Fri. No credit cards. Tube: King's Cross.*

Blue Note. Many say this dance club's one-nighters offer the best variety of music in London. Sundays feature "Metalheadz," Mondays worldbeat "Anokha." This place refuses to rest on its reputation and is always hunting for the next totally weird, new, cutting-edge group on tap. ⊠ *1 Hoxton Sq., N1,* ☎ *0171/729–8440.* ☒ *£5–£10.* ☉ *Fri.– Sat. 9:30–5, Mon.–Thurs. 9:30–3, Sun. 7–midnight. AE, MC, V. Tube: Old St.*

Camden Palace. It would be difficult to find a facial wrinkle in this huge place, even if you could see through the laser lights and find your way around the three floors of bars. There's often a live band. ⊠ *1A Camden High St., NW1,* ☎ *0171/387–0428.* ☒ *£3–£9.* ☉ *Tues.–Sat. 9–3. No credit cards. Tube: Mornington Crescent or Camden Town.*

Gardening Club. Next door to the Rock Garden, but far hipper than that ancient dive, this club has different music, ambience, and groovers on alternating nights. ⊠ *4 The Piazza, WC2,* ☎ *0171/497–3154.* ☒ *£5–£13.* ☉ *Mon.–Wed. 10–3, Fri. and Sat. 11–6. AE, DC, MC, V. Tube: Covent Garden.*

Hanover Grand. A swank and opulent big West End club, the Hanover attracts TV stars and footballers whose exploits here you can later read about in the tabloids. The "Haute Couture" one-nighter takes over on Fridays, while Saturday's glam disco "Malibu Stacey" pulls in all those who want to be seen. The lines outside get long, so dress up to impress the bouncers. ⊠ *6 Hanover Sq., W1,* ☎ *0171/499–7977.* ☒ *£5–£15.* ☉ *Wed.–Sat. 10:30–4. AE, MC, V. Tube: Oxford Circus.*

Ministry of Sound. This is more of an industry than a club, with its own record label, line of apparel, and, of course, DJs. Inside, there are chill-out rooms, dance floors, promotional Sony Playstations, Absolut shot bars—all the club kid's favorite things. If you are one, and you only have time for one night out, make it here. ⊠ *103 Gaunt St., SE1,* ☎ *0171/378–6528.* ☒ *£10–£15.* ☉ *Wed.–Sat. 11–8. MC, V. Tube: Elephant & Castle.*

Stringfellows. Peter Stringfellow's nightclub is not at all hip, but it *is* glitzy, with mirrored walls, the requisite dance-floor light show, and an expensive art deco–style restaurant. Suburbanites and middle-aged swingers frequent it. ⊠ *16–19 Upper St. Martin's La., WC2,* ☎ *0171/ 240–5534.* ☒ *Mon.–Wed. £8, Thurs. £10, Fri. and Sat. £15 (£10 before 10).* ☉ *Mon.–Sat. 8–3:30. AE, DC, MC, V. Tube: Charing Cross.*

The Wag. This tenacious representative of Soho's club circuit takes on a different character according to the night and which DJ is spinning. One extremely loud, sweaty level houses bars and dance spaces, and on a quieter, cooler floor there's a restaurant serving dinner and breakfast. ⊠ *33–35 Wardour St., W1,* ☎ *0171/437–5534.* ☒ *£5–£10.* ☉ *Mon.–Thurs. 10:30–3, Fri. and Sat. 10:30–6. No credit cards. Tube: Piccadilly Circus.*

Jazz

Jazz Café. This palace of high-tech cool in a converted bank in bohemian Camden remains an essential hangout both for fans of the mainstream end of the repertoire and younger crossover performers. It's way north, but steps from Camden Town tube. ⊠ *5–7 Pkwy., NW1,* ☎ *0171/ 344–0044 .* ☒ *£8–£14.* ☉ *Mon.–Sat. 7–late. AE, DC, MC, V. Tube: Camden Town.*

100 Club. The best for blues, trad, and Dixie, plus the occasional straight rock-and-roll, this Oxford Street subterranean has the correct paint-peeling, smoke-choked, dance-inducing atmosphere. There's a food counter most nights. ⊠ *100 Oxford St., W1,* ☎ *0171/636–0933.* ☞ *£4–£10.* ☉ *Mon.–Wed. 7:30–midnight, Thurs.–Sat. 8:30–1, Sun. 7:30–11:30. No credit cards. Tube: Oxford Circus.*

Pizza Express. It may seem strange, since Pizza Express is the capital's best-loved chain of pizza houses, but this is one of London's principal jazz venues, with music every night except Monday in the basement restaurant. The subterranean interior is darkly lighted, the lineups (often featuring visiting U.S. performers) are interesting, and the Italian-style thin-crust pizzas are great! Eight other branches also have live music; check the listings for details. ⊠ *10 Dean St., W1,* ☎ *0171/437–9595.* ☞ *£8–£20.* ☉ *From noon for food, music Tues.–Sun. 9:30–1. AE, DC, MC, V. Tube: Tottenham Court Rd.*

Ronnie Scott's. Since opening in the '60s, this legendary Soho jazz club has attracted all the big names. It's usually packed and hot, the food isn't great, and service is slow—the staff can't move through the crowds, either—but the atmosphere can't be beat, and it's probably still London's best, even since the sad departure of its eponymous founder and saxophonist. ⊠ *47 Frith St., W1,* ☎ *0171/439–0747.* ☞ *£10–£15 nonmembers.* ☉ *Mon.–Sat. 8:30–3, Sun. 8–11:30. Reservations essential. AE, DC, MC, V. Tube: Leicester Sq.*

606 Club. In deepest Fulham, this is a civilized sit-down club with late hours, showcasing mainstream and fusion mediums—basically, well-known artists from here and across the Atlantic. You have to be a member to drink alcohol, unless you're eating. ⊠ *90 Lots Rd., SW10,* ☎ *0171/352–5953.* ☞ *£7.50–£24.* ☉ *Mon.–Sat. 8:30–2, Sun. 8:30–midnight. AE, MC, V. Tube: Fulham Broadway.*

Rock

The Astoria. Very central and quite hip, this place hosts bands that there's a buzz about, plus it has late club nights. ⊠ *157 Charing Cross Rd., W1,* ☎ *0171/434–0403.* ☞ *£8–£12.* ☉ *Check listings. No credit cards. Tube: Tottenham Court Rd.*

Barfly Club. Formerly known as the Splash Club (the people who gave Skunk Anansie, Kula Shaker, and Oasis their big breaks), this is the finest and most eclectic small club in the capital. There are three bands seven nights a week, with events regularly scheduled by some of the top rocker magazines. ⊠ *The Falcon Pub, 234 Royal College St., NW1,* ☎ *0171/482–4884.* ☞ *£3–£6.* ☉ *7:30–late. MC, V. Tube: Camden Town.*

The Forum. This ex-ballroom with balcony and dance floor packs in the customers, and it consistently attracts the best medium-to-big-name performers, too. ⊠ *9–17 Highgate Rd., NW5,* ☎ *0171/284–2200.* ☞ *£8–£12.* ☉ *Most nights 7–11. AE, MC, V. Tube: Kentish Town.*

The Roadhouse. True to its name, this spot pays homage to the American dream of the open road, with a Harley behind the bar and much memorabilia. Music fits into the feel-good, tuneful, middle-of-the-road end of the R&B/blues/rock/soul spectrum. ⊠ *Jubilee Hall, Covent Garden, WC2,* ☎ *0171/240–6001.* ☞ *£3–£6.* ☉ *Mon.–Wed. 5:30–1, Thurs.–Sat. 5:30–3, Sun. 12:30 PM–5:30 PM. AE, MC, V. Tube: Covent Garden.*

Shepherd's Bush Empire. Converted from the BBC TV theater, where Terry Wogan, the United Kingdom's Johnny Carson, recorded his show for years and years, this venue now hosts the same kind of medium-big names as the north London Forum. ⊠ *Shepherd's Bush Green, W12,* ☎ *0181/740–7474.* ☞ *£8–£12.* ☉ *Most nights 7:30–11. AE, MC, V. Tube: Shepherd's Bush.*

Station Tavern. For a taste of local life, head into the wastelands for a (usually) completely unfamous R&B band in a lover'ly un-redone old-fashioned London pub. Bob's aptly named Goodtime Blues has been honking here forever. It's opposite the tube, luckily. ✉ *41 Bramley Rd., W10,* ☎ *0171/727–4053.* 🎟 *Free–£3.* ☉ *Most nights 8:30–11. Tube: Latimer Rd.*

The Gay Scene

Since February 1994, with the long-overdue lowering of the age of consent from 21, 18-year-old gay men in Britain have had the blessing of the law in doing what they've always done. The change did not extend to lesbians, nor did it need to, because there has never been any legislation that so much as mentions gay women—a circumstance that, believe it or not, dates from Queen Victoria's point-blank refusal to believe that women paired off with women. AIDS is, of course, a large issue, but the epidemic hasn't yet had quite as devastating an impact on the London scene as it has had in San Francisco and New York.

The whole of London has benefited hugely from the blossoming of gay nightlife. Soho, especially Old Compton Street, has gone through something of a pre-AIDS Christopher Street atmosphere, with gay shops, bars, restaurants, and even beauty salons (get your chest waxed here) jostling for space, and it has now settled into happy coexistence with club kids, restaurant patrons and tourists. Though lesbians are included in the gay clubbing scene (as are anyone's straight friends), it's predominantly men-for-men. The dyke scene certainly exists, and lesbian chic is as trendy in London as it is in New York or Los Angeles, but it has a lower profile, generally, than the male equivalent, and it also tends to be more politically strident. Any women-only event in London attracts a large proportion of gay women.

Check the listings in *Time Out,* the weekly *MetroXtra (MX),* and the monthly *Gay Times* for events.

Bars, Cafés, and Pubs

Pub hours for the listings in this section are the same as for all London pubs, with drinks available up to 11 PM.

The Box. On two floors, one bright, one dark, there's good, light food and (at least at press time) the Sunday night Box Babes, which wows all London dykes. ✉ *Seven Dials, Monmouth St., WC2,* ☎ *0171/240–5828. Tube: Leicester Sq.*

The Edge. Poseurs are welcome at this hip Soho hangout, where straight groovers mix in over the four floors, and there are sidewalk tables in summer. Risk the vodkas infused with candy. ✉ *11 Soho Sq., W1,* ☎ *0171/439–1313. Tube: Oxford Circus.*

Freedom. This is a popular café/bar central to the Soho scene. In addition, it has a late-night club downstairs for dancing; there's a rigid and sometimes frigid door policy, enforced by bouncers, and a cover charge after 11 PM. ✉ *60–66 Wardour St., W1,* ☎ *0171/734–0071. Tube: Piccadilly Circus.*

Substation Soho. This is a huge and centrally located dive with everything—three bars, dancing, top DJs, videos, pool tables, and a very cruisy atmosphere. ✉ *1A Dean St., W1,* ☎ *0171/287–9608. Tube: Leicester Sq.*

The Yard. This is Soho's best-looking and biggest bar/café, centered around the eponymous courtyard, and getting very full and smoky at night. Upstairs is a little more genteel, with sofas. Get a bottomless coffee, or a club sandwich, or an entire night out here. ✉ *57 Rupert St., W1,* ☎ *0171/437–2652. Tube: Piccadilly Circus.*

Cabaret

Madame Jo Jos. By no means devoid of straight spectators, this place has long been one of the most fun drag cabarets in town, with a civilized atmosphere (despite bare-chested bar boys). There are various club events, too, including London's first drag king night, held on Mondays. ⊠ *8 Brewer St.,* ☎ *0171/287–1414.* ▣ *Mon.–Thurs. £6, Fri. and Sat. £8.* ⊙ *Doors open most nights at 10, shows nightly at 12:15 and 1:15. Tube: Piccadilly Circus.*

Vauxhall Tavern. This venerable, curved pub had a drag cabaret before the Lady Bunny was born. Sometimes it's full of gay mafia, other times it's local media folk having a different night out, and Friday is the night for the lesbian cabaret, Vixens. ⊠ *372 Kennington La., SE11,* ☎ *0171/582–0833.* ▣ *Free.* ⊙ *Mon. 8–1, Tues., Thurs.–Sat. 8–2, Wed. 8–midnight, Sun. 7–10:30. Tube: Oval.*

Clubs

Heaven. Aptly named, it has by far the best light show on any London dance floor, and it's unpretentious, *loud,* and huge, with a labyrinth of quiet rooms, bars, and live-music parlors. If you go to just one club, this is the one to choose. Thursday is straight night. ⊠ *The Arches, Villiers St., WC2,* ☎ *0171/839–2520.* ▣ *£5–£12.* ⊙ *Tues.–Sat. 10:30–3:30. Tube: Charing Cross.*

One-Nighters

Some of the best gay dance clubs are held once a week in mixed clubs. The following are well established, and likely still to be going strong, but it's best to call first.

Jo's Original Tea Dance. A longtime fave with the girls, this is a very camp and very fun Sunday ballroom, line-dance, time-warp disco, now in a new home after many years. ⊠ *BJ's White Swan, 556 Commercial Rd., E14,* ☎ *0171/780–9870.* ▣ *£4.* ⊙ *Sun. 5:30–midnight. DLR: Limehouse.*

Love Muscle. A steaming mixed-gender Saturday-night party, this blast offers eight hours of dance classics at a big Brixton club. ⊠ *The Fridge, Town Hall Parade, Brixton Hill, SW2,* ☎ *0171/326–5100.* ▣ *£6 before 11 PM, £8 before midnight, £10 midnight–3 AM.* ⊙ *Sat. 10–6. Tube: Brixton.*

THE ARTS

There isn't *a* London arts scene—there are lots of them. As long as there are audiences for Feydeau revivals, drag queens, obscure teenage rock bands, hit musicals, body-painted Parisian dancers, and improvised stand-up comedy, someone will stage them in London. Commercial sponsorship of the arts is in its infancy here compared to what it is in the United States, and most major arts companies, as well as those smaller ones lucky enough to be grant-aided, are dependent, to some extent, on (inadequate) government subsidy. This ought to mean low ticket prices, but it doesn't necessarily work that way. Even so, when you consider how much a London hotel room costs, the city's arts are a bargain.

We've attempted a representative selection in the following listings, but to find out what's showing now, the weekly magazine *Time Out* (issued every Wednesday in central London) is invaluable. The *Evening Standard* also carries listings, especially in the supplement *Hot Tickets* that comes with the Thursday edition, as do the "quality" Sunday papers and the Saturday *Independent, Guardian,* and *Times.* You'll find leaflets and flyers in most cinema and theater foyers, too, and you can pick up the free fortnightly *London Theatre Guide* leaflet from hotels and tourist information centers.

Theaters and Concert Halls

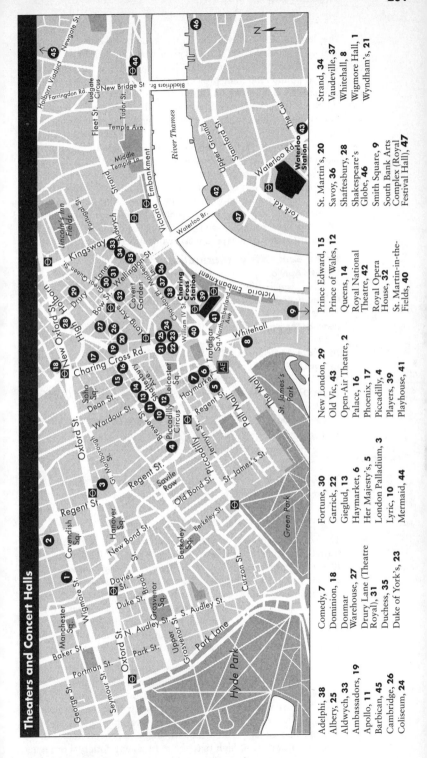

Adelphi, **38**
Albery, **25**
Aldwych, **33**
Ambassadors, **19**
Apollo, **11**
Barbican, **45**
Cambridge, **26**
Coliseum, **24**

Comedy, **7**
Dominion, **18**
Donmar Warehouse, **27**
Drury Lane (Theatre Royal), **31**
Duchess, **35**
Duke of York's, **23**

Fortune, **30**
Garrick, **22**
Gielgud, **13**
Haymarket, **6**
Her Majesty's, **5**
London Palladium, **3**
Lyric, **10**
Mermaid, **44**

New London, **29**
Old Vic, **43**
Open-Air Theatre, **2**
Palace, **16**
Phoenix, **17**
Piccadilly, **4**
Players, **39**
Playhouse, **41**

Prince Edward, **15**
Prince of Wales, **12**
Queens, **14**
Royal National Theatre, **42**
Royal Opera House, **32**
St. Martin-in-the-Fields, **40**

St. Martin's, **20**
Savoy, **36**
Shaftesbury, **28**
Shakespeare's Globe, **46**
Smith Square, **9**
South Bank Arts Complex (Royal Festival Hall), **47**

Strand, **34**
Vaudeville, **37**
Whitehall, **8**
Wigmore Hall, **1**
Wyndham's, **21**

Ballet

The Royal Opera House has been the traditional home of the world-famous Royal Ballet, but change is in the wind: The beloved opera house is now closed for a renovation that should take two years, and the multi-million-pound rebuilding project includes, in fact, monies set aside for a completely new and separate theater for the ballet. During construction, the Royal Ballet will be performing at the Labatt's Apollo Theatre and also at the Royal Festival Hall. Prices are slightly more reasonable than they are for the opera, but bookings should be made well in advance, as tickets sell out fast. The **English National Ballet** and visiting international companies perform at the Coliseum—but that theater, too, is scheduled for a renovation program lasting several seasons and resident troupes will be performing elsewhere (call the Coliseum Box Office for further information). In addition, the **City Ballet of London** performs at the Peacock Theatre. **Sadler's Wells Theatre** also hosts various other ballet companies and regional and international modern dance troupes. Modern and experimental work is best viewed at the Place.

Ballet Box Office Information

Labatt's Apollo, ⊠ *Hammersmith Broadway, W6,* ☎ *0171/304–4000. Tube: Hammersmith.*

Coliseum, ⊠ *St. Martin's La., WC2N 4ES,* ☎ *0171/632–8300. Tube: Leicester Sq.*

Peacock Theatre, ⊠ *Portugal St., WC2,* ☎ *0171/314–8800. Tube: Holborn.*

The Place, ⊠ *17 Duke's Rd, WC1,* ☎ *0171/387–8800. Tube: Euston.*

Festival Hall, ⊠ *South Bank Arts Complex, SE1 8XX,* ☎ *0171/928–8800. Tube: Waterloo or Embankment Station.*

Royal Opera House, ⊠ *Covent Garden, WC2E 9DD,* ☎ *0171/304–4000. Tube: Covent Garden.*

Sadler's Wells, ⊠ *Rosebery Ave., EC1R 4TN,* ☎ *0171/713–6000. Tube: Angel.*

Concerts

The ticket prices to symphony-size orchestral concerts are fortunately still relatively moderately priced, usually ranging from £5 to £35. If you can't book in advance, then arrive at the hall an hour before the performance for a chance at returns.

The London Symphony Orchestra is in residence at the **Barbican Centre,** although other top orchestras—including the Philharmonia and the Royal Philharmonic—also perform here. The **South Bank Arts Complex,** which includes the **Royal Festival Hall,** the **Queen Elizabeth Hall,** and the small **Purcell Room,** forms another major venue; the Royal Festival Hall is one of the finest concert halls in Europe. Between the Barbican and South Bank, there are concert performances almost every night of the year. The Barbican also features chamber music concerts with such celebrated orchestras as the City of London Sinfonia.

For a different concert-going experience, as well as the chance to take part in a great British tradition, try the **Royal Albert Hall** during the Promenade Concert season: eight weeks lasting from July to September. The usual chestnuts are featured, along with some novelties, but the capper is the last night, a madly jingoistic display of singing "Land of Hope and Glory," Union Jack waving, and general madness. Demand for tickets is so high that you must enter a lottery. For regular "proms," tickets run £3–£30; special "promenade" (standing) tickets usually cost half the price of normal tickets and are available at the hall on the night of the concert. Note, too, that the concerts have begun to be jumbo-screen broadcast in Hyde Park, but even here a seat on the grass requires a paid ticket. Call 0171/589–82122 for further information. Another summer pleasure is the outdoor concert series by the lake at **Kenwood** (⊠ Hampstead Heath, ☎ 0181/348–6684). Concerts are also part of the program at the open-air theater in **Holland Park** (☎ 0171/602–7856). Check the listings for details.

You should also look for the lunchtime concerts that take place all over the city in smaller concert halls, the big arts center foyers, and churches; they usually cost less than £5 or are free and will feature string quartets, singers, jazz ensembles, or gospel choirs. **St. John's, Smith Square,** and **St. Martin-in-the-Fields** are two of the more popular locations. Performances usually begin about 1 PM and last an hour.

Concert Hall Box Office Information

Barbican Centre, ⊠ *Barbican, EC2Y 8DS,* ☎ *0171/638–8891 or 0171/638–4141. Tube: Moorgate.*

Royal Albert Hall, ⊠ *Kensington Gore, SW7 2AP,* ☎ *0171/589–8212. Tube: Gloucester Rd.*

St. John's, Smith Square, ⊠ *SW1P 3HA,* ☎ *0171/222–1061. Tube: Westminster.*

St. Martin-in-the-Fields, ⊠ *Trafalgar Sq., WC2N 4JJ,* ☎ *0171/839–1930. Tube: Charing Cross.*

South Bank Arts Complex, ⊠ *South Bank, SE1 8XX,* ☎ *0171/928–8800 or 0171/928–3002. Tube: Waterloo.*

Wigmore Hall, ⊠ *36 Wigmore St., W1H 9DF,* ☎ *0171/935–2141. Tube: Bond St.*

Modern Dance

Contemporary dance thrives in London, with innovative young choreographers and companies constantly emerging (and then, it often seems, moving to New York). Michael Clark was one of the first of the new wave; Yolanda Snaith, Bunty Matthias, and choreographer Lea Anderson's troupe, the Cholmondeleys (pronounced Chumleys), are more examples of home-grown talent. In addition to the many fringe theaters that produce the odd dance performance, the following theaters showcase contemporary dance:

The Place, ⊠ *17 Duke's Rd., WC1,* ☎ *0171/387–0031. Tube: Euston.*
Riverside Studios (☞ Fringe Theater, *below*).
Sadler's Wells (☞ Opera, *below,* and Ballet, *above*).

Movies

Despite the video invasion, West End movie theaters continue to do good business. Most of the major houses (Odeon, ABC, etc.) are in the Leicester Square/Piccadilly Circus area, where tickets average £7.50. Mondays and matinees are often cheaper, at around £4, and there are also fewer crowds. Prices drop to around £5 as you get out of the West End, and are even lower in the suburbs, but unless you're staying there, any savings could be eaten up by transportation costs.

The few movie clubs and repertory cinemas that still exist screen a wider range of movies, including classic, Continental, and underground, as well as rare or underrated masterpieces. Some charge a membership fee of less than £1. The king is the **National Film Theatre** (⊠ South Bank Arts Complex, ☎ 0171/928–3232), where the London Film Festival is based in the fall; there are also lectures and presentations. Annual membership costs £11.95 and entitles you to £1 off the ticket price. Also worth checking out are the **Everyman** (⊠ Hollybush Vale, Hampstead, ☎ 0171/435–1525; ✉ membership £1/year), the **Rio** (⊠ Kingsland High St., Hackney E8, ☎ 0171/254–6677), though it's a bit of a trek, and the **Riverside** (☞ Fringe Theater, *below*).

Opera

The main venue for opera in London is the **Royal Opera House,** which ranks with the Metropolitan Opera House in New York—in every way, including expense. However, the famous opera house is now closed for at least two years, owing to a massive renovation program. For the 1998–99 season, most productions should be concentrated in the newly refurbished Sadler's Wells Theatre. In general, prices will probably have the same range—from £5 to more than £100 (for the best seats), and performances will probably still be divided into booking periods and sell out early, although returns and standing spaces are sold on the day. Conditions of purchase vary—call for information.

English-language productions are staged at the **Coliseum** in St. Martin's Lane, home of the English National Opera Company. Prices are lower than for the Royal Opera, ranging from £8 to £45, and productions are often innovative and exciting. The ENO sells same-day seats for as low as £2.50.

Opera Box Office Information

Barbican Centre, Albert Hall, Royal Festival Hall (South Bank Arts Complex) *See* Concert Hall Box Office Information, *above.*

Coliseum, ⊠ *St. Martin's La., WC2N 4ES,* ☎ *0171/632–8300. Tube: Leicester Sq.*

Royal Opera House, ⊠ *Covent Garden, WC2E 9DD,* ☎ *0171/304–4000. Tube: Covent Garden.*

Sadler's Wells, ⊠ *Rosebery Ave., EC1R 4TN,* ☎ *0171/713–6000. Tube: Angel.*

Shaftesbury, ⊠ *Shaftesbury Ave., WC2H 8DP,* ☎ *0171/379–5399. Tube: Holborn.*

Theater

Although the price of a seat rarely falls below a tenner, London's West End theaters still pull in enough punters to cause a mini traffic jam each night before the house lights dim and the curtain rises. From Shakespeare to the umpteenth year of *Les Misérables* (or *The Glums,* as it's affectionately known), the West End has what visitors think of as London theater. But there's more to see in London than the offerings of Theatreland and the national companies.

Of the 100 or so legitimate theaters in the capital, 50 are officially "West End," while the remainder go under the blanket title of "fringe." Much like New York's off- and off-off Broadway, tringe theater encompasses everything from off-the-wall "physical theater" pieces to first runs of new plays and revivals of old ones. A recent typical selection of fringe offerings had two Strindbergs, a Sartre, a Kafka, an Anouilh, an Ionesco, and two Molière productions—all in competition. There was a production of Sheridan's *School for Scandal* in far-off-off-off Ealing, and a feminist staging of *Ben Hur* in even farther-off Croydon. You could catch such diverse offerings as Fassbinder's *The Bitter Tears of Petra von Kant* in a pub in Camden, *The Complete History of America* (abridged) by the *other* RSC (the Reduced Shakespeare Company), an amateur production of *Godspell,* or a long-running show in which tube passengers are the unwitting actors, as the audience secretly follows a lone performer posing as a klutzy commuter. That's just the fringe.

For serious theatergoers, the top of the line is still the **Royal Shakespeare Company** and the **Royal National Theatre Company,** which perform at London's two main arts complexes, the **Barbican Centre** and the **Royal National Theatre.** Both companies mount consistently excellent productions and are usually a safe option for anyone having trouble choosing which play to see. A great hue-and-cry has gone up concerning the RSC's plans to tour the provinces during summer months—thereby depriving many tourists of seeing the best of all theater companies. Plans are still tentative at press time, so be sure to telephone before departing home. Happily and however, it is exactly during those summer months (and only then), that you can now see the Bard served up in his most spectacular manifestation—at the new open-air reconstruction of **Shakespeare's Globe Theatre,** which officially opened in June 1997. For complete information, ☞ For complete information, *see* Shakespeare's Globe *in* Chapter 2.

Most theaters have matinees twice a week (Wednesday or Thursday, and Saturday) and evening performances that begin at 7:30 or 8; performances on Sunday are rare, but not unknown. Prices vary, but in the West End you should expect to pay from £10 for a seat in the upper balcony to at least £25 for a good one in the stalls (orchestra) or dress circle (mezzanine). Tickets may be booked at the individual theater box offices or over the phone by credit card (some box offices or agents have special numbers for these, marked "cc" in the phone book); most theaters still don't charge a fee for the latter. You can also book through ticket agents, such as **First Call** (☎ 0171/240–7941) or **Ticketmaster** (☎ 0171/344–0055 or 800/775–2525 in the U.S.), although these usually do charge a booking fee. **Keith Prowse** has a New York office (⊠ 234 W. 44th St., Suite 1000, New York, NY 10036, ☎ 212/398–1430 or 800/669–8687), as does **Edwards & Edwards** (⊠ 1 Times Sq. Plaza, 12th floor, New York, NY 10036, ☎ 212/944–0290 or 800/223–6108). If you're a theater junkie and want to put together a West End package, the *Complete Guide to London's West End Theatres* has seating plans and booking information for all the houses. It costs £10.95 (plus postage) from the Society of London Theatres (☞ *below*). Alternatively, the SOLT Half Price Ticket Booth (no phone) on the southwest corner of Leicester Square sells up to four half-price tickets per purchaser on the day of performance for about 25 theaters (subject to availability). It's open Monday–Saturday 1–6:30 and from noon for matinees; there is a £2 service charge, and only cash is accepted. Note that these "half-price" tickets are invariably for orchestra ("stall," as they call them in England) seats; for more reasonably priced seats, it may be better to go to the theater box office. All the larger hotels offer theater bookings, but as they tack on a hefty service charge, you would do better visiting the box offices yourself. You might, however, consider using one particular booking line that doubles the price of tickets: **West End Cares** (☎ 0171/976–8100) donates half of what it charges to AIDS charities.

Warning: Be *very* careful of scalpers outside theaters and working the line at the Half Price Ticket Booth; they have been known to charge £200 or more for a sought-after ticket. In recent years, there has been another problem: unscrupulous ticket agents, who sell tickets at four or five times their price from the ticket box offices. Although a service charge is legitimate, this type of scalping certainly isn't, especially because the vast majority of theaters have some tickets (returns and "house seats") available on the night of performance.

Theater Directory
The following is a list of West End theaters:

Adelphi, ⊠ *Strand, WC2E 7NA,* ☎ *0171/379–8884 or 0171/344– 0055. Tube: Charing Cross.*
Albery, ⊠ *St. Martin's La., WC2N 4AH,* ☎ *0171/867–1115 or 0171/ 369–1730. Tube: Leicester Sq.*

Aldwych, ✉ *Aldwych, WC2B 4DF,* ☎ *0171/836–6404 or 0171/416–6003. Tube: Covent Garden.*

Apollo, ✉ *Shaftesbury Ave., W1V 7HD,* ☎ *0171/494–5070. Tube: Piccadilly Circus.*

Apollo Victoria, ✉ *Wilton Rd., SW1V ILL,* ☎ *0171/416–6070. Tube: Victoria.*

Arts Theatre, ✉ *6–7 Great Newport St., WC2H 7JB,* ☎ *0171/836–2132. Tube: Leicester Sq.*

Barbican (RSC), ✉ *Barbican, EC2Y 8DS,* ☎ *0171/638–8891 or 0171/628–2295. Tube: Moorgate.*

Cambridge, ✉ *Earlham St., WC2H 9HU,* ☎ *0171/379–5299 or 0171/494–5080. Tube: Covent Garden.*

Comedy, ✉ *Panton St., SW1Y 4DN,* ☎ *0171/494–5080 or 0171/369–1731. Tube: Piccadilly Circus.*

Dominion, ✉ *Tottenham Court Rd., W1 0AG,* ☎ *0171/656–1888. Tube: Tottenham Court Rd.*

Donmar Warehouse, ✉ *41 Earlham St., WC2H 9LD,* ☎ *0171/867–1150 or 0171/369–1732. Tube: Covent Garden.*

Drury Lane (Theatre Royal), ✉ *Catherine St., WC2B 5JF,* ☎ *0171/494–5000. Tube: Covent Garden.*

Duchess, ✉ *Catherine St., WC2B 5LA,* ☎ *0171/494–5075. Tube: Covent Garden.*

Fortune, ✉ *Russell St., WC2B 5HH,* ☎ *0171/836–2238. Tube: Covent Garden.*

Garrick, ✉ *Charing Cross Rd., WC2H 0HH,* ☎ *0171/494–5085. Tube: Leicester Sq.*

Gielgud, ✉ *Shaftesbury Ave., W1V 8AR,* ☎ *0171/494–5065. Tube: Piccadilly Circus.*

Globe (Shakespeare's Globe), ✉ *New Globe Walk, Bankside,* ☎ *0171/928–6406. Tube: Mansion House, then walk across Southwark Bridge, or Blackfriars, then walk across Blackfriars Bridge.*

Haymarket Theatre Royal, ✉ *Haymarket, SW1Y 4HT,* ☎ *0171/930–8800. Tube: Piccadilly Circus.*

Her Majesty's, ✉ *Haymarket, SW1Y 4QR,* ☎ *0171/494–5400. Tube: Piccadilly Circus.*

London Palladium, ✉ *8 Argyll St., W1V 1AD,* ☎ *0171/494–5020. Tube: Oxford Circus.*

Lyceum, ✉ *Wellington St., WC2,* ☎ *0171/656–1803. Tube: Charing Cross.*

Lyric, ✉ *Shaftesbury Ave., W1V 7HA,* ☎ *0171/494–5045. Tube: Piccadilly Circus.*

Lyric Hammersmith, ✉ *King St., W6 0QL,* ☎ *0181/741–2311. Tube: Hammersmith.*

Mermaid, ✉ *Puddle Dock, EC4 3DB,* ☎ *0171/410–0000 or 0171/236–2211. Tube: Blackfriars.*

New London, ✉ *Drury La., WC2B 5PW,* ☎ *0171/405–0072. Tube: Covent Garden.*

Old Vic, ✉ *Waterloo Rd., SE1 8NB,* ☎ *0171/928–7616. Tube: Waterloo.*

Open-Air Theatre, ✉ *Inner Circle, Regent's Park, NW1 4NP,* ☎ *0171/935–5884. Tube: Regent's Park.*

Palace, ✉ *Shaftesbury Ave., W1V 8AY,* ☎ *0171/434–0909. Tube: Leicester Sq.*

Phoenix, ✉ *Charing Cross Rd., WC2H 0JP,* ☎ *0171/867–1044 or 0171/369–1733. Tube: Leicester Sq.*

Piccadilly, ✉ *Denman St., W1V 8DY,* ☎ *0171/867–1118 or 0171/369–1734. Tube: Piccadilly Circus.*

Players, ✉ *The Arches, Villiers St., WC2N 6NQ,* ☎ *0171/839–1134 or 0171/976–1307. Tube: Charing Cross.*

Playhouse, ⊠ Northumberland Ave., WC2N 6NN, ☎ 0171/839–4401. Tube: Embankment.

Prince Edward, ⊠ Old Compton St., W1V 8AH, ☎ 0171/734–8951 or 0171/447–5400. Tube: Leicester Sq.

Prince of Wales, ⊠ 31 Coventry St., W1V 8AS, ☎ 0171/839–5987. Tube: Leicester Sq.

Queens, ⊠ 51 Shaftesbury Ave., W1V 8BA, ☎ 0171/494–5040. Tube: Leicester Sq.

Royal Court Downstairs at the Duke of York's, ⊠ St. Martin's La., WC2, ☎ 0171/565–5000. Tube: Leicester Sq.

Royal Court Upstairs at the Ambassadors, ⊠ West St., WC2, ☎ 0171/565–5000. Tube: Leicester Sq.

Royal National Theatre, (Cottesloe, Lyttelton, and Olivier), ⊠ South Bank Arts Complex, SE1 9PX, ☎ 0171/928–2252. Tube: Waterloo.

St. Martin's, ⊠ West St., WC2H 9NH, ☎ 0171/836–1443. Tube: Leicester Sq.

Savoy, ⊠ Strand, WC2R 0ET, ☎ 0171/836–8888. Tube: Aldwych.

Shaftesbury, ⊠ Shaftesbury Ave., WC2H 8DP, ☎ 0171/379–5399. Tube: Holborn.

Strand, ⊠ Aldwych, WC2B 5LD, ☎ 0171/930–8800. Tube: Covent Garden.

Vaudeville, ⊠ Strand, WC2R 0NH, ☎ 0171/836–9987. Tube: Charing Cross.

Victoria Palace, ⊠ Victoria St., SW1E 5EA, ☎ 0171/834–1317. Tube: Victoria.

Whitehall, ⊠ 14 Whitehall, SW1A 2DY, ☎ 0171/369–1735 or 0171/344–4444. Tube: Charing Cross.

Wyndhams, ⊠ Charing Cross Rd., WC2H 0DA, ☎ 0171/867–1116 or 0171/369–1736. Tube: Leicester Sq.

Fringe

Shows can be straight plays, circus, comedy, musicals, readings, or productions every bit as polished and impressive as those in the West End—except for their location and the price of the seat. Fringe tickets are always considerably less expensive than tickets for West End productions. The following theaters are among the better-known fringe venues:

Almeida, ⊠ Almeida St., N1 1AT, ☎ 0171/359–4404. Tube: Angel.

BAC, ⊠ 176 Lavender Hill, Battersea SW11 1JX, ☎ 0171/223–2223. BR: Clapham Junction.

Bush, ⊠ Shepherds Bush Green, W12 8QD, ☎ 0181/743–3388. Tube: Goldhawk Rd.

Canal Café Theatre, ⊠ Bridge House, Delamere Terr., W2, ☎ 0171/289–6054. Tube: Warwick Ave.

Drill Hall, ⊠ 16 Chenies St., WC1E 7EX, ☎ 0171/637–8270. Tube: Goodge St.

The Gate, ⊠ The Prince Albert, 11 Pembridge Rd., W11 3HQ, ☎ 0171/229–0706. Tube: Notting Hill Gate.

Grace Theatre at the Latchmere, ⊠ 503 Battersea Park Rd., SW11 3BW, ☎ 0171/223–3549. BR: Clapham Junction.

Hackney Empire, ⊠ 291 Mare St., E8 1EJ, ☎ 0181/985–2424. BR: Hackney Central.

Hampstead, ⊠ Swiss Cottage, NW3 3EX, ☎ 0171/722–9301. Tube: Swiss Cottage.

ICA Theatre, ⊠ The Mall, SW1Y 5AH, ☎ 0171/930–3647. Tube: Charing Cross.

Kings Head, ⊠ 115 Upper St., N1 1QN, ☎ 0171/226–1916. Tube: Highbury & Islington.

Lyric Studio, ⊠ Lyric Theatre, King St., W6 9JT, ☎ 0181/741–2311. Tube: Hammersmith.

New End Theatre, ⊠ *27 New End, NW3 1JD,* ☎ *0171/794–0022. Tube: Hampstead.*

Orange Tree, ⊠ *1 Clarence St., Richmond, TW9 1SA,* ☎ *0181/940– 3633. Tube: Richmond.*

Riverside Studios, ⊠ *Crisp Rd., W6 9RL,* ☎ *0181/237–1111. Tube: Hammersmith.*

Theatre Royal, ⊠ *Stratford East, E15 1BN,* ☎ *0181/534–0310. Tube: Stratford.*

Tricycle Theatre, ⊠ *269 Kilburn High Rd., NW6 7JR,* ☎ *0171/328– 1000. Tube: Kilburn.*

Watermans Arts Centre, ⊠ *40 High St., Brentford, TW8 0DS,* ☎ *0181/568–1176. BR: Kew Bridge.*

Young Vic, ⊠ *66 The Cut, SE1 8LZ,* ☎ *0171/928–6363. Tube: Waterloo.*

6 Outdoor Activities and Sports

Some days you win, some you lose, and some you get rained out. But that never puts a damper on one of the liveliest sports calendars around. Tennis, of course, means Wimbledon (if center court is sold out, try for an outer-court game). In summer, Her Majesty makes an appearance at Ascot, while the World Series of Cricket, the Tests, are played at the fields of Lord's. In cooler weather, football (also known as soccer) takes over, and in any season you can enjoy Pilates and yoga indoors, and let it rain, rain, rain.

THERE ARE THE WIMBLEDON TENNIS CHAMPIONSHIPS, and there's cricket, and then there's soccer, and that's about it for the sports fan in London, right? Wrong. London is a great city for the weekend player of almost anything. It really comes into its own in summer, when the parks sprout nets and goals and painted white lines, outdoor swimming pools open, and a season of spectator events gets under way. The listings below concentrate on facilities available to the casual visitor in a whole range of sports and on the more accessible or well-known spectator events. Bring your gear, and branch out from that hotel gym.

By Kate
Sekules

PARTICIPANT SPORTS AND FITNESS

If your sport is missing from those listed below, or if you need additional information, **Sportsline** (☎ 0171/222–8000), staffed weekdays 10–6, supplies details about London's clubs, events, and facilities. It's a free service.

Aerobics
You don't need to buy a membership at any of the following studios, which offer a range of classes for all levels of fitness and are open daily. The average cost for an hour of sweating is £5.

Go West Studio. About seven daily classes are graded from beginner to pro, with step, yoga, circuit training, and aquaerobics included in the mix. ⊠ *Porchester Centre, Queensway, W2,* ☎ *0171/792–2919. Tube: Bayswater.*

Jubilee Hall. Many are addicted to the "Fatbuster" classes, but there are plenty more, from body sculpting and step to Pilates and jazz dance. ⊠ *30 The Piazza, Covent Garden, WC2,* ☎ *0171/379–0008. Tube: Covent Garden.*

Portobello Green Fitness Centre. It's under the Westway overpass, and you'll have to battle through flea-market shoppers on weekends to reach these popular classes. ⊠ *3–5 Thorpe Close, W10,* ☎ *0181/960–2221. Tube: Ladbroke Grove.*

Bicycling
London is reasonably cycle-friendly for a big city, with special lanes marked for bicycles on some major roads, but it is never safe to ride without a helmet. **Bikepark** can rent anything you want—mountain, hybrid, or road bike—from £10/day, £30/weekend, or by the week, plus a deposit (MC, V) of 75%–100% of the bike's value. All machines are new models and are issued with locks; accessories are available, too. Reserve ahead in summer. ⊠ *14 Stukeley St., WC2,* ☎ *0171/430–0083. Tube: Covent Garden.*

Gyms
Albany Fitness Centre. This is a deconsecrated church (buy a WORK OFF THY LAST SUPPER T-shirt), which means tons of space. There's Keiser equipment, free weights, cardio machines, and aerobics/sculpting classes. The cost is around £15/day, with lower weekly rates negotiable. ⊠ *St. Bede's Church, Albany St., NW1,* ☎ *0171/383–7131. Tube: Great Portland St.*

Central YMCA. As you'd expect from the Y, this place boasts every facility and sport, including a great 25-meter pool and a very well-equipped gym. Weekly membership costs £32; the daily rate is £15. ⊠ *112 Great Russell St., WC1,* ☎ *0171/637–8131. Tube: Tottenham Court Rd.*

Jubilee Hall. The day rate is £6, monthly £45, at this very crowded, but happening and super well-equipped central gym. ⊠ *30 The Piazza, Covent Garden, WC2,* ☎ *0171/379–0008. Tube: Covent Garden.*

The Peak. This hotel club is expensive (£1250 /year plus £800 joining fee) but has top equipment, a pool, great ninth-floor views over Knightsbridge, and a sauna—with TV—in the full beauty spa. Day memberships are no longer available, but the 20-visit pass for £550 is fully transferrable, so a whole family can share one—as long as they use up the visits within the six-month expiration date. ⊠ *Hyatt Carlton Tower Hotel, 2 Cadogan Pl., SW1,* ☎ *0171/235–1234. Tube: Sloane Sq.*

Horseback Riding

Hyde Park Riding Stables. One of the very few public stables left for riding in Hyde Park keeps a range of horses for hacking the sand tracks. ⊠ *63 Bathurst Mews, W2,* ☎ *0171/723–2813. Tube: Lancaster Gate.*

Ross Nye's. And here's the other one. About 16 horses and ponies are kept here for lessons as well as for hacking. ⊠ *8 Bathurst Mews, W2,* ☎ *0171/262–3791. Tube: Lancaster Gate.*

Running

London is perfect for joggers. If you're after a crowd, the more popular routes include **Green Park,** which gets a stream of runners armed with maps from the Piccadilly hotels, and—to a lesser extent—adjacent **St. James's Park.** Both can get perilous with deck chairs on summer days. **Hyde Park and Kensington Gardens** together supply a 4-mi perimeter route, or you can do a 2½-mi run in **Hyde Park** alone if you start at Hyde Park Corner or Marble Arch and encircle the Serpentine. Most Park Lane hotels offer jogging maps for this, their local green space. **Regent's Park** has probably the most populated track because it's a sporting kind of place; the Outer Circle loop measures about 2½ mi.

Away from the center, there are longer, scenic runs over more varied terrain at **Hampstead Heath,** connecting with **Kenwood** and **Parliament Hill,** London's highest point, where you'll get a fabulous panoramic sweep over the entire city. **Richmond Park** is the biggest green space of all, but watch for deer during rutting season (October and November). Back in town, there's a rather traffic-heavy 1½-mi riverside run along **Victoria Embankment** from Westminster Bridge to the Embankment at Blackfriars Bridge, or a beautiful mile among the rowing clubs and ducks along the Malls—Upper, Lower, and Chiswick—from **Hammersmith Bridge.**

GROUP RUNS

If you don't want to run alone, call the **London Hash House Harriers** (☎ 0181/995–7879), or the **City Hash Hotline** (☎ 0181/749–2646). They organize noncompetitive hour-long runs around interesting bits of town, with loops and checkpoints built in. Cost: £1.

Softball

Control your mirth—the sport is huge here; in fact, it's the fastest-growing participatory sport in England. Pick up a game Sunday afternoon in **Regent's Park** or on the south edge of **Hyde Park.**

Squash

Ironmonger Row. There are 10 squash courts in this popular city sports center. You can't book by phone without a membership, but you're likely to get a court if you show up to play during Londoners' regular office hours, or possibly on weekends when courts are less busy. ⊠ *Ironmonger Row, EC1,* ☎ *0171/253–4011. Tube: Old St.*

Portobello Green Fitness Centre. There are only three courts here, but they're inexpensive. ⊠ *3–5 Thorpe Close, W10,* ☎ *0181/960–2221. Tube: Ladbroke Grove.*

Swimming

BEACHES

Hampstead Ponds. These Elysian little lakes are surrounded by grassy lounging areas. The women's one is particularly secluded—and crowded in summer, though it's open all year. The Mixed Pond is open May–September. Both have murky-looking, but clean, fresh water. *Co-ed,* ⊠ *E. Heath Rd., NW3,* ☎ *0171/435–2366. Women only,* ⊠ *Millfield La., N6,* ☎ *0171/348–1033. BR: Hampstead Heath.*

Serpentine Lido. Okay, so it's a beach on a lake, but a hot day in Hyde Park is surreally reminiscent of the seaside. There are changing facilities, and the swimming section is chlorinated. ⊠ *Hyde Park, W2,* ☎ *0171/262–5484.* ⊙ *May–Sept. Tube: Knightsbridge.*

INDOOR POOLS

Chelsea. This renovated turn-of-the-century 27-by-10-yard pool is just off King's Road, so it's usually busy, and it's packed with kids on weekends. ⊠ *Chelsea Manor St., SW3,* ☎ *0171/352–6985. Tube: South Kensington.*

INDOOR/OUTDOOR POOLS

Oasis. And it is just that, with a heated pool (open May–September) right in Covent Garden, and a 30-by-10-yard one indoors. Needless to say, they both get packed in summer. ⊠ *32 Endell St., WC2,* ☎ *0171/ 831–1804. Tube: Covent Garden.*

SPA POOLS

Ironmonger Row (☞ *above*). This 33-by-12-yard city pool is in a '30s complex that includes a Turkish bath, not quite as beautiful as Porchester's (☞ *below*). There are separate sessions for men and women.

Porchester Baths. Here there's a 33-by-11-yard pool for serious lap swimmers, plus a 1920s Turkish bath, sauna, and spa of gorgeous, though slightly faded grandeur. It has separate sessions for men and women. ⊠ *Queensway, W2,* ☎ *0171/229–9950. Tube: Queensway.*

Tennis

Holland Park. This is the prettiest place to play, with six hard courts available from April through September. ⊠ *Kensington High St., W8,* ☎ *0171/602–2226. Tube: Holland Park.*

Islington Tennis Centre. It's about the only place where you don't need membership to play indoors (year-round), though you need it to reserve by phone. There are four outdoor courts, too, and coaching is available. ⊠ *Market Rd., N7,* ☎ *0171/700–1370. Tube: Caledonian Rd.*

Paddington Sports Club. A surprisingly large and busy green space provides a set of eight hard courts where you compete for attention with track runners and soccer, cricket, and softball players. ⊠ *Castelain Rd., W9,* ☎ *0171/286–4515. Tube: Maida Vale.*

Yoga

Life Centre. London's best yoga school specializes in the dynamic, energetic Vinyasa technique. Beautiful premises enhance the experience. A huge range of holistic health therapies are available upstairs. ⊠ *15 Edge St., W8,* ☎ *0171/221–4602. Tube: Notting Hill Gate.*

SPECTATOR SPORTS

Boating

One of London's most beloved sporting events (since 1845) is also the easiest to see, and it's free. The only problem with the late-March

Beefeater Gin Oxford and Cambridge Boat Race is securing a position among the crowds that line the Putney-to-Mortlake route (mostly at pubs along the Hammersmith Lower and Upper Malls, or on Putney Bridge). The Saturday start time varies from year to year according to the tides but is usually around 2:30 PM. The **Head of the River Race** is the professional version, only this time up to 420 crews of eight row the university course in the other direction. It usually happens the Saturday before the university race, beginning at 10 AM; the best view is from above Chiswick Bridge.

Cricket

Lord's (✉ St. John's Wood, NW8, ☎ 0171/289–1611) has been hallowed turf for worshipers of England's summer game since 1811. The World Series of cricket, the Tests, are played here, but tickets are hard to procure. One-day internationals, though, can usually be seen by lining up on the day, and top-class county matches are similarly accessible—whether the rules are is quite another matter.

The Oval (✉ Kennington Oval, SE11, ☎ 0171/582–6660) is a far easier place to witness the *thwack* of leather on willow. At London's second-string ground, you can see county games of very high standard.

Equestrian Events

RACING

The main events of "the Season," as much social as sporting, occur just outside the city. Her actual Majesty attends **Royal Ascot** (✉ Grand Stand, Ascot, Berkshire, ☎ 01344/22211) in mid-June, driving from Windsor in an open carriage, and processing before the plebs daily at 2. You'll need to book good seats far in advance for this event, although some tickets—far away from the Royal Enclosure and winning post—can be bought on the day of the race for £6. There are also Ascot Heath tickets available for a mere £2, but these only admit you to a picnic area in the middle of the race course. You'll be able to see the horses, of course, but that's not why people come to Ascot. The real spectacle is the crowd itself: Enormous headgear is de rigeur on Ladies Day—usually the Thursday of the meet—and those who arrive dressed inappropriately (jeans, shorts, tank tops) will be turned away from their grandstand seats. **Derby Day** (✉ The Grandstand, Epsom Downs, Surrey, ☎ 01372/726311), usually held on the first Wednesday in June, is the other big one. One of the world's greatest races for three-year-olds, it kicks off at 3:45.

SHOW JUMPING

The **Horse of the Year Show** (✉ Wembley Arena, ☎ 0181/902–8833) in late September is the top international competition, with lots of fun events held alongside the serious. Best of all are the Pony Club Games, where child riders perform virtual gymnastics on horseback.

Marathon

Starting at 9 AM on the third Sunday in April, some 25,000 runners in the huge **Flora London Marathon** (☎ 01891/234234) race from Blackheath or Greenwich to Westminster Bridge or the Mall. Entry forms for the following year are available starting in May.

Rugby

This is not a million miles different from gridiron, but team members play unpadded. It raises the British and (especially) Welsh blood pressure like no other sport, and it has recently undergone a revolution, with the amateur Rugby Union, and the professional Rugby League, once distinct, more or less merging with the advent of major sponsorship of the amateur game. The **Rugby League Challenge Cup Final** is played at Wembley Stadium (✉ Wembley, Middlesex, ☎ 0181/900–1234) on the last Saturday in April or the first one in May, while the Rugby Union **Pilkington Cup** is traditionally fought a week later at the Twickenham Rugby Football Ground (✉ Whitton Rd., Twickenham, Middlesex, ☎ 0181/892–8161). Tickets for both are more precious than gold. But you can see international matches at Twickenham during the September-to-April season or catch the local Super League team, the London Broncos, hosting teams from the north of England, Paris, and Australia (✉ The Athletic Ground, Kew Foot Rd., Richmond, Surrey TW9, ☎ 0181/332–7112). For diehard fans, there's also the Museum of Rugby and the "Twickenham Experience" stadium tour at, yes, Twickenham.

Soccer

To refer to the national winter sport as "soccer" is to blaspheme. It is football, and the British season culminates in the televised Wembley Stadium **FA Cup Final,** for which tickets are about as easy to get as they are for the Super Bowl. International matches at Wembley (☎ 0181/900–1234) during the August-to-May season are easier to attend.

For a real taste of this British obsession, though, nothing beats a match at the home ground of one of the three London clubs competing in the Premier League. More than likely you won't see a hint of the infamous hooliganism, but you will be quite carried away by the electric atmosphere only a vast football crowd can generate. **Tottenham Hotspur,** or "Spurs" (✉ White Hart Lane, 748 High Rd., N17, ☎ 0181/808–3030), and **Arsenal** (✉ Avenell Rd., Highbury, N5, ☎ 0171/359–0131) have north Londoners' loyalties about equally divided, while **Chelsea** (✉ Stamford Bridge, Fulham Rd., SW6, ☎ 0171/385–5545) is adored by the slightly more genteel west London fan.

Tennis

The Wimbledon Lawn Tennis Championships—famous among fans for the green, green grass of Centre Court, for strawberries and cream, and for rain, which always falls, despite the last-week-of-June/first-week-of-July high-summer timing—comprise, of course, one of the top four Grand Slam events of the tennis year. Whether you can get tickets is literally down to the luck of the draw, because there's a ballot system for advance purchase. To apply, send a self-addressed, stamped envelope between October and December to the All England Lawn Tennis & Croquet Club (✉ Box 98, Church Rd., Wimbledon SW19 5AE, ☎ 0181/946–2244), then fill in the application form, and hope.

But there are other ways to see the tennis. A block of Centre Court tickets is kept back to sell each day, but fanatics line up all night for these, especially in the second week. Each afternoon, though, tickets collected from early departing spectators are resold (profits go to charity). These can provide grandstand seats (with plenty to see—play continues till dusk), because those who can afford to care so little about tennis are often on expensive business freebies or company season tickets. You can also buy entry to the grounds to roam matches on the outer courts, where even the top-seeded players compete early in the fortnight.

For up-to-date information, the London Tourist Board operates a **Wimbledon Information Line** (☎ 01839/123417), at a cost of 49p per minute from the beginning of June.

7 Shopping

Napoléon must have known what he was talking about when he called Britain a nation of shopkeepers. The finest emporiums are in London, still. You can shop like royalty at Her Majesty's glove maker, run down a leather-bound copy of Wuthering Heights *at a Charing Cross bookseller, find antique Toby jugs on Portobello Road, or drop in on clothier Paul Smith—a fave of Sir Paul McCartney. Whether you're out for fun—there's nothing like street markets to stimulate the acquisitive juices—or for fashion, London can be the most rewarding of hunting grounds.*

By Kate
Sekules

WHEN IT COMES TO LONDON, shopping can be a transforming experience. It's an open secret Cary Grant was virtually "created" by a bespoke suit from Kilgour, French & Stanbury (the tailors extended the shoulders of his jackets six and a half inches to improve his form and draped the material to slim his hips). Then there was that other fashion plate, the Duchess of Windsor—for at-home style, she couldn't be beat, thanks in part to the soigné accessories she bought at Colefax & Fowler, still purveying the "country-house look" from its shop on Brook Street. Today, London's stores continue to create icons and make styles—as you can see from a visit to Harvey Nichols, shrine of the *Absolutely Fabulous* crowd.

As befits one of the great trading capitals of the world, London's shops have been known to boast, "You name it, we sell it." If you have a yen to keep up with the Windsors, look for the BY APPOINTMENT logo, which means that this particular emporium supplies Her Majesty the Queen, the Queen Mother, Prince Philip, or the Prince of Wales—check the small print and the insignia to find out which. More fashionable types will prefer to check out the ever-expanding Browns of South Molton Street—a label-hunter's heaven—while the surrounding small stores there and along quaint St. Christopher's Place ain't bad either. London's emporiums have gifts in every price range. Head to Bond Street if you're looking for the sort of thing you would find in every Rockefeller's Christmas stocking; if you're bargain-hunting, try one of the street-scene antiques fairs (it wasn't so long ago that an original Wordsworth manuscript of "When Severn's sweeping flood" was discovered in Brick Lane Market for less than $50). Then there are always Harrods' post-Christmas sales, but beware: The sidewalks get so crowded you have to walk on the streets, and if the cars or buses don't run you over, shoppers in search of their blue-light specials will.

If you have only limited time, zoom in on one or two of the West End's grand department stores, where you'll find enough booty for your entire gift list. Marks & Spencer is one of Britain's largest, and most beloved, chain stores, legendary primarily for its women's lingerie, its men's knitwear, and its range of food, good enough to pass off as home-cooked. Selfridges, London's answer to Macy's in New York, is a splendid pile of '20s architecture, which dominates the whole of one block toward Marble Arch and is increasingly fashion-conscious and up to date. Liberty is famous for its Liberty prints—multitudes of floral designs, which you can buy as fabric, or have made into everything from book covers to dresses. It may be hokey, but Harrods is not to be missed; apart from anything else, it's one of the best free shows in the city. And though Harrods trumpets that it can supply anything to anyone anywhere in the world (once, a baby elephant to Ronald Reagan) and boasts that the Queen sometimes does her Christmas shopping here, you can just pick up one of their distinctive green-and-gold-logo totes—a perfect touch of class for your veggie marketing back home.

No matter where you head in this city, you'll find you can melt as much plastic as your wallet can stand. Just remember: Credit cards are accepted virtually everywhere, but to make sure that your Cirrus or Plus card (to cite just two of the leading names) works in European ATMs, have your bank reset it to use a four-digit PIN number before your departure. Apart from bankrupting yourself, the only problem you'll encounter is exhaustion, since London is a town of many far-flung shopping areas.

For those who can make their way across the map faster than Napoléon and only have a few hours to spare, here's a suggested plan of action. Just keep in mind that shop-till-you-droppers will return to their hotel rooms weary, wiped-out, and their bathroom scales will show they've become three pounds lighter! Let's start with a great London trademark: **Harrods**. Be there when the doors open—this is one-stop shopping at its best (and one of the city's great sights). If you're chic-to-the-cuticles, then make a beeline for **Harvey Nichols**, just a few blocks away. Harvey Nicks always has the best in modern Brit style, be it couture, menswear, or home furnishings. Want a more traditional gift that would please any Lord and Lady Fitzuppity? Head to the nearby **General Trading Co.** on Sloane Street for that lovely Staffordshire spaniel, or run down to Pimlico to see the objets d'art and furniture of **David Linley**, the most talented royal around. For still more decorative goodies, tube or cab it over to Regent Street—one of London's main consumer heavens—and **Liberty** (which actually helped create the Arts and Crafts style of the Edwardian era). High rollers should walk east several blocks to Bond Street, Old and New. Of course, there's nothing like a visit to **Asprey** or the other Gold Platinum stores here to make you acutely aware of how poor you are. *Fashionistas* should then stroll up through Mayfair several blocks to the northwest and South Moulton Street to find **Brown's**, flooded with Linda Evangelista lookalikes, then head down Davies Street to the couture salon of **Vivienne Westwood**. On Davies Street you'll also find **Gray's Antique Market** and **Gray's Mews**—just the places to find a Charles II silver spoon. For gifts with gentler price tags, tube or cab it south to Piccadilly and **Hatchards**—London largest bookstore—or nearby **Fortnum & Mason**, the Queen's grocers, to buy some tea. Speaking of which, head upstairs and collapse for the high tea here, or make a last stop at **Floris**, a few blocks south on Jermyn Street—it's one of London's prettiest parfumiers. Opt for a scent once favored by Queen Victoria or—at almost pocket-money prices—a natural-bristle toothbrush. Oh, yes: If you want to add the very latest stores to this list, check out the suggestions in the monthly glossies, such as *Tatler*'s magazine's "I Can't Live Without . . . " shopping pages or *World of Interiors'* "Antennae" section. Whew! Sorry we can't tell you where to rent a forklift to bring all those purchases home!

Shopping Districts

Camden Town

Crafts and vintage-clothing markets and shops are clustered in and around picturesque but over-renovated canal-side buildings in this frenetic mecca for the world's youth. It's a good place for boots, T-shirts, inexpensive leather jackets, ethnic crafts, antiques, and recycled trendy wear. Things are quieter midweek.

Chelsea

Chelsea centers on King's Road, which is no longer synonymous with ultra fashion, but still harbors some designer boutiques, plus antiques and home-furnishings emporiums.

Covent Garden

A something-for-everyone neighborhood, the restored 19th-century market building features mainly high-class clothing chains, plus good-quality crafts stalls. Neal Street and the surrounding alleys offer amazing gifts of every type—bikes, kites, tea, herbs, beads, hats . . . you name it. Floral Street and Long Acre have designer and chain-store fashion in equal measure, while Monmouth Street and Shorts Gardens and

Shopping A (Mayfair, Soho, and Covent Garden)

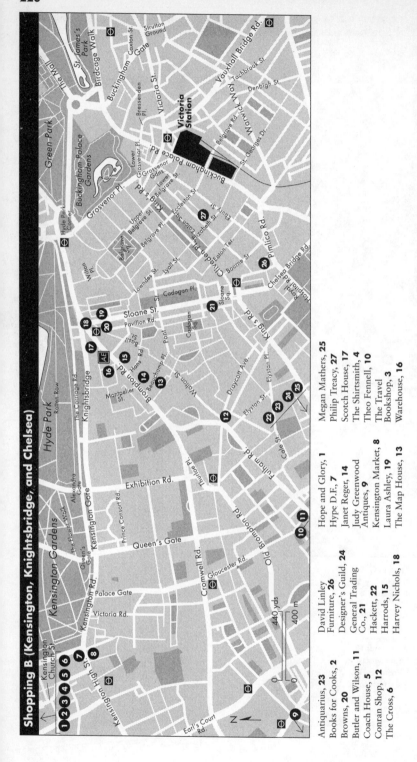

220

Shopping B (Kensington, Knightsbridge, and Chelsea)

Antiquarius, 23
Books for Cooks, 2
Browns, 20
Butler and Wilson, 11
Coach House, 5
Conran Shop, 12
The Cross, 6

David Linley
Furniture, 26
Designer's Guild, 24
General Trading
Co., 21
Hackett, 22
Harrods, 15
Harvey Nichols, 18

Hope and Glory, 1
Hype D.F., 7
Janet Reger, 14
Judy Greenwood
Antiques, 9
Kensington Market, 8
Laura Ashley, 19
The Map House, 13

Megan Mathers, 25
Philip Treacy, 27
Scotch House, 17
The Shirtsmith, 4
Theo Fennell, 10
The Travel
Bookshop, 3
Warehouse, 16

440 yds
400 m

the Thomas Neal's sort-of-mall in Earlham Street offer trendy clothes for club kids. The whole area is good for people-watching, too.

Hampstead
For picturesque peace and quiet with your shopping, stroll around here midweek. Upscale clothing stores and representatives of the better chains share the half-dozen streets with cozy boutique-size shops catering to the home and stomach.

Kensington
Kensington Church Street features expensive antiques, plus a little fashion. The main drag, Kensington High Street, is a smaller, less crowded, and classier version of Oxford Street, with a selection of clothing chains and larger stores at the eastern end.

Knightsbridge
Harrods dominates Brompton Road, but there's plenty more, especially for the well-heeled and fashion-conscious. Harvey Nichols is the top clothes stop, with many expensive designers' boîtes along Sloane Street. Walton Street and narrow Beauchamp (pronounced Beecham) Place offer more of the same, plus home furnishings and knickknacks; and Brompton Cross, at the start of Fulham Road, is the most design-conscious corner of London, with the Conran Shop and Joseph leading the field.

Mayfair
Here is Bond Street, Old and New, with desirable dress designers, jewelers, plus fine art (old and new) on Old Bond Street and Cork Street. South Molton Street has high-priced, high-style fashion—especially at Browns—and the tailors of Savile Row are of worldwide renown.

Oxford Street
Overcrowded Oxford Street is past its prime and is lined with tawdry discount shops. But many still flock here for some of London's great department stores—particularly Selfridges, John Lewis, and Marks & Spencer—and the interesting boutiques secreted in little St. Christopher's Place and Gees Court.

Notting Hill
Branching off from the famous Portobello Road market are various enclaves of boutiques selling young designers' wares, antiques, and things for the home—now favored stops for trendsetters. Explore the Ledbury Road/Westbourne Grove axis, Clarendon Cross, and Kensington Park Road, as well as Portobello Road itself.

Piccadilly
Though the actual number of shops is small for a street of its length (Green Park takes up a lot of space), Piccadilly manages to fit in several quintessential British emporiums. Fortnum and Mason is its star, and the arcades are an elegant experience even for shop-phobics.

Regent Street
At right angles to Oxford Street, this wider, curvier version has another couple of department stores, including what is possibly London's most pleasant, Liberty. Hamleys is the capital's toy center; other shops tend to be clothing stores—some stylish men's chain stores—or airline offices, though there are also shops selling china and bolts of English tweed. "West Soho," around Carnaby Street, stocks designer youth paraphernalia.

St. James's
Where the English gentleman shops, this district has some of the most elegant emporiums for hats, handmade shirts and shoes, and silver shav-

ing kits and flasks. Here, too, you'll find the Prince of Wales's after-shave supplier and possibly the world's best cheese shop. Nothing is cheap, in any sense.

Department Stores

London's department stores range from Harrods—which every tourist is obliged to visit—through many serviceable middle-range stores, devoted to the middle-of-the-road tastes of the middle class, to a few cheapjack ones that sell merchandise you would find at a better rate back home. Most of the best and biggest department stores are grouped in the West End around Regent Street and Oxford Street, with two notable exceptions out in Knightsbridge.

Liberty (✉ 200 Regent St., W1, ☎ 0171/734–1234) has one of London's most distinctive facades—a wonderful black-and-white mock-Tudor facade, making it a peacock among pigeons in humdrum Regent Street. Inside, it is a labyrinthine building, full of nooks and crannies stuffed with goodies, like a dream of an Eastern bazaar. Famous principally for its fabrics, it also has an Oriental department, rich with color; menswear that tends toward the traditional; and women's wear that has lately been spiced up with extra designer ranges. It is a hard store to resist, where you may well find an original gift—especially one made from those classic Liberty prints (☞ Map A).

John Lewis (✉ 278 Oxford St., W1, ☎ 0171/629–7711) is a short distance from Liberty, two blocks west on Oxford Street. This store's motto is "Never knowingly undersold," and for sensible goods at sensible prices John Lewis is hard to beat. For the visitor to London who's handy with the needle, John Lewis has a wonderful selection of dress and furnishing fabrics. Many's the American home with John Lewis drapes (☞ Map A).

Selfridges (✉ 400 Oxford St., W1, ☎ 0171/629–1234) is near the Marble Arch end of Oxford Street, where blocks are crowded in the middle of the day and at sale time. This giant, bustling store was started early this century by an American, though it's now British-owned. If this all-rounder has one outstanding department, it has to be its Food Hall, or else its frenetic cosmetics department—the largest in Europe—which seems to perfume the air the whole length of Oxford Street. In recent years, Selfridges has made a specialty of high-profile popular designer fashions and has spent a lot of money sprucing up. There's also a branch of the London Tourist Board, a theater ticket counter, and, in the basement, a branch of Thomas Cook, the travel agent (☞ Map A).

Harrods (✉ 87 Brompton Rd., SW1, ☎ 0171/730–1234), the only English department store classed among monuments and museums on every visitor's list, hardly needs an introduction. It is swanky and plush and as deep-carpeted as ever, its spectacular food halls are alone worth the trip, and it stands out from the pack for fashion, too. You can forgive the store its immodest motto, *Omnia, omnibus, ubique* ("everything, for everyone, everywhere"), because there are more than 230 departments, including a pet shop rumored to supply you with anything from aardvarks to zebras on request, and the toy department—sorry, *kingdom*—which does the same for its plush versions. During the pre-Christmas period and the sale—the legendary one is usually held during the last three weeks of January, but another storewide event, usually only one week, is held in mid-July—the entire store is a menagerie (☞ Map B).

Harvey Nichols (✉ 109 Knightsbridge, SW1, ☎ 0171/235–5000) is just a few blocks from Harrods, but it's not competing on the same turf, because its passion is fashion, all the way. There are nearly six floors of it, including departments for dressing homes and men, but the woman who invests in her wardrobe is the main target. Accessories are strong suits, especially jewelry, scarves, and makeup—England's first MAC counter here was 10-deep for months. The fourth floor now has a chic home design department, featuring such names as Nina Campbell, Mulberry, Ralph Lauren, and Designer's Guild. A reservation at the Fifth Floor restaurant is still coveted, too (☞ Map B).

Specialty Stores

Antiques

Investment quality or lovable junk, London has lots. Try markets first—even for pedigree silver, the dealers at these places often have the best wares and the knowledge to match. Camden Passage and Bermondsey (☞ Street Markets, *below*) are the best; the Portobello market has become a bit of a tourist trap, but its side streets are filled with interesting shops that are open outside market hours. Kensington Church Street is *the* antiques shopping street, with prices and quality both high. Of the hundreds of stores, we list 10 to whet your appetite.

Alfie's Antique Market (✉ 13–25 Church St., NW8, ☎ 0171/723–6066) is a huge and exciting labyrinth on several floors, with dealers specializing in anything and everything. You won't be deliberately stiffed, but it's a caveat emptor kind of place, thanks to the wide range of merchandise (☞ Map A).

Antiquarius (✉ 131–141 King's Rd., SW3, ☎ 0171/351–5353), at the Sloane Square end of King's Road, is an indoor antiques market with more than 200 stalls offering a wide variety of collectibles, including things that won't bust your baggage allowance: Art Deco brooches, meerschaum pipes, silver salt cellars . . . (☞ Map B).

Coach House (✉ 189 Westbourne Grove, W11, ☎ 0171/229–8306) is one reason why Westbourne Grove is one of the chicest style addresses around. A 19th-century garage has been restored by four antiques dealers, and behind a modest street facade extends a vast showroom, with neo-Gothic armoires, Arts and Crafts chairs, and lovely objets d'art. (☞ Map B).

Christopher Gibbs (✉ 8 Vigo St., ☎ 0171/439–4557) attracts such leading London tastemakers as J. Paul Getty Jr. and Mick Jagger, who, the society columns note, will hardly make a move without the judgment of Mr. Gibbs's legendary eye. If you're in the market for *Louis Quatorzième* marble busts, priceless Elizabethan embroidery, and truly one-of-a-kind antiques from all ages, this is the place to go and dream (☞ Map A).

Gallery of Antique Costume and Textiles (✉ 2 Church St., NW8, ☎ 0171/723–9981) attracts numerous movie directors who come here to get the period just right, because everything on the premises, from bedspreads to bloomers, was stitched before 1930—except for the wonderful range of copycat brocade vests. Models and Hollywood actors find incredible (and expensive) clothes here, too. It lies off our maps, but it is easily found three blocks north of the Edgware Road tube.

Colefax & Fowler (✉ 39 Brook St., W1, ☎ 0171/493–2231) is one of the most beautiful interior decorating shops in London—the virtual birthplace of the "English country-house look." John Fowler, Lady Colefax, and, most importantly, Virginia-born Nancy Lancaster, together created that cozy yet grand style, and their legacy is preserved here through wonderful wallpapers, pretty painted-wood flower holders, and assorted antique accents. If you want to make your apartment back home a mini-Chatsworth, be sure to stop in here, if only to soak up the style (☞ Map A).

Gray's Antique Market (✉ 58 Davies St., W1, ☎ 0171/629–7034) is conveniently central and assembles dealers specializing in everything from Sheffield plate to Chippendale furniture all under one roof. Bargains are not impossible, and proper pedigrees are guaranteed (☞ Map A). Also try **Gray's in the Mews** (✉ 1–7 Davies Mews, W1, ☎ 0171/629–7034) around the corner.

Hope and Glory (✉ 131A Kensington Church St., W8, ☎ 0171/727–8424) is one of the many specialty stores in the Kensington district with commemorative china and glass from 1887 to the present; there are also many affordable lesser pieces (☞ Map B).

Judy Greenwood Antiques (✉ 657 Fulham Rd., SW6, ☎ 0171/736–6037) beckons with its glowing red walls and a delightful selection of high-style antiques: Miss Havisham-y settees, vintage fabrics and textiles, gilded mirrors, and side tables (☞ Map B).

London Silver Vaults (✉ Chancery House, 53–63 Chancery La., WC2, ☎ 0171/242–3844), a basement conglomeration of around 40 dealers, is a treasure trove for the average Joe. Some pieces are spectacular, of course, but you can also pick up a set of Victorian cake forks or a dented candelabrum for less than £50 (☞ Map A).

Megan Mathers (✉ 571 Kings Rd., SW6, ☎ 0171/371–7837) offers one of London's most delectable assortments of stylish antiques: decoupaged 19th-century table obelisks, mini–Nelson's Columns, Venetian blackamoor figures—perfect *touches finales* for any high-style room (☞ Map B).

Rupert Cavendish (✉ 610 King's Rd., SW6, ☎ 0171/731–7041), this most elevated of dealers, has the Biedermeier market cornered, with Empire and Deco bringing up the rear. The shop is a museum experience (☞ Map B).

Books, CDs, and Records

Charing Cross Road is London's booksville, with a couple of dozen stores here or hereabout. The many antiquarian booksellers tend to look daunting (deceptively, as Helene Hanff found by correspondence with No. 84), but there are many new bookshops, too.

Foyles (✉ 119 Charing Cross Rd., WC2, ☎ 0171/437–5660) is especially large—so vast it can be confusing—but it is the place to come to find almost anything. **Waterstone's** (✉ 121–125 Charing Cross Rd., WC2, ☎ 0171/434–4291) is part of an admirable, and expanding, chain with long hours and a program of author readings and signings. **Hatchards** (✉ 187–188 Piccadilly, WC2, ☎ 0171/439–9921), one of London's largest bookstores, is well-stocked and old-fashioned, with helpful staff. **Dillons** (✉ 82 Gower St., WC1, ☎ 0171/636–1577) has a huge stock and a well-informed staff to help you choose (☞ Map A). **Books for Cooks** (✉ 4 Blenheim Cres., W11, ☎ 0171/221–1992) and its near neighbor, **The Travel Bookshop** (✉ No. 13, ☎ 0171/229–5260), are exactly what they say, and worth the trip for enthusiasts (☞ Map B). Travel books and maps are the specialty of **Stanfords** (✉ 12 Long Acre, WC2, ☎ 0171/836–1321). For art books, head for **Zwemmer** (✉ 24 Litchfield St., WC2, ☎ 0171/240–4158), just off Charing Cross Road. Sci-fi, fantasy, horror, and comic books are found by the mile at **Forbidden Planet** (✉ 71 New Oxford St., WC1, ☎ 0171/836–4179) (☞ Map A). On Charing Cross Road, **Silver Moon** (✉ No. 64, ☎ 0171/836–7906) is an accessible and friendly women's bookshop, and just off there, **Sportspages** (Caxton Walk, ✉ 94–96 Charing Cross Rd., ☎ 0171/240–9604) is an excellent place to start your cricket library (☞ Map A).

Just off the south end of Charing Cross is Cecil Court—a pedestrians-only lane where every shop is a specialty bookstore.

Bell, Book and Radmall (⊠ 4 Cecil Ct., WC2, ☎ 0171/240–2161) offers quality antiquarian volumes and specializes in modern first editions. **Marchpane** (⊠ 16 Cecil Ct., ☎ 0171/836–8661) stocks covetable rare and antique illustrated children's books. **Dance Books** (⊠ Cecil Ct., ☎ 0171/836–2314) has—yes—dance books. **Pleasures of Times Past** (⊠ 11 Cecil Ct., ☎ 0171/836–1142) indulges the collective nostalgia for Victoriana (☞ Map A).

London created the great megastores that have taken over the globe. These three stock most, if not all, of your CD, record, and video needs.

HMV (⊠ 150 Oxford St., W1, ☎ 0171/631–3423) has branches everywhere, but make a special trip to the HMV (did you know this stands for His Majesty's Voice?) flagship store for the widest selection. There are lots of autograph sessions and free shows, too (☞ Map A).
Tower Records (⊠ 1 Piccadilly Circus, W1, ☎ 0171/439–2500) doesn't carry records—go figure. Overlook that and you'll find its specialty departments are some of the best in London (☞ Map A).
Virgin Megastore (⊠ 14–16 Oxford St., W1, ☎ 0171/631–1234) is Richard Branson's pride and joy (though his New York City store is even bigger). It's nice to have it all under one roof, we suppose—all 8 billion selections. (☞ Map A).

China and Glass

English Wedgwood and Minton china are as collectible as they ever were, and most large department stores carry a selection, alongside lesser varieties with smaller price tags. Regent Street has several off-price purveyors, and, if you're in search of a bargain, Harrods' sale (usually held during the last three weeks of January) can't be beat—but sharpen your elbows first.

Thomas Goode (⊠ 19 S. Audley St., W1, ☎ 0171/499–2823) is one of the world's top shops for formal china and leaded crystal. On display are dinner plates designed and made for Dame Nellie Melba, Edward VII, Queen Victoria, and the last viceroy of India (☞ Map A).

Clothing

London is one of the world's four fashion capitals (along with Paris, Milan, and New York), and every designer you've ever heard of is sold here somewhere. As well as the top names, though, London retains a reputation for quirky street style, and many an exciting young designer has cut his or her teeth selling early collections at a London street market. Don't just go by the label, and you could be the first to wear clothes by a future star. Traditional British men's outfitters are also rather well known. From the Savile Row suit, handmade shirt, and custom shoes to the Harris-tweeds-and-Oxford-brogues English country look that Ralph Lauren purloined, England's indigenous garments make for real investment dressing.

GENERAL

Aquascutum (⊠ 100 Regent St., W1, ☎ 0171/734–6090) is known for its classic raincoats, but it also stocks the garments to wear underneath, for both men and women. Style keeps up with the times but is firmly on the safe side, making this a good bet for solvent professionals with an anti-fashion-victim attitude (☞ Map A).
Burberrys (⊠ 161–165 Regent St., W1, ☎ 0171/734–4060; ⊠ 18–22 The Haymarket, SW1, ☎ 0171/930–3343) tries to evoke an English Heritage ambience, with mahogany closets and stacks of neatly folded neckerchiefs alongside the trademark "Burberry Check" tartan, which adorns—in addition to those famous raincoat linings—scarves, umbrellas, and even pots of passion-fruit curd and tins of shortbread, in the British provisions line (☞ Map A).

Favourbrook (⊠ 19–21 Piccadilly Arcade, W1, ☎ 0171/491–2337) tailors exquisite handmade vests and jackets, ties and cummerbunds, all crafted from silks and brocades, velvets and satins, embroidered linens and chenilles. There's a range made up for both men and women, or order your own *Four Weddings and a Funeral* outfit (☞ Map A).

Herbert Johnson (⊠ 30 New Bond St., W1, ☎ 0171/408–1174) is one of a handful of gentlemen's hatters who still knows how to construct deerstalkers, bowlers, flat caps, and panamas—all the classic headgear, with some Ascot-worthy hats for women, too (☞ Map A).

Kensington Market (⊠ 49–53 Kensington High St., W8, ☎ 0171/938–4343) is the diametric opposite of British stiff-upper-lip anti-fashion. For more than two decades it has been a principal purveyor of the constantly changing, frivolous, hip London street style. Hundreds of stalls—some shop-size, others tiny—are crammed into this building, where you can get lost for hours trying to find the good bits (☞ Map B).

Marks & Spencer (main store, ⊠ 458 Oxford St., W1, ☎ 0171/935–7954) is a major chain of stores that's an integral part of the British way of life—sturdy practical clothes, good materials and workmanship, and basic accessories, all at moderate, though not bargain-basement, prices. "Marks and Sparks," as they are popularly known, has never been renowned for its high style, though that is changing as it continues to bring in (anonymously) big-name designers to spice up its ranges. What it *is* renowned for is underwear; all of England buys theirs here. This holds true for knitwear as well. This Marble Arch branch has the highest stock turnover of any shop in the land (☞ Map A).

Mulberry (⊠ 11–12 Gees Ct., W1, ☎ 0171/493–2546) outdoes Ralph Lauren in packaging the English look. Covetable, top-quality leather bags, belts, and cases, wool riding jackets, coats, sweaters, and corduroy and linen pants are the sorts of things found here—at a price (☞ Map A).

Scotch House (⊠ 2 Brompton Rd., SW3, ☎ 0171/581–2151), as you'd guess, is the place to buy your kilts, tartan scarves, and argyle socks without going to Edinburgh. It's also well stocked with cashmere and accessories (☞ Map B).

Simpson (⊠ 203 Piccadilly, W1, ☎ 0171/734–2002) is a quiet, pleasant store with a well-thought-out variety of designer and leisure wear, luggage, and gifts. There are a barbershop, restaurant, and wine bar here, plus the most disturbing nonreflective glass in its windows on Piccadilly (☞ Map A).

HIGH STYLE

Koh Samui (⊠ 50 Monmouth St., WC2, ☎ 0171/240–4280) stocks the clothing of around 20 young designers, nearly all of them British, some exclusive to this store, and all on the cutting edge. See the clothes you've read about by Christa Davies, Ruti Danan, and Marcus Constable, among others, and discover the next wave before *Vogue* gets there (☞ Map A).

Philip Treacy (⊠ 69 Elizabeth St., SW1, ☎ 0171/259–9605) is the name that tops every fashion maven's Santa Claus list. His magnificent hats regularly grace the pages of *Harper's Bazaar*; one-half Mad Hatter, one-half Cecil Beaton, Treacy's creations always guarantee Making an Entrance. Only the most serious fashion plates need apply—literally: the atelier is open by appointment only (☞ Map B).

Vivienne Westwood (⊠ 6 Davies St., W1, ☎ 0171/629–3757) is probably today's greatest British designer. If McQueen and Galliano have stolen a bit of her thunder recently, her Pompadour-punk ball gowns, Lady Hamilton vest coats, and foppish getups still represent the apex of high-style British couture. Her boutique is as intoxicatingly glamorous as her creations (☞ Map A).

MENSWEAR

Most stores we list above under General Clothing stock excellent menswear. Try Aquascutum, Burberrys, and Simpson. All the large department stores, too, carry a wide range of men's clothing, Selfridges and Harrods especially.

Blazer (⊠ 36 Long Acre, WC2, ☎ 0171/379–6258; ⊠ 117 Long Acre, WC2, ☎ 0171/379–0456) stocks medium-price formal wear at the first branch and a casual range at the second. Clothes tend toward the classic, but with style-conscious details and rich colors (☞ Map A).

Duffer of St. George (⊠ 29 Shorts Gardens, WC2, ☎ 0171/379–4660) has a collection of hip designers of street style in several cities, as well as its own label of sporty and dress-up lines for clubbing and posing with attitude (☞ Map A).

Hackett (main store, ⊠ 65B New King's Rd., SW6, ☎ 0171/371–7964) started as a posh thrift shop, recycling cricket flannels, hunting pinks, Oxford brogues, and similar British wear. Now they make their own, and they have become a genuine—and very good—gentlemen's outfitter (☞ Map B).

Kilgour, French & Stanbury (⊠ 8 Savile Row, W1, ☎ 0171/734–6905) is the classic and highly expensive bespoke tailors. Suits and shirts are custom cut (but note the cutters all go to lunch between 1:30 and 2:30 every afternoon). The 11th commandment here: You know a man looks like an English gentleman only when you do not notice that he is well dressed (☞ Map A).

Paul Smith (⊠ 41 Floral St., WC2, ☎ 0171/379–7133) is your man if you don't want to look outlandish, but you're bored with plain pants and sober jackets. His well-tailored suits have a subtle quirkiness, his shirts and ties a sense of humor, and his jeans and sweats a good cut. Customers include Paul McCartney, Harrison Ford, and David Hockney. The boutique is worth seeing itself—it's re-created from a Victorian chemist's shop (☞ Map A).

Tom Gilbey (⊠ 2 New Burlington Pl., W1, ☎ 0171/734–4877) is a custom tailor, but the exciting part of his shop is the Waistcoat Gallery, where exquisite vests—some in silk or brocade or embroidered by hand, others marginally plainer—are essential accessories for the dandy (☞ Map A).

Top Shop/Top Man (⊠ 214 Oxford St., W1, ☎ 0171/636–7700) is one of London's niftiest mega-chains. Head for the faux-vintage "souled-out" section (☞ Map A).

Turnbull & Asser (⊠ 70 Jermyn St., W1, ☎ 0171/930–0502) is *the* custom shirtmaker. Unfortunately for those of average means, the first order must be for a minimum of six shirts, from around £100 each. But there's a range of less expensive, still exquisitely made ready-to-wear shirts, too (☞ Map A).

WOMEN'S WEAR

Browns (⊠ 23–27 S. Molton St., W1, ☎ 0171/491–7833; ⊠ 6C Sloane St., SW1, ☎ 0171/493–4232) was the first notable store to populate the South Molton Street pedestrian mall, and it seems to sprout more offshoots every time you see it. Well-established, collectible designers (Donna Karan, Romeo Gigli, Jasper Conran, Jil Sander, Yohji Yamamoto) rub shoulder pads here with younger, funkier names (Dries Van Noten, Clements Ribiero, Anne Demeulemeester, Hussein Chalayan), and Browns also has its own label. Its July and January sales are famed (☞ Maps A and B).

Droopie & Browns (⊠ 99 St. Martin's La., WC2, ☎ 0171/379–4514) features beautifully constructed, extravagantly theatrical frocks and suits, made up in raw silks, fine linens, brocades, and velvets. Colors are strong, tailoring is unimpeachable, and kind salespeople don't turn up their noses at larger ladies (☞ Map A).

Hype D.F. (✉ 48–52 Kensington High St., W8, ☎ 0171/938–4343) is the biggest new store for designer collections to open in London in years, featuring the coolest, hottest fashions for the 18–40 crowd. There are some nifty bargains, too (☞ Map B).

Janet Reger (✉ 2 Beauchamp Pl., SW3, ☎ 0171/584–9360) is still queen of the silk teddy, having become synonymous with the ultimate in luxurious negligees and lingerie many years ago (☞ Map B).

Jigsaw (main store, ✉ 21 Long Acre, Covent Garden, WC2, ☎ 0171/240–3855) is popular for its separates that don't sacrifice quality to fashion, are reasonably priced, and suit women in their twenties to forties (☞ Map A).

Laura Ashley (main store, ✉ 256–258 Regent St., W1, ☎ 0171/437–9760) offers design from the firm founded by the late high priestess of English traditional. Country dresses, blouses, skirts, plus wallpapers and fabrics in dateless patterns that rely heavily on flowers, fruit, leaves, or just plain stripes, have captured the nostalgic imagination of the world (☞ Map A).

Nicole Farhi (main stores, ✉ 25–26 St. Christopher's Pl., W1, ☎ 0171/486–3416; ✉ 27 Hampstead High St., NW3, ☎ 0171/435–0866) suits the career woman who requires quality, cut, *and* style in a suit, plus weekend wear in summer linens and silks, or winter hand-knit woolens. Prices are on the high side, but there is some affordable wear as well, especially the sporty, casual Diversion label. Farhi offers an equally desirable men's line (☞ Map A).

Paddy Campbell (✉ 8 Gees Ct., W1, ☎ 0171/493–5646) designs elegant matching separates in natural fabrics and subtle colors. Prices are reasonable for this level of workmanship, and the staff will alter garments for a perfect fit (☞ Map A).

Pellicano (✉ 63 S. Molton St., W1, ☎ 0171/629–2205) stocks only cutting-edge designers, like Brit phenoms Bella Freud, Copperwheat Blundell, and Sonnentag Mulligan, and the *Vogue*-ier of the internationals—including Martine Sitbon and Eric Bergère—in a salon that virtually opens onto the street. The sales staff can be unbelievably snobby (☞ Map A).

The Shirtsmith (✉ 38A Ledbury Rd., W11, ☎ 0171/229–3090) does bespoke and ready-made shirts, suits, and jackets for women, using fine cottons and Indian silks. Some designs are classic and fitted, and others are slightly outrageous, like the Chatterton shirt, with more ruffles at the neck than a chrysanthemum has petals (☞ Map B).

Warehouse (main store, ✉ 19 Argyll St., W1, ☎ 0171/437–7101) stocks practical, stylish, reasonably priced separates in easy fabrics and lots of fun colors. The finishing isn't so hot, but style, not substance, counts here, and the shop's youthful fans don't seem to mind. The stock changes very quickly, so it always presents a new face to the world (☞ Maps A and B).

Whistles (main store, ✉ The Market, Covent Garden, WC2, ☎ 0171/379–7401; also at ✉ Heath St., Hampstead, ☎ 0171/431–2395) is a small chain stocking its own high-fashion, mid-price label, plus several European (mostly French) designers. Clothes are hung in color-coordinated groupings in shops that resemble designers' ateliers (☞ Map A).

Design

There's been a tremendous resurgence of interest in objects not mass-produced, and London is currently breeding innovators in the field of design at the rate of knots. Forget the dirty word "crafts"—this work is often more modern than modems.

Contemporary Applied Arts (⊠ 43 Earlham St., WC2, ☎ 0171/836–6993) has a mixed bag of designers and craftspeople displaying their wares over two floors. Anything from glassware and jewelry to furniture and lighting can be found here (☞ Map A).

Contemporary Ceramics (⊠ 7 Marshall St., W1, ☎ 0171/437–7605) was formed by some of the best British potters as a cooperative venture to market their wares. The result is a store that carries a wide spectrum of the potter's art, from thoroughly practical pitchers, plates, and bowls to ceramic sculptures. Prices range from the reasonable to way up (☞ Map A).

David Linley Furniture (⊠ 60 Pimlico Rd., SW1, ☎ 0171/730–7300) is the outpost for Viscount Linley—the only gentleman in the kingdom who can call the Queen "Auntie" and, more importantly, one of the finest furniture designers of today. Heirlooms of the future, his desks and chairs have one foot in the 18th century, another in the 21st. The large pieces are suitably expensive, but small desk accessories and objets d'art are also available (☞ Map B).

Designer's Guild (⊠ 227 King's Rd., SW3, ☎ 0171/351–5775) is where Tricia Guild shows her fabrics and accessories of fabulous, saturated colors. Inspirational, many designers vouch (☞ Map B).

Gabriel's Wharf (⊠ Upper Ground, SE1, ☎ 0171/620–0544) consists of a collection of craftspeople who have set up a cute, brightly painted village near the South Bank Centre, selling porcelain, jewelry, mirrors, clothes, toys, papier mâché wares, and more. This complex is off our map, but near the Thames on the South Bank.

The Glasshouse (⊠ 21 St. Albans Pl., N1, ☎ 0171/359–8162) is off our map, but for indigenous glassware it's about the only place, and you can drop in while visiting nearby Camden Passage. See glass being blown by several artists, then buy it.

OXO Tower (⊠ Bargehouse St., ☎ 0171/401–3610) is one of London's newest shopping meccas. Many and varied designers/makers have to pass rigorous selection procedures to set up in prime riverside workshops to make, display, and sell their work. The workshops are glass-walled, and you're invited in, even if you're just browsing or chatting. You can commission, too—anything from a cushion cover to a steel hoverbed (☞ Map A).

Space (⊠ 28 All Saints Rd., W11, ☎ 0171/229–6533) is where star designer Tom Dixon sells his own work—mostly furniture—and also that of his favorite peers. A great place for lighting fixtures, it's off our map.

Gifts

Of course, virtually anything from any shop in this chapter has gift potential, but these selections lean toward stores with a lot of choice, both in merchandise and price. Chances are you'll be wanting the recipients of your generous bounty to know how far you traveled to procure it for them, so our suggestions tend toward identifiable Britishness. You should also investigate the possibilities in the shops attached to the major museums, most of which offer far more than racks of souvenir postcards these days. Some of the best are at the **British Museum**, the **V & A**, the **Royal Academy**, and the **London Transport Museum**.

The Armoury of St. James's (⊠ 17 Piccadilly Arcade, SW1, ☎ 0171/493–5082) offers perfect playthings for overgrown schoolkids in the form of antique and newly painted lead soldiers (most wars with British involvement can be fought in miniature), plus medals, brass buttons, and military prints (☞ Map A).

Conran Shop (⊠ Michelin House, 81 Fulham Rd., SW3, ☎ 0171/589–7401) is the domain of Sir Terence Conran, of course, who has been informing British middle-class taste since he opened Habitat in the '60s;

this is the grown-up, upmarket version. Home enhancers from furniture to stemware, both handmade and mass-produced, famous name and young designer, are displayed in a suitably gorgeous building (☞ Map B).

Floris (✉ 89 Jermyn St., W1, ☎ 0171/930–2885) is probably the most beautiful shop in London, with gleaming glass and Spanish mahogany showcases (acquired from the Great Exhibition of 1851) filled with swan's-down powder puffs, cut-glass bottles, and the elegant ivory and faux tortoiseshell combs that the shop has sold since the place opened in 1730. Queen Victoria used to daub her favorite Floris fragrance on her lace handkerchief (☞ Map A).

Fortnum & Mason (✉ 181 Piccadilly, W1, ☎ 0171/734–8040), the Queen's grocer, is, paradoxically, the most egalitarian of gift stores, with plenty of irresistibly packaged luxury foods, stamped with the gold BY APPOINTMENT crest, for less than £5. Try the teas, preserves, blocks of chocolate, tins of pâté, or a box of Duchy Originals oatcakes—like Paul Newman, the Prince of Wales has gone into the retail food business (☞ Map A).

General Trading Co. (✉ 144 Sloane St., SW1, ☎ 0171/730–0411) "does" just about every upper-class wedding gift list, but caters also to slimmer pockets with merchandise shipped from farther shores (as the name suggests), but moored securely to English taste (☞ Map B).

Hamleys (✉ 188–196 Regent St., W1, ☎ 0171/734–3161) has six floors of toys and games for children and adults. The huge stock ranges from traditional teddy bears to computer games and all the latest technological gimmickry. Try to avoid it at Christmas, when police have to rope off a section of Regent Street for Hamleys customers (☞ Map A).

Lush (✉ 7 The Piazza, Covent Garden, WC2, ☎ 01202/668545 mail order) is crammed with fresh, pure, very wacky, handmade cosmetics. "13 Rabbit" is chocolate and spice for the shower; "Angels on Bare Skin" is divine lavender cleansing mush; soaps ("Banana Moon," "Dirty Boy," "Pineapple Grunt") are sliced off huge slabs like cheese, and are paper-wrapped as in an old-fashioned grocer; Bath Bombs fizz furiously, then leave the water scattered with rosebuds or scented with honey and vanilla. Quite irresistible (☞ Map A).

Neal Street East (✉ 5 Neal St., WC2, ☎ 0171/240–0135) isn't big on British, no, but this importer of Oriental everything does carry stock with universal appeal. There are several floors of what you'd expect in the way of woks, chopsticks, bowls, books, kimonos, and toys, but there are also glorious lacquered boxes, woven baskets, amber and silver jewelry, silk flowers, Japanese kites, and loads of fun gifts for less than a fiver (☞ Map A).

Neal's Yard Remedies (✉ 15 Neal's Yard, WC2, ☎ 0171/379–7222, and branches) has exquisitely fragranced bath oils, shampoos, massage lotions, soaps, and so on, plus some of the purest essential oils money can buy, complete with burners for scenting the air back home; all are packaged in their distinctive cobalt-blue apothecary bottles (☞ Map A).

Penhaligon's (main stores, ✉ 41 Wellington St., WC2, ☎ 0171/836–2150; ✉ 16 Burlington Arcade, W1, ☎ 0171/629–1416) was established by William Penhaligon, court barber at the end of Queen Victoria's lengthy reign. He blended perfumes and toilet waters in the back of his shop, often creating private blends for such customers as Lord Rothschild and Winston Churchill, using essential oils and natural, often exotic ingredients. You can buy the very same formulations today, along with soaps, talcs, bath oils, and accessories, with the strong whiff of Victoriana both inside and outside the pretty bottles and boxes. Although constructed only a decade ago, the shop is sumptuously outfitted with 19th-century perfumer furnishings (☞ Map A).

The Tea House (✉ 15A Neal St., WC2, ☎ 0171/240–7539) purveys everything to do with the British national drink; you can dispatch your entire gift list here. Alongside every variety of tea—including strange or rare brews like orchid, banana, Japanese Rice, and Russian Caravan—are teapots in the shape of a British bobby or a London taxi, plus books, and what the shop terms "teaphernalia"—strainers, trivets, and infusers, plus some gadgets that need explaining (☞ Map A).

Jewelry

Jewelry—precious, semiprecious, and totally fake—can be had by just rubbing an Aladdin's lamp in London's West End. Of the department stores, Liberty and Harvey Nichols are particularly known for their fashion jewelry, but here are a few more suggestions for baubles, bangles, and beads.

Asprey's (⊠ 165–169 New Bond St., W1, ☎ 0171/493–6767) has been described as the "classiest and most luxurious shop in the world." It offers a range of exquisite jewelry and gifts, both antique and modern. If you're in the market for a six-branched Georgian candelabrum or a six-carat emerald-and-diamond brooch, you won't be disappointed (☞ Map A).

Butler and Wilson (⊠ 20 South Molton St., W1, ☎ 0171/409–2955; ⊠ 189 Fulham Rd., SW3, ☎ 0171/352–8255) is designed to set off its irresistible costume jewelry to the very best advantage—against a dramatic black background. It has some of the best displays in town, and it keeps very busy marketing silver, diamanté, French gilt, and pearls by the truckload (☞ Maps A and B).

Cartier (⊠ 175 New Bond St., W1, ☎ 0171/493–6962) exudes an exclusivity that captures the very essence of Bond Street. It combines royal connections—Cartier was granted its first royal warrant in 1902—with the last word in luxurious good taste. The store also sells glassware, leather goods, and stationery (☞ Map A).

Garrard (⊠ 112 Regent St., W1, ☎ 0171/734–7020) has connections with the Royal Family going back to 1722 and is still in charge of the upkeep of the Crown Jewels. But they are also family jewelers, and they offer an enormous range of items, from antique to modern (☞ Map A).

The Outlaws Club (⊠ 49 Endell St., WC2, ☎ 0171/379–6940) stocks the work of around 100 designers, with prices ranging from a few pounds up to £200. The dominant style is avant-garde, meaning that this shop has been a favorite with fashion stylists for a decade (☞ Map A).

Theo Fennell (⊠ 177 Fulham Rd., SW3, ☎ 0171/376–4855) designs pieces that are instantly recognizable—exquisitely detailed miniatures and covetable jewelry (in gold studded with precious stones) reminiscent of the ecclesiastical (☞ Map B).

Prints

London harbors trillions of prints, and they make great gifts—for yourself, perhaps. We list two West End stores, but try also street markets and Cecil Court (☞ Books, CDs, and Records, *above*), just north of Trafalgar Square.

Grosvenor Prints (⊠ 28–32 Shelton St., WC2, ☎ 0171/836–1979) sells antiquarian prints, but with an emphasis on views and architecture of London—and dogs! It's an eccentric collection, and the prices range widely, but the stock is so odd that you are bound to find something interesting and unusual to meet both your budget and your taste (☞ Map A).

The Map House (⊠ 54 Beauchamp Pl., SW3, ☎ 0171/589–4325) has antique maps that can run from a few pounds to several thousand, but the shop also has excellent reproductions of maps and prints, especially of botanical subjects and cityscapes (☞ Map B).

Street Markets

London is as rich in street markets as it is in parks, and they contribute as much to the city's thriving culture. Practically every neighborhood has its own cluster of fruit-and-vegetable stalls, but we list here the bigger, specialist sort of market, which provides not only (if you luck out) a bargain, but also a great day out. A Sunday morning strolling the stalls of Brick Lane and breakfasting on the native bagels (smaller than New York's, but just as good), or a Saturday antiquing in Portobello Road, are Londoners' pastimes as much as they are tourist activities, and markets are a great way to see the city from the inside out.

Bermondsey (⊠ Tower Bridge Rd., SE1). Also known as the New Caledonian Market, this is London's best antiques market, one of the largest, and the one the dealers frequent. Due to its professional needs, the Fridays-only market starts at the unearthly hour of 4 AM, and it's then that the really great buys will be snapped up. You should still be able to find a bargain or two if you turn up a bit later. *Bus 15 or 25 to Aldgate, then Bus 42 over Tower Bridge to Bermondsey Sq.; or Tube to London Bridge (now being rebuilt, so head for St. Thomas St. and ask for directions).* ⊙ *Fri. 4 AM–noon.*

Camden Lock Market (⊠ NW1). Visit the lock on a sunny August Sunday if you want your concept of a crowd redefined. Camden is actually several markets gathered around a pair of locks in the Regent's Canal, and it was once very pretty. Now that further stalls and a new faux warehouse have been inserted into the surrounding brick railway buildings, the haphazard charm of the place is largely lost, although the variety of merchandise is mind-blowing—vintage and new clothes (design stars have been discovered here), antiques and junk, jewelry and scarves, candlesticks, ceramics, mirrors, toys . . . But underneath it's really a date spot for hip teens. The neighborhood is bursting with shops and cafés, and other markets, and it's a whole lot calmer, if stall-free, at midweek. *Tube or Bus 24 or 29 to Camden Town.* ⊙ *Shops Tues.–Sun. 9:30–5:30, stalls weekends 8–6.*

Camden Passage (⊠ Islington, N1). Despite the name, this one is not in Camden but a couple of miles away in Islington, a neighborhood first gentrified by media hippies in the '60s. Around 350 antiques dealers set up stalls here Saturdays and Wednesdays, with a curtailed version on Thursdays, and it remains a fruitful, fair-priced, and picturesque hunting ground. *Bus 19 or 38 or Tube to Angel.* ⊙ *Wed. and Sat. 8:30–3.*

Greenwich Antiques Market (⊠ Greenwich High Rd., SE10). If you're planning to visit Greenwich, then combine your trip with a wander around this open-air market near St. Alfege Church. You'll find one of the best selections of secondhand and antique clothes in London—quality tweeds and overcoats can be had at amazing prices. The market for antiques is open on weekends only. *British Rail to New Gate Cross, then Bus 117; or bus direct to Greenwich.* ⊙ *Antiques, crafts, and clothes weekends 9–5; fruit and vegetables weekdays 9–5.*

Leadenhall Market (⊠ EC3). The draw here is not so much what you can buy—plants and food, mainly—as the building itself. It's a handsome late-Victorian structure, ornate and elaborate, with plenty of atmosphere. *Tube to Bank or Monument.* ⊙ *Weekdays 7–4.*

Petticoat Lane (⊠ Middlesex St., E1). Actually, Petticoat Lane doesn't exist, and this Sunday clothing and fashion market centers on Middlesex Street, then sprawls in several directions, including east to Brick Lane. Between them, the crammed streets turn up items of dubious parentage (CD players, bikes, car radios), alongside clothes (vintage, new, and just plain tired), jewelry, books, underwear, antiques, woodworking tools, bed linens, jars of pickles, and outright junk in one of London's most entertaining diversions. ☉ *Sun. 9–2. Tube: Liverpool St., Aldgate, or Aldgate East.*

Portobello Market (✉ Portobello Rd., W11). London's most famous market still wins the prize for the all-round best. It sits in a most lively and multicultural part of town, the 1,500-odd antiques dealers don't rip you off, and it stretches over a mile, changing character completely as it goes. The top end (Notting Hill Gate) is antiques-land (with shops midweek); the middle is where locals buy fruit and vegetables and hang out in trendy restaurants; the section under the elevated highway called the Westway boasts the best flea market in town; and then it tails off into a giant rummage sale among record stores, vintage clothing boutiques, and art galleries. *Bus 52 or Tube to Ladbroke Grove or Notting Hill Gate.* ☉ *Fruit and vegetables Mon.–Wed. and Fri. 8–5, Thurs. 8–1; antiques Fri. 8–3; both food market and antiques Sat. 6–5.*

Spitalfields (✉ Brushfield St., E1). Until it eventually becomes shops and offices, this old 3-acre indoor fruit market near Petticoat Lane will be home to food, crafts, and clothes stalls, cafés, performance and sports facilities, and a city farm. There's a different market every day; Saturday is antiques, Sunday a greenmarket. *For directions,* see *Petticoat Lane,* above. ☉ *Weekdays 11–3, Sun. 9–3.*

VAT Refunds

To the eternal fury of Britain's storekeepers, who struggle under cataracts of paperwork, Britain is afflicted with a 17½% Value Added Tax. Foreign visitors, however, need not pay VAT if they take advantage of the Personal Export Scheme. Of the various ways to get a VAT refund, the most common are **Over the Counter** and **Direct Export.** Note that though practically all larger stores operate these schemes, information about them is not always readily forthcoming, so it is important to ask. Once you have gotten on the right track, you'll find that almost all of the larger stores have export departments that will be able to give you all the help you need.

The easiest and most usual way of getting your refund is the **Over the Counter** method. There is normally a minimum of £75, below which VAT cannot be refunded. You must also be able to supply proof of identity—your passport is best. The salesclerk will then fill out the necessary paperwork, Form 407 VAT. (Be sure to get an addressed envelope as well.) Keep the form and give it to customs when you leave the country. Lines at major airports are usually long, so allow plenty of time, and pack the goods you have purchased in your carry-on bags—you'll sometimes need to be able to produce them. The form will then be returned to the store and the refund forwarded to you, minus a small service charge, usually around $3. You can specify how you want the refund. Generally, the easiest way is to have it credited to your charge card. Alternatively, you can have it in the form of a sterling check, but your bank will charge a fee to convert it. Note also that it can take up to eight weeks to receive the refund.

The **Direct Export** method—whereby you have the store send the goods to your home—is more cumbersome. You must have the VAT Form 407 certified by customs, police, or a notary public when you get home and then send it back to the store. They, in turn, will refund your money.

If you are traveling to any other EC country from Britain, the same rules apply, except in France, where you can claim your refund as you leave the country.

However, in 1988 the **Tourist Tax-Free Shopping** service came into operation. This service, which uses special VAT refund vouchers, rather than Form 407, expedites your refund, provided that you make your purchases at a store (identified by the red, white, and blue TAX-FREE FOR TOURISTS sign) offering the service. If you are going on from Britain to the Continent, you can even get cash refunds. Full details and a list of stores offering the Tax-Free service are available from the British Tourist Authority (⊠ 551 5th Ave., 7th floor, New York, NY 10176, ☎ 212/986–2200 or 800/462–2748) and the British Travel Centre (⊠ 12 Regent St., London SW1Y 4PQ).

Clothing Sizes

Men
Suit and shirt sizes in the United Kingdom and the Republic of Ireland are the same as U.S. sizes.

Women

DRESSES/COATS

U.S.	4	6	8	10	12	14	16
U.K./Ireland	6	8	10	12	14	16	18

BLOUSES/SWEATERS

U.S.	30	32	34	36	38	40	42
U.K./Ireland	32	34	36	38	40	42	44

SHOES

U.S.	4	5	6	7	8	9	10
U.K./Ireland	2	3	4	5	6	7	8

8 Side Trips from London

Sometimes you really need to get away from Old Smoke, and just because you only have two weeks doesn't mean you won't feel the urge to see trees and sky and stately homes. Take any of these side trips and you'll feel—such is the change of pace you'll experience—as though you added another week to your vacation. England is so much more than its capital—a fact that Londoners tend to forget.

LONDONERS ARE UNDENIABLY LUCKY. Few populaces enjoy such glorious—and easily accessible—options for day-tripping. This chapter presents five of the most popular destinations: Bath, Cambridge, Oxford, Stratford-upon-Avon, and Windsor. Each can easily be done as a day trip, but is also well worth considering for an overnight. Then you could add a glimpse of the English countryside to your repertoire, perhaps dropping into a stately home or two, visiting a garden, or embarking on a hike with the aid of an Ordnance Survey map—which reveals every feature of the landscape, once you learn how to read it. These are high English pleasures, to be sure.

The fastest countryside fix of the five can be had at royal Windsor, perhaps the Queen's most spectacular home, situated less than an hour from London by train. The farthest is Stratford, birthplace of the Bard of Avon, old Will Shakespeare himself. Oxford and Cambridge, home to England's most celebrated, oldest, and finest pair of universities—the Ivy League equivalents—are also easily accessible; both are vibrant cities, best visited during term time. Bath is exquisite, and Jane Austen fans should have this Georgian city with its Roman baths at the very top of their must-do list—read the novels, or catch any of the numerous recent film versions for explication.

All five of these places are best reached by train (for general train information, the main telephone number is 0345/484950; to access information from overseas, dial 0161/236–3522); bus travel is a viable alternative to Oxford, Cambridge, and Windsor (to contact National Express coach lines, dial 0990/808080, which can also be accessed from overseas). Be sure to plan on an early start for all these side trips—if going by train or bus, it's a good idea to check schedules ahead of time. Below, the sights for each town are ordered in sequence to ensure the most expedient walking tour of the varied attractions.

BATH

"I really believe I shall always be talking of Bath. . . . I do like it so very much. Oh! who can ever be tired of Bath," wrote Jane Austen in *Northanger Abbey,* and, today, thousands of visitors heartily agree with the great 19th-century author. A remarkably unsullied Georgian city, Bath still looks as if John Wood, its chief architect, "Beau" Nash, its principal dandy, and Jane Austen (1775–1817) might still be strolling on the promenade here. Stepping out of the train station plumps you right in the center, and Bath is compact enough to explore on foot. A single day is sufficient for you to take in the glorious yellow stone buildings, tour the Roman baths, and stop for tea, though it will give only a brief hint of the thriving cultural life that still goes on in this vibrant place.

Bath Spa is easily reached by hourly trains from Paddington Station (about 1 hour, 25 minutes journey time), or by **National Express** coach (☎ 0990/808080) from Victoria Coach Station: journey time is 3 hours (coaches run about every 2 hours). The **Tourist Information Centre** (☎ 01225/477101) is on Bath Street in the Colonnades.

A Good Walk

The first sight you come to, having followed signs from the train station, is the **Pump Room and Roman Baths.** Built by the Romans when they settled here in AD 43, it became famous as the temple to Minerva, goddess of wisdom. Legend has it that the first taker of these sacred waters was King Lear's leprous father, Prince Bladud, in the 9th century BC. Yes, it was claimed he was cured. The waters can still be taken, and they anciently gush at a constant temperature of 46.5°C (116°F). Below the gorgeous and recently restored 18th-century Pump Room (as described in Austen's *Mansfield Park, Emma, Northanger Abbey,* et al.) is a museum of objects found during excavations. ⊠ *Abbey Churchyard,* ☎ *01225/477776.* ⊡ *£5, combined ticket with Assembly Rooms, £8.* ☉ *Apr.–Sept., daily 9–6; Oct.–Mar., Mon.–Sat. 9:30–5, Sun. 10–5.*

Opposite the Pump Room and Roman Baths is **Bath Abbey.** This was commissioned by God. Really. The current design came to a bishop in a dream, but it was actually built by the Vertue brothers during the 16th century. In the **Heritage Vaults** (☎ 01225/422462) is a museum of archeological finds, with a scale model of 13th-century Bath. Look up at the fan-vaulted ceilings in the nave, and the carved angels on the newly restored West Front. ☎ *01225/422462.* ⊡ *Abbey free; Heritage Vaults £2.*☉ *Abbey April–Oct., Mon.–Sat. 9–6, Sun. 1–2:30, 4:30–5:30; Nov.–Mar., Mon.–Sat. 9–4:30, Sun. 1–2:30, 4:30–5:30; Heritage Vaults Mon.–Sat. 10–4.*

For the perfect Bath time-out, head for **Sally Lunn's** (⊠ North Parade Passage, ☎ 01225/461634). A popular tourist trap, but one loved equally by locals, this is possibly the world's only tearoom with its own museum. A Sally Lunn is a sweet cross between an English muffin and a brioche measuring a foot in diameter, which is toasted and plied with toppings such as cinnamon butter, orange curd, or coffee-walnut.

Eastward of the Abbey, Bridge Street leads to one of the most famous landmarks of the city, **Pulteney Bridge.** This was the great Georgian architect Robert Adam's sole contribution to Bath, and is, in its way, as fine as the only other bridge in the world with shops lining either side: the Ponte Vecchio in Florence. Find it on the River Avon back down the hill, after wandering around up at the top, exploring the many nooks and crannies, secret passageways, and cobbled streetlets.

North of Saw Close and the Theatre Royal is **The Circus.** You can also reach it from Bath Abbey by heading north up Union Passage, to Milsom Street and Gay Street. This is a perfectly circular ring of Bath stone houses, designed by John Wood. On the east side of the circus are more thrills for Austen readers: her much-mentioned **Assembly Rooms,** now containing the self-explanatory Museum of Costume. ⊠ *Bennett St.,* ☎ *01225/477785.*⊡ *£3.60, combined ticket with Roman Baths £8.*☉ *Mon.–Sat. 10–5, Sun. 11–5.*

West of the Circus is the most famous sight in Bath, the **Royal Crescent,** and you can't help but see why. Designed by John Wood the younger, it's perfectly proportioned and beautifully sited, with views sweeping over parkland. A marvelous museum at **No. 1 Royal Crescent** shows life as Beau Nash would have lived it circa 1765. ☎ *01225/ 428126.*⊡ *£3.50.* ☉ *Mid-Feb.–mid-Dec., Tues.–Sun. 10:30–5 (Nov.–Dec. open till 4 PM only).*

CAMBRIDGE

Having trouble distinguishing the two Ivy League of England college towns, Oxford and Cambridge? That's not surprising, because in the United Kingdom, these two important educational institutions are often elided into the term "Oxbridge," and British people themselves— aside from Oxbridge graduates, of course—are hazy about the distinction. Cambridge lies in East Anglia, a quartet of counties consisting of Norfolk, Suffolk, Essex, and Cambridgeshire. It's a city of some 100,000 souls, dominated culturally and architecturally by its famous university—which is divided into colleges—and beautified by parks and gardens and the quietly flowing River Cam. Punting on the Cam is a quintessential Cambridge pursuit, followed by a stroll along the Backs, the quaintly entitled left bank of the Cam, to which Magdalen (pronounced maudlin), St. John's, Trinity, Clare, King's, and Queen's colleges show their beautiful backsides.

Need a key to the city? Think Rupert Brooke, the short-lived World War I–era poet ("There is some corner of a foreign field/That is forever England"), a Cambridgeshire lad, who called his county "The shire for Men who Understand." Think Wordsworth and Thackeray, Byron and Tennyson, E. M. Forster and C. S. Lewis. Exquisite King's College Chapel's equally exquisite-sounding choir defines the season for an entire nation, when the *Festival of Nine Lessons and Carols* is broadcast live on Christmas Eve. Cambridge may be one of the most beautiful cities in Britain, but it is no museum. Even if the students are on vacation, there's a strong pulse here, and the city can trace its history back to the 1st century BC, when an Iron Age tribe settled on what's now Castle Hill. By the end of the 16th century, there were 16 colleges; there are now 31. Students apply not to the university of Cambridge, but to one of the individual colleges, and inter-college rivalry is not unknown.

Trains to Cambridge leave King's Cross Station and Liverpool Street Station every hour, and take an hour (☎ 0345/484950).

By **National Express** coach (☎ 0990/808080) from Victoria Coach Station, the journey takes 2 hours; coaches run hourly.

Cambridge Tourist Information Centre is in Wheeler Street, an extension of Benet Street, off King's Parade (☎ 01223/322640).

VISITING THE COLLEGES

College visits are certainly a highlight of a Cambridge tour, but you must remember that these are private homes and workplaces, even out of term. Some are closed to the public, and access to others is restricted to the chapels and dining rooms (called halls) and sometimes the libraries, too (and you are politely requested to refrain from picnicking in the quadrangles). Some colleges charge a small fee for the privilege of nosing around. All are closed during exams, usually from mid-April to late June, when the May Balls are held, and everyone lets down their hair along with whatever else they can find. By far the best way to gain access without annoying anyone is to join a walking tour led by an official Blue Badge guide—in fact, many areas are off-limits unless you do. The two-hour tours leave up to five times daily from the Tourist Information Centre. Below is a walk that takes in most of the colleges, but it's best to set off with a map from the local tourist office and just tackle a portion of the city.

A Good Walk

On Trumpington Street is **Peterhouse,** the oldest college, founded in 1281 by the Bishop of Ely. Take a tranquil walk through its former deer park, by the river side of its ivy-clad buildings. Nearby is Cambridge's finest art gallery, the **Fitzwilliam Museum.** This contains outstanding collections of art, including several Constable paintings, and antiquities—starring some objects from ancient Egypt. ⊠ *Trumpington St.,* ☎ *01223/332900.* ☜ *Free.* ۞ *Tues.–Sat. 10–5, Sun. 2:15–5.*

Across from Peterhouse is Pembroke College (1347), with delightful gardens and bowling greens. Head down Pembroke Street to reach **Emmanuel College.** Harvard grads are especially obliged to make a pilgrimage to the Wren Chapel here to see the plaque to former student, John Harvard, who, fresh off the *Mayflower,* gave his name to that Boston institution. A number of the Pilgrims were Emmanuel alumni, and they remembered their alma mater by naming Cambridge, Massachusetts.

Westward from Jesus College, along Sidney Street, is **St. John's College.** The second-largest college in Cambridge, St. John's boasts noted alumni—Wordsworth had his rooms here—and two of the finest sights in town—the School of Pythagoras, the oldest house in Cambridge, and a copy of the Bridge of Sighs in Venice that reaches across the Cam to the mock-Gothic New Court (1825), whose white crenellations have earned it the nickname "the wedding cake." From here, it's most pleasant to head along the river and through the narrow lanes past Clare College and Trinity Hall to Trinity College.

Trinity College was founded by Henry VIII in 1546 and is the largest of all the colleges. Many of Trinity's features match its size, not least its 17th-century "great court" and the massive gatehouse that houses Great Tom, a giant clock that strikes each hour with high and low notes. Don't miss the wonderful library by Christopher Wren. Alumni include Sir Isaac Newton, Byron, Tennyson, and Thackeray, and the future King Charles III.

South of Trinity College is **King's College,** site of the world-famous Gothic-style (1446) **King's College Chapel,** which, with its great fan-vaulted roof supported by a delicate tracery of columns, is the final and, some would say, most glorious flowering of Perpendicular Gothic in Britain. "The noblest barn in Europe," it's truly a lovely sight and the home of the famous choristers. To cap it all, Rubens's *Adoration of the Magi* is secreted behind the altar.

Reached along the Backs and tucked away on Queens Lane, **Queens College** was built around 1446 and is one of Cambridge's most eye-catching colleges. The best way to enter it is over the **Mathematical Bridge.** Isaac Newton fashioned this arched wooden structure without benefit of any binding thing save gravity. Unfortunately, the curious scholars couldn't leave well enough alone and dismantled it to find Newton's secret; they failed and had to nail it back together like any other bridge. Be sure to take in the half-timber President's Lodge. In from the river is **Peterhouse.** Along King's Parade is **Corpus Christi College.** If you see only one quadrangle, make it the medieval Old Court here.

OFF THE BEATEN PATH   **GRANTCHESTER –** This pretty little village 2 mi up the river from the center of Cambridge is a delightful walk or bicycle ride along a path that follows the river through college playing fields and the Grantchester Meadows. Grantchester was put on the map by its famous son, Rupert Brooke, whose very famous line "Stands the church clock at ten to three? And is there honey still for tea?" is from his poem *The Vicarage, Grantchester.* You can still reach the village most enjoyably, if challengingly, by punt (hired at Silver Street Bridge or Mill Lane) upstream along the Cam, or by walking along the Backs past St. John's. On a sunny day, there's no better way of absorbing Cambridge's unique atmosphere—you will seem to have all the time in the world.

OXFORD

To get Oxford fixed in your mind's eye, say the phrase "Dreaming Spires" over and over—all the tour guides do—and think *Brideshead Revisited*, Sebastian Flyte, and Evelyn Waugh, in general. Think Rhodes scholar—President Clinton was one, of course—and think J. R. R. Tolkien and Percy Bysshe Shelley, and W. H. Auden and C. S. Lewis. (Wait—wasn't he in Cambridge? Yes, he *studied* here, but *taught* there.) Two more recent graduates were Margaret Thatcher and . . . Kris Kristofferson. Truly. The University of Oxford is older than Cambridge, dating from the 11th century (only the Sorbonne in Paris is older), but once again, newcomers need to learn that the University is not one unified campus, but a collection of many colleges scattered across the city.

Oxford is a bigger and much more cosmopolitan city than Cambridge, though here, too, there is no shortage of hushed quadrangles, chapels, and gardens. Bikes are propped, unlocked, against wrought-iron railings, and punting is popular along the Cherwell (rent one yourself from the foot of Magdalen Bridge), but Oxford is also quite a major industrial center, with large car and steel plants based in its suburbs. The same guidelines apply here as in Cambridge for visiting the colleges, with only the chapels and halls generally viewable.

Get here by hourly train from Paddington Station (0345/484950). The journey takes 55 minutes, or 1 hour 40 minutes by coach from Victoria Coach Station (0990/808080). Several companies operate services, so buses leave every 20 minutes or so. The **Oxford Information Centre** is in the Old School, Gloucester Green, ☎ 01865/726871.

VISITING THE COLLEGES

See general information for Cambridge (☞ *above*). Guided city walking tours leave the Oxford Information Centre several times a day.

A Good Walk

This tour encompasses much of the city; for those with limited time, get a detailed map from the tourist office and focus on selected sights.

Any tour of Oxford should begin at its very center—actually a pleasant walk of 10 minutes or so eastward of the train station—with the splendid university church of **St. Mary the Virgin,** on High Street. From its 14th-century tower, you can get a Cinerama view of the entire city. The church's interior is crowded with 700 years' worth of funeral monuments. Just north of the church is one of Oxford's most famous sights, the **Radcliffe Camera,** which holds the august **Bodleian Library.** Don't get too excited because not very much of this—one of the planet's best book collections—is on view to non-dons, but you can see part of the 2-million-volume library on a tour of the Camera— a magnificent building topped by one of Britain's biggest domes—and at the former Divinity School, where there's a changing exhibit of manuscripts and rare books, and a magnificent Gothic interior. ⊠ *Broad St.,* ☎ *01865/277165.* ☒ *£3.50.* ☾ *Tour mid-Mar.–Oct., weekdays at 10:30, 11:30, 2, and 3; Nov.–mid-Mar., weekdays at 2 and 3; occasional Sat.-morning tours (call for availability).*

A minute's stroll from the Radcliffe Camera is the **Sheldonian Theatre.** Built in 1663, the Sheldonian was Sir Christopher Wren's first work, modeled on a Roman amphitheater, and is where students' graduation ceremonies are still held, entirely in Latin, as befits the building's spirit. Outside is one of Oxford's most striking sights—a metal fence topped with stone busts of 18 Roman emperors (modern reproductions of the originals, which were eaten away by pollution). ⊠ *Sheldonian Theatre, Broad St.,* ☎ *01865/277–299.* ☒ *£1.50.* ☾ *Mon.–Sat. 10–12:45* *and 2–4:30; mid-Nov.–Feb. only till 4; closed for 10 days at Christmas and at Easter; closed for degree ceremonies and events (call ahead to check).*

Along Broad Street, you can stop in at **The Oxford Story.** Take your place at a medieval student's desk, as it trundles through 800 years of Oxford history. The multimedia ride concentrates on University life, visiting famous former students in dioramas of their workplaces. See Edmund Halley discover that comet! Watch the Scholastica's Day Riot of 1355! You can choose grown-up's or kid's commentary. ⊠ *6 Broad St.,* ☎ *01865/790055.* ▨ *£4.95.* ☉ *Apr.– Oct., daily 9:30–5; July and Aug., daily 9–6; Nov.–Mar., daily 10–4:30.*

Broad Street leads into Giles Street and prestigious **Balliol College** (1263). The doors between the inner and outer quadrangles of Christ Church's neighbor still bear the scorch marks from the flames that roasted Archbishop Cranmer and Bishops Latimer and Ridley in 1555, during Mary I's reign, for their Protestant beliefs.

Westward from Giles Street, Beaumont Street is the site of the **Ashmolean Museum,** Britain's oldest public museum, no less, in which some of the world's most precious things are stashed, all the property of the University. See Egyptian, Greek, and Roman artifacts, Michelangelo drawings, and European silverware and ceramics, Oriental paintings, and more. In 1996 a new café opened, serving snacks and meals to the culturally replete. ⊠ *Beaumont St.,* ☎ *01865/278000.* ☉ *Tues.–Sat. 10– 4, Sun. 2–4.*

North and across St. Giles Road from the Ashmolean Museum is **St. John's College.** This one was founded in 1555 and is worth visiting for its very large and lovely gardens.

The leading college of the southern half of Oxford is **Christ Church College,** found along the major road of St. Aldate's. Called "the House" by its modest members, Christ Church boasts the largest quadrangle in town, named **Tom Quad,** after the over-six-ton bell in the gate tower. This is where Charles Dodgson, better known as Lewis Carroll, was a math don; a shop opposite the meadows in St. Aldate's was the inspiration for the shop in *Through the Looking Glass.* Don't miss the 800-year-old chapel, nor the medieval dining hall, with its portraits of former students—John Wesley, William Penn, and 14 prime ministers. Also go to the **Canterbury Quadrangle,** whose gallery contains works by Leonardo, Michelangelo, and Rubens.

STRATFORD-UPON-AVON

Stratford-upon-Avon has become very adept at accommodating the hordes of visitors who come hoping for a taste of Shakespeare (1564– 1616), and getting more than they bargained for. What we mean is that Stratford is a handsome town in its own right, punctuated with those distinctive black-and-white Tudor half-timber buildings that survive from its 16th-century heyday as a crafts and trading center. Shakespeare's father participated in that boom—he was a glove maker and wool dealer who rose to the rank of town bailiff. There are also fine shopping opportunities, including the Friday market, and various little side sights, but what we're really all here for is Shakespeare. It's difficult to avoid feeling like a herd animal as you board the Shakespeare bus, but there is something to be said for taking advantage of packaged tours like **Stratford and the Shakespeare Story,** which allows you to come and go as you please around the five Shakespeare Properties, especially if your time is limited. If you can manage an overnight stay, taking in a production at one of the three Royal Shakespeare

Company's Stratford theaters will satisfyingly deepen your immersion in the Bard's works.

Try to catch the direct train each morning from **Paddington Station** (☎ 0345/484950 for times), or else you'll be doomed to at least one change, at Leamington Spa. There are two direct trains back from Stratford each afternoon, too, and the journey time is 2 hours, 20 minutes. It takes no longer to go by **National Express** (☎ 0990/808080) from Victoria Coach Station, and there are eight coaches daily, though the fastest route is by train *and* bus using the "Shakespeare Connection Road & Rail Link" from **Euston Station** to Coventry, then switching to a Guide Friday bus. This trip takes 2 hours, and there are four departures daily Monday through Friday—the three that would allow you to catch an evening performance in Stratford are at 9:15 AM, 10:45 AM, and 4:55 PM; Saturday departures are at 9:05 AM, 10:35 AM, and 5:05 PM; the Sunday departure is 9:45 AM. Returns back to London usually depart around 11:15 PM (☎ 0171/387–7070; Guide Friday offices, 01789/294466). **Stratford Tourist Information Centre** is at Bridge Foot, by the bridge (☎ 01789/293127).

GUIDED TOURS

Many people like to see Stratford from the top of an open-top double-decker bus and the **Guide Friday's Stratford and Shakespeare Story Tour** is one of the better choices. It allows you to alight and reboard at any of the Bard sights on a ticket valid all day—a particularly handy mode of transport, as two of the five sights are out of town. ⊠ *14 Rother St.,* ☎ *01789/294466.* ☞ *£8 Stratford only, £16 includes Warwick.*☉ *Tour May–Sept., daily every 15 mins; Oct.–Nov. and mid-Feb.–Apr., daily every 30 mins; late Nov.–mid-Feb., daily hourly.*

A Good Walk

Most Stratford visitors begin at **Shakespeare's Birthplace.** With the Shakespeare Centre inside, this is the perfect place to start your Bard odyssey. The half-timber building in which William grew has been a national memorial since 1847, and it is now split in half: One part is a re-creation of a typical home of the time, while the other contains a new exhibit about the historical characters in the Shakespeare canon, plus a history of the house itself. ⊠ *Henley St.,* ☎ *01789/204016.* ☞ *£4.50, combined admission for Shakespeare Birthplace Trust properties £9, 3 in-town properties £7.* ☉ *Mar.–Oct., Mon.–Sat. 9–5, Sun. 10–5; Nov.–Feb., Mon.–Sat. 9:30–4, Sun. 10:30–4.*

On High Street, the center road of Stratford, is **New Place.** What there is to see now, next to Nash's House—which belonged to Thomas Nash, first husband of Shakespeare's granddaughter, Elizabeth Hall—is an Elizabethan knot garden, planted over the foundations of the house where the Bard spent his last years, and died, in 1616. In Nash's House, see an exhibit about Stratford, and a Tudor decor job. ⊠ *Chapel St.,* ☎ *01789/292325.* ☞ *£3, or joint ticket (☞ above).* ☉ ☞ *Shakespeare's Birthplace, above.*

Along Chapel Street is one of the most picturesque set pieces of Stratford—the Guildhall buildings, comprising the Guildhall Chapel, the Almshouses, and **King Edward's Grammar School,** where Master Shakespeare learned "little Latin and less Greek." The chapel is open daily 9–5, but the schoolhouse is still used by students and can only be visited by prior arrangement (☎ 01789/293351) during after-school hours or vacation time.

On the venerable road called Old Town you'll find Stratford's most beautiful Tudor town house, **Hall's Croft.** This was—almost definitely—the home of Shakespeare's daughter, Susanna, and her husband, Dr.

John Hall. It's rather charmingly outfitted, complete with furniture of the period and the doctor's dispensary, and the walled garden is delightful. ⊠ *Old Town,* ☎ *01789/292107.* 🖼 *£3, or joint ticket (☞ above).* ⊙ *Mar.–Oct., Mon.–Sat. 9:30–5, Sun. 10:30–5; Nov.–Feb., Mon.–Sat. 10:30–4, Sun. 1:30–4.*

At the end of Old Town is "Shakespeare's church," **Holy Trinity,** along the banks of the Avon, and fronted by a beautiful avenue of lime trees. Here, in the chancel, the Bard is buried, alongside his wife, his daughter, his son-in-law, and his granddaughter's husband. The bust of Shakespeare is thought to be an authentic likeness, executed a few years after his death. ⊠ *Trinity St., Waterside.*

Perfectly positioned on the banks of the Avon not far from Holy Trinity Church, the **Royal Shakespeare Theatre** is where the Royal Shakespeare Company (known as the RSC) lives outside London, mounting several productions each season. The design of the smaller **Swan Theatre,** in the same building, is based on the original Elizabethan Globe. It's best to book well in advance, but day-of-performance tickets are nearly always available. ⊠ *Waterside, Stratford-upon-Avon, CV37 6BB,* ☎ *01789/295623.*⊙ *Tours weekdays (except matinee days) at 1:30 and 5:30; matinee days 5:30 and after show; Sun. at 12:30, 1:45, 2:35, and 3:45. Exhibition Mon.–Sat. 9:30–6:30, Sun. noon–4:30.*

STRATFORD ENVIRONS

The two remaining stops on the Shakespeare trail are just outside Stratford. **Anne Hathaway's Cottage,** the early home of the playwright's wife, is possibly the most picturesque abode in Britain—a rather substantial thatched cottage, it has been restored to reflect the comfortable middle-class Hathaway life. You can walk—it's just over a mile from downtown Stratford in Shottery. **Mary Arden's House** is probably where Shakespeare's mother was raised, and if that doesn't get you interested, perhaps **Warwick Castle**—some 8 mi away—will. This place fulfills anyone's most clichéd Camelot daydreams, being a medieval, fortified, much-restored, castellated, moated, landscaped (by Capability Brown) castle, complete with dungeons and a torture chamber, state rooms, and the occasional battle reenactment. ⊠ *Warwick,* ☎ *01926/ 495421.* 🖼 *£9.25; July–Aug. £9.95.* ⊙ *Apr.–mid-Oct., daily 10–6; mid-Oct.–Mar., daily 10–5.*

WINDSOR

The star sight of this quiet Berkshire town is, without a shadow of a doubt, the largest inhabited castle in the world—Windsor Castle. Windsor Great Park, however, shouldn't be forgotten, and Eton College, England's most famous public school, is also here. There's also now a brand-new attraction to add to the Windsor value: the kid's paradise of Legoland.

Windsor Castle is the most impressive and the longest-serving of all England's royal palaces. It's the only royal residence to have been in continuous royal use since the days of William the Conqueror, who chose this site to build a timber stockade soon after his conquest of Britain in 1066. It was Edward III in the 1300s who really founded the castle, building the Norman gateway, the great round tower, and new state apartments, then subsequent monarchs added new buildings or improved existing ones according to their tastes and their finances. Charles II restored the state apartments during the 1600s, and during the 1820s George IV, that most extravagant of kings with a mania for building, converted what was still essentially a medieval castle into the royal palace you see today. The Queen uses Windsor a lot, spending most weekends here, often joined by family and friends. She's here when the Royal Standard is flown above the Round Tower, but not when you see the Union Jack.

Windsor is easy to reach by train, either from Waterloo direct to Windsor and Eton Riverside (50 minutes), or from Paddington to Windsor Central, changing at Reading (45 minutes); there are two trains per hour on each route. The **Green Line** bus (☎ 01737/242411) leaves from Eccleston Bridge, behind Victoria train station, *not* from the Coach Station itself. Make sure you catch the fast direct service, which takes 45 minutes and runs hourly; the stopping services take up to 1 hour, 15 minutes. Windsor's **Tourist Information Centre** (☎ 01753/743900) is in Central Station.

WINDSOR CASTLE

The massive citadel occupies 13 acres, but the first part you notice on entering is the massive **Round Tower** on top of which the standard is flown, and at the base of which is the 11th-century Moat Garden, which you can occasionally visit in summer. Passing through the portcullised **Norman Gate,** you reach the **Upper Ward,** the quadrangle containing the State Apartments—which you may tour when the Queen is out—and the sovereign's Private Apartments, which you may not. Big ceremonies, like processions for foreign heads of state, go on here, as does the Changing of the Guard, when the Queen is in. Next you reach the **Lower Ward,** where the high point is the magnificent **St. George's Chapel,** symbolic and actual guardian of the Order of the Garter, the highest chivalric order in the land, founded in 1348 by Edward III. Ten sovereigns are buried in the chapel—a fantastic Gothic Perpendicular vision, 230 ft long, complete with gargoyles, buttresses, banners, swords, choir stalls, and enameled plates displaying arms of the Knights of the Order of the Garter.

The **State Apartments** are grander than Buckingham Palace's, and have the added attraction of a few gems from the Queen's vast art collection: choice canvasses by Rubens, Rembrandt, Van Dyck, Gainsborough, Canaletto, and Holbein; da Vinci drawings; Gobelin tapestries, and limewood carvings by Grinling Gibbons. The views across to Windsor Great Park, the remains of a former royal hunting forest, are magnificent, too. One unmissable treat—and not only for children— is **Queen Mary's Dolls' House,** a 12:1 scale, seven-story palace, complete with electricity, running water, and working elevators, designed in 1924 by Sir Edwin Lutyens. The detail is literally incredible—for example, some of the miniature books in the library are by Kipling, Conan Doyle, Thomas Hardy, and G. K. Chesterton—written by the great authors in their own hand.

The terrible fire of November 1992, which started in the Queen's private chapel, totally gutted some of the State Apartments. A swift rescue effort meant that, miraculously, hardly any works of art were lost. Reopened to the public in December 1997 with grand fanfare, the castle has never looked more impressive. Costing a total of £37 million, phenomenal repair work has restored the Grand Reception Room, the Green and Crimson Drawing Rooms, and the State and Octagonal Dining Rooms to their former, if not greater, glory. The private chapel of the Royal Family has also been redesigned, with a new stained-glass window commemorating the fire of 1992 and the restoration work that subsequently took place. All restored rooms are open to the public, except the private chapel. ⊠ *Windsor Castle,* ☎ *01753/868286.* 🎫 *£8.50; Dolls' House additional £1; tickets are £1.10 less on Sun. when St. George's Chapel is closed.*☉ *Mar.–Oct., daily 10–5:30 (last admission at 4); Nov.–Feb., daily 10–4 (last admission at 3).*

INDEX

NOTES

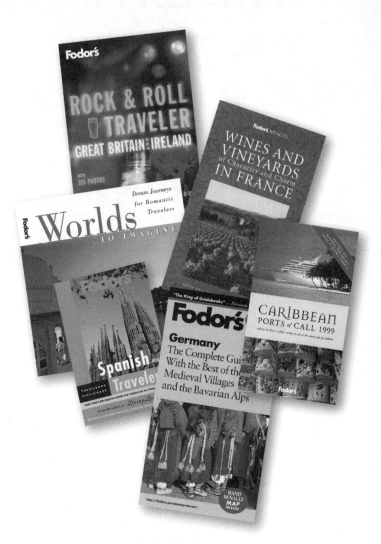

Looking for a different kind of vacation?

Fodor's makes it easy with a full line of international guidebooks to suit a variety of interests—from adventure to romance to language help.

At bookstores everywhere.
www.fodors.com

WHEREVER
YOU TRAVEL,
*H*ELP IS NEVER
FAR AWAY.

From planning your trip to providing travel assistance
along the way, American Express® Travel Service Offices
are always there to help you do more.

London

American Express Travel Service
1 Savoy Court
0171/240-1521

American Express Travel Service
6 Haymarket
0171/930-4411

American Express Travel Service
78 Brompton Road
0171/584-6182

American Express Travel Service
89 Mount Street Mayfair
0171/499-4436

American Express Travel Service
111 Cheapside
0171/600-5522

American Express Travel Service
102 Victoria Street
0171/828-7411

Travel

http://www.americanexpress.com/travel

**American Express Travel Service Offices are located
throughout the United Kingdom.**